the Bible
Search Engine

FIND KEY REFERENCES FOR

1,001 TOPICS

BOTH BIBLICAL AND CONTEMPORARY

the Bible
Search Engine

Pamela L. McQuade

BARBOUR
PUBLISHING

Published by Barbour Publishing, Inc., P.O. Box 719, Uhrichsville, Ohio 44683, www.barbourbooks.com

Our mission is to publish and distribute inspirational products offering exceptional value and biblical encouragement to the masses.

 Member of the
Evangelical Christian
Publishers Association

Printed in China.

Introduction

Like the first page of a computer search engine's results, The Bible Search Engine *provides key verses on a broad range of topics— some crucial to the Christian faith and others simply interesting.*

Unlike a computer search engine, *The Bible Search Engine* is not exhaustive. It is a quick snapshot of each topic and does not require readers to search through thousands of entries in order to find one crucial verse. Where a topic has limited references in the Bible, every one may be here. But where a subject is dealt with extensively in scripture, I have chosen those related to major events in the Bible or that have a clear practical application to the Christian walk. Not all the references here have the topic word in them. Where possible, I have tried to include helpful references that use a similar word. This may allow readers to have a more complete view of these subjects. The focus of this work is to include verses that help, encourage, and provide clear direction for a searching believer.

Since similar verses often appear in several Gospels, I have chosen verses from one, usually the book of Matthew. Readers may want to use a study Bible to compare these to the other Gospels.

Where longer passages cover a topic, I have included a few key references. Often I have included the first and last references in a chapter to bracket the topic. Readers may want to study the verses between them for a more complete view of the subject.

All in all, my goal is to encourage readers to study and understand the scriptures and to make God's Word a consistent part of their lives.

Pamela L. McQuade

1. Abide/Abideth

To abide in God is to habitually trust Him and live in a way that glorifies Him.

a under the shadow of the Almighty. . .Ps. 91:1
should not *a* in darkness. . .John 12:46
that he may *a* with you for ever. . .John 14:16
A in me, and I in you. . .John 15:4
If a man *a* not in me. . .John 15:6
a in me, and my words *a* in you. . .John 15:7
ye shall *a* in my love. . .John 15:10
a not still in unbelief. . .Rom. 11:23
Let that therefore *a* in you. . .1 John 2:24
received of him *a'th* in you. . .1 John 2:27
little children, *a* in him. . .1 John 2:28

2. Ability

They gave after their *a*. . .Ezra 2:69
such as had *a* in them. . .Dan. 1:4
according to his several *a*. . .Matt. 25:15
every man according to his *a*. . .Acts 11:29
the *a* which God giveth. . .1 Pet. 4:11

See *Skill*.

3. Abomination

An abomination is something detestable to God and therefore also to those who are righteous.

it is *a*. . .Lev. 18:22
have committed an *a*. . .Lev. 20:13
an *a* to the LORD. . .Deut. 7:25
a before the LORD. . .Deut. 24:4
an *a* unto the LORD. . .Deut. 27:15
the froward is *a*. . .Prov. 3:32

wickedness is an *a*. . .Prov. 8:7
Lying lips are *a*. . .Prov. 12:22
thoughts of the wicked are an *a*. . .Prov. 15:26
a to kings to commit wickedness.. . .Prov. 16:12
the scorner is an *a* to men. . .Prov. 24:9
an *a* to the just. . .Prov. 29:27
a with his neighbour's wife. . .Ezek. 22:11
a in the sight of God. . .Luke 16:15
whatsoever worketh *a*. . .Rev. 21:27

See *Obscenity*.

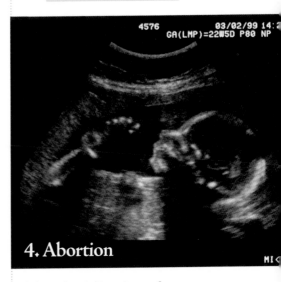

4. Abortion

God created man in his own image. . .Gen. 1:27
Thou shalt not kill. . .Exod. 20:13
hurt a woman with child. . .Exod. 21:22
did not one fashion us in the womb?. . .Job 31:15
was not hid from thee, when I was made. . .Ps. 139:15
the womb of her that is with child. . .Eccles. 11:5
formed thee in the belly I knew thee. . .Jer. 1:5
ripped up the women with child. . .Amos 1:13
even from his mother's womb. . .Luke 1:15

5. Abstain/ Abstinence

a from pollutions of idols. . .Acts 15:20

a from meats offered to idols. . .Acts 15:29

long *a'ence* Paul stood forth. . .Acts 27:21

a from fornication. . .1 Thess. 4:3

A from all appearance of evil. . .1 Thess. 5:22

a from meats, which God hath created. . .1 Tim. 4:3

a from fleshly lusts. . .1 Pet. 2:11

6. Abundance/ Abundant/Abundantly

and *a't* in goodness. . .Exod. 34:6

a of all things. . .Deut. 28:47

he giveth meat in *a*. . .Job 36:31

trusted in the *a* of his riches. . .Ps. 52:7

he shall have more *a*. . .Matt. 13:12

did cast in of their *a*. . .Mark 12:44

not in the *a* of the things. . .Luke 12:15

the *a't* grace. . .2 Cor. 4:15

to do exceeding *a'ly*. . .Eph. 3:20

shed on us *a'ly* through Jesus. . .Titus 3:6

according to his *a't* mercy. . .1 Pet. 1:3

7. Abundant Life

They shall be abundantly satisfied. . .Ps. 36:8

thee the desires of thine heart. . .Ps. 37:4

things shall be added unto you. . .Matt.6:33

life for my sake shall find it. . .Matt. 16:25

In him was life. . .John 1:4

have it more abundantly. . .John 10:10

ask any thing in my name. . .John 14:14

able to do exceeding abundantly. . .Eph. 3:20

my God shall supply all your need. . .Phil. 4:19

8. Abuse/ Abusers/Abused

they knew her, and *a'd* her all the night . Judg.19:25

nor *a'rs* of themselves with mankind. . .1 Cor. 6:9

I *a* not my power in the gospel. . .1 Cor. 9:18

See *Rape.*

9. Accept/ Acceptable/ Accepted/ Accepteth

shalt thou not be *a'ed?*. . .Gen. 4:7

The LORD thy God *a* thee. . .2 Sam. 24:23

a'able to the LORD than sacrifice. . .Prov. 21:3

God now *a'eth* thy works. . .Eccles. 9:7

worketh righteousness, is *a'ed*. . .Acts 10:35

sacrifice, holy, *a'able* unto God. . .Rom. 12:1

serveth Christ is *a'able* to God. . .Rom. 14:18

the Gentiles might be *a'able*. . .Rom. 15:16

we may be *a'ed* of him. . .2 Cor. 5:9

a'ed in the beloved. . .Eph. 1:6

what is *a'able* unto the Lord. . .Eph. 5:10

a'able in the sight of God. . .1 Tim. 2:3

good and *a'able* before God. . .1 Tim. 5:4

this is *a'able* with God. . .1 Pet. 2:20

10. Accomplishments

in all manner of workmanship. . .Exod. 31:3

giveth thee power to get wealth. . .Deut. 8:18

every willing skilful man. . .1 Chron. 28:21

I have created the smith. . .Isa. 54:16

God gave them knowledge and skill. . .Dan. 1:17

gifts differing according to the grace. . .Rom. 12:6

11. Acquaintance

mine *a* are verily estranged. . .Job 19:13

a fear to mine *a*. . .Ps. 31:11

put away mine *a* far from me. . .Ps. 88:8

sought him among their kinsfolk and *a*. . .Luke 2:44

should forbid none of his *a* to minister. . .Acts 24:23

12. Addiction

Though scripture does not specifically deal with the subject of drugs, its principles for drinking can be applied to any physical addiction.

the drunkard and the glutton. . .Prov. 23:21

not for drunkenness. . .Eccles. 10:17

as a drunken man staggereth. . .Isa. 19:14

surfeiting, and drunkenness. . .Luke 21:34

is the servant of sin. . .John 8:34

not in rioting and drunkenness. . .Rom. 13:13

nor drunkards, nor revilers. . .1 Cor. 6:10

temple of the Holy Ghost. . .1 Cor. 6:19

drunkenness, revellings. . .Gal. 5:21

be not drunk with wine. . .Eph. 5:18

See *Alcohol, Drink/Drinking, Wine.*

13. Admired/ Admiration

to be *a* in all them that believe. . .2 Thess. 1:10

having men's persons in *a'ation*. . .Jude 1:16

I wondered with great *a'ation*. . .Rev. 17:6

14. Admonish/ Admonished/ Admonishing

I have *a'ed* you. . .Jer. 42:19

able also to *a* one another. . .Rom. 15:14

a'ing one another in psalms. . .Col. 3:16

a him as a brother. . .2 Thess. 3:15

as Moses was *a'ed* of God. . .Heb. 8:5

15. Adolescence

See *Youth.*

Thou shalt not commit *a*. . .Exod. 20:14
a with another man's wife. . .Lev. 20:10
Neither shalt thou commit *a*. . .Deut. 5:18
a with their neighbours' wives. . .Jer. 29:23
a with her already in his heart. . .Matt. 5:28
a woman taken in *a*. . .John 8:3
dost thou commit *a*?. . .Rom. 2:22
A, fornication, uncleanness. . .Gal. 5:19
Having eyes full of *a*. . .2 Pet. 2:14
a with her into. . .Rev. 2:22

16. Adoption
God uses adoption as a picture of His
relationship with us, as His children.

received the Spirit of *a*. . .Rom. 8:15
waiting for the *a*. . .Rom. 8:23
to whom pertaineth the *a*. . .Rom. 9:4
that we might receive the *a* of sons. . .Gal. 4:5
us unto the *a* of children. . .Eph. 1:5

19. Advantage/ Advantaged/ Advantageth
a'd, if he gain the whole world. . .Luke 9:25
What *a* then hath the Jew?. . .Rom. 3:1
a'th it me, if the dead rise not?. . .1 Cor. 15:32
Lest Satan should get an *a* of us. . .2 Cor. 2:11
admiration because of *a*. . .Jude 1:16

17. Adorn/Adorned/ Adorneth/Adorning
as a bride *a'eth* herself. . .Isa. 61:10
women *a* themselves. . .1 Tim. 2:9
a the doctrine of God. . .Titus 2:10
that outward *a'ing* of plaiting. . .1 Pet. 3:3
a'ed themselves, being in subjection. . .1 Pet. 3:5
as a bride *a'ed* for her husband. . .Rev. 21:2

20. Adversary/Adversaries

18. Adultery
The scriptures condemn the act of adultery
between a man and woman but also use it as a
picture of Israel's spiritual unfaithfulness to God.

an *a* unto thine *a'ies*. . .Exod. 23:22
render vengeance to his *a'ies*. . .Deut. 32:43
a'ies of the Lord shall. . .1 Sam. 2:10
for good are mine *a'ies*. . .Ps. 38:20

how long shall the *a* reproach?. . .Ps. 74:10

mine *a'ies* from the Lᴏʀᴅ. . .Ps. 109:20

vengeance on his *a'ies*. . .Nah.1:2

Agree with thine *a* quickly. . .Matt. 5:25

a'ies shall not be able. . .Luke 21:15

nothing terrified by your *a'ies*. . .Phil. 1:28

to the *a* to speak reproachfully. . .1 Tim. 5:14

your *a* the devil. . .1 Pet. 5:8

See *Enemy/Enemies*.

21. Adversity

my soul out of all *a*. . .2 Sam. 4:9

God did vex them with all *a*. . .2 Chron.15:6

But in mine *a* they rejoiced. . .Ps. 35:15

brother is born for *a*.. . .Prov. 17:17

faint in the day of *a*. . .Prov. 24:10

give you the bread of *a*. . .Isa. 30:20

22. Advice

the counsel of the wicked. . .Job 21:16

darkeneth counsel by words. . .Job 38:2

walketh not in the counsel. . .Ps.1:1

Lᴏʀᴅ, who hath given me counsel. . .Ps. 16:7

The counsel of the Lᴏʀᴅ. . .Ps. 33:11

guide me with thy counsel. . .Ps. 73:24

counsel of the most High. . .Ps. 107:11

attain unto wise counsels. . .Prov. 1:5

Counsel is mine. . .Prov. 8:14

the counsels of the wicked. . .Prov. 12:5

Hear counsel, and receive

instruction. . .Prov. 19:20

counsel of the Lᴏʀᴅ. . .Prov. 19:21

See *Counsel/Counsels*.

23. Affairs

guide his *a* with discretion. . .Ps. 112:5

exercise myself in great matters. . .Ps. 131:1

unworthy to judge the smallest

matters?. . .1 Cor. 6:2

with the *a* of this life. . .2 Tim. 2:4

24. Affection/ Affectioned/Affections

kisses of an enemy are deceitful. . .Prov. 27:6

kiss me with the kisses. . .Song of Sol. 1:2

Whomsoever I shall kiss. . .Matt. 26:48

and kissed his feet. . .Luke 7:38

not ceased to kiss my feet. . .Luke 7:45

disciples, and embraced them. . .Acts 20:1

gave them up unto vile *a's*. . .Rom. 1:26

without natural *a*, implacable. . .Rom. 1:31

Be kindly *a'ed* one to another. . .Rom. 12:10

Salute one another with an holy kiss. . .Rom. 16:16

inward *a* is more abundant. . .2 Cor. 7:15

Set your *a* on things above. . .Col. 3:2

inordinate *a*, evil concupiscence. . .Col. 3:5

Without natural *a*. . .2 Tim. 3:3

with a kiss of charity. . .1 Pet. 5:14

25. Affirmations

not fail thee, nor forsake thee. . .Deut. 31:6
The Lord is my shepherd. . .Ps. 23:1
Ye are blessed of the Lord. . .Ps. 115:15
loved thee with an everlasting love. . .Jer. 31:3
are the light of the world. . .Matt. 5:14
For God so loved the world. . .John 3:16
I will not leave you comfortless. . .John 14:18
hath begun a good work in you. . .Phil. 1:6
do all things through Christ. . .Phil. 4:13
I will never leave thee. . .Heb. 13:5
faithful and just to forgive us. . .1 John 1:9

26. Affliction/ Afflictions

a cometh not forth. . .Job 5:6
the poor in his *a*. . .Job 36:15
the *a* of the afflicted. . .Ps. 22:24
Look upon mine *a*. . .Ps. 25:18
a's of the righteous. . .Ps. 34:19
my comfort in my *a*. . .Ps. 119:50
my refuge in the day of *a*. . .Jer. 16:19
a they will seek me. . .Hosea 5:15
For our light *a*. . .2 Cor. 4:17
great trial of *a*. . .2 Cor. 8:2
the word in much *a*. . .1 Thess. 1:6
partaker of the *a*'s of the gospel. . .2 Tim. 1:8
endure *a*'s. . .2 Tim. 4:5
Choosing rather to suffer *a*. . .Heb. 11:25
widows in their *a*. . .James 1:27

See *Trouble, Vexation/Vexations.*

27. Affluence

See *Financial Gain, Rich/Riches, Wealth.*

28. Afraid

a, because I was naked. . .Gen. 3:10
a to look upon God. . .Exod. 3:6
not be *a* of ten thousands. . .Ps. 3:6
of whom shall I be *a*?. . .Ps. 27:1
a when one is made rich. . .Ps. 49:16
What time I am *a*. . .Ps. 56:3
a what man can do. . .Ps. 56:11
a for the terror by night. . .Ps. 91:5
thou shalt not be *a*. . .Prov. 3:24
Be not *a* of sudden fear. . .Prov. 3:25
I will trust, and not be *a*. . .Isa. 12:2
a of them that kill. . .Luke 12:4
that which is evil, be *a*. . .Rom. 13:4
be not *a* of their terror. . .1 Pet. 3:14

See *Fear/Feared/Fears.*

29. Age

mine *a* is as nothing before thee. . .Ps. 39:5
Cast me not off in the time of old *a*. . .Ps. 71:9
They shall still bring forth fruit in old *a*. . .Ps. 92:14
And even to your old *a* I am he. . .Isa. 46:4

See *Elderly, the; Seasons of Life.*

30. Agree/Agreed

together, except they be *a'd?*. . .Amos 3:3

A with thine adversary. . .Matt. 5:25

you shall *a* on earth. . .Matt. 18:19

these three *a* in one. . .1 John 5:8

31. Agriculture

every beast of the field. . .Gen. 2:19

not sow thy field. . .Lev. 19:19

shalt sow thy field. . .Lev. 25:3

increase thereof out of the field. . .Lev. 25:12

shall yield their fruit. . .Lev. 26:4

send grass in thy fields. . .Deut. 11:15

thou be in the field. . .Deut. 28:3

the fruit of thy cattle. . .Deut. 30:9

sendeth waters upon the fields. . .Job 5:10

the cattle upon a thousand hills. . .Ps. 50:10

thy barns be filled with plenty. . .Prov. 3:10

considereth a field, and buyeth it. . .Prov. 31:16

himself is served by the field. . .Eccles. 5:9

The beast of the field. . .Isa. 43:20

pull down my barns. . .Luke 12:18

See *Crops*.

32. Ailments

consumption, and with a fever. . .Deut. 28:22

smote them with emerods. . .1 Sam. 5:6

emerods in their secret parts. . .1 Sam. 5:9

those that had the palsy. . .Matt. 4:24

man sick of the palsy. . .Matt. 9:2

had an issue of blood. . .Mark 5:25

taken with a great fever. . .Luke 4:38

the fever left him. . .John 4:52

sick of the palsy. . .Acts 9:33

fever and of a bloody flux. . .Acts 28:8

See *Blind/Blinded, Deaf, Disabilities, Diseases, Dumb, Sick/Sickly/Sickness/Sicknesses*.

33. Alcohol

he drank of the wine. . .Gen. 9:21

from wine and strong drink. . .Num. 6:3

glutton, and a drunkard. . .Deut. 21:20

drink not wine nor strong drink. . .Judg. 13:4

neither wine nor strong drink. . .1 Sam. 1:15

Wine is a mocker. . .Prov. 20:1

drunkard and the glutton. . .Prov. 23:21

not for kings to drink wine. . .Prov. 31:4

not for drunkenness!...Eccles. 10:17
as a drunken man staggereth...Isa. 19:14
drunkards of Ephraim...Isa. 28:3
drink neither wine nor strong drink...Luke 1:15
not in rioting and drunkenness...Rom. 13:13
drunkard, or an extortioner...1 Cor. 5:11
be not drunk with wine...Eph. 5:18

See *Addiction, Debauchery, Drink/Drinking,*
Drunkenness, Revelry.

34. Alien

I have been an *a* in a strange land...Exod. 18:3
mayest sell it unto an *a*...Deut. 14:21
an *a* in their sight...Job 19:15
an *a* unto my mother's children...Ps. 69:8

See *Stranger/Strangers.*

35. Alive

I kill, and I make *a*...Deut. 32:39
saved Rahab the harlot *a*...Josh. 6:25
keep *a* his own soul...Ps. 22:29
thou hast kept me *a*...Ps. 30:3
keep him *a*...Ps. 41:2
save his soul *a*...Ezek. 18:27
heard that he was *a*...Mark 16:11
he shewed himself *a*...Acts 1:3
presented her *a*...Acts 9:41
Paul affirmed to be *a*...Acts 25:19
but *a* unto God...Rom. 6:11
I was *a* without the law...Rom. 7:9
Christ shall all be made *a*...1 Cor. 15:22
we which are *a* and remain...1 Thess. 4:15
I am *a* for evermore...Rev. 1:18

36. Allure

behold, I will *a* her...Hosea 2:14
a through the lusts of the flesh...2 Pet. 2:18

37. Almighty

I am the *A* God...Gen. 17:1
God *A* bless thee...Gen. 28:3
God *A*: be fruitful...Gen. 35:11
the *A*, who shall bless thee...Gen. 49:25
the name of God *A*...Exod. 6:3
I would speak to the *A*...Job 13:3
the inspiration of the *A*...Job 32:8
the *A* hath given me life...Job 33:4
the *A* pervert judgment...Job 34:12
under the shadow of the *A*...Ps. 91:1
which is to come, the *A*...Rev. 1:8
Holy, holy, holy, Lord God *A*...Rev. 4:8
thy works, Lord God *A*...Rev. 15:3

38. Alms

Alms were gifts to the poor, an essential part
of society in an age without public welfare.
Generous giving was expected of believers.

do not your *a* before men...Matt. 6:1
when thou doest thine *a*...Matt. 6:2

But when thou doest *a*. . .Matt. 6:3
thine *a* may be in secret. . .Matt. 6:4
give *a* of such things as ye have. . .Luke 11:41
Sell that ye have, and give *a*. . .Luke 12:33

See *Give/Given/Giveth*; *Poor, the*; *Welfare*.

39. Altar/Altars

During the Old Testament era, altars were employed as part of ritual sacrifices, as described in detail in the books of Exodus and Leviticus. Before Jerusalem's temple was established, altars to the Lord were built in many places, by various people.

make me an *a* of stone. . .Exod. 20:25
build an *a* unto the Lord. . .Deut. 27:5
Joshua built an *a*. . .Josh. 8:30
throw down their *a's*. . .Judg. 2:2
he hath thrown down his *a*. . .Judg. 6:32
David built there an *a*. . .2 Sam. 24:25
hold on the horns of the *a*. . .1 Kings 2:28
Solomon stood before the *a*. . .1 Kings 8:22
they leaped upon the *a*. . .1 Kings 18:26
repaired the *a* of the Lord. . .1 Kings 18:30
Ye shall worship before one *a*. . .2 Chron. 32:12
offer polluted bread upon mine *a*. . .Mal. 1:7
bring thy gift to the *a*. . .Matt. 5:23
greater, the gift, or the *a*. . .Matt. 23:19
Isaac his son upon the *a*?. . .James 2:21

40. Amend/Amends

he shall make *a's* for the harm. . .Lev. 5:16
A your ways and your doings. . .Jer. 7:3
a your ways and your doings. . .Jer. 7:5

a your ways and your doings. . .Jer. 26:13
and *a* your doings. . .Jer. 35:15

41. Angel/Angels

As messenger
there came two *a's* to Sodom. . .Gen. 19:1
a's of God ascending. . .Gen. 28:12
a of God spake unto me. . .Gen. 31:11
a spake unto me. . .1 Kings 13:18
a said unto her, Fear not, Mary. . .Luke 1:30
the *a* of the Lord spake unto Philip. . .Acts 8:26
warned from God by an holy *a*. . .Acts 10:22

As protection
he shall send his *a* before thee. . .Gen. 24:7
a of God, which went before. . .Exod. 14:19
a of the Lord encampeth. . .Ps. 34:7
give his *a's* charge over thee. . .Ps. 91:11
sent his *a*, and hath. . .Dan. 6:22

Fallen
the devil and his *a's*. . .Matt. 25:41
spared not the *a's* that sinned. . .2 Pet. 2:4

Jesus and

give his *a's* charge concerning thee. . .Matt. 4:6

a's came and ministered. . .Matt. 4:11

shall send forth his *a's*. . .Matt. 13:41

his Father with his *a's*. . .Matt. 16:27

a's with a great sound. . .Matt. 24:31

no, not the *a's* of heaven. . .Matt.24:36

and all the holy *a's*. . .Matt. 25:31

twelve legions of *a's*?. . .Matt. 26:53

a of the Lord descended. . .Matt. 28:2

named of the *a* before. . .Luke 2:21

appeared an *a* unto him. . .Luke 22:43

a's of God ascending. . .John 1:51

Spirit, seen of *a's*. . .1 Tim. 3:16

the *a's* said he at any time. . .Heb. 1:5

Father, and before his *a's*. . .Rev. 3:5

People and

their *a's* do always behold. . .Matt. 18:10

as the *a's* of God in heaven. . .Matt. 22:30

confess before the *a's*. . .Luke 12:8

a's of God over one sinner. . .Luke 15:10

are equal unto the *a's*. . .Luke 20:36

a went down at a certain. . .John 5:4

a of the Lord by night. . .Acts 5:19

a of the Lord came. . .Acts 12:7

nor life, nor *a's*. . .Rom. 8:38

that we shall judge *a's*?. . .1 Cor. 6:3

tongues of men and of *a's*. . .1 Cor. 13:1

a from heaven, preach any other. . .Gal. 1:8

a little lower than the *a's*. . .Heb. 2:7

entertained *a's* unawares. . .Heb. 13:2

the *a's* desire to look into. . .1 Pet. 1:12

a's of the seven churches. . .Rev. 1:20

Qualities of

wisdom of an *a* of God. . .2 Sam. 14:20

a little lower than the *a's*. . .Ps. 8:5

Who maketh his *a's* spirits. . .Ps. 104:4

Type of Christ

I send an *A* before thee. . .Exod. 23:20

A which redeemed me from. . .Gen. 48:16

See *Angel of the Lord*.

42. Angel of the Lord

An angel who appears at important moments in Israel's history. In the Old Testament, sometimes this appears to be a preincarnate manifestation of Jesus.

And the *a o t L* found her. . .Gen. 16:7

the *a o t L* called. . .Gen. 22:11

a o t L appeared unto him. . .Exod. 3:2

a o t L stood in the way. . .Num 22:22

a o t L appeared unto him. . .Judg. 6:12

a o t L appeared unto the woman. . .Judg. 13:3

the *a o t L* went out. . .2 Kings 19:35
a o t L appeared unto him. . .Matt. 1:20
a o t L had bidden him. . .Matt. 1:24
a o t L appeareth in a dream. . .Matt. 2:19
appeared unto him an *a o t L*. . .Luke 1:11
a o t L came upon them. . .Luke 2:9

See *Angel: Type of Christ.*

43. Anger of the Lord
Against idolatry
lest the *a* of the Lord. . .Deut. 6:15
a of the Lord was hot. . .Judg. 2:14

Against sin
a of the Lord was kindled. . .Exod. 4:14
and his *a* was kindled. . .Num. 11:1
God's *a* was kindled. . .Num. 22:22
Lord's *a* was kindled against Israel. . .Num. 32:13
a of the Lord was kindled. . .Josh. 7:1
a of the Lord was kindled. . .2 Sam. 6:7
we are consumed by thine *a*. . .Ps. 90:7
the wrath of God is revealed. . .Rom. 1:18
Because the law worketh wrath. . .Rom. 4:15
shall be saved from wrath through him. . .Rom. 5:9

Judgment and
his *a*, wrath, and indignation. . .Ps. 78:49
both with wrath and fierce *a*. . .Isa. 13:9

Limitations of
gracious and merciful, slow to *a*. . .Neh. 9:17
his *a* endureth but a moment. . .Ps. 30:5
a shut up his tender mercies?. . .Ps. 77:9
turned he his *a* away. . .Ps. 78:38
slow to *a*, and plenteous. . .Ps. 103:8

slow to *a*, and of great. . .Ps. 145:8
a is not turned away. . .Isa. 9:17
I defer mine *a*. . .Isa. 48:9

Provoking
abominations provoked they him
    to *a*. . .Deut. 32:16
provoked him to *a*. . .Ps. 78:58
only provoked me to *a*. . .Jer. 32:30

See *Wrath of God.*

44. Anger, Righteous/Angry
Moses' *a* waxed hot. . .Exod. 32:19
And his *a* was kindled. . .Judg. 14:19
about on them with *a*. . .Mark 3:5
Be ye *a'ry*, and sin not. . .Eph. 4:26

45. Anger, Sin of/Angry
Angry people
a contentious and an *a'ry* woman. . .Prov. 21:19
friendship with an *a'ry* man. . .Prov. 22:24

An *a'ry* man stirreth up strife. . .Prov. 29:22

not selfwilled, not soon *a'ry*. . .Titus 1:7

Avoiding

thine *a* be hot against me. . .Judg. 6:39

Kiss the Son, lest he be *a*. . .Ps. 2:12

rebuke me not in thine *a*. . .Ps. 6:1

thine *a* toward us to cease. . .Ps. 85:4

all these; *a*, wrath, malice. . .Col. 3:8

Examples of

Balaam's *a* was kindled. . .Num. 22:27

Saul's *a* was kindled. . .1 Sam. 20:30

his *a* burned in him. . .Esther 1:12

he was very *a'ry*. . .Jon. 4:1

were filled with wrath. . .Luke 4:28

they were full of wrath. . .Acts 19:28

Foolishness of

wrath killeth the foolish man. . .Job 5:2

fool's wrath is presently known. . .Prov. 12:16

soon *a'ry* dealeth foolishly. . .Prov. 14:17

a fool's wrath is heavier. . .Prov. 27:3

a resteth in the bosom. . .Eccles. 7:9

Provoking

grievous words stir up *a*. . .Prov. 15:1

whoso provoketh him to *a*. . .Prov. 20:2

wrath bringeth forth strife. . .Prov. 30:33

foolish nation I will *a* you. . .Rom. 10:19

provoke not your children to *a*. . .Col. 3:21

Results of

God will not withdraw his *a*. . .Job 9:13

God distributeth sorrows in his *a*. . .Job 21:17

Thy wrath lieth hard upon me. . .Ps. 88:7

Unto whom I sware in my wrath. . .Ps. 95:11

of great wrath shall suffer punishment. . .Prov. 19:19

Slow to

slow to wrath is of great. . .Prov. 14:29

slow to *a* appeaseth strife. . .Prov. 15:18

He that is slow to *a*. . .Prov. 16:32

a man deferreth his *a*. . .Prov. 19:11

slow to speak, slow to wrath. . .James 1:19

Warnings against

Cease from *a*, and forsake wrath. . .Ps. 37:8

A gift in secret pacifieth *a*. . .Prov. 21:14

a'ry countenance a backbiting tongue. . .Prov. 25:23

wise men turn away wrath. . .Prov. 29:8

flee from the wrath to come?. . .Matt. 3:7

a'ry with his brother. . .Matt. 5:22

give place unto wrath. . .Rom. 12:19

bitterness, and wrath, and *a*. . .Eph. 4:31

without wrath and doubting. . .1 Tim. 2:8

the wrath of man worketh not. . .James 1:20

See *Sin*.

46. Anguish

saw the *a* of his soul. . .Gen. 42:21

Moses for *a* of spirit. . .Exod. 6:9

Trouble and *a* have taken hold. . .Ps. 119:143

she remembereth no more the *a*. . .John 16:21

Tribulation and *a*, upon every soul. . .Rom. 2:9

much affliction and *a* of heart. . .2 Cor. 2:4

47. Animals

It is not clear what the Old Testament means when it refers to dragons, and modern scholars have considered a number of

possibilities. Psalm 148:7 obviously refers to a sea creature; another term used for it is "leviathan." But Isaiah 34:14 clearly refers to a land creature. In the New Testament, the term "dragon" refers to the snake Satan. The unicorn, sometimes translated "wild ox" in modern versions, may be the oryx.

Dragon/Dragons

is the poison of dragons. . .Deut. 32:33
dragon shalt thou trample. . .Ps. 91:13
ye dragons, and all deeps. . .Ps. 148:7
an habitation of dragons. . .Isa. 34:13
the dragons and the owls. . .Isa. 43:20
and a den of dragons. . .Jer. 9:11
snuffed up the wind like dragons. . .Jer. 14:6
behold a great red dragon. . .Rev. 12:3

Frogs

river shall bring forth frogs. . .Exod. 8:3
frogs, which destroyed them. . .Ps. 78:45
brought forth frogs in abundance. . .Ps. 105:30
three unclean spirits like frogs. . .Rev. 16:13

Mole/Moles

and the snail, and the mole. . .Lev. 11:30
moles and to the bats. . .Isa. 2:20

Mouse

the weasel, and the mouse. . .Lev. 11:29
the abomination, and the mouse. . .Isa. 66:17

Snail

the lizard, and the snail. . .Lev. 11:30
As a snail which melteth. . .Ps. 58:8

Unicorn/Unicorns

the strength of an unicorn. . .Num. 23:22
horn of an unicorn. . .Ps. 92:10
unicorns shall come down. . .Isa. 34:7

See *Livestock, Mammals, Reptiles, Sea Creatures.*

48. Anointed/ Anointing

Oils and ointments were commonly used for anointing, for grooming or healing purposes, in the biblical era. In a religious sense, anointing was a sign that God had chosen a place, priest, prophet, or leader to fulfill His holy purpose.

spices for *a'ing* oil. . .Exod. 25:6
take the *a'ing* oil, and pour it. . .Exod. 29:7
a'ed therein, and to be consecrated. . .Exod. 29:29
an holy *a'ing* oil. . .Exod. 30:25
a'ed the tabernacle. . .Lev. 8:10
a'ed him, to sanctify him. . .Lev. 8:12
walk before mine *a'ed*. . .1 Sam. 2:35
Lord *a'ed* thee king over Israel?. . .1 Sam. 15:17
horn of oil, and *a'ed* him. . .1 Sam. 16:13
my master, the Lord's *a'ed*. . .1 Sam. 24:6
washed, and *a'ed* himself. . .2 Sam. 12:20
Saying, Touch not mine *a'ed*. . .1 Chron. 16:22
saving strength of his *a'ed*. . .Ps. 28:8
a'ed me to preach good tidings. . .Isa. 61:1
a'ed with oil many. . .Mark 6:13
a'ed them with the ointment. . .Luke 7:38
God *a'ed* Jesus of Nazareth. . .Acts 10:38
hath *a'ed* us, is God. . .2 Cor. 1:21

49. Anxiety

Take no thought for your life. . .Matt. 6:25
take ye thought for raiment?. . .Matt. 6:28
no thought for the morrow. . .Matt. 6:34
take no thought how or what. . .Matt. 10:19
be ye not troubled. . .Mark 13:7
troubled about many things. . .Luke 10:41
Why are ye troubled?. . .Luke 24:38

Let not your heart be troubled. . .John 14:1
we were troubled on every side. . .2 Cor. 7:5
shaken in mind, or be troubled. . .2 Thess. 2:2
their terror, neither be troubled. . .1 Pet. 3:14

See *Worry*.

50. Apologizing

Blessed are the peacemakers. . .Matt. 5:9
have peace one with another. . .Mark 9:50
fruit of the Spirit is love, joy, peace. . .Gal. 5:22
For he is our peace. . .Eph. 2:14
forbearing one another in love. . .Eph. 4:2
unity of the Spirit in the bond of peace. . .Eph. 4:3
be at peace among yourselves. . .1 Thess. 5:13
Follow peace with all men. . .Heb. 12:14
seek peace, and ensue it. . .1 Pet. 3:11

51. Apostasy

Apostasy is defined as a renunciation of faith, a turning away from a previous loyalty.

in time of temptation fall away. . .Luke 8:13
come a falling away. . .2 Thess. 2:3
If they shall fall away. . .Heb. 6:6

52. Apostle/ Apostles

the names of the twelve *a's*. . .Matt. 10:2
send them prophets and *a's*. . .Luke 11:49
numbered with the eleven *a's*. . .Acts 1:26
a's were many signs and wonders. . .Acts 5:12
brought him to the *a's*. . .Acts 9:27
the *a's*, Barnabas and Paul. . .Acts 14:14
to Jerusalem unto the *a's* and elders. . .Acts 15:2

54. Appearance, Physical

men of a great stature. . .Num. 13:32

man looketh on the outward *a*. . .1 Sam. 16:7

a man of great stature. . .2 Sam. 21:20

a man of great stature. . .1 Chron. 11:23

add one cubit unto his stature?. . .Matt. 6:27

increased in wisdom and stature. . .Luke 2:52

Judge not according to the *a*. . .John 7:24

them which glory in *a*. . .2 Cor. 5:12

look on things after the outward *a*?. . .2 Cor. 10:7

See *Outward Appearance*.

a's and elders came together. . .Acts 15:6

ordained of the *a's* and elders. . .Acts 16:4

called to be an *a*. . .Rom. 1:1

the *a* of the Gentiles. . .Rom. 11:13

first *a's*, secondarily prophets. . .1 Cor. 12:28

least of the *a's*. . .1 Cor. 15:9

the *A* and High Priest. . .Heb. 3:1

the commandment of us the *a's*. . .2 Pet. 3:2

53. Apparel

king's gate clothed with sackcloth. . .Esther 4:2

drowsiness shall clothe a man with rags. . .Prov. 23:21

the body than raiment?. . .Matt. 6:25

why take ye thought for raiment?. . .Matt. 6:28

Wherewithal shall we be clothed?. . .Matt. 6:31

John was clothed with camel's hair. . .Mark 1:6

wrapped him in swaddling clothes. . .Luke 2:7

having food and raiment. . .1 Tim. 6:8

a poor man in vile raiment. . .James 2:2

clothed in white raiment. . .Rev. 3:5

clothed with white robes. . .Rev. 7:9

clothed in pure and white linen. . .Rev. 15:6

clothed with a vesture. . .Rev. 19:13

See *Attire/Attired; Clothe/Clothed/Clothes/Clothing, Physical; Fashion; Garment/Garments*.

55. Appetite

a man given to *a*. . .Prov. 23:2

yet the *a* is not filled. . .Eccles. 6:7

56. Approve/ Approved/Approvest/ Approveth

the LORD *a'th* not. . .Lam. 3:36
a man *a'd* of God. . .Acts 2:22
his will, and *a'st* the things. . .Rom. 2:18
and *a'd* of men. . .Rom. 14:18
Salute Apelles *a'd* in Christ. . .Rom. 16:10
commendeth himself is *a'd*. . .2 Cor. 10:18
a things that are excellent. . .Phil. 1:10
shew thyself *a'd* unto God. . .2 Tim. 2:15

57. Arguments

And the mouth

and fill my mouth with *a*. . .Job 23:4
the strife of tongues. . .Ps. 31:20
no talebearer, the strife ceaseth. . .Prov. 26:20

And sin

froward man soweth strife. . .Prov. 16:28
loveth transgression that loveth strife. . .Prov. 17:19
a strife among them. . .Luke 22:24
envying, and strife, and divisions. . .1 Cor. 3:3
wraths, strifes, backbitings. . .2 Cor. 12:20

questions and strifes of words. . .1 Tim. 6:4
strife is, there is confusion. . .James 3:16

Avoiding

house full of sacrifices with strife. . .Prov. 17:1
a man to cease from strife. . .Prov. 20:3
strife and reproach shall cease. . .Prov. 22:10
they do gender strifes. . .2 Tim. 2:23
if any man have a quarrel against any. . .Col. 3:13

Stirring up

a strife unto our neighbours. . .Ps. 80:6
Hatred stirreth up strifes. . .Prov. 10:12
A wrathful man stirreth up strife. . .Prov. 15:18
The beginning of strife. . .Prov. 17:14
contentious man to kindle strife. . .Prov. 26:21
a proud heart stirreth up strife. . .Prov. 28:25
An angry man stirreth up strife. . .Prov. 29:22
forcing of wrath bringeth forth strife. . .Prov. 30:33

58. Ark of the Covenant

the *a o t c* of the LORD. . .Num. 10:33
nevertheless the *a o t c*. . .Num. 14:44
to bear the *a o t c*. . .Deut. 10:8
put it in the side of the *a o t c*. . .Deut. 31:26
see the *a o t c* of the LORD. . .Josh. 3:3
which bare the *a o t c* stood. . .Josh. 4:9
a o t c of the LORD came into. . .1 Sam. 4:5
stood before the *a o t c*. . .1 Kings 3:15
bring up the *a o t c*. . .1 Kings 8:1
went to bring up the *a o t c*. . .1 Chron. 15:25
he left there before the *a o t c*. . .1 Chron. 16:37
house of cedars, but the *a o t c*. . .1 Chron. 17:1
and covered the *a o t c*. . .1 Chron. 28:18

priests brought in the *a o t c*. . .2 Chron. 5:7
a o t c overlaid round about with gold. . .Heb. 9:4

---

59. Armageddon

Only mentioned once in scripture, this place where evil is to be finally overthrown is not clearly identified. Based on Revelation 16:12, some scholars believe it will be near the Euphrates River. Others posit that this place is the same as Megiddo, in the Plain of Jezreel (or Esdraelon); below this fortified city many battles have been fought.

by the waters of Megiddo. . .Judg. 5:19
in the valley of Jezreel. . .Judg. 6:33
upon the great river Euphrates. . .Rev. 16:12
battle of that great day. . .Rev. 16:14
called in the Hebrew tongue *A*. . .Rev. 16:16

---

60. Arms

a of his hands were made. . .Gen. 49:24
is broken by mine *a*. . .2 Sam. 22:35
will break his *a*. . .Ezek. 30:22
a of the king of Babylon. . .Ezek. 30:24
a of the south shall not withstand. . .Dan. 11:15

---

61. Army

Assyrian
unto king Hezekiah with a great *a*. . .Isa. 36:2

Babylonian
Babylon's *a* besieged Jerusalem. . .Jer. 32:2
king of Babylon, and all his *a*. . .Jer. 34:1
Babylon's *a* fought against Jerusalem. . .Jer. 34:7
hand of the king of Babylon's *a*. . .Jer. 34:21
the king of Babylon's *a*. . .Jer. 38:3
all his *a* against Jerusalem. . .Jer. 39:1
his *a*, against Jerusalem. . .Jer. 52:4
the wages for his *a*. . .Ezek. 29:19

Chaldean
a of the Chaldees pursued. . .2 Kings 25:5
all the *a* of the Chaldees. . .2 Kings 25:10
fear of the *a* of the Chaldeans. . .Jer. 35:11
the whole *a* of the Chaldeans. . .Jer. 37:10
Chaldeans' *a* pursued after them. . .Jer. 39:5
all the *a* of the Chaldeans. . .Jer. 52:14

Egyptian
a, and overtook them encamping. . .Exod. 14:9
the *a* of Egypt. . .Deut. 11:4
Then Pharaoh's *a* was come. . .Jer. 37:5
his *a* slain by the sword. . .Ezek. 32:31

God's
his will in the *a* of heaven. . .Dan. 4:35
and against his *a*. . .Rev. 19:19

Of Israel
slew of the *a* in the field. . .1 Sam. 4:2
and ran toward the *a*. . .1 Sam. 17:48
number thee an *a*. . .1 Kings 20:25
Joab led forth the power of the *a*. . .1 Chron. 20:1
given to the *a* of Israel?. . .2 Chron. 25:9

soldiers of the *a* which Amaziah. . .2 Chron. 25:13

Of Judah
a of valiant men of war. . .2 Chron. 13:3
Asa had an *a* of men. . .2 Chron. 14:8
they went out before the *a*. . .2 Chron. 20:21
a of Israel go with thee. . .2 Chron. 25:7

62. Arrogance/ Arrogancy
let not *a'y* come out of your mouth. . .1 Sam. 2:3
hate evil: pride, and *a'y*. . .Prov. 8:13
high wall in his own conceit. . .Prov. 18:11
wise in his own conceit. . .Prov. 26:5
wise in his own conceit?. . .Prov. 26:12
wiser in his own conceit. . .Prov. 26:16
wise in his own conceit. . .Prov. 28:11
a'y of the proud to cease. . .Isa. 13:11
his loftiness, and his *a'y*. . .Jer. 48:29
wise in your own conceits. . .Rom. 11:25
wise in your own conceits. . .Rom. 12:16

63. Art

Though Exodus 20:4 forbade Israel from making graven images for purposes of

idolatry, Israel had a rich history of the arts. First Kings 5–7 describes the architecture of Jerusalem's temple and the king's palace. The literary arts are obvious in the written scriptures.

Idolatrous
he had made it a molten calf. . .Exod. 32:4
every form of creeping things. . .Ezek. 8:10

Music and dance
with timbrels and with dances. . .Exod. 15:20
David took an harp, and played. . .1 Sam. 16:23
the congregation with singing. . .1 Chron. 6:32
cornet, and with trumpets. . .1 Chron. 15:28
upon the harp will I praise. . .Ps. 43:4
joyful noise unto the Lord. . .Ps. 98:4
praise his name in the dance. . .Ps. 149:3
psalms and hymns and spiritual songs. . .Eph. 5:19

Smiths'
cunning works, to work in gold. . .Exod. 31:4

Visual arts
in cutting of stones. . .Exod. 31:5
two cherubims of olive tree. . .1 Kings 6:23
carved all the walls of the house. . .1 Kings 6:29

64. Ascension, the
Thou hast ascended on high. . .Ps. 68:18
he was received up into heaven. . .Mark 16:19
no man hath ascended up to heaven. . .John 3:13
I ascend unto my Father. . .John 20:17
he was taken up. . .Acts 1:9
ascended into the heavens. . .Acts 2:34
Who shall ascend into heaven?. . .Rom. 10:6

he ascended up on high. . .Eph. 4:8
ascended up far above all heavens. . .Eph. 4:10

65. Assault/ Assaulted

that would *a* them. . .Esther 8:11
there was an *a* made. . .Acts 14:5
a'ed the house of Jason. . .Acts 17:5

66. Assembly/ Assemblies/ Assembling

Of saints

a of the congregation. . .Exod. 12:6
the *a* was gathered together. . .Lev. 8:4
a of the children of Israel. . .Num. 8:9
the *a* of the saints. . .Ps. 89:7
the *a* of the elders. . .Ps. 107:32
the *a* of the upright. . .Ps. 111:1

forsaking the *a'ing* of ourselves. . .Heb. 10:25
a and church of the firstborn. . .Heb. 12:23
if there come unto your *a*. . .James 2:2

Of sinners

a'ies of violent men. . .Ps. 86:14
the congregation and *a*. . .Prov. 5:14
an *a* of treacherous men. . .Jer. 9:2
a of the mockers. . .Jer. 15:17
determined in a lawful *a*. . .Acts 19:39

67. Assurance

quietness and *a* for ever. . .Isa. 32:17
given *a* unto all men. . .Acts 17:31
full *a* of understanding. . .Col. 2:2
full *a* of hope. . .Heb. 6:11
in full *a* of faith. . .Heb. 10:22

68. Astrologers

lift up thine eyes unto heaven. . .Deut. 4:19
the *a*, the stargazers. . .Isa. 47:13
be not dismayed at the signs of heaven. . .Jer. 10:2
better than all the magicians and *a*. . .Dan. 1:20

cannot the wise men, the *a*. . .Dan. 2:27
the magicians, the *a*. . .Dan. 4:7
to bring in the *a*. . .Dan. 5:7
the wise men, the *a*. . .Dan. 5:15
we have seen his star in the east. . .Matt. 2:2
the star, which they saw. . .Matt. 2:9

See *Magic/Magicians*.

69. Athletics
wrestled a man with him. . .Gen. 32:24
a strong man to run a race. . .Ps. 19:5
they which run in a race run all. . .1 Cor. 9:24
I therefore so run. . .1 Cor. 9:26
Ye did run well. . .Gal. 5:7
I have not run in vain. . .Phil. 2:16
bodily exercise profiteth little. . .1 Tim. 4:8
run with patience the race. . .Heb. 12:1

70. Atonement
*The books of Leviticus and Numbers prescribe
the various and extensive atonement offerings made by the priests for sinners. These Old
Testament sacrifices prefigured Jesus' sacrifice
on the cross.*

for a sin offering for *a*. . .Exod. 29:36
an *a* for your sin. . .Exod. 32:30
to make an *a* for Israel. . .1 Chron. 6:49
we have now received the *a*. . .Rom. 5:11

71. Attire/Attired
a woman with the *a* of an harlot. . .Prov. 7:10
or a bride her *a*?. . .Jer. 2:32
linen mitre shall he be *a'ed*. . .Lev. 16:4

See *Apparel; Clothe/Clothed/Clothes/Clothing,
Physical; Fashion; Garment/Garments*.

72. Attitude
Gentle
be gentle unto all men. . .2 Tim. 2:24
but gentle, shewing all meekness. . .Titus 3:2

Humble
humble himself as this little child. . .Matt. 18:4
humbleness of mind. . .Col. 3:12
be clothed with humility. . .1 Pet. 5:5

Joyful
put their trust in thee rejoice. . .Ps. 5:11
rejoice, ye righteous. . .Ps. 32:11
Rejoice in the Lord always. . .Phil. 4:4

Meek

The meek will he guide. . .Ps. 25:9

The Lord lifteth up the meek. . .Ps. 147:6

Meekness, temperance. . .Gal. 5:23

With all lowliness and meekness. . .Eph. 4:2

Quiet

ye study to be quiet. . .1 Thess. 4:11

a meek and quiet spirit. . .1 Pet. 3:4

73. Attributes of God

Eternal

the Lord, the everlasting God. . .Gen. 21:33

Lord shall reign for ever. . .Exod. 15:18

eternal God is thy refuge. . .Deut. 33:27

his eternal power and Godhead. . .Rom. 1:20

unto the King eternal. . .1 Tim. 1:17

Holy

for I am holy. . .Lev. 11:44

for he is an holy God. . .Josh. 24:19

none holy as the Lord. . .1 Sam. 2:2

thou Holy One of Israel. . .Ps. 71:22

the Holy One of God. . .Mark 1:24

the holy Spirit of God. . .Eph. 4:30

Infinite

his understanding is infinite. . .Ps. 147:5

Invisible

invisible, the only wise God. . .1 Tim. 1:17

Longsuffering

merciful and gracious, longsuffering. . .Exod. 34:6

The Lord is longsuffering. . .Num. 14:18

endured with much longsuffering. . .Rom. 9:22

the God of patience. . .Rom. 15:5

longsuffering to us-ward. . .2 Pet. 3:9

the longsuffering of our Lord. . .2 Pet. 3:15

Loving

thy lovingkindness, O God!. . .Ps. 36:7

according to thy lovingkindness. . .Ps. 51:1

the love of God. . .Luke 11:42

God so loved the world. . .John 3:16

separate us from the love of God. . .Rom. 8:39

the love of Christ. . .Eph. 3:19

love the Father hath bestowed. . .1 John 3:1

perceive we the love of God. . .1 John 3:16

God is love. . .1 John 4:8

Merciful

shewing mercy unto thousands. . .Exod. 20:6

merciful and gracious. . .Exod. 34:6

the greatness of thy mercy. . .Neh. 13:22

trust in the mercy of God. . .Ps. 52:8

our God is merciful. . .Ps. 116:5

his mercy endureth for ever. . .Ps. 136:2

God, who is rich in mercy. . .Eph. 2:4

Omnipotent

the power, and the glory. . .1 Chron. 29:11

power and might. . .2 Chron. 20:6

ruleth by his power for ever. . .Ps. 66:7
Lord God omnipotent reigneth. . .Rev. 19:6

Omnipresent

shall I flee from thy presence?. . .Ps. 139:7
and move, and have our being. . .Acts 17:28
never leave thee, nor forsake thee. . .Heb. 13:5

Omniscient

art acquainted with all my ways. . .Ps. 139:3
his understanding is infinite. . .Ps. 147:5
thee in the belly I knew thee. . .Jer. 1:5

Powerful

with great power. . .Exod. 32:11
the power of his works. . .Ps. 111:6
made the earth by his power. . .Jer. 10:12
by my great power. . .Jer. 27:5
power on earth to forgive sins. . .Mark 2:10
in the power of the Spirit. . .Luke 4:14
power he commandeth. . .Luke 4:36
the power of the Lord. . .Luke 5:17
Holy Ghost and with power. . .Acts 10:38
the glory of his power. . .2 Thess. 1:9

Righteous

God of Israel, thou art righteous. . .Ezra 9:15
righteous God trieth the hearts. . .Ps. 7:9
heavens shall declare his righteousness. . .Ps. 50:6
Gracious is the Lord, and righteous. . .Ps. 116:5
God, and his righteousness. . .Matt. 6:33

74. Authority

righteous are in *a*. . .Prov. 29:2
taught them as one having *a*. . .Matt. 7:29
I am a man under *a*. . .Matt. 8:9
by what *a* I do. . .Matt. 21:24
with *a* commandeth he. . .Mark 1:27
power and *a* over all devils. . .Luke 9:1
a to execute judgment. . .John 5:27
all *a* and power. . .1 Cor. 15:24
for all that are in *a*. . .1 Tim. 2:2
usurp *a* over the man. . .1 Tim. 2:12
rebuke with all *a*. . .Titus 2:15

75. Avenge / Avenged / Avenger / Avengeth

Thou shalt not *a*. . .Lev. 19:18
a the quarrel of my covenant. . .Lev. 26:25
refuge from the *a'r*. . .Num. 35:12
Lest the *a'r* of the blood. . .Deut. 19:6

a the blood of his servants. . .Deut. 32:43
people had *a'd* themselves. . .Josh. 10:13
the Lord *a* me of thee. . .1 Sam. 24:12
a themselves on their enemies. . .Esther 8:13
still the enemy and the *a'r*. . .Ps. 8:2
It is God that *a'th* me. . .Ps. 18:47
a me of mine enemies. . .Isa. 1:24
God *a* his own elect. . .Luke 18:7
Dearly beloved, *a* not yourselves. . .Rom. 12:19
Lord is the *a'r* of all. . .1 Thess. 4:6
judge and *a* our blood. . .Rev. 6:10
hath *a'd* the blood. . .Rev. 19:2

76. Awe

Stand in *a*, and sin not. . .Ps. 4:4
the world stand in *a* of him. . .Ps. 33:8
standeth in *a* of thy word. . .Ps. 119:161

77. Babble/Babbler/ Babbling/Babblings

who hath *b'ing*?. . .Prov. 23:29
a *b'r* is no better. . .Eccles. 10:11
What will this *b'r* say?. . .Acts 17:18
avoiding profane and vain *b'ings*. . .1 Tim. 6:20
shun profane and vain *b'ings*. . .2 Tim. 2:16

78. Babies

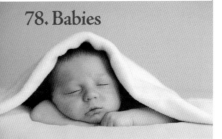

behold, the babe wept. . .Exod. 2:6
suckling also with the man. . .Deut. 32:25
infant and suckling. . .1 Sam. 15:3
an infant of days. . .Isa. 65:20
child and suckling. . .Jer. 44:7
shall bring forth a son. . .Matt. 1:23
babe leaped in her womb. . .Luke 1:41
babe wrapped in swaddling clothes. . .Luke 2:12

See *Boys, Child/Children, Girls.*

79. Backbiting/ Backbitings

slandereth his neighbour. . .Ps. 101:5
he that uttereth a slander. . .Prov. 10:18
A talebearer revealeth secrets. . .Prov. 11:13
a whisperer separateth chief friends. . .Prov. 16:28
words of a talebearer are as wounds. . .Prov. 18:8
a talebearer revealeth secrets. . .Prov. 20:19
where there is no talebearer. . .Prov. 26:20
words of a talebearer. . .Prov. 26:22
a murmuring of the Grecians. . .Acts 6:1
Being defamed. . .1 Cor. 4:13
strifes, *b's*, whisperings. . .2 Cor. 12:20
without murmurings and disputings. . .Phil. 2:14
wives be grave, not slanderers. . .1 Tim. 3:11
tattlers also and busybodies. . .1 Tim. 5:13
prating against us. . .3 John 1:10

80. Backslider/ Backsliding/ Backslidings

The *b* in heart. . .Prov. 14:14
b'ings shall reprove thee. . .Jer. 2:19
which *b'ing* Israel hath done?. . .Jer. 3:6

Turn, O *b'ing* children. . .Jer. 3:14
our *b'ings* are many. . .Jer. 14:7
I will heal their *b'ing*. . .Hosea 14:4

81. Bake/Baked/Baken/Bakers

b unleavened bread. . .Gen. 19:3
the chief of the *b'rs*. . .Gen. 40:2
b'd unleavened cakes of the dough. . .Exod. 12:39
shall not be *b'n* with leaven. . .Lev. 6:17
to be cooks, and to be *b'rs*. . .1 Sam. 8:13
a cake *b'n* on the coals. . .1 Kings 19:6

82. Balance

Meekness, temperance. . .Gal. 5:23
moderation be known unto all men. . .Phil. 4:5
to temperance patience. . .2 Pet. 1:6

83. Bald/Baldness

he is *b*; yet is he clean. . .Lev. 13:40
They shall not make *b'ness*. . .Lev. 21:5
Go up, thou *b* head. . .2 Kings 2:23
to mourning, and to *b'ness*. . .Isa. 22:12

84. Banquet/Banqueting/Banquetings

b that I have prepared. . .Esther 5:4
at the *b* of wine. . .Esther 7:2
to the *b'ing* house. . .Song of Sol. 2:4
came into the *b* house. . .Dan. 5:10
revellings, *b'ings*. . .1 Pet. 4:3

See *Entertained/Entertainment, Revelry.*

85. Baptism/Baptized
And the Holy Ghost

b'd with the Holy Ghost. . .Acts 1:5
that these should not be *b'd*. . .Acts 10:47
b'd with the Holy Ghost. . .Acts 11:16
Spirit are we all *b'd*. . .1 Cor. 12:13

And Jesus

Jesus, when he was *b'd*. . .Matt. 3:16
b'd with the *b*. . .Matt. 20:22
a *b* to be *b'd* with. . .Luke 12:50
Jesus made and *b'd* more disciples. . .John 4:1
received his word were *b'd*. . .Acts 2:41

Repent, and be *b'd*. . .Acts 2:38
b'd, both men and women. . .Acts 8:12
b'd in the name of the Lord. . .Acts 8:16
hinder me to be *b'd*?. . .Acts 8:36
b'd in the name of the Lord. . .Acts 19:5
b'd into Jesus Christ. . .Rom. 6:3
b'd into Christ. . .Gal. 3:27

Examples of
arose, and was *b'd*. . .Acts 9:18
when she was *b'd*. . .Acts 16:15
b'd, he and all his. . .Acts 16:33
believed, and were *b'd*. . .Acts 18:8
arise, and be *b'd*. . .Acts 22:16

Of John
were *b'd* of him. . .Matt. 3:6
The *b* of John. . .Matt. 21:25
publicans to be *b'd*. . .Luke 3:12
b'd with the *b* of John. . .Luke 7:29
Unto what then were ye *b'd*?. . .Acts 19:3

Salvation and
the *b* of repentance. . .Mark 1:4
is *b'd* shall be saved. . .Mark 16:16

See *Great Commission*.

86. Barren
But Sarai was *b*. . .Gen. 11:30
because she was *b*. . .Gen. 25:21
but Rachel was *b*. . .Gen. 29:31
male or female *b*. . .Deut. 7:14
was *b*, and bare not. . .Judg. 13:2
b woman to keep house. . .Ps. 113:9
the *b* womb. . .Prov. 30:16

Sing, O *b*. . .Isa. 54:1
Elisabeth was *b*. . .Luke 1:7
Blessed are the *b*. . .Luke 23:29

87. Bastard
she is with child by whoredom. . .Gen. 38:24
A *b* shall not enter. . .Deut. 23:2
And a *b* shall dwell in Ashdod. . .Zech. 9:6
he was the son of an harlot. . .Judg. 11:1

See *Harlot/Harlot's/Harlots*, *Whore/Whoredom/Whoremonger/Whoremongers*.

88. Bathe
As a sign of hospitality, a host would bathe guests' feet after they traveled to his home. Under the Old Testament law, ceremonial washing was part of the ritual purification process.

wash your feet. . .Gen. 18:4
b himself in water. . .Lev. 15:5
nor *b* his flesh. . .Lev. 17:16
Wash thyself therefore. . .Ruth 3:3
saw a woman washing herself. . .2 Sam. 11:2

washed, and anointed himself. . .2 Sam. 12:20
wash in Jordan seven times. . .2 Kings 5:10
wash myself with snow water. . .Job 9:30
wash mine hands in innocency. . .Ps. 26:6

89. Beauty/ Beautiful

Human
Rachel was *b'iful*. . .Gen. 29:17
of a *b'iful* countenance. . .1 Sam. 16:12
and of a *b'iful* countenance. . .1 Sam. 25:3
very *b'iful* to look upon. . .2 Sam. 11:2
as Absalom for his *b*. . .2 Sam. 14:25
the princes her *b*. . .Esther 1:11
the maid was fair and *b'iful*. . .Esther 2:7
his *b* to consume away. . .Ps. 39:11
greatly desire thy *b*. . .Ps. 45:11
their *b* shall consume. . .Ps. 49:14
Lust not after her *b*. . .Prov. 6:25
the *b* of old men. . .Prov. 20:29
and *b* is vain. . .Prov. 31:30
b'iful, O my love. . .Song of Sol. 6:4
How *b'iful* are thy feet. . .Song of Sol. 7:1

b is a fading flower. . .Isa. 28:1
no *b* that we should desire. . .Isa. 53:2
appear *b'iful* outward. . .Matt. 23:27

Of the gospel
How *b'iful* upon the mountains. . .Isa. 52:7
How *b'iful* are the feet of them. . .Rom. 10:15

Of holiness
b of holiness. . .1 Chron. 16:29
b of the LORD. . .Ps. 27:4
the perfection of *b*. . .Ps. 50:2
b are in his sanctuary. . .Ps. 96:6
b for ashes. . .Isa. 61:3

Of things
precious stones for *b*. . .2 Chron. 3:6
B'iful for situation. . .Ps. 48:2
every thing *b'iful* in his time. . .Eccles. 3:11

90. Beggar/ Begging

lifteth up the *b*. . .1 Sam. 2:8
nor his seed *b'ing* bread. . .Ps. 37:25
b named Lazarus. . .Luke 16:20
the *b* died. . .Luke 16:22
by the highway side *b'ing*. . .Mark 10:46

See *Lack/Lacked; Poor, the; Poverty.*

91. Behead/Beheaded

heifer that is *b'ed*. . .Deut. 21:6

slew him, and *b'ed* him. . .2 Sam. 4:7

b'ed John in the prison. . .Matt. 14:10

John, whom I *b'ed*. . .Mark 6:16

b'ed him in the prison. . .Mark 6:27

them that were *b'ed*. . .Rev. 20:4

---

92. Believe/Believed/ Believeth/Believest

In God

he *b'd* in the Lord. . .Gen. 15:6

b that the Lord. . .Exod. 4:5

b the voice of the latter sign. . .Exod. 4:8

b'd the Lord. . .Exod. 14:31

will it be ere they *b* me. . .Num. 14:11

b'd to see the goodness. . .Ps. 27:13

b'd they his words. . .Ps. 106:12

b'd thy commandments. . .Ps. 119:66

b'th shall not make haste. . .Isa. 28:16

because he *b'd* in his God. . .Dan. 6:23

people of Nineveh *b'd* God. . .Jon. 3:5

as Abraham *b'd* God. . .Gal. 3:6

must *b* that he is. . .Heb. 11:6

b'st that there is one God. . .James 2:19

In Jesus

as thou hast *b'd*. . .Matt. 8:13

B ye that I am able. . .Matt. 9:28

little ones which *b* in me. . .Matt. 18:6

b'ing, ye shall receive. . .Matt. 21:22

b the gospel. . .Mark 1:15

possible to him that *b'th*. . .Mark 9:23

I *b*; help thou mine unbelief. . .Mark 9:24

Fear not: *b* only. . .Luke 8:50

all men through him might *b*. . .John 1:7

b on his name. . .John 1:12

his disciples *b'd* on him. . .John 2:11

whosoever *b'th* in him. . .John 3:16

He that *b'th* on the Son. . .John 3:36

work of God, that ye *b*. . .John 6:29

b'th on me shall never thirst. . .John 6:35

He that *b'th* on me. . .John 7:38

he that *b'th* in me. . .John 11:25

b that thou hast sent me. . .John 11:42

b in the light. . .John 12:36

b that I am he. . .John 13:19

b in God, *b* also in me. . .John 14:1

b'th on me, the works. . .John 14:12

b'd that I came out. . .John 16:27

all that *b* are justified. . .Acts 13:39

ordained to eternal life *b'd*. . .Acts 13:48

B on the Lord Jesus Christ. . .Acts 16:31

Gentiles which *b*. . .Acts 21:25

justifier of him which *b'th*. . .Rom. 3:26

b that we shall also live. . .Rom. 6:8

b in thine heart that God. . .Rom. 10:9

b that Jesus died and rose again. . .1 Thess. 4:14

b to the saving of the soul. . .Heb. 10:39

which *b* he is precious. . .1 Pet. 2:7

b'th that Jesus is the Son. . .1 John 5:5

In truth

Beareth all things, *b'th* all things. . .1 Cor. 13:7

Salvation and

b'th and is baptized. . .Mark 16:16

b and be saved. . .Luke 8:12

Scripture

they *b'd* the scripture. . .John 2:22

For had ye *b'd* Moses. . .John 5:46

See *Coming to Christ, Conversion, Repentance, Salvation, Unbelief.*

93. Beloved

The *b* of the Lᴏʀᴅ. . .Deut. 33:12

who was *b* of his God. . .Neh. 13:26

thy *b* may be delivered. . .Ps. 60:5

he giveth his *b* sleep. . .Ps. 127:2

dearly *b* of my soul. . .Jer. 12:7

O Daniel, a man greatly *b*. . .Dan. 10:11

This is my *b* Son. . .Matt. 3:17

whom I have chosen; my *b*. . .Matt. 12:18

b of God, called. . .Rom. 1:7

b for the father's sakes. . .Rom. 11:28

my *b* brethren. . .1 Cor. 15:58

accepted in the *b*. . .Eph. 1:6

elect of God, holy and *b*. . .Col. 3:12

Luke, the *b* physician. . .Col. 4:14

brethren *b* of the Lord. . .2 Thess. 2:13

See *Special to God.*

94. Benevolence

hath not left off his kindness. . .Ruth 2:20

this kindness unto your lord. . .2 Sam. 2:5

shew the kindness of God. . .2 Sam. 9:3

desire of a man is his kindness. . .Prov. 19:22

tongue is the law of kindness. . .Prov. 31:26

render unto the wife due *b*. . .1 Cor. 7:3

bowels of mercies, kindness. . .Col. 3:12

having compassion one of another. . .1 Pet. 3:8

to brotherly kindness charity. . .2 Pet. 1:7

of some have compassion. . .Jude 1:22

95. Bereaved

b'd of my children. . Gen. 42:36

b'd of my children. . .Gen. 43:14

grief were throughly weighed. . .Job 6:2

consumed because of grief. . .Ps. 6:7

sorrows of death compassed me. . .Ps. 18:4

my life is spent with grief. . .Ps. 31:10

to the house of mourning. . .Eccles. 7:2

great mourning, Rachel weeping. . .Matt. 2:18

96. Betray/Betrayed/Betrayers

b me to mine enemies. . .1 Chron. 12:17

Judas Iscariot, who also *b'ed* him. . .Matt. 10:4

Son of man shall be *b'ed*. . .Matt. 17:22

shall *b* one another. . .Matt. 24:10

b'ed to be crucified. . .Matt. 26:2

one of you shall *b* me. . .Matt. 26:21

b'ed the innocent blood. . .Matt. 27:4

brother shall *b* the brother. . .Mark 13:12

b'ers and murderers. . .Acts 7:52

b'ed took bread. . .1 Cor. 11:23

97. Betroth/Betrothed

In the biblical time, a betrothal, or engagement, was considered as binding as a marriage. A betrothed woman who was unfaithful to her betrothed could be stoned. This relationship is also a picture of the relationship between God and His people.

entice a maid that is not *b'ed*.. . .Exod. 22:16

hath *b'ed* a wife. . .Deut. 20:7

I will *b* thee unto me. . .Hosea 2:19

Mary was espoused to Joseph. . .Matt. 1:18

Mary his espoused wife. . .Luke 2:5

I have espoused you. . .2 Cor. 11:2

See *Courtship*, *Dating*, *Marriage/Marry/Marrying*.

98. Bird/Birds

every *b* of every sort. . .Gen. 7:14

he sent forth a dove. . .Gen. 8:8

turtledoves, or of young pigeons. . .Lev. 1:14

owl, and the night hawk. . .Lev. 11:16

swan, and the pelican. . .Lev. 11:18

brought quails from the sea. . .Num. 11:31

all clean *b's* ye shall eat. . .Deut. 14:11

stork, and the heron. . .Deut. 14:18

If a *b's* nest chance to be. . .Deut. 22:6

apes, and peacocks. . .1 Kings 10:22

feathers unto the ostrich?. . .Job 39:13

sparrow alone upon the house top. . .Ps. 102:7

Where the *b's* make their nests. . .Ps. 104:17

crane or a swallow. . .Isa. 38:14

mount up with wings as eagles. . .Isa. 40:31

stork in the heaven. . .Jer. 8:7

b's of the air have nests. . .Matt. 8:20

two sparrows sold for a farthing?. . .Matt. 10:29

99. Birth

day of one's *b*. . .Eccles. 7:1

b of Jesus Christ. . .Matt. 1:18

rejoice at his *b*. . .Luke 1:14

I travail in *b*. . .Gal. 4:19

100. Blame/Blamed

the ministry be not *b'd*. . .2 Cor. 6:3
no man should *b* us. . .2 Cor. 8:20
he was to be *b'd*. . .Gal. 2:11

101. Blameless

sabbath, and are *b*. . .Matt. 12:5
ordinances of the Lord *b*. . .Luke 1:6
that ye may be *b*. . .1 Cor. 1:8
shall have put on incorruption. . .1 Cor. 15:54
holy and without blame. . .Eph. 1:4
b and harmless. . .Phil. 2:15
in the law, *b*. . .Phil. 3:6
be preserved *b*. . .1 Thess. 5:23
A bishop then must be *b*. . .1 Tim. 3:2
deacon, being found *b*. . .1 Tim. 3:10
without spot, and *b*. . .2 Pet. 3:14

102. Blaspheme/ Blasphemed/ Blasphemeth/ Blasphemest

b'th the name of the Lord. . .Lev. 24:16
enemies of the Lord to *b*. . .2 Sam. 12:14
Thou *b'st*. . .John 10:36
themselves, and *b'd*. . .Acts 18:6
name of God is *b'd*. . .Rom. 2:24
doctrine be not *b'd*. . .1 Tim. 6:1
word of God be not *b'd*. . .Titus 2:5

103. Blasphemy/ Blasphemer/ Blasphemers

b against the Holy Ghost. . .Matt. 12:31
He hath spoken *b*. . .Matt. 26:65
b, pride, foolishness. . .Mark 7:22
anger, wrath, malice, *b*. . .Col. 3:8
Who was before a *b'r*. . .1 Tim. 1:13
boasters, proud, *b'rs*. . .2 Tim. 3:2

See *Idolatry*.

104. Blemish/ Blemishes

In the Old Testament sacrifices, unblemished, perfectly healthy animals were to be offered to God. The lack of blemish was a picture of holiness.

lamb shall be without *b*. . .Exod. 12:5
two rams without *b*. . .Exod. 29:1
No man that hath a *b*. . .Lev. 21:21
b, that shall ye not offer. . .Lev. 22:20

cause a *b* in his neighbour. . .Lev. 24:19

there was no *b* in him. . .2 Sam. 14:25

Children in whom was no *b*. . .Dan. 1:4

holy and without *b*. . .Eph. 5:27

without *b* and without spot. . .1 Pet. 1:19

Spots they are and *b'es*. . .2 Pet. 2:13

105. Bless/ Blessed

God gives His people many blessings, or good things, of which these are a sampling.

By God

God *b'ed* them. . .Gen. 1:22

I will *b* thee. . .Gen. 12:2

b'ed the Egyptian's house. . .Gen. 39:5

b'ed the sabbath day. . .Exod. 20:11

The Lord *b* thee. . .Num. 6:24

B'ed shalt thou be. . .Deut. 28:6

thou wouldest *b* me indeed. . .1 Chron. 4:10

b his people with peace. . .Ps. 29:11

b them that fear the Lord. . .Ps. 115:13

b'ed art thou among women. . .Luke 1:28

b'ed is the fruit of thy womb. . .Luke 1:42

b'ed are they that hear. . .Luke 11:28

B'ed are they whose iniquities. . .Rom. 4:7

The obedient believer

B'ed is the man that walketh. . .Ps. 1:1

B'ed are all they. . .Ps. 2:12

B'ed is he whose transgression. . .Ps. 32:1

B'ed is the nation. . .Ps. 33:12

b'ed is the man. . .Ps. 34:8

B'ed is that man. . .Ps. 40:4

B'ed is he that considereth. . .Ps. 41:1

B'ed are they that dwell. . .Ps. 84:4

B'ed are they that keep. . .Ps. 106:3

B'ed are the undefiled. . .Ps. 119:1

B'ed is every one. . .Ps. 128:1

his children are *b'ed*. . .Prov. 20:7

B'ed is the man that trusteth. . .Jer. 17:7

B'ed are the poor in spirit. . .Matt. 5:3

b'ed to give than to receive. . .Acts 20:35

B'ed is the man that endureth. . .James 1:12

Praise

b'ed be my rock. . .2 Sam. 22:47

Every day will I *b* thee. . .Ps. 145:2

doth not *b* their mother. . .Prov. 30:11

arise up, and call her *b'ed*. . .Prov. 31:28

b them that curse you. . .Matt. 5:44

b'ed is he. . .Matt. 11:6

B'ed is he that cometh. . .Matt. 21:9

B them which persecute you. . .Rom. 12:14

106. Blessing/Blessings

b and a curse. . .Deut. 11:26

b's shall come on thee. . .Deut. 28:2

B's are upon the head. . .Prov. 10:6

b of the Lord. . .Prov. 10:22

b of the upright. . .Prov. 11:11

shall abound with *b's*. . .Prov. 28:20

pour you out a *b*. . .Mal. 3:10

b of Abraham. . .Gal. 3:14

107. Blind/Blinded

Scripture refers to physical blindness, but it also uses this disability as a picture of those who are spiritually unseeing.

the seeing, or the *b*?. . .Exod. 4:11

stumblingblock before the *b*. . .Lev. 19:14

openeth the eyes of the *b*. . .Ps. 146:8

eyes of the *b* shall be opened. . .Isa. 35:5

b men came to him. . .Matt. 9:28

b receive their sight. . .Matt. 11:5

if the *b* lead the *b*. . .Matt. 15:14

lame, *b*, dumb, maimed. . .Matt. 15:30

Woe unto you, ye *b* guides. . .Matt. 23:16

b Bartimaeus. . .Mark 10:46

ye say was born *b*?. . .John 9:19

b'ed their eyes, and hardened. . .John 12:40

thou shalt be *b*. . .Acts 13:11

their minds were *b'ed*. . .2 Cor. 3:14

hath *b'ed* the minds. . .2 Cor. 4:4

darkness hath *b'ed* his eyes. . .1 John 2:11

See *Ailments, Deaf, Disabilities, Diseases, Dumb.*

108. Blood

Animals'

ye shall not eat the *b*. . .Deut. 12:16

idols, and from *b*. . .Acts 21:25

Jesus'

my *b* of the new testament. . .Matt. 26:28

I have betrayed the innocent *b*. . .Matt. 27:4

His *b* be on us. . .Matt. 27:25

great drops of *b* falling down. . .Luke 22:44

and drink his *b*. . .John 6:53

out *b* and water. . .John 19:34

purchased with his own *b*. . .Acts 20:28

propitiation through faith in his *b*. . .Rom. 3:25

the *b* of Christ?. . .1 Cor. 10:16

new testament in my *b*. . .1 Cor. 11:25

body and *b* of the Lord. . .1 Cor. 11:27

redemption through his *b*. . .Eph. 1:7

redemption through his *b*. . .Col. 1:14

made peace through the *b*. . .Col. 1:20

by his own *b* he entered. . .Heb. 9:12

the *b* of Jesus Christ. . .1 Pet. 1:2

precious *b* of Christ. . .1 Pet. 1:19

b of Jesus Christ his Son. . .1 John 1:7

came by water and *b*. . .1 John 5:6

from our sins in his own *b*. . .Rev. 1:5

the *b* of the Lamb. . .Rev. 7:14

Man's

Whoso sheddeth man's *b*. . .Gen. 9:6

they shall take of the *b*. . .Exod. 12:7

hands that shed innocent *b*. . .Prov. 6:17

flesh and *b* hath not revealed. . .Matt. 16:17

born, not of *b*. . .John 1:13

one *b* all nations of men. . .Acts 17:26

swift to shed *b*. . .Rom. 3:15

flesh and *b* cannot inherit. . .1 Cor. 15:50

wrestle not against flesh and *b*. . .Eph. 6:12

109. Boast//Boasteth/Boasters

the wicked *b'eth*. . .Ps. 10:3

In God we *b*. . .Ps. 44:8

trust in their wealth, and *b*. . .Ps. 49:6

B not thyself of to morrow. . .Prov. 27:1

despiteful, proud, *b'ers*. . .Rom. 1:30

lest any man should *b*. . .Eph. 2:9

covetous, *b'ers*, proud. . .2 Tim. 3:2

b'eth great things. . .James 3:5

110. Body, Church

communion of the *b* of Christ?. . .1 Cor. 10:16

For as the *b* is one. . .1 Cor. 12:12

baptized into one *b*. . .1 Cor. 12:13

the *b* is not one member. . .1 Cor. 12:14

111. Body, Human

Blessed shall be the fruit of thy *b*. . .Deut. 28:4

worms destroy this *b*. . .Job 19:26

fearfully and wonderfully made. . .Ps. 139:14

whole *b* should be cast into hell. . .Matt. 5:29

light of the *b* is the eye. . .Matt. 6:22

nor yet for your *b*. . .Matt. 6:25

them which kill the *b*. . .Matt. 10:28

Take, eat; this is my *b*. . .Matt. 26:26

the temple of his *b*. . .John 2:21

the *b* is dead. . .Rom. 8:10

b is not for fornication. . .1 Cor. 6:13

joined to an harlot is one *b*?. . .1 Cor. 6:16

sinneth against his own *b*. . .1 Cor. 6:18

not power of her own *b*. . .1 Cor. 7:4

b, and bring it into subjection. . .1 Cor. 9:27

b and blood of the Lord. . .1 Cor. 11:27

neglecting of the *b*. . .Col. 2:23

112. Bold/Boldness/Boldly

righteous are *b* as a lion. . .Prov. 28:1
b'ness of Peter and John. . .Acts 4:13
word of God with *b'ness*. . .Acts 4:31
Paul and Barnabas waxed *b*. . .Acts 13:46
In whom we have *b'ness*. . .Eph. 3:12
I may open my mouth *b'ly*. . .Eph. 6:19
we were *b* in our God. . .1 Thess. 2:2
b'ly unto the throne of grace. . .Heb. 4:16
b'ness to enter into the holiest. . .Heb. 10:19
we may *b'ly* say. . .Heb. 13:6

See *Courage*.

113. Bondage

lives bitter with hard *b*. . .Exod. 1:14
unto God by reason of the *b*. . .Exod. 2:23
I will rid you out of their *b*. . .Exod. 6:6
and for cruel *b*. . .Exod. 6:9
out of the house of *b*. . .Exod. 13:3
a little reviving in our *b*. . .Ezra 9:8
God hath not forsaken us in our *b*. . .Ezra 9:9
we bring into *b* our sons. . .Neh. 5:5
the *b* was heavy. . .Neh. 5:18
from the hard *b*. . .Isa. 14:3
not received the spirit of *b*. . .Rom. 8:15
delivered from the *b* of corruption. . .Rom. 8:21
is not under *b* in such cases. . .1 Cor. 7:15
if a man bring you into *b*. . .2 Cor. 11:20
that they might bring us into *b*. . .Gal. 2:4
in *b* under the elements. . .Gal. 4:3
desire again to be in *b*?. . .Gal. 4:9
mount Sinai, which gendereth to *b*. . .Gal. 4:24
again with the yoke of *b*. . .Gal. 5:1

all their lifetime subject to *b*. . .Heb. 2:15
same is he brought in *b*. . .2 Pet. 2:19

See *Servant/Servants*.

114. Born Again

Except a man be *b a*. . .John 3:3
b a, not of corruptible seed. . .1 Pet. 1:23

See *New Life*, *Regeneration*, *Salvation*.

115. Borrow/Borroweth/Borrower

b ought of his neighbour. . .Exod. 22:14
but thou shalt not *b*. . .Deut. 15:6

The wicked *b'eth*, and payeth not. . .Ps. 37:21

B'er is servant to the lender. . .Prov. 22:7

from him that would *b* of thee. . .Matt. 5:42

116. Bounty/ Bountiful/ Bountifully/ Bountifulness

he hath dealt *b'ifully* with me. . .Ps. 13:6

Lord hath dealt *b'ifully*. . .Ps. 116:7

Deal *b'ifully* with thy servant. . .Ps. 119:17

thou shalt deal *b'ifully*. . .Ps. 142:7

a *b'iful* eye shall be blessed. . .Prov. 22:9

b, and not as of covetousness. . .2 Cor. 9:5

He which soweth *b'ifully* shall reap. . .2 Cor. 9:6

every thing to all *b'ifulness*. . .2 Cor. 9:11

117. Boys

a child is known by his doings. . .Prov. 20:11

Train up a child. . .Prov. 22:6

little child shall lead them. . .Isa. 11:6

as a little child. . .Mark 10:15

receive this child in my name. . .Luke 9:48

I spake as a child. . .1 Cor. 13:11

from a child thou hast known. . .2 Tim. 3:15

See *Babies, Child/Children, Son/Sons, Youth.*

118. Branch, Jesus as the

stem of Jesse, and a *B.*. .Isa. 11:1

unto David a righteous *B.*. .Jer. 23:5

the *B* of righteousness. . .Jer. 33:15

bring forth my servant the *B.*. .Zech. 3:8

man whose name is The *B.*. .Zech. 6:12

119. Bribe/Bribes/ Bribery

after lucre, and took *b's.*. .1 Sam. 8:3

the tabernacles of *b'ry.*. .Job 15:34

right hand is full of *b's.*. .Ps. 26:10

hands from holding of *b's.*. .Isa. 33:15

they take a *b.*. .Amos 5:12

120. Bride

on thee, as a *b* doeth. . .Isa. 49:18

b adorneth herself. . .Isa. 61:10

bridegroom rejoiceth over the *b.*. .Isa. 62:5

or a *b* her attire?. . .Jer. 2:32

the voice of the *b.*. .Jer. 33:11

hath the *b* is the bridegroom. . .John 3:29

prepared as a *b.*. .Rev. 21:2

b, the Lamb's wife. . .Rev. 21:9

Spirit and the *b.*. .Rev. 22:17

See *Bridegroom.*

121. Bridegroom

as a *b* coming out. . .Ps. 19:5
as a *b* decketh himself. . .Isa. 61:10
the voice of the *b.* . .Jer. 33:11
b is with them?. . .Matt. 9:15
to meet the *b.* . .Matt. 25:1
called the *b.* . .John 2:9

See *Bride*.

122. Broken/Brokenhearted

he hath *b* me asunder. . .Job 16:12
I am like a *b* vessel. . .Ps. 31:12
them that are of a *b* heart. . .Ps. 34:18
I am feeble and sore *b.* . .Ps. 38:8
are a *b* spirit. . .Ps. 51:17
Reproach hath *b* my heart. . .Ps. 69:20
He healeth the *b* in heart. . .Ps. 147:3
b spirit drieth. . .Prov. 17:22
the spirit is *b.* . .Prov. 15:13
bind up the *b'hearted.* . .Isa. 61:1
sent me to heal the *b'hearted.* . .Luke 4:18
which is *b* for you. . .1 Cor. 11:24
be *b* to shivers. . .Rev. 2:27

123. Brother/Brother's/Brotherly/Brotherhood

Caring for

Am I my *b's* keeper?. . .Gen. 4:9
shall the weak *b* perish. . .1 Cor. 8:11
b or sister be naked. . .James 2:15

Hatred for

b shall deliver up the *b.* . .Matt. 10:21
hateth his *b* is in darkness. . .1 John 2:11

Judging

dost thou judge thy *b*?. . .Rom. 14:10
occasion to fall in his *b's* way. . .Rom. 14:13

Loving

to another with *b'ly* love. . .Rom. 12:10
as touching *b'ly* love ye. . .1 Thess. 4:9
b'ly love continue. . .Heb. 13:1
Love the *b'hood.* . .1 Pet. 2:17
He that loveth his *b.* . .1 John 2:10
loveth not his *b.* . .1 John 3:10
godliness *b'ly* kindness. . .2 Pet. 1:7

Offenses

b hath ought against thee. . .Matt. 5:23
mote that is in thy *b's* eye. . .Matt. 7:3

his *b* their trespasses. . .Matt. 18:35
If thy *b* trespass. . .Luke 17:3
if thy *b* be grieved. . .Rom. 14:15

Sinning
if thy *b* shall trespass. . .Matt. 18:15
oft shall my *b* sin. . .Matt. 18:21
whereby thy *b* stumbleth. . .Rom. 14:21
a *b* be a fornicator. . .1 Cor. 5:11
b goeth to law with *b*. . .1 Cor. 6:6
defraud his *b*. . .1 Thess. 4:6
every *b* that walketh disorderly. . .2 Thess. 3:6
admonish him as a *b*. . .2 Thess. 3:15

Who is?
the same is my *b*. . .Matt. 12:50

124. Build/Builder/ Builders/Buildest/ Building/Builded
And God
stone which the *b'ers* rejected. . .Matt. 21:42
b'er and maker is God. . .Heb. 11:10

stone which the *b'ers* disallowed. . .1 Pet. 2:7
the *b'ing* of the wall. . .Rev. 21:18

Church
I will *b* my church. . .Matt. 16:18

Physical buildings
my barns, and *b* greater. . .Luke 12:18
intending to *b* a tower. . .Luke 14:28
they planted, they *b'ed*. . .Luke 17:28
what house will ye *b* me?. . .Acts 7:49
house is *b'ed* by some man. . .Heb. 3:4

Spiritual building
able to *b* you up. . .Acts 20:32
lest I should *b* upon. . .Rom. 15:20
ye are God's *b'ing*. . .1 Cor. 3:9
b'ing of God. . .2 Cor. 5:1
b'ed together for an habitation. . .Eph. 2:22

Temple
to *b* it in three days. . .Matt. 26:61
b'est it in three days. . .Matt. 27:40
Seest thou these great *b'ings*?. . .Mark 13:2
b again the tabernacle. . .Acts 15:16

125. Building Supplies
Brick/Bricks
let us make brick. . .Gen. 11:3
straw to make brick. . .Exod. 5:7
deliver the tale of bricks. . .Exod. 5:18

Morter
in morter, and in brick. . .Exod. 1:14
daub it with untempered morter. . .Ezek. 13:11
tread the morter. . .Nah. 3:14

Nails

nails for the doors of the gates. . .1 Chron. 22:3

weight of the nails was fifty shekels. . .2 Chron. 3:9

with nails and with hammers. . .Jer. 10:4

126. Bury/Burial/ Buried

there will I be *b'ied*. . .Ruth 1:17

first to go and *b* my father. . .Matt. 8:21

she did it for my *b'ial*. . .Matt. 26:12

carried Stephen to his *b'ial*. . .Acts 8:2

b'ied with him by baptism. . .Rom. 6:4

B'ied with him in baptism. . .Col. 2:12

See *Death*, *Mortal/Mortality*.

127. Burden/ Burdened/Burdens

as an heavy *b*. . .Ps. 38:4

Cast thy *b* upon the LORD. . .Ps. 55:22

no greater *b* than these. . .Acts 15:28

do groan, being *b'ed*. . .2 Cor. 5:4

Bear ye one another's *b's*. . .Gal. 6:2

bear his own *b*. . .Gal. 6:5

all your care upon him. . .1 Pet. 5:7

128. Business

he be charged with any *b*. . .Deut. 24:5

have a perfect and just weight. . .Deut. 25:15

sell the oil, and pay thy debt. . .2 Kings 4:7

that do *b* in great waters. . .Ps. 107:23

Divers weights are an abomination. . .Prov. 20:23

a man diligent in his *b*?. . .Prov. 22:29

maketh fine linen, and selleth it. . .Prov. 31:24

Not slothful in *b*. . .Rom. 12:11

Lydia, a seller of purple. . .Acts 16:14

to do your own *b*. . .1 Thess. 4:11

buy and sell, and get gain. . .James 4:13

See *Honest/Honestly/Honesty*, *Partner/Partners*.

129. Busybody/ Busybodies

he soweth discord. . .Prov. 6:14

A talebearer revealeth secrets. . .Prov. 11:13

a whisperer separateth chief friends. . .Prov. 16:28

words of a talebearer are as wounds. . .Prov. 18:8

a talebearer revealeth secrets. . .Prov. 20:19

where there is no talebearer. . .Prov. 26:20

words of a talebearer. . .Prov. 26:22

a murmuring of the Grecians. . .Acts 6:1

strifes, backbitings, whisperings. . .2 Cor. 12:20

without murmurings and disputings. . .Phil. 2:14

tattlers also and *b's*. . .1 Tim. 5:13

b in other men's matters. . .1 Pet. 4:15

prating against us. . .3 John 1:10

130. Buy/Buyer/ Buyest/Buyeth

to Joseph for to *b* corn. . .Gen. 41:57

b'est ought of thy neighbour's. . .Lev. 25:14

B it before the inhabitants. . .Ruth 4:4

it is naught, saith the *b'er*. . .Prov. 20:14

B the truth. . .Prov. 23:23

considereth a field, and *b'eth* it. . .Prov. 31:16

b themselves victuals. . .Matt. 14:15

b themselves bread. . .Mark 6:36

b and sell, and get gain. . .James 4:13

no man might *b* or sell. . .Rev. 13:17

no man *b'eth* their merchandise. . .Rev. 18:11

131. Calling

the gifts and *c* of God. . .Rom. 11:29

ye see your *c*, brethren. . .1 Cor. 1:26

abide in the same *c*. . .1 Cor. 7:20

the hope of his *c*. . .Eph. 1:18

in one hope of your *c*. . .Eph. 4:4

prize of the high *c* of God. . .Phil. 3:14

132. Calvary

Calvary is the Latin name for the place also called Golgotha in scripture, where Jesus died.

come unto a place called Golgotha. . .Matt. 27:33

bring him unto the place Golgotha. . .Mark 15:22

the place, which is called *C*. . .Luke 23:33

which is called in the Hebrew Golgotha. . .John 19:17

See *Cross.*

133. Capital Punishment

Though it is not popular in our day, scripture clearly prescribes capital punishment for numerous serious offenses, of which the following are just a sampling. Scripture also prescribes the methods of judgment that should be used and requires judges to be honest and unbiased. Of course, this punishment was misused in the Crucifixion.

by man shall his blood be shed. . .Gen. 9:6

shall surely be put to death. . .Exod. 31:14

surely be put to death. . .Lev. 20:2

shall surely be put to death. . .Lev. 20:10

worthy of death be put to death. . .Deut. 17:6

life shall go for life. . .Deut. 19:21

delivered him to be crucified. . .Matt. 27:26

beareth not the sword in vain. . .Rom. 13:4

See *Death Penalty.*

134. Captive/Captives

c's a beautiful woman. . .Deut. 21:11
lead thy captivity c. . .Judg. 5:12
two wives were taken c's. . .1 Sam. 30:5
c out of the land of Israel. . .2 Kings 5:2
carried them c to Assyria. . .2 Kings 15:29
proclaim liberty to the c's. . .Isa. 61:1
preach deliverance to the c's. . .Luke 4:18
led away c into all nations. . .Luke 21:24
he led captivity c. . .Eph. 4:8
who are taken c. . .2 Tim. 2:26
lead c silly women. . .2 Tim. 3:6

See *Captive/Captivity*, *Prisoner/Prisoners*.

135. Captive/Captivity

God will turn thy *city*. . .Deut. 30:3
lead thy *city* c. . .Judg. 5:12
into *city* from Jerusalem to Babylon. . .2 Kings 24:15
which were come out of the *city*. . .Ezra 8:35
God bringeth back the *city*. . .Ps. 53:6
delivered his strength into *city*. . .Ps. 78:61
my people are gone into *city*. . .Isa. 5:13
I will cause to return the *city*. . .Jer. 33:11
Nebuchadrezzar carried away c. . .Jer. 52:28
I turn back your *city*. . .Zeph. 3:20
city to the law of sin. . .Rom. 7:23
bringing into *city* every thought. . .2 Cor. 10:5
he led *city* c. . .Eph. 4:8
leadeth into *city* shall go into *city*. . .Rev. 13:10

See *Captive/Captives*, *Prisoner/Prisoners*.

136. Care/Careful/ Cares

the c of this world. . .Matt. 13:22
the c's of this world. . .Mark 4:19
choked with c's and riches. . .Luke 8:14
c's of this life. . .Luke 21:34
Be c'ful for nothing. . .Phil. 4:6
Casting all your c upon him. . .1 Pet. 5:7

137. Carnal/Carnally

thou shalt not lie c'ly. . .Lev. 18:20
I am c, sold under sin. . .Rom. 7:14
to be c'ly minded is death. . .Rom. 8:6
c mind is enmity. . .Rom. 8:7
ye are yet c. . .1 Cor. 3:3
weapons of our warfare are not c. . .2 Cor. 10:4
law of a c commandment. . .Heb. 7:16
c ordinances, imposed on them. . .Heb. 9:10

138. Chance

a c that happened to us. . .1 Sam. 6:9
c happeneth to them all. . .Eccles. 9:11
by c there came down. . .Luke 10:31

139. Change/ Changed/ Changeth/Changes

and *c'th* not. . .Ps. 15:4

they have no *c's*. . .Ps. 55:19

and they shall be *c'd*. . .Ps. 102:26

with them that are given to *c*. . .Prov. 24:21

he *c'th* the times and the seasons. . .Dan. 2:21

will I *c* their glory into shame. . .Hosea 4:7

I am the Lord, I *c* not. . .Mal. 3:6

but we shall all be *c'd*. . .1 Cor. 15:51

c'd into the same image. . .2 Cor. 3:18

Who shall *c* our vile body. . .Phil. 3:21

and they shall be *c'd*. . .Heb. 1:12

140. Characteristics of God

Eternal

the Lord, the everlasting God. . .Gen. 21:33

Lord shall reign for ever and ever. . .Exod. 15:18

eternal God is thy refuge. . .Deut. 33:27

his eternal power and Godhead. . .Rom. 1:20

unto the King eternal. . .1 Tim. 1:17

Holy

for I am holy. . .Lev. 11:44

for he is an holy God. . .Josh. 24:19

There is none holy as the Lord. . .1 Sam. 2:2

thou Holy One of Israel. . .Ps. 71:22

the Holy One of God. . .Mark 1:24

the holy Spirit of God. . .Eph. 4:30

Infinite

his understanding is infinite. . .Ps. 147:5

Invisible

invisible, the only wise God. . .1 Tim. 1:17

Longsuffering

merciful and gracious, longsuffering. . .Exod. 34:6

The Lord is longsuffering. . .Num. 14:18

endured with much longsuffering. . .Rom. 9:22

the God of patience. . .Rom. 15:5

longsuffering to us-ward. . .2 Pet. 3:9

the longsuffering of our Lord. . .2 Pet. 3:15

Loving

thy lovingkindness, O God!. . .Ps. 36:7

according to thy lovingkindness. . .Ps. 51:1

the love of God. . .Luke 11:42

God so loved the world. . .John 3:16

separate us from the love of God. . .Rom. 8:39

the love of Christ. . .Eph. 3:19

the love of Christ. . .Eph. 3:19

love the Father hath bestowed. . .1 John 3:1
perceive we the love of God. . .1 John 3:16
God is love. . .1 John 4:8

Merciful

shewing mercy unto thousands. . .Exod. 20:6
merciful and gracious. . .Exod. 34:6
the greatness of thy mercy. . .Neh. 13:22
trust in the mercy of God. . .Ps. 52:8
our God is merciful. . .Ps. 116:5
his mercy endureth for ever. . .Ps. 136:2
God, who is rich in mercy. . .Eph. 2:4

Omnipotent

the power, and the glory. . .1 Chron. 29:11
power and might. . .2 Chron. 20:6
He ruleth by his power for ever. . .Ps. 66:7
Lord God omnipotent reigneth. . .Rev. 19:6

Omniscient

art acquainted with all my ways. . .Ps. 139:3
his understanding is infinite. . .Ps. 147:5
Before I formed thee in the belly
    I knew thee. . .Jer. 1:5

Powerful

with great power. . .Exod. 32:11
the power of his works. . .Ps. 111:6
made the earth by his power. . .Jer. 10:12
by my great power. . .Jer. 27:5
power on earth to forgive sins. . .Mark 2:10
in the power of the Spirit. . .Luke 4:14
power he commandeth. . .Luke 4:36
the power of the Lord. . .Luke 5:17
Holy Ghost and with power. . .Acts 10:38
the glory of his power. . .2 Thess. 1:9

Omnipresent

shall I flee from thy presence?. . .Ps. 139:7
him we live, and move, and have
    our being. . .Acts 17:28
never leave thee, nor forsake thee. . .Heb. 13:5

Righteous

God of Israel, thou art righteous. . .. . .Ezra 9:15
righteous God trieth the hearts. . .Ps. 7:9
heavens shall declare his righteousness. . .Ps. 50:6
Gracious is the Lord, and righteous. . .Ps. 116:5
God, and his righteousness. . .Matt. 6:33

whatsoever things are pure. . .Phil. 4:8

keep thyself pure. . .1 Tim. 5:22

discreet, chaste, keepers at home. . .Titus 2:5

the bed undefiled. . .Heb. 13:4

behold your *c* conversation. . .1 Pet. 3:2

See Modest/Modesty, Virgin/Virginity/Virgins.

141. Charity

In the King James Version of the Bible, "charity" is another word for "love."

puffeth up, but *c* edifieth. . .1 Cor. 8:1

have not *c*, I am become. . .1 Cor. 13:1

C never faileth. . .1 Cor. 13:8

now abideth faith, hope, *c*. . .1 Cor. 13:13

Follow after *c*. . .1 Cor. 14:1

put on *c*. . .Col. 3:14

c out of a pure heart. . .1 Tim. 1:5

faith, *c*, peace. . .2 Tim. 2:22

above all things have fervent *c*. . .1 Pet. 4:8

to brotherly kindness *c*. . .2 Pet. 1:7

142. Chastise/ Chastisement

will *c* you seven times. . .Lev. 26:28

I have borne *c'ment*. . .Job 34:31

c'ment of our peace. . .Isa. 53:5

c him, and let him go. . .Luke 23:22

if ye be without *c'ment*. . .Heb. 12:8

143. Chaste/Chastity

Though chastity implies the absence of improper sexual activity, it also refers to personal purity and integrity.

144. Cheating

hath deceived his neighbour. . .Lev. 6:2

Divers weights are an abomination. . .Prov. 20:23

deceive not with thy lips. . .Prov. 24:28

dishonest gain. . .Ezek. 22:13

cursed be the deceiver. . .Mal. 1:14

ye do wrong, and defraud. . .1 Cor. 6:8

hidden things of dishonesty. . .2 Cor. 4:2

See Deceit/Deceitful/Deceitfully/Deceitfulness.

145. Cheerful/ Cheerfulness

maketh a *c* countenance. . .Prov. 15:13

mercy, with *c'ness*. . .Rom. 12:8

God loveth a *c* giver. . .2 Cor. 9:7

146. Child/Children

he was a goodly *c*. . .Exod. 2:2

c'ren are an heritage. . .Ps. 127:3

blessed thy *c'ren* within thee. . .Ps. 147:13

glory of *c'ren* are their fathers. . .Prov. 17:6

c'ren arise up, and call her blessed. . .Prov. 31:28

unto us a *c* is born. . .Isa. 9:6

a little *c* shall lead them. . .Isa. 11:6

woman forget her sucking *c*. . .Isa. 49:15

such *c'ren* in my name. . .Mark 9:37
kingdom of God as a little *c*. . .Mark 10:15
parents for the *c'ren*. . .2 Cor. 12:14
C'ren, obey your parents. . .Eph. 6:1
from a *c* thou hast known. . .2 Tim. 3:15

See *Babies, Boys, Daughter/Daughters, Family,*
Girls, Son/Sons, Youth.

147. Child Rearing

child is known by his doings. . .Prov. 20:11
Train up a child in the way. . .Prov. 22:6
in the heart of a child. . .Prov. 22:15
a child left to himself. . .Prov. 29:15
I understood as a child. . .1 Cor. 13:11
Study to shew thyself approved. . .2 Tim. 2:15
from a child thou hast known. . .2 Tim. 3:15

148. Children of Light

wiser than the *c o l*. . .Luke 16:8
may be the *c o l*. . .John 12:36

walk as *c o l*. . .Eph. 5:8
are all the *c o l*. . .1 Thess. 5:5

149. Choices

choose you this day. . .Josh. 24:15
chosen the way of truth. . .Ps. 119:30
I have chosen thy precepts. . .Ps. 119:173
choose the fear of the LORD. . .Prov. 1:29
choose none of his ways. . .Prov. 3:31
name is rather to be chosen. . .Prov. 22:1

150. Chosen People

c thee to be a peculiar *p*. . .Deut. 14:2
p whom he hath *c*. . .Ps. 33:12
ye are a chosen generation. . .1 Pet. 2:9

151. Christian/ Christians

Before Christians received that name in
Antioch, they were known as followers of the
Way. Scripture only uses the word "Christian"
three times.

found any of this way. . .Acts 9:2
called *C's* first in Antioch. . .Acts 11:26
spake evil of that way. . .Acts 19:9
no small stir about that way. . .Acts 19:23
I persecuted this way. . .Acts 22:4
the way which they call heresy. . .Acts 24:14
knowledge of that way. . .Acts 24:22
persuadest me to be a *C*. . .Acts 26:28
any man suffer as a *C*. . .1 Pet. 4:16

See *Christianity; Church, Congregation/Churches.*

152. Christianity

The word "Christianity" is nowhere used in scripture to define the belief or body of believers in Jesus. But the concept of faith in Christ and a unified church body runs throughout the Bible.

the faith in Christ. . .Acts 24:24
by faith in Christ Jesus. . .Gal. 3:26
your faith in Christ Jesus. . .Col. 1:4
your faith in Christ. . .Col. 2:5

See *Christian/Christians; Church, Congregation/Churches.*

153. Church, Congregation/ Churches

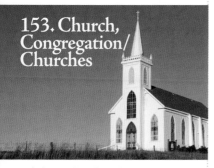

c which was at Jerusalem. . .Acts 8:1
ordained them elders in every *c*. . .Acts 14:23
gathered the *c* together. . .Acts 14:27
c that is in their house. . .Rom. 16:5
c of God which is at Corinth. . .1 Cor. 1:2
c may receive edifying. . .1 Cor. 14:5
care of the *c* of God?. . .1 Tim. 3:5
call for the elders of the *c*. . .James 5:14
John to the seven *c*'es. . .Rev. 1:4

See *Christian/Christians; Church Leaders; Church, Universal Congregation; Christianity.*

154. Church Leaders

Bishop
bishop, he desireth a good work. . .1 Tim. 3:1
bishop then must be blameless. . .1 Tim. 3:2
bishop must be blameless. . .Titus 1:7
Bishop of your souls. . .1 Pet. 2:25

Deacon/Deacons
must the deacons be grave. . .1 Tim. 3:8
use the office of a deacon. . .1 Tim. 3:10
deacons be the husbands of one wife. . .1 Tim. 3:12
used the office of a deacon. . .1 Tim. 3:13

Evangelist/Evangelists
Philip the evangelist. . .Acts 21:8
and some, evangelists. . .Eph. 4:11
do the work of an evangelist. . .2 Tim. 4:5

Minister/Ministers
Scripture uses the word "minister" to describe those who do God's work. It is not necessarily a paid church leadership position.

let him be your minister. . .Matt. 20:26
ministers of the word. . .Luke 1:2
he is the minister of God. . .Rom. 13:4
minister of the circumcision. . .Rom. 15:8

minister of Jesus Christ. . .Rom. 15:16
ministers by whom ye believed. . .1 Cor. 3:5
ministers of Christ. . .1 Cor. 4:1
ministers of the new testament. . .2 Cor. 3:6
ourselves as the ministers of God. . .2 Cor. 6:4
ministers of righteousness. . .2 Cor. 11:15
I was made a minister. . .Eph. 3:7
faithful minister in the Lord. . .Eph. 6:21
Paul am made a minister. . .Col. 1:23
good minister of Jesus Christ. . .1 Tim. 4:6

See *Pastor.*

155. Church, Universal

I will build my *c*. . .Matt. 16:18
Lord added to the *c*. . .Acts 2:47
feed the *c* of God. . .Acts 20:28
hath set some in the *c*. . .1 Cor. 12:28
I persecuted the *c* of God. . .1 Cor. 15:9
all things to the *c*. . .Eph. 1:22
known by the *c*. . .Eph. 3:10
Christ is the head of the *c*. . .Eph. 5:23
a glorious *c*. . .Eph. 5:27
head of the body, the *c*. . .Col. 1:18

156. Circumcision

gave unto you *c*. . .John 7:22
covenant of *c*. . .Acts 7:8
c which believed. . .Acts 10:45
c contended with him. . .Acts 11:2
c is made uncircumcision. . .Rom. 2:25
profit is there of *c*?. . .Rom. 3:1
justify the *c* by faith. . .Rom. 3:30
sign of *c*. . .Rom. 4:11
minister of the *c*. . .Rom. 15:8

C is nothing. . .1 Cor. 7:19
neither *c* availeth. . .Gal. 5:6
c, which worship God. . .Phil. 3:3
c made without hands. . .Col. 2:11

157. Clean/Cleanse/ Cleansed/Cleanseth/ Cleansing

In the scriptures, cleanliness has both a physical and a spiritual dimension. When lepers were healed, they were "clean" according to the Old Testament law.

Physical

thou canst make me *c*. . .Matt. 8:2
c the outside of the cup. . .Matt. 23:25
offer for thy *c'sing*. . .Mark 1:44
all things are *c* unto you. . .Luke 11:41

Spiritual

ye are *c*. . .John 13:10

c through the word. . .John 15:3

What God hath *c'sed*. . .Acts 10:15

let us *c'se* ourselves. . .2 Cor. 7:1

he might sanctify and *c'se*. . .Eph. 5:26

C'se your hands. . .James 4:8

those that were *c*. . .2 Pet. 2:18

c'seth us from all sin. . .1 John 1:7

c'se us from all unrighteousness. . .1 John 1:9

158. Clothe/Clothed/ Clothes/Clothing, Physical

Wearing sackcloth was a sign of mourning, while bright colors showed that the wearer was prosperous.

Fine

c'd with scarlet. . .Prov. 31:21

c'd thee also with broidered work. . .Ezek. 16:10

c'd Daniel with scarlet. . .Dan. 5:29

they that wear soft *c'ing*. . .Matt. 11:8

love to go in long *c'ing*. . .Mark 12:38

c'd him with purple. . .Mark 15:17

weareth the gay *c'ing*. . .James 2:3

c'd in white raiment. . .Rev. 3:5

In mourning

my *c'ing* was sackcloth. . .Ps. 35:13

c'd in sackcloth. . .Rev. 11:3

Needed

and *c'd* them. . .Gen. 3:21

their *c's* waxed not old. . .Neh. 9:21

not much more *c* you. . .Matt. 6:30

ye *c'd* me. . .Matt. 25:36

Poor

c a man with rags. . .Prov. 23:21

c'd with camel's hair. . .Mark 1:6

wrapped him in swaddling *c's*. . .Luke 2:7

wrapped him in swaddling clothes. . .Luke 2:7

See *Apparel, Attire/Attired, Fashion, Garment/ Garments.*

159. Clothed/ Clothing, Spiritually

righteousness, and it *c* me. . .Job 29:14

be *c* with shame. . .Ps. 35:26

c himself with cursing. . .Ps. 109:18

be *c* with righteousness. . .Ps. 132:9

honour are her *c'ing*. . .Prov. 31:25

c upon, that mortality. . .2 Cor. 5:4

be *c* with humility. . .1 Pet. 5:5

160. Comfort, Physical

My bed shall *c* me. . .Job 7:13

c me with apples. . .Song of Sol. 2:5

See *Comfort/Comforted/Comforteth/ Comforts, Spiritual.*

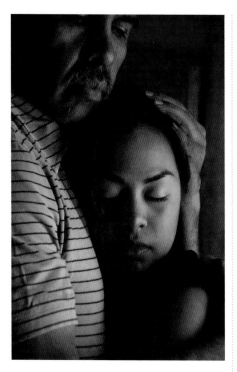

God of all *c*. . .2 Cor. 1:3

ourselves are *c'ed* of God. . .2 Cor. 1:4

See *Comfort, Physical; Consolation/Consolations; Encouragement.*

162. Comforter (Holy Spirit)

he shall give you another *C*. . .John 14:16

C, which is the Holy Ghost. . .John 14:26

when the *C* is come. . .John 15:26

the *C* will not come. . .John 16:7

See *Holy Ghost, Spirit, Holy.*

163. Coming to Christ

whosoever believeth in him. . .John 3:16

believeth on him that sent me. . .John 5:24

he that believeth on me. . .John 6:35

Believe on the Lord Jesus Christ. . .Acts 16:31

shalt believe in thine heart. . .Rom. 10:9

See *Believe/Believed/Believeth/Believest, Conversion, Repentance, Salvation.*

164. Commandment/ Commandments

God gave His people many commandments. Perhaps the best known are the Ten Commandments, which appear in Exodus 20:2–17 and Deuteronomy 5:6–21.

love me, and keep my *c's*. . .Exod. 20:6

keep my *c's*, and do them. . .Lev. 26:3

161. Comfort/ Comforted/ Comforteth/ Comforts, Spiritual

thy staff they *c* me. . .Ps. 23:4

c me on every side. . .Ps. 71:21

soul refused to be *c'ed*. . .Ps. 77:2

thy *c's* delight my soul. . .Ps. 94:19

c ye my people. . .Isa. 40:1

am he that *c'eth* you. . .Isa. 51:12

c all that mourn. . .Isa. 61:2

for they shall be *c'ed*. . .Matt. 5:4

and *c'ed* her. . .John 11:31

c of the Holy Ghost. . .Acts 9:31

c of the scriptures. . .Rom. 15:4

and exhortation, and *c*. . .1 Cor. 14:3

his statutes, and his c's...Deut. 4:40
love me and keep my c's...Deut. 5:10
diligently keep the c's...Deut. 6:17
all his c's are sure...Ps. 111:7
delighteth greatly in his c's...Ps. 112:1
love thy c's above gold...Ps. 119:127
break one of these least c's...Matt. 5:19
which is the great c...Matt. 22:36
love me, keep my c's...John 14:15
if we keep his c's...1 John 2:3

See *Law, the*; *Laws*.

165. Communication/ Communications
writing was the writing of God...Exod. 32:16
writing, the ten commandments...Deut. 10:4
your c be, Yea, yea...Matt. 5:37
word that men shall speak...Matt. 12:36
evil c's corrupt...1 Cor. 15:33
great plainness of speech...2 Cor. 3:12
no corrupt c proceed...Eph. 4:29
nor foolish talking...Eph. 5:4
filthy c out of your mouth...Col. 3:8

speech be alway with grace...Col. 4:6
Sound speech...Titus 2:8
speak evil of no man...Titus 3:2

See *Eloquent*.

166. Communion
Jesus took bread, and blessed it...Matt. 26:26
Jesus took bread, and blessed...Mark 14:22
he took the cup...Luke 22:17
c of the blood of Christ?...1 Cor. 10:16
not to eat the Lord's supper...1 Cor. 11:20

167. Companion
c of all them that fear thee...Ps. 119:63
c of fools...Prov. 13:20
c of riotous men...Prov. 28:7
thy c, and the wife...Mal. 2:14

168. Compassion/ Compassions
art a God full of c...Ps. 86:15
c on the son of her womb?...Isa. 49:15
his c's fail not...Lam. 3:22
to have c upon thee...Ezek. 16:5
shew mercy and c's...Zech. 7:9
moved with c on them...Matt. 9:36
having c one of another...1 Pet. 3:8
shutteth up his bowels of c...1 John 3:17
of some have c...Jude 1:22

See *Concern for Others*, *Pity*.

169. Complain/ Complained/ Complainers/ Complaint

c'ed, it displeased the LORD. . .Num. 11:1

I mourn in my *c't*. . .Ps. 55:2

I *c'ed*, and my spirit. . .Ps. 77:3

poured out my *c't* before him. . .Ps. 142:2

Wherefore doth a living man *c*. . .Lam. 3:39

These are murmurers, *c'ers*. . .Jude 1:16

See *Contention/Contentions/Contentious, Discontentment/Discontented, Murmur/Murmured/ Murmurers/Murmuring/Murmurings.*

170. Comprehend/ Comprehended

which we cannot *c*. . .Job 37:5

c'ed the dust of the earth. . .Isa. 40:12

darkness *c'ed* it not. . .John 1:5

c with all saints. . .Eph. 3:18

See *Understanding.*

171. Conceit/Conceits

high wall in his own *c*. . .Prov. 18:11

wise in his own *c*. . .Prov. 26:5

wise in his own *c?*. . .Prov. 26:12

wiser in his own *c*. . .Prov. 26:16

wise in his own *c*. . .Prov. 28:11

wise in your own *c's*. . .Rom. 11:25

Be not wise in your own *c's*. . .Rom. 12:16

172. Concern for Others

pity should be shewed. . .Job 6:14

no man cared for my soul. . .Ps. 142:4

hath pity upon the poor. . .Prov. 19:17

took care of him. . .Luke 10:34

dost thou not care. . .Luke 10:40

not that he cared for the poor. . .John 12:6

have the same care. . .1 Cor. 12:25

pray one for another. . .James 5:16

See *Compassion/Compassions.*

173. Condemnation

art in the same *c?*. . .Luke 23:40

c, that light is come. . .John 3:19

shall not come into *c*. . .John 5:24

judgment was by one to *c*. . .Rom. 5:16

therefore now no *c*. . .Rom. 8:1

ministration of *c*. . .2 Cor. 3:9

c of the devil. . .1 Tim. 3:6

receive the greater *c*. . .James 3:1

lest ye fall into *c*. . .James 5:12

ordained to this *c*. . .Jude 1:4

See *Consequences of Sin.*

174. Conduct

even he shall live by me. . .John 6:57

The just shall live by faith. . .Rom. 1:17
he liveth unto God. . .Rom. 6:10
live peaceably with all men. . .Rom. 12:18
live of the gospel. . .1 Cor. 9:14
live in peace. . .2 Cor. 13:11
also walk in the Spirit. . .Gal. 5:25
liveth in pleasure is dead. . .1 Tim. 5:6
live soberly, righteously. . .Titus 2:12
live the rest of his time. . .1 Pet. 4:2
lay down our lives. . .1 John 3:16

See *Conversation.*

175. Confess/ Confesseth

I will *c* my transgressions. . .Ps. 32:5
whoso *c'eth* and forsaketh. . .Prov. 28:13
c me before men. . .Matt. 10:32
c with thy mouth. . .Rom. 10:9
every tongue shall *c*. . .Rom. 14:11
every tongue should *c*. . .Phil. 2:11
C your faults one to another. . .James 5:16
If we *c* our sins. . .1 John 1:9
c that Jesus is the Son. . .1 John 4:15

176. Confident/ Confidence

in this will I be *c*. . .Ps. 27:3
who art the *c'ce*. . .Ps. 65:5

than to put *c'ce* in man. . .Ps. 118:8
the Lord shall be thy *c'ce*. . .Prov. 3:26
fear of the Lord is strong *c'ce*. . .Prov. 14:26
we are always *c*. . .2 Cor. 5:6
access with *c'ce* by the faith. . .Eph. 3:12
Being *c* of this very thing. . .Phil. 1:6
have no *c'ce* in the flesh. . .Phil. 3:3
I can do all things through Christ. . .Phil. 4:13
Cast not away therefore your *c'ce*. . .Heb. 10:35
we may have *c'ce*. . .1 John 2:28
c'ce toward God. . .1 John 3:21

177. Conflict

strength unto the battle. . .Ps. 18:39
them that fight against me. . .Ps. 35:1
in peace from the battle. . .Ps. 55:18
fighting daily oppresseth me. . .Ps. 56:1
Having the same *c*. . .Phil. 1:30
Fight the good fight of faith. . .1 Tim. 6:12
I have fought a good fight. . .2 Tim. 4:7
fightings among you?. . .James 4:1

See *Contention/Contentions/Contentious.*

178. Confusion

brought to *c*. . .Ps. 35:4
My *c* is continually. . .Ps. 44:15
let me never be put to *c*. . .Ps. 71:1
not the author of *c*. . .1 Cor. 14:33
perplexed, but not in despair. . .2 Cor. 4:8
strife is, there is *c*. . .James 3:16

179. Congregation

the *c* of the righteous. . .Ps. 1:5

in the midst of the *c*. . .Ps. 22:22
thanks in the great *c*. . .Ps. 35:18
Remember thy *c*. . .Ps. 74:2
c of saints. . .Ps. 149:1
shewed before the whole *c*. . .Prov. 26:26

180. Conscience

convicted by their own *c*. . .John 8:9
c void of offence toward God. . .Acts 24:16
their *c* also bearing witness. . .Rom. 2:15
c of him which is weak. . .1 Cor. 8:10
C, I say, not thine own. . .1 Cor. 10:29
and of a good *c*. . .1 Tim. 1:5
faith, and a good *c*. . .1 Tim. 1:19
c seared with a hot iron. . .1 Tim. 4:2
mind and *c* is defiled. . .Titus 1:15
purge your *c*. . .Heb. 9:14
Having a good *c*. . .1 Pet. 3:16

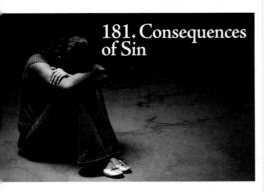

181. Consequences of Sin

the workers of iniquity?. . .Job 31:3
wickedness overthroweth the sinner. . .Prov. 13:6
Evil pursueth sinners. . .Prov. 13:21
forsake the LORD shall. . .Isa. 1:28
soul that sinneth, it shall die. . .Ezek. 18:4
ye shall die in your sins. . .John 8:24

God heareth not sinners. . .John 9:31
the wages of sin is death. . .Rom. 6:23

See *Condemnation*.

182. Conservation

Though God does not use the word "conservation" in scripture, Genesis 1 clearly describes His loving creation of the earth and humankind's responsibility for its care. When we care for the earth, we care for His creation as good stewards.

created the heaven and the earth. . .Gen. 1:1
and over all the earth. . .Gen. 1:26
replenish the earth. . .Gen. 1:28
into your hand are they delivered. . .Gen. 9:2
all flesh that is upon the earth. . .Gen. 9:16
earth brought forth by handfuls. . .Gen. 41:47
for all the earth is mine. . .Exod. 19:5
LORD made heaven and earth. . .Exod. 20:11
regardeth the life of his beast. . .Prov. 12:10
the earth is the Lord's. . .1 Cor. 10:26
precious fruit of the earth. . .James 5:7

See *Earth, Ecology*.

183. Consolation/ Consolations

Are the *c*'s of God small. . .Job 15:11
ye have received your *c*. . .Luke 6:24
God of patience and *c*. . .Rom. 15:5
c also aboundeth. . .2 Cor. 1:5
hath given us everlasting *c*. . .2 Thess. 2:16
we might have a strong *c*. . .Heb. 6:18

See *Comfort/Comforted/Comforteth/Comforts,*
Spiritual; Encouragement.

184. Contend/ Contendeth

neither *c* with them in battle. . .Deut. 2:9

c with him in battle. . .Deut. 2:24

will ye *c* for God?. . .Job 13:8

such as keep the law *c*. . .Prov. 28:4

c with him that is mightier. . .Eccles. 6:10

I will *c* with him that *c'eth*. . .Isa. 49:25

who will *c* with me?. . .Isa. 50:8

For I will not *c* for ever. . .Isa. 57:16

them that *c* with me. . .Jer. 18:19

earnestly *c* for the faith. . .Jude 1:3

185. Content/ Contentment

be *c* with your wages. . .Luke 3:14

therewith to be *c*. . .Phil. 4:11

godliness with *c'ment* is great gain. . .1 Tim. 6:6

let us be therewith *c*. . .1 Tim. 6:8

be *c* with such things. . .Heb. 13:5

186. Contention/ Contentions/ Contentious

Only by pride cometh *c*. . .Prov. 13:10

therefore leave off *c*. . .Prov. 17:14

A fool's lips enter into *c*. . .Prov. 18:6

c's are like the bars. . .Prov. 18:19

c's of a wife. . .Prov. 19:13

c'us and an angry woman. . .Prov. 21:19

c shall go. . .Prov. 22:10

c'us man to kindle strife. . .Prov. 26:21

c'us woman are alike. . .Prov. 27:15

them that are *c'us*. . .Rom. 2:8

there are *c's* among you. . .1 Cor. 1:11

c's, and strivings. . .Titus 3:9

See *Complain/Complained/Complainers/Complaint,*
    Conflict, Discontentment/Discontented,
    Murmur/Murmured/Murmurers/
    Murmuring/Murmurings, Quarrel.

187. Conversation

In the King James Bible, "conversation"
means more than "speech." It also
describes a consistent lifestyle of faith
and conduct.

ordereth his *c* aright. . .Ps. 50:23

our *c* in the world. . .2 Cor. 1:12

my *c* in time past. . .Gal. 1:13

we all had our *c*. . .Eph. 2:3

concerning the former *c*. . .Eph. 4:22

c be as it becometh the gospel. . .Phil. 1:27

in *c*, in charity. . .1 Tim. 4:12

c be without covetousness. . .Heb. 13:5

good *c* his works. . .James 3:13

holy in all manner of *c*. . .1 Pet. 1:15
c honest among the Gentiles. . .1 Pet. 2:12
your good *c* in Christ. . .1 Pet. 3:16
holy *c* and godliness. . .2 Pet. 3:11

See *Conduct*.

188. Conversion

whosoever believeth in him. . .John 3:16
believeth on him that sent me. . .John 5:24
he that believeth on me. . .John 6:35
converted, and I should heal. . .Matt. 13:15
Except ye be converted. . .Matt. 18:3
be converted, that your sins. . .Acts 3:19
Believe on the Lord Jesus Christ. . .Acts 16:31
shalt believe in thine heart. . .Rom. 10:9

See *Believe/Believed/Believeth/Believest, Coming
to Christ, Knowing God, New Life, Repentance,
Salvation*.

189. Corporal Punishment

Forty stripes he may give him. . .Deut. 25:3
their transgression with the rod. . .Ps. 89:32
rod is for the back of him. . .Prov. 10:13
spareth his rod hateth his son. . .Prov. 13:24
the rod of correction. . .Prov. 22:15
beatest him with the rod. . .Prov. 23:13
rod and reproof give wisdom. . .Prov. 29:15

See *Spanking*.

190. Correction

neither be weary of his *c*. . .Prov. 3:11
C is grievous unto him. . .Prov. 15:10
the rod of *c*. . .Prov. 22:15
Withhold not *c* from the child. . .Prov. 23:13
for reproof, for *c*. . .2 Tim. 3:16

191. Corruption

their *c* is in them. . .Lev. 22:25
and not see *c*. . .Ps. 49:9
from the pit of *c*. . .Isa. 38:17
brought up my life from *c*. . .Jon. 2:6
neither his flesh did see *c*. . .Acts 2:31
no more to return to *c*. . .Acts 13:34
from the bondage of *c*. . .Rom. 8:21
It is sown in *c*. . .1 Cor. 15:42

doth *c* inherit incorruption. . .1 Cor. 15:50
flesh reap *c*. . .Gal. 6:8
having escaped the *c*. . .2 Pet. 1:4

192. Counsel/Counsels

he hath *c* and understanding. . .Job 12:13
walketh not in the *c*. . .Ps. 1:1
who hath given me *c*. . .Ps. 16:7
c of the heathen to nought. . .Ps. 33:10
guide me with thy *c*. . .Ps. 73:24
walked in their own *c's*. . .Ps. 81:12
shall attain unto wise *c's*. . .Prov. 1:5
no *c* is, the people fall. . .Prov. 11:14
hearkeneth unto *c* is wise. . .Prov. 12:15
Without *c* purposes are disappointed. . .Prov. 15:22
purpose is established by *c*. . .Prov. 20:18
c of his own will. . .Eph. 1:11

See *Advice, Decision Making.*

193. Countenance

Lord lift up his *c*. . .Num. 6:26
Look not on his *c*. . .1 Sam. 16:7
through the pride of his *c*. . .Ps. 10:4
c doth behold the upright. . .Ps. 11:7
the help of his *c*. . .Ps. 42:5
in the light of thy *c*. . .Ps. 89:15
maketh a cheerful *c*. . .Prov. 15:13
sadness of the *c*. . .Eccles. 7:3

194. Courage

Be strong and of a good *c*. . .Deut. 31:6
Be strong and of a good *c*. . .Josh. 1:9
be of good *c*. . .Ps. 27:14

Be of good *c*. . .Ps. 31:24
thanked God, and took *c*. . .Acts 28:15

See *Bold/Boldness/Boldly.*

195. Courtship

In biblical times, courtship was not a protracted relationship-building period as it is today. Instead, a woman was chosen by a man, or more often, his parents. A bride typically received gifts from her suitor, and they built a relationship after marriage. Scripture provides some guidelines for the actions of unmarried people and how they should treat each other. Christians should always treat others with respect.

take a wife unto my son. . .Gen. 24:38
jewels of silver, and jewels of gold. . .Gen. 24:53
serve thee seven years for Rachel. . .Gen. 29:18
get her for me to wife. . .Judg. 14:2
Mary was espoused to Joseph. . .Matt. 1:18
unequally yoked together. . .2 Cor. 6:14
younger as sisters, with all purity. . .1 Tim. 5:2
and the bed undefiled. . .Heb. 13:4

See *Betroth/Betrothed, Dating, Marriage/Marry/Marrying*.

196. Covenant

I will establish my *c*. . .Gen. 9:11
a token of a *c*. . .Gen. 9:13
made a *c* with Abram. . .Gen. 15:18
token of the *c*. . .Gen. 17:11
mindful always of his *c*. . .1 Chron. 16:15
make a *c* with our God. . .Ezra 10:3
keep his *c* and his testimonies. . .Ps. 25:10
My *c* will I not break. . .Ps. 89:34
my *c* unto them. . .Rom. 11:27
the *c*, that was confirmed. . .Gal. 3:17
mediator of a better *c*. . .Heb. 8:6
c that I will make. . .Heb. 10:16
mediator of the new *c*. . .Heb. 12:24
blood of the everlasting *c*. . .Heb. 13:20

197. Covet/Covetous/Covetousness

not *c* thy neighbour's house. . .Exod. 20:17
c thy neighbour's house. . .Deut. 5:21

Thefts, *c'ousness*. . .Mark 7:22
beware of *c'ousness*. . .Luke 12:15
wickedness, *c'ousness*. . .Rom. 1:29
the *c'ous*, or extortioners. . .1 Cor. 5:10
c earnestly the best gifts. . .1 Cor. 12:31
uncleanness, or *c'ousness*. . .Eph. 5:3
and *c'ousness*, which is idolatry. . .Col. 3:5
c'ous, boasters, proud. . .2 Tim. 3:2
exercised with *c'ous* practices. . .2 Pet. 2:14

198. Crafty/Craftiness

disappointeth the devices of the *c*. . .Job 5:12
tongue of the *c*. . .Job 15:5
c counsel against thy people. . .Ps. 83:3
wise in their own *c'iness*. . .1 Cor. 3:19
not walking in *c'iness*. . .2 Cor. 4:2
cunning *c'iness*, whereby. . .Eph. 4:14

199. Create/Created

God *c'd* the heaven. . .Gen. 1:1
God *c'd* great whales. . .Gen. 1:21
God *c'd* man in his own image. . .Gen. 1:27
earth when they were *c'd*. . .Gen. 2:4
Male and female *c'd* he them. . .Gen. 5:2
behold who hath *c'd* these things. . .Isa. 40:26
I have *c'd* him for my glory. . .Isa. 43:7
light, and *c* darkness. . .Isa. 45:7
hath not one God *c'd* us?. . .Mal. 2:10
man *c'd* for the woman. . .1 Cor. 11:9
c'd all things by Jesus Christ. . .Eph. 3:9
after God is *c'd* in righteousness. . .Eph. 4:24
God hath *c'd* to be received. . .1 Tim. 4:3
thou hast *c'd* all things. . .Rev. 4:11

See *Creation*.

200. Creation

from the beginning of the *c*. . .Mark 10:6
invisible things of him from the *c*. . .Rom. 1:20
the whole *c* groaneth. . .Rom. 8:22

See *Create/Created*.

201. Creator

Remember now thy *C* in. . .Eccles. 12:1
C of the ends of the earth. . .Isa. 40:28
c of Israel, your King. . .Isa. 43:15
creature more than the *C*. . .Rom. 1:25
as unto a faithful *C*. . .1 Pet. 4:19

202. Credit

If thou lend money. . .Exod. 22:25
nor lend him thy victuals. . .Lev. 25:37
shalt lend unto many nations. . .Deut. 15:6
lend him sufficient for his need. . .Deut. 15:8
not lend upon usury. . .Deut. 23:19
thou dost lend thy brother. . .Deut. 24:10
wicked borroweth, and payeth not. . .Ps. 37:21

sheweth favour, and lendeth. . .Ps. 112:5
pity upon the poor lendeth. . .Prov. 19:17
borrower is servant to the lender. . .Prov. 22:7
lender, so with the borrower. . .Isa. 24:2
from him that would borrow. . .Matt. 5:42
if ye lend to them. . .Luke 6:34

See *Gambling, Money*.

203. Crime
Extortion
thy neighbours by extortion. . .Ezek. 22:12
full of extortion and excess. . .Matt. 23:25

Theft/Thefts
shall be sold for his theft. . .Exod. 22:3
fornications, thefts. . .Matt. 15:19
Thefts, covetousness. . .Mark 7:22
nor of their thefts. . .Rev. 9:21

See *Adultery, Blasphemy/Blasphemer/
Blasphemers, Criminals, Homosexuality, Idolatry,
Murder/Murders, Rape*.

204. Criminals
Extortioner/Extortioners
extortioner catch all. . .Ps. 109:11
extortioners, unjust, adulterers. . .Luke 18:11
extortioners, or with idolaters. . .1 Cor. 5:10
nor revilers, nor extortioners. . .1 Cor. 6:10

Murderer/Murderers
he is a murderer. . .Num. 35:16
shall slay the murderer. . .Num. 35:21
desired a murderer to be granted. . .Acts 3:14

murderers of fathers. . .1 Tim. 1:9

suffer as a murderer. . .1 Pet. 4:15

hateth his brother is a murderer. . .1 John 3:15

Thief

if the thief be found. . .Exod. 22:7

then that thief shall die. . .Deut. 24:7

When thou sawest a thief. . .Ps. 50:18

Men do not despise a thief. . .Prov. 6:30

Whoso is partner with a thief. . .Prov. 29:24

See *Adultery, Blasphemy/Blasphemer/ Blasphemers, Crime, Homosexuality, Idolatry, Murder/Murders, Rape.*

205. Criticism

The word "criticism" does not appear in the King James Version of the Bible, and scripture does not encourage believers to critique others' lives, but the concepts of correction by those in authority and blamelessness are important to those who seek to live a faithful life.

shall not he correct?. . .Ps. 94:10

Correction is grievous. . .Prov. 15:10

the rod of correction. . .Prov. 22:15

Judge not, that ye be. . .Matt. 7:1

ministry be not blamed. . .2 Cor. 6:3

no man should blame us. . .2 Cor. 8:20

he was to be blamed. . .Gal. 2:11

206. Crops

the firstfruits of wheat harvest. . .Exod. 34:22

homer of barley seed. . .Lev. 27:16

A land of wheat, and barley. . .Deut. 8:8

beginning of barley harvest. . .Ruth 1:22

Behold, he winnoweth barley. . .Ruth 3:2

wheat, and barley, and flour. . .2 Sam. 17:28

with the finest of the wheat. . .Ps. 81:16

with the finest of the wheat. . .Ps. 147:14

and cast in the principal wheat. . .Isa. 28:25

wheat, and barley, and beans. . .Ezek. 4:9

sowed tares among the wheat. . .Matt. 13:25

a corn of wheat fall into the ground. . .John 12:24

See *Agriculture, Food, Plant/Plants.*

207. Cross

taketh not his *c*. . .Matt. 10:38
his *c*, and follow me. . .Matt. 16:24
compelled to bear his *c*. . .Matt. 27:32
come down from the *c*. . .Matt. 27:40
bearing his *c* went forth. . .John 19:17
stood by the *c*. . .John 19:25
lest the *c* of Christ. . .1 Cor. 1:17
offence of the *c*. . .Gal. 5:11
c of our Lord Jesus. . .Gal. 6:14
one body by the *c*. . .Eph. 2:16
even the death of the *c*. . .Phil. 2:8
through the blood of his *c*. . .Col. 1:20
nailing it to his *c*. . .Col. 2:14
endured the *c*. . .Heb. 12:2

See *Calvary*.

208. Crucify/Crucified

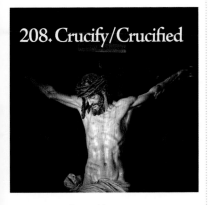

to scourge, and to *c*. . .Matt. 20:19
is betrayed to be *c'ied*. . .Matt. 26:2
delivered him to be *c'ied*. . .Matt. 27:26
And they *c'ied* him. . .Matt. 27:35
two thieves *c'ied* with him. . .Matt. 27:38
Jesus, which was *c'ied*. . .Matt. 28:5
c'ied there was a garden. . .John 19:41

Jesus, whom ye have *c'ied*. . .Acts 2:36
C'ied, whom God raised. . .Acts 4:10
our old man is *c'ied*. . .Rom. 6:6
we preach Christ *c'ied*. . .1 Cor. 1:23
Jesus Christ, and him *c'ied*. . .1 Cor. 2:2
I am *c'ied* with Christ. . .Gal. 2:20
c'ied among you?. . .Gal. 3:1
c'ied the flesh. . .Gal. 5:24
world is *c'ied* unto me. . .Gal. 6:14

209. Cruel

and for *c* bondage. . .Exod. 6:9
unrighteous and *c* man. . .Ps. 71:4
thy years unto the *c*. . .Prov. 5:9
c troubleth his own flesh. . .Prov. 11:17
mercies of the wicked are *c*. . .Prov. 12:10
Wrath is *c*. . .Prov. 27:4

210. Crying

mine eye poureth out tears unto God. . .Job 16:20
water my couch with my tears. . .Ps. 6:6
tears have been my meat. . .Ps. 42:3
Rivers of waters run down mine eyes. . .Ps. 119:136
Those that sow in tears. . .Ps. 126:5
a time to weep. . .Eccles. 3:4
Blessed are ye that weep now. . .Luke 6:21
wash his feet with tears. . .Luke 7:38
weep not for me. . .Luke 23:28
ye shall weep and lament. . .John 16:20
and as she wept. . .John 20:11
why weepest thou?. . .John 20:15
weeping, and shewing. . .Acts 9:39
great humility and with tears. . .Acts 20:19
night and day with tears. . .Acts 20:31
sorrow, nor *c*. . .Rev. 21:4

211. Currency

Originally the shekel and talent were weights, not coins, but eventually they became standardized as currency.

worth four hundred shekels. . .Gen. 23:15
half a shekel weight. . .Gen. 24:22
thirty shekels of silver. . .Exod. 21:32
a shekel is twenty gerahs. . .Exod. 30:13
half a shekel, when they give. . .Exod. 30:15
fine flour for a shekel. . .2 Kings 7:18
six hundred shekels of beaten gold. . .2 Chron. 9:15
paid the uttermost farthing. . .Matt. 5:26
sparrows sold for a farthing?. . .Matt. 10:29
labourers for a penny a day. . .Matt. 20:2
they brought unto him a penny. . .Matt. 22:19
one he gave five talents. . .Matt. 25:15
mites, which make a farthing. . .Mark 12:42
he took out two pence. . .Luke 10:35
sold for three hundred pence. . .John 12:5

See *Money*.

212. Curse/Cursed/ Cursing

profane my holy name. . .Lev. 22:32
c'd as he went. . .2 Sam. 16:13
clothed himself with c'ing. . .Ps. 109:18

hear thy servant c thee. . .Eccles. 7:21
the mouth, this defileth a man. . .Matt. 15:11
denied with an oath. . .Matt. 26:72
full of c'ing and bitterness. . .Rom. 3:14
same mouth proceedeth blessing
    and c'ing. . .James 3:10

See *Profane/Profanity*.

213. Damnation

wicked shall be turned into hell. . .Ps. 9:17
go down quick into hell. . .Ps. 55:15
shall be in danger of hell fire. . .Matt. 5:22
Gomorrha in the day of judgment. . .Matt. 10:15
forth judgment unto victory. . .Matt. 12:20
in the day of judgment. . .Matt. 12:36
prince of this world is judged. . .John 16:11
judgment seat of Christ. . .2 Cor. 5:10
and of eternal judgment. . .Heb. 6:2
but after this the judgment. . .Heb. 9:27
reserved unto judgment. . .2 Pet. 2:4
unto the day of judgment. . .2 Pet. 2:9
in the day of judgment. . .1 John 4:17
judgment of the great day. . .Jude 1:6
his judgment is come. . .Rev. 14:7
judgment of the great whore. . .Rev. 17:1

See *Hell, Unsaved*.

214. Darkness

the LORD will lighten my *d*. . .2 Sam. 22:29

d and the shadow of death. . .Job 10:21

He setteth an end to *d*. . .Job 28:3

Clouds and *d* are round. . .Ps. 97:2

brought them out of *d*. . .Ps. 107:14

d shall cover me. . .Ps. 139:11

walk in the ways of *d*. . .Prov. 2:13

body shall be full of *d*. . .Matt. 6:23

cast out into outer *d*. . .Matt. 8:12

to them that sit in *d*. . .Luke 1:79

also is full of *d*. . .Luke 11:34

ye have spoken in *d*. . .Luke 12:3

light shineth in *d*. . .John 1:5

men loved *d*. . .John 3:19

not walk in *d*. . .John 8:12

should not abide in *d*. . .John 12:46

light to shine out of *d*. . .2 Cor. 4:6

communion hath light with *d*?. . .2 Cor. 6:14

from the power of *d*. . .Col. 1:13

in him is no *d* at all. . .1 John 1:5

215. Dating

There was no such thing as dating in the biblical era. Marriages were often arranged, and the partners were expected to be virgins when they married.

take a wife unto my son. . .Gen. 24:38

jewels of silver, and jewels of gold. . .Gen. 24:53

serve thee seven years for Rachel. . .Gen. 29:18

get her for me to wife. . .Judg. 14:2

Mary was espoused to Joseph. . .Matt. 1:18

Blessed are the pure in heart. . .Matt. 5:8

unequally yoked together. . .2 Cor. 6:14

younger as sisters, with all purity. . .1 Tim. 5:2

and the bed undefiled. . .Heb. 13:4

purifieth himself. . .1 John 3:3

See *Adultery, Betroth/Betrothed, Courtship, Marriage/Marry/Marrying, Virgin/Virginity/Virgins.*

216. Daughter/ Daughters

if a man sell his *d*. . .Exod. 21:7

prostitute thy *d*. . .Lev. 19:29

d unto Benjamin to wife. . .Judg. 21:1

Michal his *d* to wife. . .1 Sam. 18:27

their *d*'s unto devils. . .Ps. 106:37

d's may be as corner stones. . .Ps. 144:12

Many *d*'s have done virtuously. . .Prov. 31:29

d against her mother. . .Matt. 10:35

he that loveth son or *d*. . .Matt. 10:37

your *d*'s shall prophesy. . .Acts 2:17

shall be my sons and *d*'s. . .2 Cor. 6:18

whose *d*'s ye are. . .1 Pet. 3:6

See *Girl/Girls, Woman, Youth.*

217. Deaf

maketh the dumb, or *d*. . .Exod. 4:11
Thou shalt not curse the *d*. . .Lev. 19:14
d shall be unstopped. . .Isa. 35:5
the *d* hear. . .Matt. 11:5
one that was *d*. . .Mark 7:32
dumb and *d* spirit. . .Mark 9:25

See *Ailments, Blind/Blindness, Disabilities, Diseases, Dumb.*

218. Death

d of the righteous. . .Num. 23:10
d part thee and me. . .Ruth 1:17
valley of the shadow of *d*. . .Ps. 23:4
belong the issues from *d*. . .Ps. 68:20
shall not see *d*?. . .Ps. 89:48
swallow up *d* in victory. . .Isa. 25:8
d of him that dieth. . .Ezek. 18:32
passed from *d* unto life. . .John 5:24
he shall never see *d*. . .John 8:51
and *d* by sin. . .Rom. 5:12
d hath no more dominion. . .Rom. 6:9
wages of sin is *d*. . .Rom. 6:23
since by man came *d*. . .1 Cor. 15:21
obedient unto *d*. . .Phil. 2:8
bringeth forth *d*. . .James 1:15

See *Bury/Burial/Buried, Death Penalty, Mortal/ Mortality.*

219. Death Penalty

surely be put to death. . .Exod. 21:16
surely be put to death. . .Lev. 20:10
surely be put to death. . .Lev. 20:13
surely be put to death. . .Lev. 20:15
that man shall die. . .Deut. 17:12
that prophet shall die. . .Deut. 18:20
lay with her shall die. . .Deut. 22:25
that thief shall die. . .Deut. 24:7

See *Capital Punishment, Death.*

220. Debauchery

chambering and wantonness. . .Rom. 13:13
fornication and lasciviousness. . .2 Cor. 12:21
uncleanness, lasciviousness. . .Gal. 5:19
wherein is excess. . .Eph. 5:18
lasciviousness, lusts. . .1 Pet. 4:3

See *Adultery, Alcohol, Drink/Drinking, Lasciviousness.*

221. Debt

See *Credit, Money.*

222. Deceit/Deceitful/ Deceitfully/ Deceitfulness

which he hath *d'fully* gotten. . .Lev. 6:4
abhor the bloody and *d'ful*. . .Ps. 5:6

nor sworn *d'fully*. . .Ps. 24:4

bloody and *d'ful* men. . .Ps. 55:23

counsels of the wicked are *d*. . .Prov. 12:5

folly of fools is *d*. . .Prov. 14:8

kisses of an enemy are *d'ful*. . .Prov. 27:6

Favour is *d'ful*. . .Prov. 31:30

The heart is *d'ful*. . .Jer. 17:9

d'fulness of riches. . .Matt. 13:22

wickedness, *d*. . .Mark 7:22

handling the word of God *d'fully*. . .2 Cor. 4:2

according to the *d'ful* lusts. . .Eph. 4:22

See *Cheating*.

223. Decision Making

choose you this day. . .Josh. 24:15

choose the fear of the Lᴏʀᴅ. . .Prov. 1:29

choose none of his ways. . .Prov. 3:31

yet what I shall choose. . .Phil. 1:22

See *Counsel/Counsels*.

224. Defile/Defiled/Defileth

lay with her, and *d'd* her. . .Gen. 34:2

every one that *d'th* it. . .Exod. 31:14

shall ye *d* yourselves. . .Lev. 11:44

D not ye yourselves. . .Lev. 18:24

d'd with their own works. . .Ps. 106:39

shall they *d* themselves. . .Ezek. 37:23

d'd my holy name. . .Ezek. 43:8

they *d* the man. . .Matt. 15:18

See *Impurity*.

225. Defraud/Defrauded

Shalt not *d* thy neighbour. . .Lev. 19:13

D not. . .Mark 10:19

suffer yourselves to be *d'ed*?. . .1 Cor. 6:7

D ye not one the other. . .1 Cor. 7:5

d his brother. . .1 Thess. 4:6

226. Deity of Christ

Son of the living God. . .Matt. 16:16
All things were made by him. . .John 1:3
making himself equal with God. . .John 5:18
Son, even as they honour the Father. . .John 5:23
bread of God is he. . .John 6:33
seen me hath seen the Father. . .John 14:9
and make our abode with him. . .John 14:23
being in the form of God. . .Phil. 2:6
image of the invisible God. . .Col. 1:15
by him were all things created. . .Col. 1:16
fulness of the Godhead bodily. . .Col. 2:9
Son he saith, Thy throne, O God. . .Heb. 1:8

227. Delay/Delayed

Thou shalt not *d* to offer. . .Exod. 22:29
Moses *d'ed* to come down. . .Exod. 32:1
d'ed not to keep thy commandments. . .Ps. 119:60
See *Patience/Patient/Patiently, Wait/Waited/
Waiteth/Waiting.*

228. Delight/ Delighted/ Delighteth

Hath the Lord as great *d*. . .1 Sam. 15:22
because he *d'ed* in me. . .2 Sam. 22:20
d is in the law. . .Ps. 1:2
because he *d'ed* in me. . .Ps. 18:19
D thyself also in the Lord. . .Ps. 37:4
he *d'eth* in his way. . .Ps. 37:23
thy comforts *d* my soul. . .Ps. 94:19
just weight is his *d*. . .Prov. 11:1
prayer of the upright is his *d*. . .Prov. 15:8
give *d* unto thy soul. . .Prov. 29:17

See *Enjoy.*

229. Deliverer

the Lord raised up a *d*. . .Judg. 3:9
my fortress, and my *d*. . .Ps. 18:2
my help and my *d*. . .Ps. 40:17
my help and my *d*. . .Ps. 70:5
my high tower, and my *d*. . .Ps. 144:2
a ruler and a *d*. . .Acts 7:35
come out of Sion the *D*. . .Rom. 11:26

230. Delusion

imaginations of the thoughts. . .1 Chron. 28:9
deviseth wicked imaginations. . .Prov. 6:18
all their imaginations against me. . .Lam. 3:60
became vain in their imaginations. . .Rom. 1:21
Casting down imaginations. . .2 Cor. 10:5

231. Demon Possession

were possessed with devils. . .Matt. 8:16
two possessed with devils. . .Matt. 8:28
man possessed with a devil. . .Matt. 9:32
one possessed with a devil. . .Matt. 12:22
vexed with a devil. . .Matt. 15:22
Jesus rebuked the devil. . .Matt. 17:18
man with an unclean spirit. . .Mark 5:2
which hath a dumb spirit. . .Mark 9:17
whom he had cast seven devils. . .Mark 16:9
vexed with unclean spirits. . .Luke 6:18
Then entered Satan into Judas. . .Luke 22:3
unclean spirits, crying. . .Acts 8:7

See *Devil/Devils; Possession, Demon.*

232. Deny/Denying

lest ye *d* your God. . .Josh. 24:27
Lest I be full, and *d* thee. . .Prov. 30:9
shall *d* me before men. . .Matt. 10:33
let him *d* himself. . .Matt. 16:24
thou shalt *d* me thrice. . .Matt. 26:34
d that there is any resurrection. . .Luke 20:27

if we *d* him. . .2 Tim. 2:12
he cannot *d* himself. . .2 Tim. 2:13
d'ing the power thereof. . .2 Tim. 3:5
in works they *d* him. . .Titus 1:16
d'ing ungodliness and worldly. . .Titus 2:12
even *d'ing* the Lord. . .2 Pet. 2:1

233. Depression

Why art thou cast down. . .Ps. 42:5
cast down, O my soul?. . .Ps. 43:5
eat the bread of sorrows. . .Ps. 127:2
comforteth those that are cast down. . .2 Cor. 7:6

See *Empty, Emptiness, Sorrow/Sorrowed/Sorrows.*

234. Desire/Desired/ Desires

boasteth of his heart's *d.* . .Ps. 10:3
the *d* of the humble. . .Ps. 10:17
given him his heart's *d.* . .Ps. 21:2
have I *d'd* of the Lord. . .Ps. 27:4
d's of thine heart. . .Ps. 37:4
d of the wicked. . .Ps. 112:10
satisfiest the *d.* . .Ps. 145:16
d of the righteous. . .Prov. 10:24
d of the slothful. . .Prov. 21:25
that we should *d* him. . .Isa. 53:2
d to be first. . .Mark 9:35
What things soever ye *d.* . .Mark 11:24
my heart's *d* and prayer. . .Rom. 10:1
d spiritual gifts. . .1 Cor. 14:1
d the office of a bishop. . .1 Tim. 3:1
d to have, and cannot. . .James 4:2

235. Desire/Desires, Sexual

d shall be to thy husband. . .Gen. 3:16
d thy neighbour's wife. . .Deut. 5:21
his *d* is toward me. . .Song of Sol. 7:10
d's of the flesh. . .Eph. 2:3

236. Despair/Despaired

d of all the labour. . .Eccles. 2:20
we *d'ed* even of life. . .2 Cor. 1:8
perplexed, but not in *d*. . .2 Cor. 4:8

237. Despise/Despised/Despisest/Despiseth

they *d'd* my judgments. . .Lev. 26:43
d me shall be lightly. . .1 Sam. 2:30
he hath not *d'd* nor abhorred. . .Ps. 22:24
not *d* their prayer. . .Ps. 102:17
fools *d* wisdom. . .Prov. 1:7
d not the chastening. . .Prov. 3:11
Whoso *d'th* the word. . .Prov. 13:13
d'th his neighbour. . .Prov. 14:21
d'th his mother. . .Prov. 15:20
d'd and rejected. . .Isa. 53:3
d the other. . .Matt. 6:24

d'th you *d'th* me. . .Luke 10:16
d'st thou the riches. . .Rom. 2:4
d him that eateth not. . .Rom. 14:3
things which are *d'd*. . .1 Cor. 1:28
D not prophesyings. . .1 Thess. 5:20
no man *d* thy youth. . .1 Tim. 4:12
d'd the poor. . .James 2:6

See *Hate/Hated/Hatest/Hateth.*

238. Destruction/Destructions

rescue my soul from their *d's*. . .Ps. 35:17
down into the pit of *d*. . .Ps. 55:23
them down into *d*. . .Ps. 73:18
turnest man to *d*. . .Ps. 90:3
thy life from *d*. . .Ps. 103:4
foolish is near *d*. . .Prov. 10:14
wide his lips shall have *d*. . .Prov. 13:3
Pride goeth before *d*. . .Prov. 16:18
that leadeth to *d*. . .Matt. 7:13
D and misery. . .Rom. 3:16
vessels of wrath fitted to *d*. . .Rom. 9:22
Whose end is *d*. . .Phil. 3:19
punished with everlasting *d*. . .2 Thess. 1:9
d and perdition. . .1 Tim. 6:9

239. Devil/Devils

to be tempted of the *d*. . .Matt. 4:1
have cast out *d's*?. . .Matt. 7:22
d's besought him. . .Matt. 8:31
He casteth out *d's*. . .Matt. 9:34
cast out *d's*. . .Matt. 10:8
your father the *d*. . .John 8:44
Can a *d* open the eyes. . .John 10:21
they sacrifice to *d's*. . .1 Cor. 10:20
Neither give place to the *d*. . .Eph. 4:27
stand against the wiles of the *d*. . .Eph. 6:11
the snare of the *d*. . .1 Tim. 3:7
doctrines of *d's*. . .1 Tim. 4:1
power of death, that is, the *d*. . .Heb. 2:14
Resist the *d*. . .James 4:7
your adversary the *d*. . .1 Pet. 5:8

See *Demon Possession; Possession Demon.*

240. Devotion

walked before thee in truth. . .2 Kings 20:3
serve him with a perfect heart. . .1 Chron. 28:9
lifted up in the ways of the LORD. . .2 Chron. 17:6
trusteth in thee. . .Ps. 86:2
the Lord without distraction. . .1 Cor. 7:35
followed every good work. . .1 Tim. 5:10
maintain good works. . .Titus 3:8

See *Good Work/Good Works.*

241. Devotions

Be still, and know that I am God. . .Ps. 46:10
daily shall he be praised. . .Ps. 72:15
my prayer be set forth. . .Ps. 141:2
ye shall ask in prayer. . .Matt. 21:22

continually to prayer. . .Acts 6:4
give yourselves to fasting and prayer. . .1 Cor. 7:5
Praying always with all prayer. . .Eph. 6:18
by prayer and supplication. . .Phil. 4:6
word of Christ dwell in you. . .Col. 3:16
Continue in prayer. . .Col. 4:2
Pray without ceasing. . .1 Thess. 5:17
rightly dividing the word of truth. . .2 Tim. 2:15
All scripture is given. . .2 Tim. 3:16
the word of God is quick. . .Heb. 4:12
desire the sincere milk of the word. . .1 Pet. 2:2

See *Prayer/Prayers, Word of God.*

242. Diet

shalt eat the herb of the field. . .Gen. 3:18
the beasts which ye shall eat. . .Lev. 11:2
not good to eat much honey. . .Prov. 25:27
let them give us pulse to eat. . .Dan. 1:12
what ye shall eat. . .Matt. 6:25
life is more than meat. . .Luke 12:23
Arise, Peter; slay and eat. . .Acts 11:7
neither to eat flesh. . .Rom. 14:21
Meats for the belly. . .1 Cor. 6:13
body is the temple of the Holy Ghost. . .1 Cor. 6:19
Whether therefore ye eat. . .1 Cor. 10:31
to abstain from meats. . .1 Tim. 4:3
having food and raiment. . .1 Tim. 6:8

See *Fasting/Fastings.*

243. Differ/ Difference/Differences

no *d'ence* between us and them. . .Acts 15:9
for there is no *d'ence*. . .Rom. 3:22
maketh thee to *d* from another?. . .1 Cor. 4:7
d'ences of administrations. . .1 Cor. 12:5
making a *d'ence*. . .Jude 1:22

244. Diligent/ Diligently/Diligence

If thou wilt *d'ly*. . .Exod. 15:26
keep thy soul *d'ly*. . .Deut. 4:9
teach them *d'ly*. . .Deut. 6:7
d'ly keep the commandments. . .Deut. 6:17
Keep thy heart with all *d'ce*. . .Prov. 4:23
d maketh rich. . .Prov. 10:4
d'ly seeketh good. . .Prov. 11:27
substance of a *d* man. . .Prov. 12:27
d in his business?. . .Prov. 22:29
them that *d'ly* seek him. . .Heb. 11:6
give *d'ce* to make your calling. . .2 Pet. 1:10
be *d* that ye may be found. . .2 Pet. 3:14

See *Industry*.

245. Disabilities

he fell, and became lame. . .2 Sam. 4:4
I was eyes to the blind. . .Job 29:15
Then shall the lame man leap. . .Isa. 35:6
and the lame walk. . .Matt. 11:5
lame, blind, dumb, maimed. . .Matt. 15:30
blind and the lame. . .Matt. 21:14
the maimed, the lame, the blind. . .Luke 14:13
a certain man lame. . .Acts 3:2
palsies, and that were lame. . .Acts 8:7

See *Ailments, Blind/Blinded, Deaf, Diseases, Dumb, Sick/Sickly/Sickness/Sicknesses*.

246. Disappoint/ Disappointed

d him, cast him down. . .Ps. 17:13
and were not confounded. . .Ps. 22:5
Without counsel purposes are *d'ed*. . .Prov. 15:22
ashamed that wait for me. . .Isa. 49:23
hope maketh not ashamed. . .Rom. 5:5

247. Disasters, Natural
Drought
shall not be dew nor rain. . .1 Kings 17:1
in the year of drought. . .Jer. 17:8

Earthquake
saw the earthquake. . .Matt. 27:54
there was a great earthquake. . .Acts 16:26
there was a great earthquake. . .Rev. 6:12

Famine
there was a famine. . .Gen. 26:1
seven years of famine. . .Gen. 41:27

Either three years' famine. . .1 Chron. 21:12
in the days of famine. . .Ps. 37:19
or persecution, or famine. . .Rom. 8:35

Hail

So there was hail. . .Exod. 9:24
there followed hail and fire. . .Rev. 8:7
an earthquake, and great hail. . .Rev. 11:19

Pestilence/Pestilences

with the pestilence. . .Num. 14:12
the LORD sent a pestilence. . .2 Sam. 24:15
pestilences, and earthquakes. . .Matt. 24:7

Plague/Plagues

one plague more upon Pharaoh. . .Exod. 11:1
the plague was stayed. . .Num. 16:48
make thy plagues wonderful. . .Deut. 28:59
any plague come nigh. . .Ps. 91:10
as many as had plagues. . .Mark 3:10
healed of that plague. . .Mark 5:29
plagues yet repented not. . .Rev. 9:20

248. Discern/ Discerned/Discerner/ Discerneth/Discerning

to *d* judgment. . .1 Kings 3:11
wise man's heart *d'eth*. . .Eccles. 8:5
ye do not *d* this time?. . .Luke 12:56
they are spiritually *d'ed*. . .1 Cor. 2:14
another *d'ing* of spirits. . .1 Cor. 12:10
d'er of the thoughts. . .Heb. 4:12

249. Disciple

d is not above his master. . .Matt. 10:24
only in the name of a *d*. . .Matt. 10:42
himself was Jesus' *d*. . .Matt. 27:57
he cannot be my *d*. . .Luke 14:26
d, whom Jesus loved. . .John 20:2
d named Tabitha. . .Acts 9:36
d was there, named Timotheus. . .Acts 16:1

250. Disciples

Believers

d were called Christians. . .Acts 11:26
d were filled with joy. . .Acts 13:52
yoke upon the neck of the *d*. . .Acts 15:10
strengthening all the *d*. . .Acts 18:23
d came together to break bread. . .Acts 20:7
draw away *d* after them. . .Acts 20:30

The Twelve

his *d* came unto him. . .Matt. 5:1
his *d* came to him. . .Matt. 8:25
commanding his twelve *d*. . .Matt. 11:1
thy *d* do that which. . .Matt. 12:2

Jesus constrained his *d*. . .Matt. 14:22
and gave to his *d*. . .Matt. 15:36
d, saying, Whom do men. . .Matt. 16:13
When his *d* heard it. . .Matt. 19:25
d came unto him privately. . .Matt. 24:3
d, and said, Take, eat. . .Matt. 26:26
d, and findeth them asleep. . .Matt. 26:40
his *d* that he is risen. . .Matt. 28:7

251. Discipline

if ye will obey my voice. . .Exod. 19:5
openeth also their ear to *d*. . .Job 36:10
that ye should obey it. . .Rom. 6:12
be done decently and in order. . .1 Cor. 14:40

See *Obedience*.

252. Discontentment/ Discontented

every one that was *d'ed*. . .1 Sam. 22:2
neither will he rest content. . .Prov. 6:35
and not content therewith. . .3 John 1:10

See *Complain/Complained/Complainers/Complaint, Contention/Contentions/Contentious*.

253. Discord

he soweth *d*. . .Prov. 6:14
soweth *d* among brethren. . .Prov. 6:19
had no small dissension. . .Acts 15:2
arose a great dissension. . .Acts 23:10
not in strife and envying. . .Rom. 13:13
divisions and offences. . .Rom. 16:17
the disputer of this world?. . .1 Cor. 1:20
envying, and strife. . .1 Cor. 3:3
have a quarrel against any. . .Col. 3:13

254. Discretion

guide his affairs with *d*. . .Ps. 112:5
knowledge and *d*. . .Prov. 1:4
D shall preserve thee. . .Prov. 2:11
keep sound wisdom and *d*. . .Prov. 3:21
That thou mayest regard *d*. . .Prov. 5:2
woman which is without *d*. . .Prov. 11:22
d of a man deferreth his anger. . .Prov. 19:11
God doth instruct him to *d*. . .Isa. 28:26

255. Discrimination

Scripture admonishes believers not to discriminate against anyone on the basis of their nationality. All Christians are to love one another.

Love your enemies. . .Matt. 5:44
love thy neighbour as thyself. . .Matt. 19:19
that ye love one another. . .John 15:17
not call any man common or unclean. . .Acts 10:28
for there is no difference. . .Rom. 3:22
no difference between the Jew. . .Rom. 10:12

are one body in Christ. . .Rom. 12:5
kindly affectioned one to another. . .Rom. 12:10
ye are all one in Christ Jesus. . .Gal. 3:28
neither Greek nor Jew. . .Col. 3:11

See *Equality*, *Favoritism*.

256. Diseases

one plague more upon Pharaoh. . .Exod. 11:1
none of these *d*. . .Exod. 15:26
consumption, and the burning. . .Lev. 26:16
died by the plague. . .Num. 14:37
the plague is begun. . .Num. 16:46
those that died in the plague. . .Num. 25:9
plague among the congregation. . .Num. 31:16
Take heed in the plague of leprosy. . .Deut. 24:8
smite thee with a consumption. . .Deut. 28:22
plague was on you all. . .1 Sam. 6:4
plague may be stayed. . .2 Sam. 24:21
he would recover him of his leprosy. . .2 Kings 5:3
healeth all thy *d*. . .Ps. 103:3
divers *d* and torments. . .Matt. 4:24
immediately his leprosy was cleansed. . .Matt. 8:3
as many as had plagues. . .Mark 3:10
and to cure *d*. . .Luke 9:1
not killed by these plagues. . .Rev. 9:20

See *Ailments*, *Blind/Blinded*, *Deaf*, *Disabilities*,
Dumb, *Sick/Sickly/Sickness/Sicknesses*.

257. Disgrace

O my God, I am ashamed. . .Ezra 9:6
great affliction and reproach. . .Neh. 1:3
mine enemies be ashamed. . .Ps. 6:10
shame of my face. . .Ps. 44:15

Turn away my reproach. . .Ps. 119:39
then cometh shame. . .Prov. 11:2
she that maketh ashamed. . .Prov. 12:4
sin is a reproach to any people. . .Prov. 14:34
bringeth his mother to shame. . .Prov. 29:15
worthy to suffer shame. . .Acts 5:41
lest he fall into reproach. . .1 Tim. 3:7
put him to an open shame. . .Heb. 6:6

258. Dishonest/ Dishonesty

unrighteousness in judgment. . .Lev. 19:35
all that do unrighteously. . .Deut. 25:16
false balance is abomination. . .Prov. 11:1
unjust man is an abomination. . .Prov. 29:27
thy *d* gain. . .Ezek. 22:13
hidden things of *d'y*. . .2 Cor. 4:2

259. Dishonour/ Dishonourest

my shame, and my *d*. . .Ps. 69:19
ye do *d* me. . .John 8:49

to *d* their own bodies. . .Rom. 1:24
d'est thou God?. . .Rom 2:23
another unto *d*?. . .Rom. 9:21
It is sown in *d*. . .1 Cor. 15:43
honour, and some to *d*. . .2 Tim. 2:20

260. Disobedient/ Disobedience

Nevertheless they were *d*. . .Neh. 9:26
the *d* to the wisdom. . .Luke 1:17
d to parents. . .Rom. 1:30
by one man's *d'ce*. . .Rom. 5:19
d and gainsaying people. . .Rom. 10:21
children of *d'ce*. . .Eph. 2:2
children of *d'ce*. . .Eph. 5:6

261. Disputed/ Disputer

ye *d* among yourselves. . .Mark 9:33
d against the Grecians. . .Acts 9:29
d he in the synagogue. . .Acts 17:17
the *d'r* of this world?. . .1 Cor. 1:20
contending with the devil he *d*. . .Jude 1:9

262. Disrespect

is laughed to scorn. . .Job 12:4
My friends scorn me. . .Job 16:20
sitteth in the seat of the scornful. . .Ps. 1:1
laugh me to scorn. . .Ps. 22:7
a scorn and a derision. . .Ps. 44:13
He that reproveth a scorner. . .Prov. 9:7
Scornful men bring a city. . .Prov. 29:8
laughed him to scorn. . .Matt. 9:24
scoffers, walking after their own. . .2 Pet. 3:3

263. Distress/ Distressed/Distresses

my *d* I called upon. . .2 Sam. 22:7
when I was in *d*. . .Ps. 4:1
In my *d* I called upon. . .Ps. 18:6
out of my *d*. . .Ps. 25:17
delivered them out of their *d'es*. . .Ps. 107:6
the needy in his *d*. . .Isa. 25:4
shall tribulation, or *d*. . .Rom. 8:35
on every side, yet not *d'ed*. . .2 Cor. 4:8
d'es for Christ's sake. . .2 Cor. 12:10

264. Diversity

See *Discrimination*.

265. Divinity

See *Deity of Christ*.

266. Divorce/ Divorced/Divorcement

he may not put her away. . .Deut. 22:19
write her a bill of *d'ment*. . .Deut. 24:1
he hateth putting away. . .Mal. 2:16
d'd committeth adultery. . .Matt. 5:32

put away his wife. . .Matt. 19:3

let not man put asunder. . .Matt. 19:6

shall put away his wife. . .Matt. 19:9

not the husband put away his wife. . .1 Cor. 7:11

Art thou loosed from a wife?. . .1 Cor. 7:27

See *Adultery*, *Fornication/Fornications*, *Lawsuits*.

267. Doctrine/ Doctrines

I give you good *d*. . .Prov. 4:2

astonished at his *d*. . .Matt. 7:28

d's the commandments. . .Matt. 15:9

shall know of the *d*. . .John 7:17

the apostles' *d*. . .Acts 2:42

d which was delivered you. . .Rom. 6:17

prophesying, or by *d*?. . .1 Cor. 14:6

psalm, hath a *d*. . .1 Cor. 14:26

every wind of *d*. . .Eph. 4:14

faith and of good *d*. . .1 Tim. 4:6

labour in the word and *d*. . .1 Tim. 5:17

d which is according to. . .1 Tim. 6:3

is profitable for *d*. . .2 Tim. 3:16

able by sound *d*. . .Titus 1:9

abideth not in the *d* of Christ. . .2 John 1:9

268. Dominion

God gave humankind dominion over the

earth, with the idea that humans should rule wisely and under Him.

d over the fish of the sea. . .Gen. 1:26

replenish the earth, and subdue it. . .Gen. 1:28

Thou madest him to have *d*. . .Ps. 8:6

269. Doubt/Doubted/ Doubteth/Doubtful/ Doubting/Doubts

dissolving of *d's*. . .Dan. 5:12

have faith, and *d* not. . .Matt. 21:21

but some *d'ed*. . .Matt. 28:17

shall not *d* in his heart. . .Mark 11:23

neither be ye of *d'ful* mind. . .Luke 12:29

he that *d'eth* is. . .Rom. 14:23

without wrath and *d'ing*. . .1 Tim. 2:8

See *Emotions*, *Feelings*.

Do not drink wine nor strong *d*. . .Lev. 10:9

he is a glutton, and a drunkard. . .Deut. 21:20

for he was very drunken. . .1 Sam. 25:36

and he made him drunk. . .2 Sam. 11:13

the drunkard and the glutton. . .Prov. 23:21

for strength, and not for drunkenness!. . .Eccles. 10:17

a drunken man staggereth in his vomit. . .Isa. 19:14

and to eat and *d*, and to be drunken. . .Luke 12:45

not in rioting and drunkenness. . .Rom. 13:13

a drunkard, or an extortioner. . .1 Cor. 5:11

nor drunkards, nor revilers. . .1 Cor. 6:10

drunkenness, revellings. . .Gal. 5:21

be not drunk with wine, wherein
is excess. . .Eph. 5:18

revellings, banquetings. . .1 Pet. 4:3

See *Addiction, Alcohol, Banquet/Banqueting/
Banquetings, Debauchery, Drunkenness, Revelry,
Wine.*

270. Dream/ Dreamed/Dreams

he *d'ed*, and behold. . .Gen. 28:12

Joseph *d'ed* a *d*. . .Gen. 37:5

We have *d'ed* a *d*. . .Gen. 40:8

that Pharaoh *d'ed*. . .Gen. 41:1

or a dreamer of *d's*. . .Deut. 13:1

in the multitude of *d's*. . .Eccles. 5:7

in all visions and *d's*. . .Dan. 1:17

interpreting of *d's*. . .Dan. 5:12

old men shall *d d's*. . .Joel 2:28

being warned of God in a *d*. . .Matt. 2:12

appeareth in a *d* to Joseph. . .Matt. 2:19

in a *d* because of him. . .Matt. 27:19

271. Drink/Drinking

he drank of the wine, and was drunken. . .Gen. 9:21

272. Drugs

*Though scripture does not specifically
mention drugs, it condemns the kind of
lifestyle that goes with illegal drug use and
encourages believers to care for their bodies.*

with surfeiting, and drunkenness. . .Luke 21:34

Let not sin therefore reign. . .Rom. 6:12

mortify the deeds of the body. . .Rom. 8:13

ye are the temple of God. . .1 Cor. 3:16

glorify God in your body. . .1 Cor. 6:20

body, and bring it into subjection. . .1 Cor. 9:27

drunkenness, revellings. . .Gal. 5:21

revellings, banquetings. . .1 Pet. 4:3

273. Drunkenness

Avoiding drink and drunkards

for strength, and not for d!. . .Eccles. 10:17
with surfeiting, and d. . .Luke 21:34
not in rioting and d. . .Rom. 13:13
a drunkard, or an extortioner. . .1 Cor. 5:11
be not drunk with wine, wherein
   is excess. . .Eph. 5:18

Consequences of

he drank of the wine, and was drunken. . .Gen. 9:21
he is a glutton, and a drunkard. . .Deut. 21:20
the drunkard and the glutton. . .Prov. 23:21
a drunken man staggereth. . .Isa. 19:14

Examples of

for he was very drunken. . .1 Sam. 25:36
and he made him drunk. . .2 Sam. 11:13
drink, and to be drunken. . .Luke 12:45
revellings, banquetings. . .1 Pet. 4:3

God's kingdom and

nor drunkards, nor revilers. . .1 Cor. 6:10
d, revellings. . .Gal. 5:21

See *Alcohol, Drink/Drinking, Revelry*.

274. Dumb

who maketh the d. . .Exod. 4:11
tongue of the d sing. . .Isa. 35:6
d man possessed. . .Matt. 9:32
blind, and d. . .Matt. 12:22
lame, blind, d. . .Matt. 15:30

See *Ailments, Blind/Blinded, Deaf, Disabilities, Diseases*.

275. Duty

whole d of man. . .Eccles. 12:13
that which was our d to do. . .Luke 17:10
d is also to minister. . .Rom. 15:27

276. Dwelling

heaven thy d place. . .1 Kings 8:43
d place of the wicked. . .Job 8:22
thou hast been our d place. . .Ps. 90:1
any plague come nigh thy d. . .Ps. 91:10
d of the righteous. . .Prov. 24:15
d in the light. . .1 Tim. 6:16

277. Earnest

An earnest is a deposit. God gives believers a deposit toward their future in eternity when the Holy Spirit comes to dwell in them.

the e of the Spirit. . .2 Cor. 5:5
the e of our inheritance. . .Eph. 1:14

278. Earth

created the heaven and the e. . .Gen. 1:1
Let the e bring forth grass. . .Gen. 1:11
e bring forth the living creature. . .Gen. 1:24
and over all the e. . .Gen. 1:26

replenish the *e*. . .Gen. 1:28
The *e* also was corrupt. . .Gen. 6:11
flood of waters upon the *e*. . .Gen. 6:17
While the *e* remaineth. . .Gen. 8:22
every beast of the *e*. . .Gen. 9:2
e brought forth by handfuls. . .Gen. 41:47
the *e* is the Lord's. . .1 Cor. 10:26

See *Conservation, Ecology.*

279. Ease

couch shall *e* my complaints. . .Job 7:13
His soul shall dwell at *e*. . .Ps. 25:13
those that are at *e*. . .Ps. 123:4
take thine *e*, eat, drink. . .Luke 12:19

280. Eat/Eateth/Eating

thou mayest freely *e*. . .Gen. 2:16
thy face shalt thou *e* bread. . .Gen. 3:19
e unleavened bread. . .Exod. 13:6
shall *e* and be satisfied. . .Ps. 22:26
e the labour of thine hands. . .Ps. 128:2
e the bread of wickedness. . .Prov. 4:17
righteous *e'eth* to the satisfying. . .Prov. 13:25
did *e* grass as oxen. . .Dan. 4:33
what ye shall *e*. . .Matt. 6:25
take thine ease, *e*, drink. . .Luke 12:19
e the flesh of the Son. . .John 6:53
Whether therefore ye *e*. . .1 Cor. 10:31
e of the tree of life. . .Rev. 2:7

See *Food, Health, Nourishment.*

281. Ecology

Though the word "ecology" is not used in scripture, Genesis 1 clearly describes God's loving creation of the earth and humankind's responsibility for its care. Genesis 6–9 describes the flood and God's salvation of some animals and humans, with whom God makes a covenant. When famine threatened the Near East, Joseph's wise stewardship led Egypt to store enough food to share with other nations. Repeatedly God reminds His people that He made and controls the heaven and earth. When we care for the earth, we care for His creations as stewards of His land.

created the heaven and the earth. . .Gen. 1:1
and over all the earth. . .Gen. 1:26
replenish the earth. . .Gen. 1:28
into your hand are they delivered. . .Gen. 9:2
all flesh that is upon the earth. . .Gen. 9:16
earth brought forth by handfuls. . .Gen. 41:47
for all the earth is mine. . .Exod. 19:5
a land flowing with milk and honey. . .Exod. 33:3
land which the LORD thy God careth for. . .Deut. 11:12
shall greatly bless thee in the land. . .Deut. 15:4
regardeth the life of his beast. . .Prov. 12:10

the earth is the Lord's. . .1 Cor. 10:26

precious fruit of the earth. . .James 5:7

See *Conservation*, *Earth*.

282. Edify/Edification/Edifieth/Edifying

one may *e* another. . .Rom. 14:19

his good to *e'ication*. . .Rom. 15:2

but charity *e'eth*. . .1 Cor. 8:1

all things *e* not. . .1 Cor. 10:23

speaketh unto men to *e'ication*. . .1 Cor. 14:3

Let all things be done unto *e'ing*. . .1 Cor. 14:26

hath given me to *e'ication*. . .2 Cor. 13:10

e'ing of itself in love. . .Eph. 4:16

good to the use of *e'ing*. . .Eph. 4:29

both learned, and received. . .Phil. 4:9

Ever learning, and never able. . .2 Tim. 3:7

See *Learn/Learned/Learning*.

283. Education

that ye may learn them. . .Deut. 5:1

learn to fear the LORD. . .Deut. 31:13

the priest instructed him. . .2 Kings 12:2

know wisdom and instruction. . .Prov. 1:2

Take fast hold of instruction. . .Prov. 4:13

Hear instruction, and be wise. . .Prov. 8:33

Whoso loveth instruction. . .Prov. 12:1

knowledge and skill in all learning. . .Dan. 1:17

Moses was learned. . .Acts 7:22

were written for our learning. . .Rom. 15:4

doctrine which ye have learned. . .Rom. 16:17

that all may learn. . .1 Cor. 14:31

See *Learn/Learned/Learning*.

284. Elderly, the

bear a child, which am old?. . .Gen. 18:13

aged understand judgment. . .Job 32:9

and now am old. . .Ps. 37:25

when I am old and greyheaded. . .Ps. 71:18

bring forth fruit in old age. . .Ps. 92:14

old men, and children. . .Ps. 148:12

are the crown of old men. . .Prov. 17:6

beauty of old men. . .Prov. 20:29

thy mother when she is old. . .Prov. 23:22

old men shall dream dreams. . .Acts 2:17

aged men be sober, grave. . .Titus 2:2

aged women likewise. . .Titus 2:3

See *Age*, *Seasons of Life*.

285. Elect/Elect's, the

whom I uphold; mine *e*. . .Isa. 42:1

Israel mine *e*. . .Isa. 45:4

e shall long enjoy the work. . .Isa. 65:22

but for the *e's* sake. . .Matt. 24:22

they shall deceive the very *e*. . .Matt. 24:24

his *e* from the four winds. . .Matt. 24:31

God avenge his own *e*. . .Luke 18:7

to the charge of God's *e*?. . .Rom. 8:33
e of God, holy and beloved. . .Col. 3:12
the *e* angels. . .1 Tim. 5:21
for the *e's* sakes. . .2 Tim. 2:10
E according to the foreknowledge. . .1 Pet. 1:2

See *Election.*

286. Election

God according to *e*. . .Rom. 9:11
according to the *e* of grace. . .Rom. 11:5
e hath obtained it. . .Rom. 11:7
as touching the *e*. . .Rom. 11:28
your *e* of God. . .1 Thess. 1:4
your calling and *e* sure. . .2 Pet. 1:10

See *Elect/Elect's, the; Foreknowledge of God;*
Predestinate/Predestinated.

287. Eloquent

I am not *e*. . .Exod. 4:10
the *e* orator. . .Isa. 3:3
an *e* man. . .Acts 18:24

See *Communication/Communications.*

288. Emotions

Isaac, whom thou lovest. . .Gen. 22:2
them that hated me. . .2 Sam. 22.18
I will fear no evil. . .Ps. 23:4
whom shall I fear?. . .Ps. 27:1
me from all my fears. . .Ps. 34:4
fear, where no fear was. . .Ps. 53:5
that hate thee?. . .Ps. 139:21
fear of man bringeth. . .Prov. 29:25
and a time to hate. . .Eccles. 3:8
love is strong as death. . .Song of Sol. 8:6
he that hateth his brother. . .1 John 2:11
no fear in love. . .1 John 4:18

See *Doubt/Doubted/Doubteth/Doubtful/Doubting/*
Doubts; Fear/Feared/Fears; Hate/Hated/Hatest/
Hateth; Love, Brotherly.

289. Employment

Six days shalt thou labour. . .Exod. 20:9
had a mind to work. . .Neh. 4:6
goeth forth unto his work. . .Ps. 104:23
he that gathereth by labour. . .Prov. 13:11
In all labour there is profit. . .Prov. 14:23
sleep of a labouring man. . .Eccles. 5:12
labourer is worthy of his hire. . .Luke 10:7
if any would not work. . .2 Thess. 3:10

See *Hiring, Jobs, Work.*

290. Empty/Emptiness

Scripture uses the word "empty" to describe
spiritual or emotional sorrow.

brought me home again *e*. . .Ruth 1:21

my years with sighing. . .Ps. 31:10

sadness of the countenance. . .Eccles. 7:3

his soul is *e*. . .Isa. 29:8

e the soul of the hungry. . .Isa. 32:6

he was sad at that saying. . .Mark 10:22

hath sent *e* away. . .Luke 1:53

See *Depression*.

291. Encouragement

in the comfort of the Holy Ghost. . .Acts 9:31

comforted together with you. . .Rom. 1:12

God of patience and consolation. . .Rom. 15:5

exhortation, and comfort. . .1 Cor. 14:3

consolation in Christ. . .Phil. 2:1

comfort one another. . .1 Thess. 4:18

comfort yourselves together. . .1 Thess. 5:11

given us everlasting consolation. . .2 Thess. 2:16

exhort one another daily. . .Heb. 3:13

exhorting one another. . .Heb. 10:25

See *Comfort/Comforted/Comforteth/Comforts,
Spiritual*; *Consolation/Consolations*.

292. Endure/Endured/Endureth/Enduring

e'ing for ever. . .Ps. 19:9

e'th to the end. . .Matt. 10:22

e but for a time. . .Mark 4:17

e'th all things. . .1 Cor. 13:7

effectual in the *e'ing*. . .2 Cor. 1:6

tribulations that ye *e*. . .2 Thess. 1:4

therefore *e* hardness. . .2 Tim. 2:3

e afflictions. . .2 Tim. 4:5

ye *e'd* a great fight. . .Heb. 10:32

If ye *e* chastening. . .Heb. 12:7

man that *e'th* temptation. . .James 1:12

happy which *e*. . .James 5:11

See *Perseverance*.

293. Enemy/Enemies

e be exalted over me?. . .Ps. 13:2

saved from mine *e'ies*. . .Ps. 18:3

presence of mine *e'ies*. . .Ps. 23:5

If thine *e* be hungry. . .Prov. 25:21

kisses of an *e*. . .Prov. 27:6

Love your *e'ies*. . .Matt. 5:44

when we were *e'ies*. . .Rom. 5:10

The last *e* that. . .1 Cor. 15:26

e'ies of the cross. . .Phil. 3:18

count him not as an *e*. . .2 Thess. 3:15

e of God. . .James 4:4

See *Adversary/Adversaries*.

294. Engagement

See *Betroth/Betrothed*, *Courtship*, *Dating*, *Marriage/Marry/Marrying*.

295. Enjoy

pleasures for evermore. . .Ps. 16:11
river of thy pleasures. . .Ps. 36:8
He that loveth pleasure. . .Prov. 21:17
therefore *e* pleasure. . .Eccles. 2:1
e good in his labour. . .Eccles. 2:24
mine elect shall long *e*. . .Isa. 65:22
pleasures of this life. . .Luke 8:14
she that liveth in pleasure. . .1 Tim. 5:6
all things to *e*. . .1 Tim. 6:17
lovers of pleasures. . .2 Tim. 3:4
e the pleasures of sin. . .Heb. 11:25
Ye have lived in pleasure. . .James 5:5

See *Delight/Delighted/Delighteth*.

296. Enter/Entered/ Entering

e into covenant. . .Deut. 29:12

e into my rest. . .Ps. 95:11
E into his gates. . .Ps. 100:4
e into the kingdom. . .Matt. 5:20
E ye in at the strait. . .Matt. 7:13
e into life. . .Matt. 19:17
e into the kingdom. . .Matt. 19:24
e not into temptation. . .Matt. 26:41
e'ing into him. . .Mark 7:15
his own blood he *e'ed*. . .Heb. 9:12
e'ed into the holy places. . .Heb. 9:24
boldness to *e*. . .Heb. 10:19

297. Entertained/ Entertainment

that he may make us sport. . .Judg. 16:25
lodged us three days courteously. . .Acts 28:7
e'ed angels unawares. . .Heb. 13:2
drunkenness, revellings. . .Gal. 5:21
excess of wine, revellings. . .1 Pet. 4:3

See *Banquet/Banqueting/Banquetings*.

298. Entice/Enticed/ Enticeth

Though we tend to think of enticement in sexual terms, the scriptures describe

enticement as drawing another into any
sin—sexual or otherwise.

if a man *e* a maid. . .Exod. 22:16
e thee secretly. . .Deut. 13:6
E thy husband. . .Judg. 14:15
Who shall *e* Ahab. . .2 Chron. 18:19
if sinners *e* thee. . .Prov. 1:10
A violent man *e'th*. . .Prov. 16:29
his own lust, and *e'd*. . .James 1:14

See *Lust/Lusts.*

299. Entrepreneurs

have a perfect and just weight. . .Deut. 25:15
cannot perform their enterprise. . .Job 5:12
If I have made gold my hope. . .Job 31:24
do business in great waters. . .Ps. 107:23
guide his affairs with discretion. . .Ps. 112:5
a just weight is his delight. . .Prov. 11:1
a man diligent in his business?. . .Prov. 22:29
maketh haste to be rich. . .Prov. 28:20
maketh fine linen, and selleth it. . .Prov. 31:24
Lydia, a seller of purple. . .Acts 16:14
Not slothful in business. . .Rom. 12:11
to do your own business. . .1 Thess. 4:11
buy and sell, and get gain. . .James 4:13

300. Envy/Envying/Envyings

e slayeth the silly. . .Job 5:2
E thou not the oppressor. . .Prov. 3:31
e the rottenness of. . .Prov. 14:30
heart *e* sinners. . .Prov. 23:17
stand before *e*?. . .Prov. 27:4

full of *e*, murder. . .Rom. 1:29
not in strife and *e'ing*. . .Rom. 13:13
e'ing, and strife. . .1 Cor. 3:3
debates, *e'ings*, wraths. . .2 Cor. 12:20
e'ing one another. . .Gal. 5:26
e, strife, railings. . .1 Tim. 6:4
where *e'ing* and strife. . .James 3:16

301. Equality

In the first-century church, many Jews
disapproved of the Gentiles, whom they saw
as being unclean. As apostle to the Gentiles,
Paul addressed this issue quickly and firmly.

not call any man common or unclean. . .Acts 10:28
are we better than they?. . .Rom. 3:9
for there is no difference. . .Rom. 3:22
whether we be Jews or Gentiles. . .1 Cor. 12:13
ye are all one in Christ Jesus. . .Gal. 3:28
neither Greek nor Jew. . .Col. 3:11

See *Discrimination.*

302. Error/Errors

Who can understand his *e's*?. . .Ps. 19:12
utter *e* against the LORD. . .Isa. 32:6

work of *e's*. . .Jer. 10:15
recompence of their *e*. . .Rom. 1:27
e's of the people. . .Heb. 9:7
from the *e* of his way. . .James 5:20
them who live in *e*. . .2 Pet. 2:18
e of the wicked. . .2 Pet. 3:17
spirit of *e*. . .1 John 4:6

See *Fail/Faileth*.

303. Eternity
have I in heaven but thee?. . .Ps. 73:25
One that inhabiteth *e*. . .Isa. 57:15
in earth, as it is in heaven. . .Matt. 6:10
be with me in paradise. . .Luke 23:43
hath ascended up to heaven. . .John 3:13
caught up into paradise. . .2 Cor. 12:4
laid up for you in heaven. . .Col. 1:5
paradise of God. . .Rev. 2:7

See *Eternal Life; Heaven/Heavenly/Heavens; Reward, Eternal.*

304. Eternal Life
I may have *e l?*. . .Matt. 19:16
world to come *e l*. . .Mark 10:30
but have *e l*. . .John 3:15

blood, hath *e l*. . .John 6:54
words of *e l*. . .John 6:68
give unto them *e l*. . .John 10:28
he should give *e l*. . .John 17:2
ordained to *e l*. . .Acts 13:48
immortality, *e l*. . .Rom. 2:7
gift of God is *e l*. . .Rom. 6:23
lay hold on *e l*. . .1 Tim. 6:12
In hope of *e l*. . .Titus 1:2
promised us, even *e l*. . .1 John 2:25
e l abiding in him. . .1 John 3:15

See *Eternity; Everlasting Life/Life Everlasting; Heaven/Heavenly/Heavens; Immortal/Immortality; Life Eternal; Reward, Eternal; Salvation.*

305. Eucharist
Jesus took bread, and blessed it. . .Matt. 26:26
Jesus took bread, and blessed. . .Mark 14:22
He took the cup. . .Luke 22:17
communion of the body of Christ?. . .1 Cor. 10:16
not to eat the Lord's supper. . .1 Cor. 11:20

See *Lord's Supper*.

306. Everlasting Life/ Life Everlasting
some to *e l*. . .Dan. 12:2
shall inherit *e l*. . .Matt. 19:29
world to come *l e*. . .Luke 18:30
perish, but have *e l*. . .John 3:16
on the Son hath *e l*. . .John 3:36
springing up into *e l*. . .John 4:14
on him that sent me, hath *e l*. . .John 5:24
endureth unto *e l*. . .John 6:27

e l: and I will raise him. . .John 6:40
believeth on me hath *e l*. . .John 6:47
commandment is *l e*. . .John 12:50
yourselves unworthy of *e l*. . .Acts 13:46
of the Spirit reap *l e*. . .Gal. 6:8
believe on him to *l e*. . .1 Tim. 1:16

See *Eternal Life*, *Immortal/Immortality*,
Life Eternal, *Salvation*.

307. Evil

knowledge of good and *e*. . .Gen. 2:9
imagination of man's heart is *e*. . .Gen. 8:21
I will fear no *e*. . .Ps. 23:4
lovest *e* more than good. . .Ps. 52:3
no *e* happen to the just. . .Prov. 12:21
call *e* good, and good *e*. . .Isa. 5:20
Seek good, and not *e*. . .Amos 5:14
bringeth forth *e* things. . .Matt. 12:35
e hateth the light. . .John 3:20
e which I would not. . .Rom. 7:19
Abhor that which is *e*. . .Rom. 12:9
thinketh no *e*. . .1 Cor. 13:5

See *Wickedness*.

308. Exalt/Exalted/Exalteth

I will *e* him. . .Exod. 15:2
e'ed be the God. . .2 Sam. 22:47
let us *e* his name. . .Ps. 34:3
I will be *e'ed* in the earth. . .Ps. 46:10
not the rebellious *e* themselves. . .Ps. 66:7
Be thou *e'ed*, O God. . .Ps. 108:5
the city is *e'ed*. . .Prov. 11:11
Righteousness *e'eth* a nation. . .Prov. 14:34
Every valley shall be *e'ed*. . .Isa. 40:4
e himself shall be abased. . .Matt. 23:12
God also hath highly *e'ed* him. . .Phil. 2:9
may *e* you in due time. . .1 Pet. 5:6

309. Example/Examples

I have given you an *e*. . .John 13:15
these things were our *e's*. . .1 Cor. 10:6
have us for an ensample. . .Phil. 3:17
be thou an *e*. . .1 Tim. 4:12
e of unbelief. . .Heb. 4:11
e and shadow of heavenly. . .Heb. 8:5
e of suffering affliction. . .James 5:10
leaving us an *e*. . .1 Pet. 2:21
being *e's* to the flock. . .1 Pet. 5:3
set forth for an *e*. . .Jude 1:7

310. Excellent

he is *e* in power. . .Job 37:23
how *e* is thy name. . .Ps. 8:1
his *e* greatness. . .Ps. 150:2
The righteous is more *e*. . .Prov. 12:26
he hath done *e* things. . .Isa. 12:5
e spirit, and knowledge. . .Dan. 5:12
a more *e* way. . .1 Cor. 12:31
approve things that are *e*. . .Phil. 1:10
a more *e* name. . .Heb. 1:4
a more *e* ministry. . .Heb. 8:6
a more *e* sacrifice. . .Heb. 11:4

311. Excuse

no cloak for their sin. . .John 15:22
they are without *e*. . .Rom. 1:20
thou art inexcusable. . .Rom. 2:1
e ourselves unto you?. . .2 Cor. 12:19

312. Execution

hanged the chief baker. . .Gen. 40:22
shall certainly stone him. . .Lev. 24:16
hang him on a tree. . .Deut. 21:22
hanged on a tree. . .Esther 2:23
Haman on the gallows. . .Esther 7:10
hanged Haman's ten sons. . .Esther 9:14
beheaded John in the
    prison. . .Matt. 14:10
Jews took up stones. . .John 10:31
they stoned Stephen. . .Acts 7:59
having stoned Paul. . .Acts 14:19
They were stoned. . .Heb. 11:37
beheaded for the witness. . .Rev. 20:4

313. Exercise

there wrestled a man. . .Gen. 32:24
run through a troop. . .2 Sam. 22:30
run, and not be weary. . .Isa. 40:31
the deeds of the body. . .Rom. 8:13
body is the temple. . .1 Cor. 6:19
run in a race. . .1 Cor. 9:24
keep under my body. . .1 Cor. 9:27
run with patience. . .Heb. 12:1

See *Health*.

314. Exploitation

not oppress a stranger. . .Exod. 23:9
not oppress one another. . .Lev. 25:14
not oppress an hired servant. . .Deut. 24:14
oppression of the poor. . .Ps. 12:5
Trust not in oppression. . .Ps. 62:10
Rob not the poor. . .Prov. 22:22
oppress not the widow. . .Zech. 7:10
oppress the hireling. . .Mal. 3:5
make merchandise of you. . .2 Pet. 2:3

315. Eye/Eyes, Physical

E for *e*. . .Exod. 21:24
e's of the wicked. . .Job 11:20

Mine *e* is consumed. . .Ps. 6:7

I will lift up mine *e's*. . .Ps. 121:1

e's shall behold. . .Prov. 23:33

mine *e's* desired. . .Eccles. 2:10

e's of the blind. . .Isa. 35:5

their *e's* received sight. . .Matt. 20:34

spit on his *e's*. . .Mark 8:23

fell from his *e's*. . .Acts 9:18

E hath not seen. . .1 Cor. 2:9

tears from their *e's*. . .Rev. 21:4

316. Eye/Eyes, Spiritual

e's shall be opened. . .Gen. 3:5

right in his own *e's*. . .Judg. 17:6

Open thou mine *e's*. . .Ps. 119:18

e's of the blind. . .Ps. 146:8

in thine own *e's*. . .Prov. 3:7

bountiful *e* shall be. . .Prov. 22:9

wise in their own *e's*. . .Isa. 5:21

right *e* offend thee. . .Matt. 5:29

mote that is in thy brother's *e*. . .Matt. 7:3

e's they have closed. . .Matt. 13:15

e cannot say. . .1 Cor. 12:21

e's of your understanding. . .Eph. 1:18

317. Fail/Faileth

he will not *f* thee. . .Deut. 31:6

my strength *f'eth*. . .Ps. 31:10

my spirit *f'eth*. . .Ps. 143:7

thy foot shall not stumble. . .Prov. 3:23

stumble in their ways. . .Jer. 18:15

thy faith *f* not. . .Luke 22:32

he stumbleth not. . .John 11:9

For they stumbled. . .Rom. 9:32

Have they stumbled. . .Rom. 11:11

Charity never *f'eth*. . .1 Cor. 13:8

f of the grace of God. . .Heb. 12:15

And a stone of stumbling. . .1 Pet. 2:8

See *Error/Errors*.

318. Fairness

people with equity. . .Ps. 98:9

thou dost establish equity. . .Ps. 99:4

judgment, and equity. . .Prov. 1:3

knowledge, and in equity. . .Eccles. 2:21

reprove with equity. . .Isa. 11:4

See *Justice*.

319. Faith

Doubt and

f as a grain of mustard. . .Matt. 17:20

f, and doubt not. . .Matt. 21:21

Established in

established in the *f*. . .Acts 16:5

propitiation through *f*. . .Rom. 3:25

justified by *f*. . .Rom. 5:1

f cometh by hearing. . .Rom. 10:17

saved through *f*. . .Eph. 2:8

Great

not found so great *f*. . .Matt. 8:10
f hath made thee whole. . .Matt. 9:22
great is thy *f*. . .Matt. 15:28
Stephen, a man full of *f*. . .Acts 6:5

Living in

just shall live by his *f*. . .Hab. 2:4
purifying their hearts by *f*. . .Acts 15:9
obedience to the *f*. . .Rom. 1:5
not of *f* is sin. . .Rom. 14:23
f, hope, charity. . .1 Cor. 13:13
we walk by *f*. . .2 Cor. 5:7
children of God by *f*. . .Gal. 3.26
gentleness, goodness, *f*. . .Gal. 5:22
breastplate of *f*. . .1 Thess. 5:8
I have kept the *f*. . .2 Tim. 4:7
f is the substance. . .Heb. 11:1

See *Religion*.

320. Faithful

Lᴏʀᴅ preserveth the *f*. . .Ps. 31:23
f man who can find?. . .Prov. 20:6
F are the wounds. . .Prov. 27:6
f man shall abound. . .Prov. 28:20
thou good and *f* servant. . .Matt. 25:21
f also in much. . .Luke 16:10

God is *f*. . .1 Cor. 1:9
f in all things. . .1 Tim. 3:11
he is *f* and just. . .1 John 1:9
F and True. . .Rev. 19:11

321. Faithfulness, Marital

rejoice with the wife of thy youth. . .Prov. 5:18
the wife of thy covenant. . .Mal. 2:14
against the wife of his youth. . .Mal. 2:15
faithful in all things. . .1 Tim. 3:11
Marriage is honourable in all. . .Heb. 13:4

322. Faithless

be not *f*. . .John 20:27
all men have not faith. . .2 Thess. 3:2
without faith it is impossible. . .Heb. 11:6

See *Falling into Sin*.

including Molech, Chemosh, and Baal. They lured the Israelites into such worship, drawing them away from the Lord.

through the fire to Molech. . .Lev. 18:21
Baal and Ashtaroth. . .Judg. 2:13
the altar of Baal. . .Judg. 6:30
high place for Chemosh. . .1 Kings 11:7
went and served Baal. . .1 Kings 16:31
the prophets of Baal. . .1 Kings 18:19
Jehu destroyed Baal. . .2 Kings 10:28
them that are no gods. . .Jer. 5:7
walk after other gods. . .Jer. 7:9

See *Idol/Idolater/Idolaters/Idols, Idolatry*.

323. Fall, the

Genesis 3 describes the fall of humankind when Adam and Eve ate the fruit God had forbidden them to taste. Their sin impacted the whole world, and even today we struggle under a burden of sin.

she took of the fruit thereof. . .Gen. 3:6
Hast thou eaten of the tree. . .Gen. 3:11
The serpent beguiled me. . .Gen. 3:13
So he drove out the man. . .Gen. 3:24
by one man sin entered. . .Rom. 5:12
whole creation groaneth. . .Rom. 8:22
since by man came death. . .1 Cor. 15:21

326. Falsehood

brought forth *f*. . .Ps. 7:14
their deceit is *f*. . .Ps. 119:118
right hand of *f*. . .Ps. 144:8
under *f* have we hid. . .Isa. 28:15
molten image is *f*. . .Jer. 10:14
trusted in *f*. . .Jer. 13:25

324. Falling into Sin

For all have sinned. . .Rom. 3:23
no more I that do it, but sin. . .Rom. 7:17
is not of faith is sin. . .Rom. 14:23
if we sin willfully. . .Heb. 10:26
say that we have no sin . . .1 John 1:8
If we confess our sins. . .1 John 1:9
abideth in him sinneth not. . .1 John 3:6

See *Faithless*.

327. False Teaching

prophet that teacheth lies. . .Isa. 9:15
teacher of lies. . .Hab. 2:18
sorcerer, a false prophet. . .Acts 13:6
For such are false apostles. . .2 Cor. 11:13
because many false prophets. . .1 John 4:1
which say they are apostles. . .Rev. 2:2
mouth of the false prophet. . .Rev. 16:13
false prophet that wrought miracles. . .Rev. 19:20
beast and the false prophet. . .Rev. 20:10

325. False Gods

The Canaanites worshipped many false gods,

328. Fame

his *f* was noised. . .Josh. 6:27
heard the *f* of him. . .Josh. 9:9
f of Solomon. . .1 Kings 10:1
f of David went out. . .1 Chron. 14:17
his *f* went out. . .Esther 9:4
his *f* went throughout. . .Matt. 4:24
f of Jesus. . .Matt. 14:1

329. Family

thy father and thy mother. . .Exod. 20:12
his father or his mother. . .Deut. 27:16
as a father the son. . .Prov. 3:12
keep thy father's commandment. . .Prov. 6:20
hateth his son. . .Prov. 13:24
wise son maketh a glad. . .Prov. 15:20
father of the righteous. . .Prov. 23:24
mocketh at his father. . .Prov. 30:17
Children, obey your parents. . .Eph. 6:1
provoke not your children. . .Col. 3:21
to requite their parents. . .1 Tim. 5:4
those of his own house. . .1 Tim. 5:8

See *Child/Children, Father/Fathers, Husband/
Husbands, Mother/Mother's, Parents, Wife/Wives.*

330. Fashion

jewels of gold, and raiment. . .Gen. 24:53
jewels of gold, and raiment. . .Exod. 3:22
clothed with a robe of fine linen. . .1 Chron. 15:27
in raiment of needlework. . .Ps. 45:14
changeable suits of apparel. . .Isa. 3:22
or a bride her attire?. . .Jer. 2:32
I clothed thee also with broidered
    work. . .Ezek. 16:10
shall be clothed with scarlet. . .Dan. 5:7
women adorn themselves in modest
    apparel. . .1 Tim. 2:9
that outward adorning of plaiting
    the hair. . .1 Pet. 3:3

See *Apparel; Attire/Attired; Clothe/Clothed/Clothes/
Clothing, Physical; Garment/Garments.*

331. Fasting/Fastings

f, and weeping. . .Esther 4:3
humbled my soul with *f*. . .Ps. 35:13
my soul with *f*. . .Ps. 69:10
weak through *f*. . .Ps. 109:24
supplications, with *f*. . .Dan. 9:3
f, and with weeping. . .Joel 2:12
prayer and *f*. . .Matt. 17:21
served God with *f's*. . .Luke 2:37
prayed with *f*. . .Acts 14:23
yourselves to *f* and prayer. . .1 Cor. 7:5
in watchings, in *f's*. . .2 Cor. 6:5

See *Diet.*

332. Father/Fathers

man leave his *f*. . .Gen. 2:24
f of many nations. . .Gen. 17:4
Honour thy *f*. . .Exod. 20:12
my *f* and my mother. . .Ps. 27:10
iniquity of the *f's*. . .Jer. 32:18
f's to the children. . .Mal. 4:6

He that loveth *f*. . .Matt. 10:37
Honour thy *f*. . .Matt. 15:4
f shall be divided. . .Luke 12:53

See *Family*, *Parents*.

333. Father, God the/ Father's

f of the fatherless. . .Ps. 68:5
The everlasting *F*. . .Isa. 9:6
Have we not all one *f*?. . .Mal. 2:10
Our *F* which art in heaven. . .Matt. 6:9
knoweth the Son, but the *F*. . .Matt. 11:27
be about my *F's* business?. . .Luke 2:49
F loveth the Son. . .John 3:35
F judgeth no man. . .John 5:22
man hath seen the *F*. . .John 6:46
F that sent me. . .John 8:18
I and my *F* are one. . .John 10:30
I go unto the *F*. . .John 14:28
F himself loveth you. . .John 16:27
F of lights. . .James 1:17
ye call on the *F*. . .1 Pet. 1:17

334. Faultless

Blessed are the undefiled. . .Ps. 119:1
which is in the law, blameless. . .Phil. 3:6

holy, harmless, undefiled. . .Heb. 7:26
undefiled before God. . .James 1:27
present you *f*. . .Jude 1:24

335. Favoritism

do no unrighteousness in
    judgment. . .Lev. 19:15
God is no respecter of persons. . .Acts 10:34
there is no respect of persons. . .Rom. 2:11
neither is there respect of persons. . .Eph. 6:9
there is no respect of persons. . .Col. 3:25
doing nothing by partiality. . .1 Tim. 5:21
if ye have respect to persons. . .James 2:9
without partiality. . .James 3:17

See *Discrimination*.

336. Favour

have I not found *f*. . .Num. 11:11
Let me find *f*. . .Ruth 2:13
f both with the Lord. . .1 Sam. 2:26
found *f* in my sight. . .1 Sam. 16:22
she obtained grace and *f*. . .Esther 2:17
with *f* wilt thou compass him. . .Ps. 5:12
in his *f* is life. . .Ps. 30:5
Good understanding giveth *f*. . .Prov. 13:15
obtaineth *f* of the Lord. . .Prov. 18:22

F is deceitful. . .Prov. 31:30

found *f* with God. . .Luke 1:30

f with God and man. . .Luke 2:52

337. Fear/Feared/ Fears

f'ed to say, She is my wife. . .Gen. 26:7

Esau: for I *f* him. . .Gen. 32:11

f every man his mother. . .Lev. 19:3

f'ed him, as they *f'ed* Moses. . .Josh. 4:14

I will *f* no evil. . .Ps. 23:4

whom shall I *f*?. . .Ps. 27:1

f, where no *f* was. . .Ps. 53:5

f of man bringeth a snare. . .Prov. 29:25

F thou not; for I am. . .Isa. 41:10

f not them which kill. . .Matt. 10:28

f to whom *f*. . .Rom. 13:7

within were *f's*. . .2 Cor. 7:5

not given us the spirit of *f*. . .2 Tim. 1:7

There is no *f* in love. . .1 John 4:18

See Afraid, Emotions, Feelings.

338. Fear of God/ Feared God/ Fearest God

Surely the *f o G*. . .Gen. 20:11

I know that thou *f'est G*. . .Gen. 22:12

the midwives *f'ed G*. . .Exod. 1:17

f the Lord thy God. . .Deut. 6:2

f the Lord your God for ever. . .Josh. 4:24

Behold, the *f* of the Lord. . .Job 28:28

Serve the Lord with *f*. . .Ps. 2:11

Let all the earth *f* the Lord. . .Ps. 33:8

f of the Lord is to hate evil. . .Prov. 8:13

f of the Lord prolongeth days. . .Prov. 10:27

f of the Lord is strong confidence. . .Prov. 14:26

339. Feelings

Isaac, whom thou lovest. . .Gen. 22:2

them that hated me. . .2 Sam. 22:18

I will fear no evil. . .Ps. 23:4

whom shall I fear?. . .Ps. 27:1

me from all my fears. . .Ps. 34:4

fear, where no fear was. . .Ps. 53:5

that hate thee?. . .Ps. 139:21

fear of man bringeth. . .Prov. 29:25

and a time to hate. . .Eccles. 3:8

love is strong as death. . .Song of Sol. 8:6

he that hateth his brother. . .1 John 2:11

no fear in love. . .1 John 4:18

See Doubt/Doubted/Doubteth/Doubtful/Doubting/ Doubts; Fear/Feared/Fears; Hate/Hated/Hatest/ Hateth; Love, Brotherly.

340. Fellowservant/ Fellowservants

found one of his *f's*. . .Matt. 18:28

smite his *f's*. . . Matt. 24:49

Epaphras our dear *f*. . .Col. 1:7

minister and *f* in the Lord. . .Col. 4:7

until their *f's* also. . .Rev. 6:11

I am thy *f*. . .Rev. 19:10

I am thy *f*. . .Rev. 22:9

341. Fellowship

apostles'doctrine and *f*. . .Acts 2:42

f of his Son. . .1 Cor. 1:9

have *f* with devils. . .1 Cor. 10:20

what *f* hath righteousness. . .2 Cor. 6:14

f of the ministering. . .2 Cor. 8:4

right hands of *f*. . .Gal. 2:9

f of the mystery. . .Eph. 3:9

no *f* with the unfruitful works. . .Eph. 5:11

f in the gospel. . .Phil. 1:5

f of the Spirit. . .Phil. 2:1

f of his sufferings. . .Phil. 3:10

we have *f* with him. . .1 John 1:6

342. Fight/Fighting/ Fightings

The Lord shall *f* for you. . .Exod. 14:14

f against them that fight. . .Ps. 35:1

f'ing daily oppresseth me. . .Ps. 56:1

than with a brawling woman. . .Prov. 21:9

even to *f* against God. . .Acts 5:39

so *f*I, not as one. . .1 Cor. 9:26

without were *f'ings*. . .2 Cor. 7:5

not a brawler. . .1 Tim. 3:3

f the good *f*. . .1 Tim. 6:12

I have fought a good *f*. . .2 Tim. 4:7

wars and *f'ings* among you?. . .James 4:1

will *f* against them. . .Rev. 2:16

343. Filled with the Spirit

f w t s of wisdom. . .Exod. 28:3

f him *w t s* of God. . .Exod. 31:3

filled with the Holy Ghost. . .Luke 1:15

filled with the Holy Ghost. . .Luke 1:41

filled with the Holy Ghost. . .Luke 1:67

filled with the Holy Ghost. . .Acts 2:4

Peter, filled with the Holy Ghost. . .Acts 4:8

filled with the Holy Ghost. . .Acts 4:31

filled with the Holy Ghost. . .Acts 9:17

be *f w t S*. . .Eph. 5:18

344. Filth/Filthy/ Filthiness

f'y is man. . .Job 15:16

are all together become *f'y*. . .Ps. 14:3

righteousnesses are as *f'y* rags. . .Isa. 64:6

as the *f* of the world. . .1 Cor. 4:13

cleanse ourselves from all *f'iness*. . .2 Cor. 7:1

f'iness, nor foolish talking. . .Eph. 5:4

blasphemy, *f'y* communication. . .Col. 3:8

not greedy of *f'y* lucre. . .1 Tim. 3:3

f of the flesh. . .1 Pet. 3:21

vexed with the *f'y* conversation. . .2 Pet. 2:7

f'y dreamers defile. . .Jude 1:8

let him be *f'y* still. . .Rev. 22:11

345. Financial Gain

giveth thee power to get wealth. . .Deut. 8:18
They that trust in their wealth. . .Ps. 49:6
leave their wealth to others. . .Ps. 49:10
Wealth and riches shall be. . .Ps. 112:3
He that gathereth in summer. . .Prov. 10:5
Wealth gotten by vanity. . .Prov. 13:11
than great revenues without right. . .Prov. 16:8
diligent tend only to plenteousness. . .Prov. 21:5
to increase his riches. . .Prov. 22:16
giveth him not for his work. . .Jer. 22:13
things shall be added unto you. . .Matt. 6:33
be content with your wages. . .Luke 3:14
yourselves friends of the mammon. . .Luke 16:9
lay by him in store. . .1 Cor. 16:2
rich fall into temptation. . .1 Tim. 6:9

See *Money, Rich/Riches, Wealth.*

346. Finished Work of Christ

With His death on the cross, Christ's sacrificial work was ended. All who believe in Him will be redeemed and reconciled with God.

Son therefore shall make you free. . .John 8:36
he said, It is finished. . .John 19:30

faith of Jesus Christ unto all. . .Rom. 3:22
all men unto justification of life. . .Rom. 5:18
unto eternal life by Jesus Christ. . .Rom. 5:21
as in Adam all die, even so in Christ. . .1 Cor. 15:22
he is the propitiation for our sins. . .1 John 2:2

See *Propitiation, Reconcile/Reconciled/ Reconciliation/Reconciling, Redemption.*

347. First and Last

Alpha and omega are the first and last letters of the Greek alphabet. The book of Revelation uses these symbols to describe Jesus as the One who is first and last.

I am Alpha and Omega. . .Rev. 1:8
Saying, I am Alpha and Omega. . .Rev. 1:11
I am Alpha and Omega. . .Rev. 21:6
the first and the last. . .Rev. 22:13

348. Firstborn

younger before the *f.* . .Gen. 29:26
Reuben, thou art my *f.* . .Gen. 49:3
f in the land of Egypt. . .Exod. 11:5
will smite all the *f.* . .Exod. 12:12
Sanctify unto me all the *f.* . .Exod. 13:2
f of thy sons thou shalt redeem. . .Exod. 34:20

all the *f* are mine. . .Num. 3:13

instead of all the *f*. . .Num. 3:45

I will make him my *f*. . .Ps. 89:27

brought forth her *f* son. . .Matt. 1:25

f among many brethren. . .Rom. 8:29

f of every creature. . .Col. 1:15

f from the dead. . .Col. 1:18

349. Firstfruits

f of thy labours. . .Exod. 23:16

f of wheat harvest. . .Exod. 34:22

oblation of the *f*. . .Lev. 2:12

f of the Spirit. . .Rom. 8:23

f of Achaia unto Christ. . .Rom. 16:5

f of them that slept. . .1 Cor. 15:20

Christ the *f*. . .1 Cor. 15:23

f of Achaia. . .1 Cor. 16:15

f of his creatures. . .James 1:18

being the *f* unto God. . .Rev. 14:4

350. Fish/Fishes

over the *f* of the sea. . .Gen. 1:26

all the *f'es* of the sea. . .Gen. 9:2

f that is in the river. . .Exod. 7:18

the likeness of any *f*. . .Deut. 4:18

f of the sea. . .Ps. 8:8

Jonah was in the belly of the *f*. . .Jon. 1:17

Or if he ask a *f*. . .Matt. 7:10

five loaves, and two *f'es*. . .Matt. 14:17

f that first cometh up. . .Matt. 17:27

great multitude of *f'es*. . .Luke 5:6

piece of a broiled *f*. . .Luke 24:42

net to land full of great *f'es*. . .John 21:11

351. Flatter/Flattereth/Flattery/Flattering

speaketh *f'y* to his friends. . .Job 17:5

they *f* with their tongue. . .Ps. 5:9

with *f'ing* lips. . .Ps. 12:2

For he *f'eth* himself. . .Ps. 36:2

Nevertheless they did *f* him. . .Ps. 78:36

stranger which *f'eth*. . .Prov. 2:16

f'y of the tongue. . .Prov. 6:24

meddle not with him that *f'eth*. . .Prov. 20:19

f'ing mouth worketh ruin. . .Prov. 26:28

f'eth his neighbour. . .Prov. 29:5

any time used we *f'ing*. . .1 Thess. 2:5

352. Flesh

they shall be one *f*. . .Gen. 2:24

yet in my *f* shall I see God. . .Job 19:26

unto thee shall all *f* come. . .Ps. 65:2

they were but *f*. . .Ps. 78:39

all *f* shall see it. . .Isa. 40:5

give them an heart of *f*. . .Ezek. 11:19

my spirit upon all *f*. . .Joel 2:28

f and blood hath not. . .Matt. 16:17

should no *f* be saved. . .Matt. 24:22

Word was made *f*. . .John 1:14

Whoso eateth my *f*. . .John 6:54

live after the *f*. . .Rom. 8:13
have crucified the *f*. . .Gal. 5:24
Christ is come in the *f*. . .1 John 4:2

353. Flock

thy people like a *f*. . .Ps. 77:20
in the wilderness like a *f*. . .Ps. 78:52
feed his *f* like a shepherd. . .Isa. 40:11
scattered my *f*. . .Jer. 23:2
shepherd doth his *f*. . .Jer. 31:10
my *f* was scattered. . .Ezek. 34:6
I will feed my *f*. . .Ezek. 34:15
f of his people. . .Zech. 9:16
sheep of the *f*. . .Matt. 26:31
Fear not, little *f*. . .Luke 12:32
to all the *f*. . .Acts 20:28
Feed the *f* of God. . .1 Pet. 5:2

354. Flood

bring a *f* of waters. . .Gen. 6:17
f of waters was upon. . .Gen. 7:6
waters of the *f*. . .Gen. 7:7
f was forty days. . .Gen. 7:17
any more be a *f*. . .Gen. 9:11

shall no more become a *f*. . .Gen. 9:15
Noah lived after the *f*. . .Gen. 9:28
other side of the *f*. . .Josh. 24:14
until the *f* came. . .Matt. 24:39
f upon the world. . .2 Pet. 2:5

355. Flower/Flowers

He cometh forth like a *f*. . .Job 14:2
Let thistles grow. . .Job 31:40
as a *f* of the field. . .Ps. 103:15
I am the rose of Sharon. . .Song of Sol. 2:1
The *f*'s appear on the earth. . .Song of Sol. 2:12
grape is ripening in the *f*. . .Isa. 18:5
blossom as the rose. . .Isa. 35:1
withereth, the *f* fadeth. . .Isa. 40:7
Consider the lilies of the field. . .Matt. 6:28
as the *f* of the grass. . .James 1:10

356. Following Jesus

Follow me. . .Matt. 4:19
he that followeth me. . .John 8:12
let him follow me. . .John 12:26
follow thou me. . .John 21:22
walk in newness of life. . .Rom. 6:4
walk not after the flesh. . .Rom. 8:1
Let us walk honestly. . .Rom. 13:13
therefore follow after. . .Rom. 14:19
For we walk by faith. . .2 Cor. 5:7

Walk in the Spirit. . .Gal. 5:16
we should walk in them. . .Eph. 2:10
And walk in love. . .Eph. 5:2
walk as children of light. . .Eph. 5:8
walk worthy of the Lord. . .Col. 1:10
so walk ye in him. . .Col. 2:6
if we walk in the light. . .1 John 1:7
walk after his commandments. . .2 John 1:6

357. Folly

knowest my foolishness. . .Ps. 69:5
greatness of his *f.* . .Prov. 5:23
fool layeth open his *f.* . .Prov. 13:16
f of fools is deceit. . .Prov. 14:8
The simple inherit *f.* . .Prov. 14:18
hasty of spirit exalteth *f.* . .Prov. 14:29
F is joy to him. . .Prov. 15:21
it is *f* and shame. . .Prov. 18:13
foolishness of man perverteth. . .Prov. 19:3
Foolishness is bound. . .Prov. 22:15
thought of foolishness is sin. . .Prov. 24:9
fool according to his *f.* . .Prov. 26:4
fool returneth to his *f.* . .Prov. 26:11
to them that perish foolishness. . .1 Cor. 1:18
foolishness with God. . .1 Cor. 3:19
Neither filthiness, nor foolish talking. . .Eph. 5:4
f shall be manifest. . .2 Tim. 3:9
ignorance of foolish men. . .1 Pet. 2:15

See *Fool/Fool's/Fools.*

358. Food

green herb for meat. . .Gen. 1:30
sight, and good for *f.* . .Gen. 2:9
thou shalt eat the herb. . .Gen. 3:18

f of those good years. . .Gen. 41:35
fish, which we did eat. . .Num. 11:5
A land of wheat, and barley. . .Deut. 8:8
giving him *f* and raiment. . .Deut. 10:18
Butter of kine, and milk. . .Deut. 32:14
bring forth *f* out of the earth. . .Ps. 104:14
giveth *f* to the hungry. . .Ps. 146:7
she bringeth her *f* from afar. . .Prov. 31:14
Give us this day our daily bread. . .Matt. 6:11
five loaves, and two fishes. . .Matt. 14:17
having *f* and raiment. . .1 Tim. 6:8
destitute of daily *f.* . .James 2:15

See *Crops, Eat/Eateth/Eating, Nourishment, Plant/Plants.*

359. Fool/Fool's/Fools

f hath said in his heart. . .Ps. 14:1
f and the brutish person. . .Ps. 49:10
f's despise wisdom. . .Prov. 1:7
prating *f* shall fall. . .Prov. 10:8
f shall be servant. . .Prov. 11:29
f's wrath is presently known. . .Prov. 12:16
heart of *f's* proclaimeth foolishness. . .Prov. 12:23
folly of *f's* is deceit. . .Prov. 14:8

foolishness of *f's* is folly. . .Prov. 14:24

f despiseth his father's. . .Prov. 15:5

f's mouth is his destruction. . .Prov. 18:7

trusteth in his own heart is a *f*. . .Prov. 28:26

f uttereth all his mind. . .Prov. 29:11

f also is full of words. . .Eccles. 10:14

Ye *f's* and blind. . .Matt. 23:17

they became *f's*. . .Rom. 1:22

f's for Christ's sake. . .1 Cor. 4:10

See *Folly*.

360. Forbearance/ Forbearing

By long *f'ing* is a prince. . .Prov. 25:15

f and longsuffering. . .Rom. 2:4

through the *f* of God. . .Rom. 3:25

f'ing one another in love. . .Eph. 4:2

f'ing threatening. . .Eph. 6:9

F'ing one another. . .Col. 3:13

See *Longsuffering*.

361. Forbidden Fruit

When God forbade Adam and Eve to eat from one tree in the Garden of Eden, the expression

"forbidden fruit" was coined. The scriptures forbid many kinds of sinful behavior that come naturally to sinful humanity.

thou shalt not eat of it. . .Gen. 2:17

make unto thee any graven image. . .Exod. 20:4

name of the Lord thy God in vain. . .Exod. 20:7

thou shalt not do any work. . .Exod. 20:10

Thou shalt not kill. . .Exod. 20:13

shalt not commit adultery. . .Exod. 20:14

Thou shalt not steal. . .Exod. 20:15

shalt not bear false witness. . .Exod. 20:16

shalt not covet thy neighbour's. . .Exod. 20:17

things which are forbidden. . .Lev. 5:17

thy God hath forbidden thee. . .Deut. 4:23

See *Restrictions*.

362. Foreigners

See *Alien, Stranger/Strangers*.

363. Foreknowledge of God

eyes of the Lord run. . .2 Chron. 16:9

his understanding is infinite. . .Ps. 147:5

determinate counsel and *f of G*. . .Acts 2:23

whom he did foreknow. . .Rom. 8:29

his people which he foreknew. . .Rom. 11:2

opened unto the eyes of him. . .Heb. 4:13

Elect according to the *f of G*. . .1 Pet. 1:2

knoweth all things. . .1 John 3:20

See *Election, Predestinate/Predestinated, Sovereignty of God*.

364. Forgetfulness, God's

he forgetteth not the cry. . .Ps. 9:12

shalt not be forgotten of me. . .Isa. 44:21

yet will I not forget thee. . .Isa. 49:15

forgotten before God?. . .Luke 12:6

God is not unrighteous to forget. . .Heb. 6:10

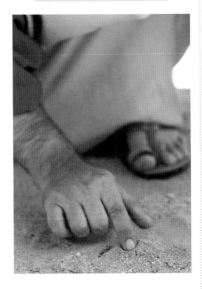

365. Forgive/Forgiven/Forgiveness/Forgiveth/Forgiving

f'ing iniquity. . .Exod. 34:7

God ready to pardon. . .Neh. 9:17

Lord, pardon mine iniquity. . .Ps. 25:11

f'n the iniquity of thy people. . .Ps. 85:2

ready to f. . .Ps. 86:5

f'th all thine iniquities. . .Ps. 103:3

he will abundantly pardon. . .Isa. 55:7

that pardoneth iniquity. . .Mic. 7:18

f us our debts. . .Matt. 6:12

power on earth to f sins. . .Matt. 9:6

shall not be f'n. . .Matt. 12:31

I f him? till seven times?. . .Matt. 18:21

when ye stand praying, f. . .Mark 11:25

f, and ye shall be f'n. . .Luke 6:37

to whom little is f'n. . .Luke 7:47

f us our sins. . .Luke 11:4

if he repent, f him. . .Luke 17:3

ought rather to f him. . .2 Cor. 2:7

the f'ness of sins. . .Eph. 1:7

f'ing one another. . .Eph. 4:32

f'n you all trespasses. . .Col. 2:13

to f us our sins. . .1 John 1:9

366. Fornication/Fornications

saving for the cause of f. . .Matt. 5:32

adulteries, f's, thefts. . .Matt. 15:19

pollutions of idols, and from f. . .Acts 15:20

unrighteousness, f, wickedness. . .Rom. 1:29

the body is not for f. . .1 Cor. 6:13

Flee f. . .1 Cor. 6:18

to avoid f. . .1 Cor. 7:2

Adultery, f, uncleanness. . .Gal. 5:19

f, and all uncleanness. . .Eph. 5:3

f, uncleanness, inordinate affection. . .Col. 3:5

abstain from f. . .1 Thess. 4:3

See *Adultery, Divorce/Divorced/Divorcement, Impurity, Living Together.*

367. Forsake/Forsaken

he will not f thee. . .Deut. 4:31

ye have f'n me. . .Judg. 10:13

if thou f him. . .1 Chron. 28:9

not f'n them that seek thee. . .Ps. 9:10
why hast thou f'n me?. . .Ps. 22:1
father and my mother f me. . .Ps. 27:10
I not seen the righteous f'n. . .Ps. 37:25
Persecuted, but not f'n. . .2 Cor. 4:9
Demas hath f'n me. . .2 Tim. 4:10
never leave thee, nor f thee. . .Heb. 13:5

368. Found

man hath f, he hideth. . .Matt. 13:44
thou hast f favour with God. . .Luke 1:30
they f him in the temple. . .Luke 2:46
not f so great faith. . .Luke 7:9
I have f my sheep. . .Luke 15:6
he was lost, and is f. . .Luke 15:24
they f not his body. . .Luke 24:23
We have f the Messias. . .John 1:41
f even to fight against God. . .Acts 5:39
I f to be unto death. . .Rom. 7:10
I was f of them. . .Rom. 10:20
that a man be f faithful. . .1 Cor. 4:2
we shall not be f naked. . .2 Cor. 5:3
ourselves also are f sinners. . .Gal. 2:17
being f in fashion as a man. . .Phil. 2:8
And be f in him. . .Phil. 3:9
being f blameless. . .1 Tim. 3:10

369. Foundation/ Foundations, Firm

laid the f on a rock. . .Luke 6:48
I have laid the f. . .1 Cor. 3:10
For other f can no man. . .1 Cor. 3:11
before the f of the world. . .Eph. 1:4
f of the apostles and prophets. . .Eph. 2:20
for themselves a good f. . .1 Tim. 6:19

f of God standeth sure. . .2 Tim. 2:19
city which hath f's. . .Heb. 11:10

370. Fountain/ Fountains

Doth a f send forth. . .James 3:11
so can no f both yield. . .James 3:12
living f's of waters. . .Rev. 7:17
upon the f's of waters. . .Rev. 8:10
f's of waters. . .Rev. 14:7
rivers and f's of waters. . .Rev. 16:4
f of the water of life. . .Rev. 21:6

371. Fraud

Defraud not. . .Mark 10:19
yourselves to be defrauded?. . .1 Cor. 6:7
ye do wrong, and defraud. . .1 Cor. 6:8
Defraud ye not one the other. . .1 Cor. 7:5
we have defrauded no man. . .2 Cor. 7:2
defraud his brother in any matter. . .1 Thess. 4:6
kept back by f. . .James 5:4

372. Freedom

liberty throughout all the land. . .Lev. 25:10

I will walk at liberty. . .Ps. 119:45

proclaim liberty to the captives. . .Isa. 61:1

in proclaiming liberty. . .Jer. 34:17

set at liberty them that are bruised. . .Luke 4:18

liberty of the children of God. . .Rom. 8:21

she is at liberty to be married. . .1 Cor. 7:39

this liberty of yours. . .1 Cor. 8:9

why is my liberty judged. . .1 Cor. 10:29

Spirit of the Lord is, there is liberty. . .2 Cor. 3:17

Stand fast therefore in the liberty. . .Gal. 5:1

called unto liberty. . .Gal. 5:13

perfect law of liberty. . .James 1:25

judged by the law of liberty. . .James 2:12

As free, and not using your liberty. . .1 Pet. 2:16

373. Free Will

therefore choose life. . .Deut. 30:19

wash thine heart from wickedness. . .Jer. 4:14

and ye would not!. . .Matt. 23:37

his heart bringeth forth. . .Luke 6:45

all men to be saved. . .1 Tim. 2:4

recover themselves. . .2 Tim. 2:26

who were once enlightened. . .Heb. 6:4

not willing that any should perish. . .2 Pet. 3:9

374. Friend/Friends/ Friendship
Faithful

A f loveth at all times. . .Prov. 17:17

Faithful are the wounds of a f. . .Prov. 27:6

a man lay down his life for his f's. . .John 15:13

God as

as a man speaketh unto his f. . .Exod. 33:11

Abraham thy f. . .2 Chron. 20:7

Job's three f's. . .Job 2:11

he was called the F of God. . .James 2:23

Making

A man that hath f's. . .Prov. 18:24

no f'ship with an angry man. . .Prov. 22:24

Mistakes concerning

if thou be surety for thy f. . .Prov. 6:1

blesseth his f with a loud voice. . .Prov. 27:14

Unfaithful

My f's scorn me. . .Job 16:20

speaketh flattery to his f's. . .Job 17:5

familiar f's have forgotten me. . .Job 19:14

my f's stand aloof. . .Ps. 38:11

mine own familiar f. . .Ps. 41:9

separateth very f's. . .Prov. 17:9

f'ship of the world is enmity. . .James 4:4

Wealth and

rich hath many f's. . .Prov. 14:20

f to him that giveth gifts. . .Prov. 19:6

375. Fruit/Fruits

f tree yielding f. . .Gen. 1:11

But of the f of the tree. . .Gen. 3:3

one cluster of grapes. . .Num. 13:23

fig trees, and pomegranates. . .Deut. 8:8

comfort me with apples. . .Song of Sol. 2:5

pomegranates, with pleasant
    f's. . .Song of Sol. 4:13

juice of my pomegranate. . .Song of Sol. 8:2

f of the vine. . .Matt. 26:29

my *f's* and my goods. . .Luke 12:18

seeking *f* on this fig tree. . .Luke 13:7

first partaker of the *f's*. . .2 Tim. 2:6

earth brought forth her *f*. . .James 5:18

yielded her *f* every month. . .Rev. 22:2

376. Fruit/Fruits, Spiritual

f's meet for repentance. . .Matt. 3:8

Ye shall know them by their *f's*. . .Matt. 7:16

good tree cannot bring forth evil *f*. . .Matt. 7:18

brought forth *f*. . .Matt. 13:8

bringeth forth much *f*. . .John 12:24

bringeth forth much *f*. . .John 15:5

What *f* had ye then. . .Rom. 6:21

bring forth *f* unto death. . .Rom. 7:5

f's of your righteousness. . .2 Cor. 9:10

But the *f* of the Spirit. . .Gal. 5:22

f's of righteousness. . .Phil. 1:11

f of our lips giving thanks. . .Heb. 13:15

full of mercy and good *f's*. . .James 3:17

377. Frustration

cursing, vexation, and rebuke. . .Deut. 28:20

vanity and vexation of spirit. . .Eccles. 1:14

this also is vexation of spirit. . .Eccles. 1:17

vexation of his heart. . .Eccles. 2:22

vanity and vexation of spirit. . .Eccles. 4:4

See *Vexation/Vexations*.

378. Full

f of the spirit of wisdom. . .Deut. 34:9

I went out *f*. . .Ruth 1:21

earth is *f* of the goodness. . .Ps. 33:5

right hand is *f* of righteousness. . .Ps. 48:10

I am *f* of heaviness. . .Ps. 69:20

God *f* of compassion. . .Ps. 86:15

my soul is *f* of troubles. . .Ps. 88:3

earth is *f* of thy riches. . .Ps. 104:24

f of compassion, and righteous. . .Ps. 112:4

f of thy mercy. . .Ps. 119:64

Lest I be *f*, and deny thee. . .Prov. 30:9

whole body shall be *f* of light. . .Matt. 6:22

Jesus being *f* of the Holy Ghost. . .Luke 4:1

Woe unto you that are *f*!. . .Luke 6:25

f of grace and truth. . .John 1:14

that your joy might be *f*. . .John 15:11

f of the Holy Ghost. . .Acts 6:3

f of faith and power. . .Acts 6:8

f of good works. . .Acts 9:36

f and to be hungry. . .Phil. 4:12

f of mercy and good fruits. . .James 3:17

your joy may be *f*. . .1 John 1:4

379. Fury

contrary unto you also in *f*. . .Lev. 26:28
God shall cast the *f* of his wrath. . .Job 20:23
render his anger with *f*. . .Isa. 66:15
poured out his *f* like fire. . .Lam. 2:4
make my *f* toward thee to rest. . .Ezek. 16:42
his *f* is poured out like fire. . .Nah. 1:6
jealous for her with great *f*. . .Zech. 8:2

380. Gain/Gained

every one that is greedy of *g*. . .Prov. 1:19
g thereof than fine gold. . .Prov. 3:14
He that is greedy of *g*. . .Prov. 15:27
He that by usury and unjust *g*. . .Prov. 28:8
if he shall *g* the whole world. . .Matt. 16:26
thou hast *g'ed* thy brother. . .Matt. 18:15
that I might *g* the more. . .1 Cor. 9:19
and to die is *g*. . .Phil. 1:21
what things were *g* to me. . .Phil. 3:7
supposing that *g* is godliness. . .1 Tim. 6:5
with contentment is great *g*. . .1 Tim. 6:6
buy and sell, and get *g*. . .James 4:13

381. Gambling

Perhaps the closest the Bible comes to the issue of gambling is when it describes Roman soldiers casting lots for Jesus' clothing during the Crucifixion. But scripture does often warn

of the love of money and a desire to gain wealth apart from hard work.

Better is little with the fear. . .Prov. 15:16
foolish man spendeth it up. . .Prov. 21:20
Lay not up for yourselves treasures. . .Matt. 6:19
where your treasure is. . .Matt. 6:21
treasure in the heavens. . .Luke 12:33
make not provision for the flesh. . .Rom. 13:14
if any provide not for his own. . .1 Tim. 5:8
love of money is the root of all evil. . .1 Tim. 6:10

See *Credit, Money*.

382. Garden/Gardens

g eastward in Eden. . .Gen. 2:8
walking in the *g*. . .Gen. 3:8
g of herbs. . .1 Kings 21:2
buried in the *g*. . .2 Kings 21:18
which is by the king's *g*. . .2 Kings 25:4
g of the king's palace. . .Esther 1:5
g's and orchards. . .Eccles. 2:5
A fountain of *g's*. . .Song of Sol. 4:15
into the *g* of nuts. . .Song of Sol. 6:11
g of cucumbers. . .Isa. 1:8
sacrificeth in *g's*. . .Isa. 65:3
plant *g's*, and eat. . .Jer. 29:28
Eden the *g* of God. . .Ezek. 28:13
brook Cedron, where was a *g*. . .John 18:1
crucified there was a *g*. . .John 19:41

383. Garment/Garments

Rending garments and wearing sackcloth were signs of mourning. Scripture also uses moth-eaten garments as a picture of the temporary nature of earthly wealth.

change your g's...Gen. 35:2
she caught him by his g...Gen. 39:12
holy g's for Aaron...Exod. 28:2
cut off their g's...1 Chron. 19:4
I rent my g...Ezra 9:3
They part my g's...Ps. 22:18
sackcloth also my g...Ps. 69:11
with light as with a g...Ps. 104:2
wax old as a g...Isa. 50:9
g of praise...Isa. 61:3
thy broidered g's...Ezek. 16:18
whose g was white as snow...Dan. 7:9
heart, and not your g's...Joel 2:13
new cloth unto an old g...Matt. 9:16
hem of his g...Matt. 9:20
spread their g's in the way...Matt. 21:8
not having a wedding g?...Matt. 22:12
borders of their g's...Matt. 23:5
parted his g's...Matt. 27:35
cast their g's on him...Mark 11:7
your g's are motheaten...James 5:2

See *Apparel; Attire/Attired; Clothe/Clothed/Clothes/ Clothing, Physical; Fashion.*

384. Gate/Gates
Lot sat in the g of Sodom...Gen. 19:1
thy house, and on thy g's...Deut. 6:9
entering of the g of the city...Josh. 20:4
Then went Boaz up to the g...Ruth 4:1
beside the way of the g...2 Sam. 15:2
king arose, and sat in the g...2 Sam. 19:8
entering of the horse g...2 Chron. 23:15

g's thereof are burned...Neh. 2:17
sitteth at the king's g...Esther 6:10
ye g's; and be ye lift up...Ps. 24:7
Enter into his g's...Ps. 100:4
g's of hell shall not prevail...Matt. 16:18
at the g's twelve angels...Rev. 21:12

385. Gender/Sex Roles
Female
he shall rule over thee...Gen. 3:16
She will do him good...Prov. 31:12
power of her own body...1 Cor. 7:4
Wives, submit yourselves...Eph. 5:22
reverence her husband...Eph. 5:33

Male
shall cleave unto his wife...Gen. 2:24
husband is known in the gates...Prov. 31:23
husband render unto the wife...1 Cor. 7:3
husband is the head...Eph. 5:23
Husbands, love your wives...Eph. 5:25
So ought men to love their wives...Eph. 5:28

386. Generosity
Thou shalt surely give him...Deut. 15:10
offer so willingly...1 Chron. 29:14

brought they in abundantly. . .2 Chron. 31:5
sheweth mercy, and giveth. . .Ps. 37:21
ever merciful, and lendeth. . .Ps. 37:26
sheweth favour, and lendeth. . .Ps. 112:5
liberal soul shall be made fat. . .Prov. 11:25
he giveth of his bread. . .Prov. 22:9
gave much alms. . .Acts 10:2
riches of their liberality. . .2 Cor. 8:2
soweth bountifully shall reap. . .2 Cor. 9:6
to all bountifulness. . .2 Cor. 9:11

See *Give/Given/Giveth*.

387. Gentiles
Come to faith
to it shall the *G* seek. . .Isa. 11:10
G shall come to thy light. . .Isa. 60:3
these things do the *G* seek. . .Matt. 6:32
his name shall the *G* trust. . .Matt. 12:21
on the *G* also was poured. . .Acts 10:45
G granted repentance unto life. . .Acts 11:18
G which believe. . .Acts 21:25
G, which have not the law. . .Rom. 2:14
salvation is come unto the *G*. . .Rom. 11:11
Praise the Lord, all ye *G*. . .Rom. 15:11

Judgment of
judgment to the *G*. . .Isa. 42:1
shew judgment to the *G*. . .Matt. 12:18

Light to
for a light of the *G*. . .Isa. 42:6
light to lighten the *G*. . .Luke 2:32

Power of
shall deliver him to the *G*. . .Matt. 20:19

princes of the *G*. . .Matt. 20:25
into the hands of the *G*. . .Acts 21:11

Times of
times of the *G* be fulfilled. . .Luke 21:24

Witness to
declare my glory among the *G*. . .Isa. 66:19
bear my name before the *G*. . .Acts 9:15
we turn to the *G*. . .Acts 13:46
apostle of the *G*. . .Rom. 11:13

See *Heathen, Pagan*.

388. Gentle/Gentleness

g'ness hath made me great. . .Ps. 18:35
g'ness of Christ. . .2 Cor. 10:1
g'ness, goodness, faith. . .Gal. 5:22

we were *g* among you. . .1 Thess. 2:7
be *g* unto all men. . .2 Tim. 2:24
g, shewing all meekness. . .Titus 3:2
then peaceable, *g*. . .James 3:17
to the good and *g*. . .1 Pet. 2:18

389. Giant/Giants

There were *g's* in the earth. . .Gen. 6:4
g's, the sons of Anak. . .Num. 13:33
Which also were accounted *g's*. . .Deut. 2:11
accounted a land of *g's*. . .Deut. 2:20
remnant of *g's*. . .Deut. 3:11
called the land of *g's*. . .Deut. 3:13
valley of the *g's*. . .Josh. 15:8
Perizzites and of the *g's*. . .Josh. 17:15
sons of the *g*. . .2 Sam. 21:16
the children of the *g*. . .1 Chron. 20:4
born unto the *g* in Gath. . .1 Chron. 20:8

390. Gift/Gifts, Spiritual

g's and calling of God. . .Rom. 11:29
Having then *g's* differing. . .Rom. 12:6
proper *g* of God. . .1 Cor. 7:7
concerning spiritual *g's*. . .1 Cor. 12:1
diversities of *g's*. . .1 Cor. 12:4
g's of healing. . .1 Cor. 12:9
then *g's* of healings. . .1 Cor. 12:28
covet earnestly the best *g's*. . .1 Cor. 12:31
have the *g* of prophecy. . .1 Cor. 13:2
desire spiritual *g's*. . .1 Cor. 14:1
zealous of spiritual *g's*. . .1 Cor. 14:12
g's of the Holy Ghost. . .Heb. 2:4

391. Girls

father's house, as in her youth. . .Lev. 22:13
her youth in her father's house. . .Num. 30:16
fear the Lord from my youth. . .1 Kings 18:12
possess the iniquities of my youth. . .Job 13:26
Remember not the sins of my youth. . .Ps. 25:7
thou hast taught me from my youth. . .Ps. 71:17
youth is renewed like the eagle's. . .Ps. 103:5
forsaketh the guide of her youth. . .Prov. 2:17
Train up a child. . .Prov. 22:6
childhood and youth are vanity. . .Eccles. 11:10
in the days of thy youth. . .Eccles. 12:1
as a little child. . .Mark 10:15
receive this child in my name. . .Luke 9:48
I spake as a child. . .1 Cor. 13:11
Flee also youthful lusts. . .2 Tim. 2:22
from a child thou hast known. . .2 Tim. 3:15

See *Babies, Child/Children, Daughter/Daughters, Youth*.

392. Give/Given/Giveth

shall *g* as he is able. . .Deut. 16:17

he hath *g'n* to the poor. . .Ps. 112:9

He that *g'th* unto the poor. . .Prov. 28:27

Cast thy bread upon the waters. . .Eccles. 11:1

G to him that asketh. . .Matt. 5:42

whosoever shall *g*. . .Matt. 10:42

g to the poor. . .Matt. 19:21

G, and it shall be *g'n*. . .Luke 6:38

whomsoever much is *g'n*. . .Luke 12:48

half of my goods I *g* to the poor. . .Luke 19:8

such as I have *g* I thee. . .Acts 3:6

all my goods to feed the poor. . .1 Cor. 13:3

so let him *g*. . .2 Cor. 9:7

he hath *g'n* to the poor. . .2 Cor. 9:9

may have to *g* to him. . .Eph. 4:28

See *Alms; Generosity; Poor, the; Welfare.*

393. Glad/Gladness

with *g'ness* of heart. . .Deut. 28:47

g'ness are in his place. . .1 Chron. 16:27

I will be *g* and rejoice. . .Ps. 9:2

Therefore my heart is *g*. . .Ps. 16:9

girded me with *g'ness*. . .Ps. 30:11

shall be *g* in the LORD. . .Ps. 64:10

earth be *g*. . .Ps. 96:11

Serve the LORD with *g'ness*. . .Ps. 100:2

be *g* in it. . .Ps. 118:24

g when they said. . .Ps. 122:1

he that is *g* at calamities. . .Prov. 17:5

be exceeding *g*. . .Matt. 5:12

shalt have joy and *g'ness*. . .Luke 1:14

g tidings of the kingdom. . .Luke 8:1

g also with exceeding joy. . .1 Pet. 4:13

394. Glory

g of the LORD. . .Exod. 16:10

for *g* and for beauty. . .Exod. 28:2

sanctified by my *g*. . .Exod. 29:43

his *g* and his greatness. . .Deut. 5:24

shield for me; my *g*. . .Ps. 3:3

heavens declare the *g*. . .Ps. 19:1

and the *g*, for ever. . .Matt. 6:13

come in the *g*. . .Matt. 16:27

riches of the *g*. . .Eph. 1:18

riches in *g* by Christ. . .Phil. 4:19

appear with him in *g*. . .Col. 3:4

obtaining of the *g*. . .2 Thess. 2:14

his *g* shall be revealed. . .1 Pet. 4:13

receive a crown of *g*. . .1 Pet. 5:4

called us to *g* and virtue. . .2 Pet. 1:3

See *Shining/Glory of God.*

395. Glutton/ Gluttonous

a *g*, and a drunkard. . .Deut. 21:20
the drunkard and the *g*. . .Prov. 23:21
Behold a man *g'ous*. . .Matt. 11:19
Behold a *g'ous* man. . .Luke 7:34

See *Obesity*.

396. Goals

teach us to number our days. . .Ps. 90:12
multitude of counsellors. . .Prov. 11:14
to them that devise good. . .Prov. 14:22
Without counsel purposes. . .Prov. 15:22
Commit thy works unto the Lord. . .Prov. 16:3
A man's heart deviseth his way. . .Prov. 16:9
nor counsel against the Lord. . .Prov. 21:30
seek that ye may excel. . .1 Cor. 14:12
I press toward the mark. . .Phil. 3:14
If the Lord will, we shall. . .James 4:15

397. God

Eternal

the Lord, the everlasting *G*. . .Gen. 21:33
Lord shall reign for ever and ever. . .Exod. 15:18
eternal *G* is thy refuge. . .Deut. 33:27
his eternal power and Godhead. . .Rom. 1:20
unto the King eternal. . .1 Tim. 1:17

Holy

for I am holy. . .Lev. 11:44
for he is an holy God. . .Josh. 24:19
There is none holy as the Lord. . .1 Sam. 2:2
thou Holy One of Israel. . .Ps. 71:22
the Holy One of *G*. . .Mark 1:24
the holy Spirit of *G*. . .Eph. 4:30

Infinite

his understanding is infinite. . .Ps. 147:5

Invisible

invisible, the only wise *G*. . .1 Tim. 1:17

Longsuffering

merciful and gracious, longsuffering. . .Exod. 34:6
The Lord is longsuffering. . .Num. 14:18
endured with much longsuffering. . .Rom. 9:22
the *G* of patience. . .Rom. 15:5
longsuffering to us-ward. . .2 Pet. 3:9
the longsuffering of our Lord. . .2 Pet. 3:15

Loving

thy lovingkindness, O *G*!. . .Ps. 36:7
according to thy lovingkindness. . .Ps. 51:1
the love of *G*. . .Luke 11:42
G so loved the world. . .John 3:16
separate us from the love of *G*. . .Rom. 8:39
the love of Christ. . .Eph. 3:19

love the Father hath bestowed. . .1 John 3:1

perceive we the love of G. . .1 John 3:16

G is love. . .1 John 4:8

Merciful

shewing mercy unto thousands. . .Exod. 20:6

merciful and gracious. . .Exod. 34:6

the greatness of thy mercy. . .Neh. 13:22

trust in the mercy of G. . .Ps. 52:8

our G is merciful. . .Ps. 116:5

his mercy endureth for ever. . .Ps. 136:2

G, who is rich in mercy. . .Eph. 2:4

Omnipotent

the power, and the glory. . .1 Chron. 29:11

power and might. . .2 Chron. 20:6

He ruleth by his power for ever. . .Ps. 66:7

Lord G omnipotent reigneth. . .Rev. 19:6

Omnipresent

shall I flee from thy presence?. . .Ps. 139:7

him we live, and move, and have
our being. . .Acts 17:28

never leave thee, nor forsake thee. . .Heb. 13:5

Omniscient

art acquainted with all my ways. . .Ps. 139:3

his understanding is infinite. . .Ps. 147:5

Before I formed thee in the belly
I knew thee. . .Jer. 1:5

Powerful

with great power. . .Exod. 32:11

the power of his works. . .Ps. 111:6

made the earth by his power. . .Jer. 10:12

by my great power. . .Jer. 27:5

power on earth to forgive sins. . .Mark 2:10

in the power of the Spirit. . .Luke 4:14

power he commandeth. . .Luke 4:36

the power of the Lord. . .Luke 5:17

Holy Ghost and with power. . .Acts 10:38

the glory of his power. . .2 Thess. 1:9

Righteous

G of Israel, thou art righteous. . .Ezra 9:15

righteous G trieth the hearts. . .Ps. 7:9

heavens shall declare his righteousness. . .Ps. 50:6

Gracious is the Lord, and righteous. . .Ps. 116:5

G, and his righteousness. . .Matt. 6:33

See *Attributes of God, Characteristics of God.*

398. Godly/Godliness

that is g for himself. . .Ps. 4:3

for the g man ceaseth. . .Ps. 12:1

every one that is g pray. . .Ps. 32:6

simplicity and g sincerity. . .2 Cor. 1:12

g sorrow worketh repentance. . .2 Cor. 7:10

peaceable life in all g'iness. . .1 Tim. 2:2

becometh women professing g'iness. . .1 Tim. 2:10

great is the mystery of g'iness. . .1 Tim. 3:16

thyself rather unto g'iness. . .1 Tim. 4:7

g'iness is profitable. . .1 Tim. 4:8

doctrine which is according to g'iness. . .1 Tim. 6:3

our God is merciful. . .Ps. 116:5
God, who is rich in mercy. . .Eph. 2:4
he is faithful and just. . .1 John 1:9

400. God's Will

Scripture is filled with commands indicating God's will for our lives. That's why it's so important for Christians to read the Bible regularly. The basis of all commands is the Ten Commandments (Exodus 20:1–17 and Deuteronomy 5:6–21).

supposing that gain is g'iness. . .1 Tim. 6:5
g'iness with contentment. . .1 Tim. 6:6
righteousness, g'iness, faith. . .1 Tim. 6:11
Having a form of g'iness. . .2 Tim. 3:5
live g in Christ. . .2 Tim. 3:12
truth which is after g'iness. . .Titus 1:1
live soberly, righteously, and g. . .Titus 2:12
that pertain unto life and g'iness. . .2 Pet. 1:3
to patience g'iness. . .2 Pet. 1:6
And to g'iness brotherly kindness. . .2 Pet. 1:7
how to deliver the g. . .2 Pet. 2:9
holy conversation and g'iness. . .2 Pet. 3:11

399. God's Condescension

shewing mercy unto thousands. . .Exod. 20:6
God, merciful and gracious. . .Exod. 34:6
LORD was gracious. . .2 Kings 13:23
the greatness of thy mercy. . .Neh. 13:22
God forgotten to be gracious?. . .Ps. 77:9
gracious, longsuffering. . .Ps. 86:15
gracious, slow to anger. . .Ps. 103:8
gracious and full of compassion. . .Ps. 111:4

have no other gods before me. . .Exod. 20:3
love the LORD thy God. . .Deut. 6:5
serve him with all your heart. . .Deut. 11:13
I will instruct thee and teach thee. . .Ps. 32:8
Thy word is a lamp. . .Ps. 119:105
Trust in the LORD. . .Prov. 3:5
Commit thy works unto the LORD. . .Prov. 16:3
love thy neighbour as thyself. . .Matt. 19:19
good, and acceptable, and perfect,
    will. . .Rom. 12:2
fervent in spirit; serving the Lord. . .Rom. 12:11
do all to the glory of God. . .1 Cor. 10:31
the mystery of his will. . .Eph. 1:9
what the will of the Lord is. . .Eph. 5:17
let your requests be made known. . .Phil. 4:6
this is the will of God. . .1 Thess. 4:3
If any of you lack wisdom. . .James 1:5

401. Good
Behavior

Teach me g judgment. . .Ps. 119:66
righteous is only g. . .Prov. 11:23
thou g and faithful servant. . .Matt. 25:21

overcome evil with *g*. . .Rom. 12:21

this is *g* and acceptable. . .1 Tim. 2:3

g and acceptable before God. . .1 Tim. 5:4

shew out of a *g* conversation. . .James 3:13

not only to the *g*. . .1 Pet. 2:18

Having a *g* conscience. . .1 Pet. 3:16

Doing

none that doeth *g*. . .Ps. 14:1

Depart from evil, and do *g*. . .Ps. 34:14

Trust in the Lord, and do *g*. . .Ps. 37:3

do *g* to them that hate. . .Matt. 5:44

He that doeth *g* is of God. . .3 John 1:11

God is

for he is *g*. . .1 Chron. 16:34

G and upright is the Lord. . .Ps. 25:8

thy judgments are *g*. . .Ps. 119:39

none *g* but one, that is, God. . .Mark 10:18

I am the *g* shepherd. . .John 10:11

Man

steps of a *g* man. . .Ps. 37:23

A *g* man sheweth favour. . .Ps. 112:5

A *g* man obtaineth favour. . .Prov. 12:2

a *g* man shall be satisfied. . .Prov. 14:14

A *g* man out of the *g* treasure. . .Matt. 12:35

peradventure for a *g* man. . .Rom. 5:7

402. Goodness

my *g* pass before thee. . .Exod. 33:19

abundant in *g* and truth. . .Exod. 34:6

g and mercy shall follow. . .Ps. 23:6

how great is thy *g*. . .Ps. 31:19

earth is full of the *g*. . .Ps. 33:5

g of God endureth. . .Ps. 52:1

thy *g* for the poor. . .Ps. 68:10

hungry soul with *g*. . .Ps. 107:9

praise the Lord for his *g*. . .Ps. 107:15

My *g*, and my fortress. . .Ps. 144:2

proclaim every one his own *g*. . .Prov. 20:6

riches of his *g*. . .Rom. 2:4

g and severity of God. . .Rom. 11:22

gentleness, *g*, faith. . .Gal. 5:22

fruit of the Spirit is in all *g*. . .Eph. 5:9

403. Good Work/ Good Works

then may ye also do good. . .Jer. 13:23

they may see your *g w's*. . .Matt. 5:16

not a terror to *g w's*. . .Rom. 13:3

abound to every *g w*. . .2 Cor. 9:8

do good unto all men. . .Gal. 6:10

in Christ Jesus unto *g w's*. . .Eph. 2:10

begun a *g w* in you. . .Phil. 1:6

fruitful in every *g w*. . .Col. 1:10

every *g* word and *w*. . .2 Thess. 2:17

with *g w's*. . .1 Tim. 2:10

g w's of some are manifest. . .1 Tim. 5:25

rich in *g w's*. . .1 Tim. 6:18

prepared unto every *g w*. . .2 Tim. 2:21

zealous of *g w's*. . .Titus 2:14

unto love and to *g w's*. . .Heb. 10:24

See *Devotion*.

404. Gospel, the

one that bringeth good tidings. . .Isa. 41:27
bringeth good tidings of good. . .Isa. 52:7
preach good tidings. . .Isa. 61:1
good tidings of great joy. . .Luke 2:10
glad tidings of good things!. . .Rom. 10:15

405. Gossip

he soweth discord. . .Prov. 6:14
A talebearer revealeth secrets. . .Prov. 11:13
whisperer separateth chief friends. . .Prov. 16:28
words of a talebearer are as. . .Prov. 18:8
a talebearer revealeth secrets. . .Prov. 20:19
where there is no talebearer. . .Prov. 26:20
words of a talebearer. . .Prov. 26:22
a murmuring of the Grecians. . .Acts 6:1
strifes, backbitings, whisperings. . .2 Cor. 12:20
without murmurings and disputings. . .Phil. 2:14
tattlers also and busybodies. . .1 Tim. 5:13
busybody in other men's matters. . .1 Pet. 4:15
prating against us. . .3 John 1:10

See *Talebearer.*

406. Government

The rulers included here are the local leaders of Israel and Judah in biblical times.

Joseph was the governor. . .Gen. 42:6
governors of Israel. . .Judg. 5:9
had made Gedaliah governor. . .2 Kings 25:23
Nehemiah the governor. . .Neh. 12:26
Governor among the nations. . .Ps. 22:28
g shall be upon his shoulder. . .Isa. 9:6
out of thee shall come a Governor. . .Matt. 2:6
before governors and kings. . .Matt. 10:18
Pontius Pilate the governor. . .Matt. 27:2
when Cyrenius was governor of Syria. . .Luke 2:2
Pontius Pilate being governor. . .Luke 3:1
unto governors, as unto them. . .1 Pet. 2:14

Leaders

and with every leader. . .1 Chron. 13:1
leaders of this people. . .Isa. 9:16
leader and commander to the people. . .Isa. 55:4

See *King, Earthly*; *Prince/Princes.*

407. Grace
Believers and

g unto the lowly. . .Prov. 3:34
g was upon them. . .Acts 4:33
g did much more abound. . .Rom. 5:20
not under the law, but under *g*. . .Rom. 6:14
all *g* abound toward you. . .2 Cor. 9:8
by *g* are ye saved. . .Eph. 2:8
unto the throne of *g*. . .Heb. 4:16

giveth *g* unto the humble. . .James 4:6
But grow in *g*. . .2 Pet. 3:18

Finding of

But Noah found *g*. . .Gen. 6:8
found *g* in my sight. . .Exod. 33:17

God and

LORD will give *g* and glory. . .Ps. 84:11
g of God was upon him. . .Luke 2:40
full of *g* and truth. . .John 1:14
g and truth came by Jesus. . .John 1:17
g of the Lord Jesus. . .Acts 15:11
justified freely by his *g*. . .Rom. 3:24
the election of *g*. . .Rom. 11:5
My *g* is sufficient. . .2 Cor. 12:9
according to the riches of his *g*. . .Eph. 1:7
g of God that bringeth. . .Titus 2:11
being justified by his *g*. . .Titus 3:7
heirs together of the *g*. . .1 Pet. 3:7

408. Gratitude

both with thanksgivings. . .Neh. 12:27
with the voice of thanksgiving. . .Ps. 26:7
Offer unto God thanksgiving. . .Ps. 50:14
magnify him with thanksgiving. . .Ps. 69:30
before his presence with thanksgiving. . .Ps. 95:2

Enter into his gates with thanksgiving. . .Ps. 100:4
supplication with thanksgiving. . .Phil. 4:6
if it be received with thanksgiving. . .1 Tim. 4:4

409. Great Commission

In Matthew 28:19–20, Jesus commanded His disciples to spread the gospel message by preaching and baptizing believers. Today this is often called the Great Commission. There is plenty of evidence in scripture that the leaders of the first-century church took this message to heart and preached and baptized many.

Go ye therefore, and teach. . .Matt. 28:19
Teaching them to observe. . .Matt. 28:20
Repent, and be baptized. . .Acts 2:38
they ceased not to teach. . .Acts 5:42
they were baptized. . .Acts 8:12
hinder me to be baptized?. . .Acts 8:36
arose, and was baptized. . .Acts 9:18
that these should not be baptized. . .Acts 10:47
teaching and preaching. . .Acts 15:35
when she was baptized. . .Acts 16:15
was baptized, he and all his. . .Acts 16:33
believed, and were baptized. . .Acts 18:8
arise, and be baptized. . .Acts 22:16
Preaching the kingdom of God. . .Acts 28:31
I teach every where. . .1 Cor. 4:17

See Baptism/Baptized, Teach/Teaching.

410. Greed/Greedily/ Greediness/Greedy

one that is *g'y* of gain. . .Prov. 1:19

He that is *g'y* of gain. . .Prov. 15:27
He coveteth *g'ily* all the day. . .Prov. 21:26
hast *g'ily* gained of thy neighbours. . .Ezek. 22:12
work all uncleanness with *g'iness*. . .Eph. 4:19
not *g'y* of filthy lucre. . .1 Tim. 3:3
not *g'y* of filthy lucre. . .1 Tim. 3:8

See *Materialism.*

411. Grief/Griefs

his *g* was very great. . .Job 2:13
my *g* were throughly weighed. . .Job 6:2
consumed because of *g*. . .Ps. 6:7
my life is spent with *g*. . .Ps. 31:10
A foolish son is a *g*. . .Prov. 17:25
much wisdom is much *g*. . .Eccles. 1:18
acquainted with *g*. . .Isa. 53:3
he hath borne our *g's*. . .Isa. 53:4
before me continually is *g*. . .Jer. 6:7
conscience toward God endure *g*. . .1 Pet. 2:19

See *Mourn/Mourning.*

412. Groan/Groaned/ Groaneth/Groaning/ Groanings

God heard their *g'ing*. . .Exod. 2:24
heavier than my *g'ing*. . .Job 23:2
weary with my *g'ing*. . .Ps. 6:6
my *g'ing* is not hid. . .Ps. 38:9
g'ing of the prisoner. . .Ps. 102:20
he *g'ed* in the spirit. . .John 11:33
the whole creation *g'eth*. . .Rom. 8:22
g within ourselves. . .Rom. 8:23
g'ings which cannot be uttered. . .Rom. 8:26

we *g*, earnestly desiring to. . .2 Cor. 5:2
do *g*, being burdened. . .2 Cor. 5:4

413. Grooming

Levitical law prohibited men from cutting their beards. Shaving a beard was an insult, part of a Levitical cleansing, or a sign of mourning. The prophets often use a shaved head as a sign of God's punishment for sin.

his head and his beard. . .Lev. 14:9
the corners of your heads. . .Lev. 19:27
shall not make baldness. . .Lev. 21:5
Nazarite shall shave the head. . .Num. 6:18
one half of their beards. . .2 Sam. 10:4
the hair was heavy. . .2 Sam. 14:26
nor trimmed his beard. . .2 Sam. 19:24
my head and of my beard. . .Ezra 9:3
plucked off their hair. . .Neh. 13:25

consume the beard. . .Isa. 7:20
every beard cut off. . .Isa. 15:2
Cut off thine hair. . .Jer. 7:29
their beards shaven. . .Jer. 41:5
every beard clipped. . .Jer. 48:37
take thee a barber's razor. . .Ezek. 5:1
if a woman have long hair. . .1 Cor. 11:15
not with broided hair. . .1 Tim. 2:9
plaiting the hair. . .1 Pet. 3:3

414. Grow/Groweth

g as the vine. . .Hosea 14:7
g up into him. . .Eph. 4:15
faith *g'eth* exceedingly. . .2 Thess. 1:3
that ye may *g* thereby. . .1 Pet. 2:2
But *g* in grace. . .2 Pet. 3:18

415. Grudge

Esau hated Jacob because. . .Gen. 27:41
requite us all the evil. . .Gen. 50:15
nor bear any *g*. . .Lev. 19:18
in wrath they hate me. . .Ps. 55:3
g if they be not. . .Ps. 59:15
Herodias had a quarrel against. . .Mark 6:19
G not one against another. . .James 5:9

416. Guests

In an age when there were few safe places to stop over during travel, hospitality was an important part of social life. The person who took in a traveler was responsible for him and his welfare. The apostles encouraged Christians to care for others, especially those bearing the gospel, by taking them in for a time.

I will fetch a morsel of bread. . .Gen. 18:5
tarry all night. . .Gen. 19:2
room to lodge in. . .Gen. 24:25
stranger that dwelleth with you. . .Lev. 19:34
loveth the stranger. . .Deut. 10:18
he brought him into his house. . .Judg. 19:21
he went into the Pharisee's. . .Luke 7:36
whatsoever house ye enter. . .Luke 9:4
given to hospitality. . .Rom. 12:13
given to hospitality. . .1 Tim. 3:2
if she have lodged strangers. . .1 Tim. 5:10
a lover of hospitality. . .Titus 1:8
received the spies with peace. . .Heb. 11:31
not forgetful to entertain strangers. . .Heb. 13:2
hospitality one to another. . .1 Pet. 4:9
ought to receive such. . .3 John 1:8

See *Hospitality*.

417. Guide/Guided/Guides

G'd them on every side. . .2 Chron. 32:22
meek will he *g*. . .Ps. 25:9
lead me, and *g* me. . .Ps. 31:3
I will *g* thee. . .Ps. 32:8
g even unto death. . .Ps. 48:14
g me with thy counsel. . .Ps. 73:24
forsaketh the *g*. . .Prov. 2:17

upright shall *g* them. . .Prov. 11:3
g thine heart. . .Prov. 23:19
Lord shall *g* thee. . .Isa. 58:11
ye blind *g's*. . .Matt. 23:16
to *g* our feet. . .Luke 1:79
g you into all truth. . .John 16:13

418. Guilty/Guiltless

will not hold him *g'less*. . .Exod. 20:7
not justify the wicked. . .Exod. 23:7
no means clear the *g*. . .Exod. 34:7
done, and are *g*. . .Lev. 4:13
yet is he *g*. . .Lev. 5:17
which is *g* of death. . .Num. 35:31
it would be sin in thee. . .Deut. 23:21
be iniquity in my hands. . .Ps. 7:3
mine iniquity have I not hid. . .Ps. 32:5
condemned the *g'less*. . .Matt. 12:7
no cloak for their sin. . .John 15:22
world may become *g*. . .Rom. 3:19
g of the body. . .1 Cor. 11:27
he is *g* of all. . .James 2:10

419. Hand of the Lord

h o t L, that it is mighty. . .Josh. 4:24
h o t L was against them. . .Judg. 2:15
h o t L is gone out against. . .Ruth 1:13
h o t L was against the city. . .1 Sam. 5:9
h o t L be against you. . .1 Sam. 12:15
fall now into the *h o t L*. . .2 Sam. 24:14
h o t L was on Elijah. . .1 Kings 18:46
strengthened as the *h o t L*. . .Ezra 7:28
h o t L doeth valiantly. . .Ps. 118:15
heart is in the *h o t L*. . .Prov. 21:1
h o t L was upon me. . .Ezek. 37:1

h o t L was with him. . .Luke 1:66
h o t L was with them. . .Acts 11:21
h o t L is upon thee. . .Acts 13:11

420. Happy

H art thou, O Israel. . .Deut. 33:29
h is the man whom God. . .Job 5:17
H is the man that hath. . .Ps. 127:5
h is that people. . .Ps. 144:15
H is the man that findeth. . .Prov. 3:13
on the poor, *h* is he. . .Prov. 14:21
trusteth in the Lord, *h*. . .Prov. 16:20
H is the man that feareth. . .Prov. 28:14
keepeth the law, *h* is he. . .Prov. 29:18
H is he that condemneth. . .Rom. 14:22
count them *h* which endure. . .James 5:11
sake, *h* are ye. . .1 Pet. 3:14
Christ, *h* are ye. . .1 Pet. 4:14

421. Hardening of the Heart

but I will harden his heart. . .Exod. 4:21
harden the hearts of the Egyptians. . .Exod. 14:17
shalt not harden thine heart. . .Deut. 15:7
Lord to harden their hearts. . .Josh. 11:20
hardened his heart from turning. . .2 Chron. 36:13

Harden not your heart. . .Ps. 95:8
he that hardeneth his heart. . .Prov. 28:14
hardness of your hearts. . .Matt. 19:8
hardness of their hearts. . .Mark 3:5
their heart was hardened. . .Mark 6:52
your heart yet hardened?. . .Mark 8:17
unbelief and hardness of heart. . .Mark 16:14
eyes, and hardened their heart. . .John 12:40
hardness and impenitent heart. . .Rom. 2:5
Harden not your hearts. . .Heb. 3:8
his voice, harden not your hearts. . .Heb. 4:7

---

422. Harlot/Harlot's/ Harlots

God uses harlotry as a picture of His people's unfaithfulness to Him.

he thought her to be an *h*. . .Gen. 38:15
h, these shall he not take. . .Lev. 21:14
came into an *h's* house, named Rahab. . .Josh. 2:1
the son of an *h*. . .Judg. 11:1
that were *h's*, unto the king. . .1 Kings 3:16

keepeth company with *h's*. . .Prov. 29:3
faithful city become an *h*!. . .Isa. 1:21
thou hast played the *h*. . .Jer. 3:1
cease from playing the *h*. . .Ezek. 16:41
mother hath played the *h*. . .Hosea 2:5
shalt not play the *h*. . .Hosea 3:3
they sacrifice with *h's*. . .Hosea 4:14
given a boy for an *h*. . .Joel 3:3
publicans and the *h's* go. . .Matt. 21:31
to an *h* is one body?. . .1 Cor. 6:16

See *Bastard*, *Seduction*, *Whore/Whoredom/ Whoremonger/Whoremongers*.

---

423. Harmony

how pleasant it is for brethren. . .Ps. 133:1
same mind one toward another. . .Rom. 12:16
what concord hath Christ. . .2 Cor. 6:15
unity of the Spirit. . .Eph. 4:3
be ye all of one mind. . .1 Pet. 3:8

See *Peace*.

---

424. Harvest

h truly is plenteous. . .Matt. 9:37
the Lord of the *h*. . .Matt. 9:38
grow together until the *h*. . .Matt. 13:30
h is the end of the world. . .Matt. 13:39
because the *h* is come. . .Mark 4:29
white already to *h*. . .John 4:35
h of the earth is ripe. . .Rev. 14:15

See *Lost/Unsaved*, *Unsaved*, *Witness/Witnessing*.

425. Hasty

h of spirit exalteth folly. . .Prov. 14:29
every one that is *h*. . .Prov. 21:5
that is *h* in his words?. . .Prov. 29:20
let not thine heart be *h*. . .Eccles. 5:2
Be not *h* in thy spirit. . .Eccles. 7:9

426. Hate/Hated/ Hatest/Hateth

Brother

Thou shalt not *h* thy brother. . .Lev. 19:17
h'th his brother. . .1 John 2:9

Enemies

enemy, and from them that *h'd* me. . .2 Sam. 22:18
suffer of them that *h* me. . .Ps. 9:13
h them, O Lord, that *h* thee?. . .Ps. 139:21
h thine enemy. . .Matt. 5:43
do good to them which *h* you. . .Luke 6:27

God and

which the Lord thy God *h'th*. . .Deut. 16:22
they that *h'd* them ruled over them. . .Ps. 106:41
they that *h* me love death. . .Prov. 8:36
love, and a time to *h*. . .Eccles. 3:8
h'd of all men. . .Matt. 10:22
when men shall *h* you. . .Luke 6:22
h not his father. . .Luke 14:26
The world cannot *h* you. . .John 7:7

Sin and

h'st all workers of iniquity. . .Ps. 5:5
h'd the congregation of evil doers. . .Ps. 26:5
they that *h* the righteous. . .Ps. 34:21
h'st wickedness. . .Ps. 45:7
Ye that love the Lord, *h* evil. . .Ps. 97:10

I *h* vain thoughts. . .Ps. 119:113
For that they *h'd* knowledge. . .Prov. 1:29
fear of the Lord is to *h* evil. . .Prov. 8:13
he that *h'th* his life. . .John 12:25
what I *h*, that do I. . .Rom. 7:15

See *Despise/Despised/Despisest/Despiseth, Emotions, Feelings.*

427. Haughty/ Haughtiness

thine eyes are upon the *h*. . .2 Sam. 22:28
h spirit before a fall. . .Prov. 16:18
heart of man is *h*. . .Prov. 18:12
Proud and *h* scorner. . .Prov. 21:24
h'iness of men. . .Isa. 2:17
h shall be humbled. . .Isa. 10:33
h'iness of the terrible. . .Isa. 13:11

428. Haves and Have Nots

leave them unto the poor. . .Lev. 23:22
hand from thy poor brother. . .Deut. 15:7
open thine hand wide. . .Deut. 15:11
he that considereth the poor. . .Ps. 41:1
maketh himself rich, yet hath nothing. . .Prov. 13:7
He that oppresseth the poor. . .Prov. 14:31

The poor useth intreaties. . .Prov. 18:23
Wealth maketh many friends. . .Prov. 19:4
He that hath pity upon the poor. . .Prov. 19:17
stoppeth his ears at the cry of the poor. . .Prov. 21:13
The rich and poor meet together. . .Prov. 22:2
the rich ruleth over the poor. . .Prov. 22:7
He that oppresseth the poor. . .Prov. 22:16
rich man is wise in his own conceit. . .Prov. 28:11
plead the cause of the poor. . .Prov. 31:9
Blessed are the poor in spirit. . .Matt. 5:3
Give, and it shall be given. . .Luke 6:38
poor widow hath cast in more. . .Luke 21:3
man with a gold ring. . .James 2:2

See *Poor, the.*

429. Heal/Healing

I wound, and I *h*. . .Deut. 32:39
behold, I will *h* thee. . .2 Kings 20:5
will *h* their land. . .2 Chron. 7:14
O Lord, *h* me. . .Ps. 6:2
h my soul. . .Ps. 41:4
a time to *h*. . .Eccles. 3:3
h your backslidings. . .Jer. 3:22
H me, O Lord. . .Jer. 17:14
he will *h* us. . .Hosea 6:1
h all manner of sickness. . .Matt. 10:1
Is it lawful to *h*. . .Matt. 12:10
I should *h* them. . .Matt. 13:15
they could not cure him. . .Matt. 17:16
all devils, and to cure diseases. . .Luke 9:1

See *Physician/Physicians, Recover/Recovered/
Recovering, Sick/Sickly/Sickness/Sicknesses.*

430. Health

the *h* of my countenance. . .Ps. 42:11
thy saving *h* among all nations. . .Ps. 67:2
It shall be *h* to thy navel. . .Prov. 3:8
tongue of the wise is *h*. . .Prov. 12:18
h to the bones. . .Prov. 16:24
A merry heart doeth good. . .Prov. 17:22
for this is for your *h*. . .Acts 27:34
prosper and be in *h*. . .3 John 1:2

See *Eat/Eateth/Eating, Exercise.*

431. Hear/Hearer/ Heareth

that they may *h*. . .Deut. 31:12
H me when I call. . .Ps. 4:1
h joy and gladness. . .Ps. 51:8
h what God the Lord. . .Ps. 85:8
h the words of the wise. . .Prov. 22:17
h, and your soul shall live. . .Isa. 55:3
He that *h'eth*, let him *h*. . .Ezek. 3:27
If they *h* not Moses. . .Luke 16:31
they that *h* shall live. . .John 5:25
God *h'eth* not sinners. . .John 9:31
any man *h* my words. . .John 12:47
truth *h'eth* my voice. . .John 18:37

how shall they *h*. . .Rom. 10:14
being not a forgetful *h'er*. . .James 1:25
he that knoweth God *h'eth* us. . .1 John 4:6

See *Listen*.

432. Heart

My *h* rejoiceth in the LORD. . .1 Sam. 2:1
man after his own *h*. . .1 Sam. 13:14
rejoicing the *h*. . .Ps. 19:8
My *h* is fixed, O God. . .Ps. 57:7
your *h* shall live. . .Ps. 69:32
froward *h* shall depart. . .Ps. 101:4
with my whole *h*. . .Ps. 111:1
A merry *h* maketh. . .Prov. 15:13
I have made my *h* clean. . .Prov. 20:9
king's *h* is in the hand. . .Prov. 21:1
as he thinketh in his *h*. . .Prov. 23:7
new *h* also will I give. . .Ezek. 36:26
h of the fathers. . .Mal. 4:6
there will your *h* be. . .Matt. 6:21
of the *h* proceed evil thoughts. . .Matt. 15:19
Let not your *h* be troubled. . .John 14:1

433. Heathen

Why do the *h* rage. . .Ps. 2:1
shall give thee the *h*. . .Ps. 2:8

h to nought. . .Ps. 33:10
exalted among the *h*. . .Ps. 46:10
God reigneth over the *h*. . .Ps. 47:8
Declare his glory among the *h*. . .Ps. 96:3
in the sight of the *h*. . .Ps. 98:2
h shall fear the name. . .Ps. 102:15
Learn not the way of the *h*. . .Jer. 10:2
from among the *h*. . .Ezek. 36:24
repetitions, as the *h* do. . .Matt. 6:7
unto thee as an *h* man. . .Matt. 18:17
preach him among the *h*. . .Gal. 1:16
we should go unto the *h*. . .Gal. 2:9
God would justify the *h*. . .Gal. 3:8

See *Gentiles*, *Pagan*.

434. Heaven/ Heavenly/Heavens

blessings of *h* above. . .Gen. 49:25
thy holy habitation, from *h*. . .Deut. 26:15
Our Father which art in *h*. . .Matt. 6:9
in earth, as it is in *h*. . .Matt. 6:10
treasures in *h*. . .Matt. 6:20
Lord of *h* and earth. . .Matt. 11:25
names are written in *h*. . .Luke 10:20
eternal in the *h's*. . .2 Cor. 5:1
right hand in the *h'ly* places. . .Eph. 1:20
our conversation is in *h*. . .Phil. 3:20
have a Master in *h*. . .Col. 4:1
shall descend from *h*. . .1 Thess. 4:16
shall be revealed from *h*. . .2 Thess. 1:7
but into *h* itself. . .Heb. 9:24
reserved in *h* for you. . .1 Pet. 1:4

See *Eternity*; *Eternal Life*; *Reward, Eternal*.

435. Hebrew/Hebrews

Abram the *H*. . .Gen. 14:13
brought in an *H*. . .Gen. 39:14
young man, an *H*. . .Gen. 41:12
H midwives. . .Exod. 1:15
to the *H* women. . .Exod. 1:16
H women are not. . .Exod. 1:19
nurse of the *H* women. . .Exod. 2:7
Egyptian smiting an *H*. . .Exod. 2:11
buy an *H* servant. . .Exod. 21:2
H of the *H's*. . .Phil. 3:5

See *Israelites, Jew/Jews.*

436. Heir/Heirs

Those who believe in Jesus are heirs, with Him, to the kingdom of God.

be *h's*, faith is made void. . .Rom. 4:14
joint-*h's* with Christ. . .Rom. 8:17
h's according to the promise. . .Gal. 3:29
I say, That the *h*. . .Gal. 4:1
h of God through Christ. . .Gal. 4:7
not be *h* with the son. . .Gal. 4:30
we should be made *h's*. . .Titus 3:7
appointed *h* of all things. . .Heb. 1:2

h's of salvation?. . .Heb. 1:14
h's of promise. . .Heb. 6:17
h of the righteousness. . .Heb. 11:7
h's of the kingdom. . .James 2:5
h's together of the grace. . .1 Pet. 3:7

437. Hell

h compassed me about. . .2 Sam. 22:6
wicked shall be turned into *h*. . .Ps. 9:17
wilt not leave my soul in *h*. . .Ps. 16:10
The sorrows of *h*. . .Ps. 18:5
my soul from the lowest *h*. . .Ps. 86:13
if I make my bed in *h*. . .Ps. 139:8
in danger of *h* fire. . .Matt. 5:22
cast into *h*. . .Matt. 5:30
soul and body in *h*. . .Matt. 10:28
h shall not prevail. . .Matt. 16:18
damnation of *h*?. . .Matt. 23:33
set on fire of *h*. . .James 3:6
cast them down to *h*. . .2 Pet. 2:4
keys of *h*. . .Rev. 1:18
And death and *h*. . .Rev. 20:14

See *Damnation, Perdition, Unsaved.*

438. Help/Helped/ Helper/Helpeth

h meet for him. . .Gen. 2:18
surely *h* with him. . .Exod. 23:5
h'er of the fatherless. . .Ps. 10:14
H, Lord; for the godly. . .Ps. 12:1
thou hast been my *h*. . .Ps. 27:9
I am *h'ed*. . .Ps. 28:7
Lord, be thou my *h'er*. . .Ps. 30:10
our *h* and our shield. . .Ps. 33:20

very present *h* in trouble. . .Ps. 46:1
him that hath no *h'er*. . .Ps. 72:12
whence cometh my *h*. . .Ps. 121:1
h thou mine unbelief. . .Mark 9:24
Macedonia, and *h* us. . .Acts 16:9
h'eth our infirmities. . .Rom. 8:26
h in time of need. . .Heb. 4:16

439. Herd/Herds

had flocks, and *h's*. . .Gen. 13:5
flocks, and *h's*. . .Gen. 24:35
h's with young. . .Gen. 33:13
flocks and your *h's*. . .Exod. 12:32
look well to thy *h's*. . .Prov. 27:23
into the *h* of swine. . .Matt. 8:31

440. Heresy

Let us go after other gods. . .Deut. 13:2
Beware of false prophets. . .Matt. 7:15
many false prophets. . .Matt. 24:11
there shall arise false Christs. . .Matt. 24:24
sorcerer, a false prophet. . .Acts 13:6
For such are false apostles. . .2 Cor. 11:13

there shall be false teachers. . .2 Pet. 2:1
forsaken the right way. . .2 Pet. 2:15
certain men crept in unawares. . .Jude 1:4
beast and the false prophet. . .Rev. 20:10

441. Heritage

give it you for an *h*. . .Exod. 6:8
h appointed unto him. . .Job 20:29
I have a goodly *h*. . .Ps. 16:6
given me the *h*. . .Ps. 61:5
taken as an *h*. . .Ps. 119:111
children are an *h*. . .Ps. 127:3
lords over God's *h*. . .1 Pet. 5:3

442. Hidden Things

See *Mystery/Mysteries*.

443. Hiring

Six days shalt thou labour. . .Exod. 20:9
the diligent maketh rich. . .Prov. 10:4
diligent shall bear rule. . .Prov. 12:24
labourer is worthy of his hire. . .Luke 10:7

See *Employment*, *Work*.

444. Holiness

glorious in *h*. . .Exod. 15:11
the beauty of *h*. . .1 Chron. 16:29
perfecting *h* in the fear. . .2 Cor. 7:1
in *h* before God. . .1 Thess. 3:13
uncleanness, but unto *h*. . .1 Thess. 4:7
h with sobriety. . .1 Tim. 2:15
behaviour as becometh *h*. . .Titus 2:3
partakers of his *h*. . .Heb. 12:10
with all men, and *h*. . .Heb. 12:14

See *Holy*.

445. Holy

standest is *h* ground. . .Exod. 3:5
sabbath day, to keep it *h*. . .Exod. 20:8
Ye shall be *h*. . .Lev. 19:2
therefore, and be ye *h*. . .Lev. 20:7
none *h* as the Lᴏʀᴅ. . .1 Sam. 2:2
Glory ye in his *h* name. . .1 Chron. 16:10
H One to see corruption. . .Ps. 16:10
But thou art *h*. . .Ps. 22:3
my soul; for I am *h*. . .Ps. 86:2
h in all his works. . .Ps. 145:17
H, h, h, is the Lᴏʀᴅ. . .Isa. 6:3
h and without blame. . .Eph. 1:4
to present you *h*. . .Col. 1:22
so be ye *h*. . .1 Pet. 1:15
for thou only art *h*. . .Rev. 15:4

See *Holiness*.

446. Holy Ghost

baptize you with the *H G*. . .Matt. 3:11
blasphemy against the *H G*. . .Matt. 12:31

Son, and of the *H G*. . .Matt. 28:19
H G shall teach you. . .Luke 12:12
filled with the *H G*. . .Acts 2:4
gift of the *H G*. . .Acts 10:45
H G which is given. . .Rom. 5:5
joy in the *H G*. . .Rom. 14:17
power of the *H G*. . .Rom. 15:13
temple of the *H G*. . .1 Cor. 6:19
power, and in the *H G*. . .1 Thess. 1:5
H G which dwelleth in us. . .2 Tim. 1:14
renewing of the *H G*. . .Titus 3:5
gifts of the *H G*. . .Heb. 2:4
partakers of the *H G*. . .Heb. 6:4

See *Comforter (Holy Spirit)*; *Spirit, Holy*.

447. Home

food of thy household. . .Prov. 27:27
giveth meat to her household. . .Prov. 31:15
snow for her household. . .Prov. 31:21
the ways of her household. . .Prov. 31:27
shew piety at *h*. . .1 Tim. 5:4
chaste, keepers at *h*. . .Titus 2:5

448. Homosexuality

Thou shalt not lie with mankind. . .Lev. 18:22
man also lie with mankind. . .Lev. 20:13
nor a sodomite of the sons. . .Deut. 23:17
God gave them up unto vile affections. . .Rom. 1:26
men with men working that. . .Rom. 1:27
nor adulterers, nor effeminate. . .1 Cor. 6:9
defile themselves with mankind. . .1 Tim. 1:10
going after strange flesh. . .Jude 1:7

449. Honest/ Honestly/Honesty

Let us walk *h'ly*. . .Rom. 13:13
do that which is *h*. . .2 Cor. 13:7
whatsoever things are *h*. . .Phil. 4:8
ye may walk *h'ly*. . .1 Thess. 4:12
all godliness and *h'y*. . .1 Tim. 2:2
h among the Gentiles. . .1 Pet. 2:12

See *Business, Truth.*

450. Honour/ Honoureth

H thy father and thy mother. . .Exod. 20:12
h me I will *h*. . .1 Sam. 2:30
Glory and *h* are in his. . .1 Chron. 16:27
riches and *h* come of thee. . .1 Chron. 29:12
crowned him with glory and *h*. . .Ps. 8:5
h of his name. . .Ps. 66:2
deliver him, and *h* him. . .Ps. 91:15
H the LORD with thy. . .Prov. 3:9
woman retaineth *h*. . .Prov. 11:16
prophet is not without *h*. . .Matt. 13:57
h'eth me with their lips. . .Matt. 15:8
all men should *h* the Son. . .John 5:23

glory, *h*, and peace. . .Rom. 2:10
one vessel unto *h*. . .Rom. 9:21
H all men. . .1 Pet. 2:17

See *Respect.*

451. Hope

So the poor hath *h*. . .Job 5:16
where is now my *h*?. . .Job 17:15

flesh also shall rest in *h*. . .Ps. 16:9
them that *h* in his mercy. . .Ps. 33:18
h thou in God. . .Ps. 42:11
I *h* in thy word. . .Ps. 119:81
h of the righteous. . .Prov. 10:28
H deferred maketh. . .Prov. 13:12
whose *h* the LORD is. . .Jer. 17:7
my *h* in the day of evil. . .Jer. 17:17
both *h* and quietly wait. . .Lam. 3:26
h of the promise. . .Acts 26:6
against *h* believed in *h*. . .Rom. 4:18
h maketh not ashamed. . .Rom. 5:5
we are saved by *h*. . .Rom. 8:24
faith, *h*, charity. . .1 Cor. 13:13
h which is laid up. . .Col. 1:5
the *h* of glory. . .Col. 1:27

452. Hospitality

given to *h*. . .Rom. 12:13
given to *h*. . .1 Tim. 3:2
lover of *h*. . .Titus 1:8
Use *h* one to another. . .1 Pet. 4:9

See *Guests*.

453. Hosts, Lord of

See *Lord of Hosts*.

454. Humble/ Humbled/Humbleness

h themselves, and pray. . .2 Chron. 7:14
thou didst *h* thyself. . .2 Chron. 34:27
forget not the *h*. . .Ps. 10:12
desire of the *h*. . .Ps. 10:17
h spirit. . .Prov. 16:19
contrite and *h* spirit. . .Isa. 57:15
shall *h* himself. . .Matt. 18:4
h himself shall be exalted. . .Matt. 23:12
he *h'd* himself. . .Phil. 2:8
h'ness of mind. . .Col. 3:12
grace unto the *h*. . .James 4:6
H yourselves. . .James 4:10
H yourselves therefore. . .1 Pet. 5:6

See *Humility*.

455. Humiliation

till they were ashamed. . .Judg. 3:25
reproach her not. . .Ruth 2:15
against me my reproach. . .Job 19:5
wait on thee be ashamed. . .Ps. 25:3
Let them be ashamed. . .Ps. 40:14
mine enemies reproach me. . .Ps. 42:10
Turn away my reproach. . .Ps. 119:39
In his *h* his judgment. . .Acts 8:33
hope maketh not ashamed. . .Rom. 5:5

See *Reproach/Reproached/Reproaches/ Reproacheth*.

456. Humility

before honour is *h*. . .Prov. 15:33
before honour is *h*. . .Prov. 18:12
By *h* and the fear. . .Prov. 22:4
all *h* of mind. . .Acts 20:19
be clothed with *h*. . .1 Pet. 5:5

See *Humble/Humbled/Humbleness*.

457. Humor

to make great mirth. . .Neh. 8:12
mirth is heaviness. . .Prov. 14:13
A merry heart maketh. . .Prov. 15:13
merry heart hath. . .Prov. 15:15
merry heart doeth good. . .Prov. 17:22
I will prove thee with mirth. . .Eccles. 2:1
mirth, What doeth it?. . .Eccles. 2:2
in the house of mirth. . .Eccles. 7:4

Then I commended mirth. . .Eccles. 8:15
eat, drink, and be merry. . .Luke 12:19
foolish talking, nor jesting. . .Eph. 5:4
Is any merry?. . .James 5:13

See *Laugh/Laughter.*

458. Hunger, Physical/Hungred

whole assembly with *h*. . .Exod. 16:3
suffered thee to *h*. . .Deut. 8:3
from heaven for their *h*. . .Neh. 9:15
idle soul shall suffer *h*. . .Prov. 19:15
If thine enemy be hungry. . .Prov. 25:21
not *h* nor thirst. . .Isa. 49:10
like to die for *h*. . .Jer. 38:9
he was afterward an *h'red*. . .Matt. 4:2
disciples were an *h'red*. . .Matt. 12:1
when he was an *h'red*. . .Matt. 12:3
For I was an *h'red*. . .Matt. 25:35
when saw we thee an *h'red*. . .Matt. 25:37
For I was an *h'red*. . .Matt. 25:42
when saw we thee an *h'red*. . .Matt. 25:44
if thine enemy *h*. . .Rom. 12:20
we both *h*, and thirst. . .1 Cor. 4:11
if any man *h*. . .1 Cor. 11:34

h and thirst after righteousness. . .Matt. 5:6
Blessed are ye that *h*. . .Luke 6:21
shall never thirst. . .John 4:14
cometh to me shall never *h*. . .John 6:35
If any man thirst. . .John 7:37
They shall *h* no more. . .Rev. 7:16

459. Hunger, Spiritual

panteth my soul after thee. . .Ps. 42:1
My soul thirsteth for God. . .Ps. 42:2
my soul thirsteth for thee. . .Ps. 63:1
Hungry and thirsty, their soul. . .Ps. 107:5
fainteth for thy salvation. . .Ps. 119:81
every one that thirsteth. . .Isa. 55:1
nor a thirst for water. . .Amos 8:11

460. Hurt/Hurtful

h a woman with child. . .Exod. 21:22
he will turn and do you *h*. . .Josh. 24:20
Thy wickedness may *h*. . .Job 35:8
sweareth to his own *h*. . .Ps. 15:4
that devise my *h*. . .Ps. 35:4
do my prophets no harm. . .Ps. 105:15
done thee no harm. . .Prov. 3:30
thereof to their *h*. . .Eccles. 5:13
after other gods to your *h*. . .Jer. 7:6
they have not *h* me. . .Dan. 6:22

it shall not *h* them. . .Mark 16:18

foolish and *h'ful* lusts. . .1 Tim. 6:9

he that will harm you. . .1 Pet. 3:13

not be *h* of the second death. . .Rev. 2:11

h men five months. . .Rev. 9:10

love their *h's*. . .Titus 2:4

to your own *h's*. . .1 Pet. 3:1

Likewise, ye *h's*. . .1 Pet. 3:7

See *Family, Marriage/Marry/Marrying, Spouse/Spouses.*

461. Husband/ Husbands

gave also unto her *h*. . .Gen. 3:6

desire shall be to thy *h*. . .Gen. 3:16

crown to her *h*. . .Prov. 12:4

heart of her *h* doth. . .Prov. 31:11

h also, and he praiseth. . .Prov. 31:28

thy Maker is thine *h*. . .Isa. 54:5

shall put away her *h*. . .Mark 10:12

woman have her own *h*. . .1 Cor. 7:2

wife depart from her *h*. . .1 Cor. 7:10

thou shalt save thy *h*?. . .1 Cor. 7:16

she may please her *h*. . .1 Cor. 7:34

if her *h* be dead. . .1 Cor. 7:39

unto your own *h's*. . .Eph. 5:22

H's, love your wives. . .Eph. 5:25

she reverence her *h*. . .Eph. 5:33

h of one wife. . .1 Tim. 3:2

462. Hypocrite/ Hypocrite's/ Hypocrites/ Hypocrisy/Hypocrisies

h's hope shall perish. . .Job 8:13

h shall not come before him. . .Job 13:16

h with his mouth. . .Prov. 11:9

h's do in the synagogues. . .Matt. 6:2

h, of a sad countenance. . .Matt. 6:16

h, first cast out. . .Matt. 7:5

scribes and Pharisees, *h's*!. . .Matt. 23:13

scribes and Pharisees, *h's*!. . .Matt. 23:29

Speaking lies in *h'sy*. . .1 Tim. 4:2

partiality, and without *h'sy*. . .James 3:17

h'sies, and envies. . .1 Pet. 2:1

463. "I Am" Statements of Jesus

Jesus' "I am" statements were based on Exodus 3:14, the name with which God described Himself to Moses when the prophet sought to identify Him to His people. When Jesus used this statement in John 8:58, His enemies clearly understood He was claiming to be God.

I that speak unto thee *a*. . .John 4:26
I a the bread of life. . .John 6:35
I a the light of the world. . .John 8:12
I a from above. . .John 8:23
Before Abraham was, *I a*. . .John 8:58
I a the door. . .John 10:9
I a the good shepherd. . .John 10:11
I a the Son of God?. . .John 10:36
I a the resurrection. . .John 11:25
may believe that *I a* he. . .John 13:19
I a the way. . .John 14:6
I a the true vine. . .John 15:1
saith unto them, *I a* he. . .John 18:5
that *I a* he. . .John 18:8
I a Alpha and Omega. . .Rev. 1:8

See *Name of Jesus/Name's*.

464. Idle/Idleness

Go to the ant, thou sluggard. . .Prov. 6:6
The soul of the sluggard. . .Prov. 13:4
i soul shall suffer hunger. . .Prov. 19:15
sluggard will not plow. . .Prov. 20:4
The sluggard is wiser. . .Prov. 26:16
eateth not the bread of *i'ness*. . .Prov. 31:27
through *i'ness* of the hands. . .Eccles. 10:18
every *i* word that men. . .Matt. 12:36
they learn to be *i*. . .1 Tim. 5:13

See *Slothful/Slothfulness*.

465. Idol/Idolater/ Idolaters/Idols

Turn ye not unto *i's*. . .Lev. 19:4
Ye shall make you no *i's*. . .Lev. 26:1

gods of the people are *i's*. . .1 Chron. 16:26
they served their *i's*. . .Ps. 106:36
Their land also is full of *i's*. . .Isa. 2:8
i he shall utterly abolish. . .Isa. 2:18
shall cast away his *i's*. . .Isa. 31:7
turn yourselves from your *i's*. . .Ezek. 14:6
abstain from pollutions of *i's*. . .Acts 15:20
from meats offered to *i's*. . .Acts 15:29
or covetous, or an *i'ater*. . .1 Cor. 5:11
nor *i'aters*, nor adulterers. . .1 Cor. 6:9
things offered unto *i's*. . .1 Cor. 8:1
i is nothing in the world. . .1 Cor. 8:4
conscience of the *i*. . .1 Cor. 8:7
that the *i* is any thing. . .1 Cor. 10:19

See *False Gods, Idolatry, Superstition/Superstitious*.

466. Idolatry

is as iniquity and *i*. . .1 Sam. 15:23
wholly given to *i*. . .Acts 17:16
flee from *i*. . .1 Cor. 10:14
I, witchcraft, hatred. . .Gal. 5:20
covetousness, which is *i*. . .Col. 3:5

See *False Gods, Idol/Idolater/Idolaters/Idols, Superstition/Superstitious*.

467. Illegitimacy

with child by whoredom. . .Gen. 38:24
A bastard shall not enter. . .Deut. 23:2
the son of an harlot. . .Judg. 11:1

468. Imagination/ Imaginations

i of the thoughts. . .Gen. 6:5
i of man's heart. . .Gen. 8:21
i of mine heart. . .Deut. 29:19
I know their *i*. . .Deut. 31:21
i's of the thoughts. . .1 Chron. 28:9
i of the thoughts. . .1 Chron. 29:18
imagine mischiefs in their heart. . .Ps. 140:2
deviseth wicked *i's*. . .Prov. 6:18
i of their evil heart. . .Jer. 3:17
proud in the *i*. . .Luke 1:51
vain in their *i's*. . .Rom. 1:21
Casting down *i's*. . .2 Cor. 10:5

469. Immortal/ Immortality

honour and *i'ity*. . .Rom. 2:7
mortal must put on *i'ity*. . .1 Cor. 15:53
shall have put on *i'ity*. . .1 Cor. 15:54
King eternal, *i*, invisible. . .1 Tim. 1:17
Who only hath *i'ity*. . .1 Tim. 6:16
brought life and *i'ity*. . .2 Tim. 1:10

See *Eternal Life, Everlasting Life/Life Everlasting, Life Eternal, Salvation.*

470. Impatience

he that is hasty of spirit. . .Prov. 14:29

every one that is hasty. . .Prov. 21:5
maketh haste to be rich. . .Prov. 28:20
hasty in his words?. . .Prov. 29:20
hasty to utter any thing. . .Eccles. 5:2
Be not hasty in thy spirit. . .Eccles. 7:9

471. Impossible

nothing shall be *i* unto you. . .Matt. 17:20
With men this is *i*. . .Matt. 19:26
with God nothing shall be *i*. . .Luke 1:37
i but that offences. . .Luke 17:1
For it is *i*. . .Heb. 6:4
i for God to lie. . .Heb. 6:18
i to please him. . .Heb. 11:6

472. Imprisonment

was there in the prison. . .Gen. 39:20
were bound in the prison. . .Gen. 40:5
shall be kept in prison. . .Gen. 42:16
bound him with fetters. . .Judg. 16:21
my soul out of prison. . .Ps. 142:7
He was taken from prison. . .Isa. 53:8
opening of the prison. . .Isa. 61:1

court of the prison. . .Jer. 32:2
John was cast into prison. . .Matt. 4:12
thou be cast into prison. . .Matt. 5:25
beheaded John in the prison. . .Matt. 14:10
I was in prison. . .Matt. 25:36
committed them to prison. . .Acts 8:3
was kept in prison. . .Acts 12:5
into the inner prison. . .Acts 16:24

See *Prisoner/Prisoners.*

473. Impurity

clean thing out of an unclean?. . .Job 14:4
purge away thy dross. . .Isa. 1:25
common or unclean. . .Acts 10:14
any man common or unclean. . .Act 10:28
gave them up to uncleanness. . .Rom. 1:24
servants to uncleanness. . .Rom. 6:19
uncleanness and fornication. . .2 Cor. 12:21
fornication, uncleanness. . .Gal. 5:19
to work all uncleanness. . .Eph. 4:19
and all uncleanness. . .Eph. 5:3
nor unclean person. . .Eph. 5:5
uncleanness, inordinate affection. . .Col. 3:5
not called us unto uncleanness. . .1 Thess. 4:7

See *Adultery, Defile/Defiled/Defileth,
Fornication/ Fornications.*

474. Impute/Imputed/ Imputeth/Imputing

Lᴏʀᴅ *i'eth* not iniquity. . .Ps. 32:2
God *i'eth* righteousness. . .Rom. 4:6
Lord will not *i* sin. . .Rom. 4:8
righteousness might be *i'ed*. . .Rom. 4:11
i'ed to him for righteousness. . .Rom. 4:22
that it was *i'ed* to him. . .Rom. 4:23
whom it shall be *i'ed*. . .Rom. 4:24
i'ed when there is no law. . .Rom. 5:13
not *i'ing* their trespasses. . .2 Cor. 5:19
it was *i'ed* unto him. . .James 2:23

475. Incest

near of kin to him. . .Lev. 18:6
nakedness of thy father's wife. . .Lev. 18:8
nakedness of thy sister. . .Lev. 18:9
nakedness of thy son's daughter. . .Lev. 18:10
she is thy sister. . .Lev. 18:11
nakedness of thy father's sister. . .Lev. 18:12
nakedness of thy mother's sister. . .Lev. 18:13
approach to his wife. . .Lev. 18:14
nakedness of thy daughter in law. . .Lev. 18:15
nakedness of thy brother's wife. . .Lev. 18:16
a woman and her daughter. . .Lev. 18:17
a wife to her sister. . .Lev. 18:18
hath humbled his sister. . .Ezek. 22:11

476. Increase

*Increase was whatever the land or cattle, or
even their investments, produced. It was one
way in which God blessed Israel. In the New
Testament, increase is often referred to in
relation to the spread of the gospel.*

usury of him, or *i*. . .Lev. 25:36
nor gather in our *i*. . .Lev. 25:20
land shall yield her *i*. . .Lev. 26:4
that ye may *i* mightily. . .Deut. 6:3
i of thy kine. . .Deut. 7:13
tithe all the *i*. . .Deut. 14:22
i of thine house. . .1 Sam. 2:33
yieldeth much *i*. . .Neh. 9:37
i unto the caterpiller. . .Ps. 78:46
firstfruits of all thine *i*. . .Prov. 3:9
i of his government. . .Isa. 9:7
God gave the *i*. . .1 Cor. 3:6
i of the body. . .Eph. 4:16
i of God. . .Col. 2:19

477. Indignation

Pour out thine *i*. . .Ps. 69:24
anger, wrath, and *i*. . .Ps. 78:49
i and thy wrath. . .Ps. 102:10
hast filled me with *i*. . .Jer. 15:17
i of the Lord. . .Mic. 7:9
stand before his *i*?. . .Nah. 1:6
were moved with *i*. . .Matt. 20:24
some that had *i*. . .Mark 14:4
unrighteousness, *i*. . .Rom. 2:8
yea, what *i*. . .2 Cor. 7:11

judgment and fiery *i*. . .Heb. 10:27
cup of his *i*. . .Rev. 14:10

478. Industry

industrious, he made him ruler. . .1 Kings 11:28
the diligent maketh rich. . .Prov. 10:4
diligent shall bear rule. . .Prov. 12:24
substance of a diligent man. . .Prov. 12:27
diligent in his business?. . .Prov. 22:29

See *Diligent/Diligently/Diligence*.

479. Infertility

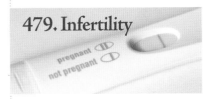

because she was barren. . .Gen. 25:21
male or female barren. . .Deut. 7:14
thou art barren. . .Judg. 13:3
barren woman to keep house. . .Ps. 113:9
and the barren womb. . .Prov. 30:16
Elisabeth was barren. . .Luke 1:7
Blessed are the barren. . .Luke 23:29
barren that bearest not. . .Gal. 4:27

480. Influence

*Christians should not give in to the influence
of other people at the cost of their own faith.*

when men shall revile you. . .Matt. 5:11
light so shine before men. . .Matt. 5:16
men should do to you. . .Matt. 7:12

hated of all men. . .Matt. 10:22
confess me before men. . .Matt. 10:32
even as ye were led. . .1 Cor. 12:2
if I yet pleased men. . .Gal. 1:10
not as pleasing men. . .1 Thess. 2:4
please them well. . .Titus 2:9

481. Inheritance

their land for an *i*. . .Deut. 4:38
the Lord is his *i*. . .Deut. 10:9
portion is his people. . .Deut. 32:9
part and thine *i*. . .Num. 18:20
portion of a wicked man. . .Job 27:13
portion of mine *i*. . .Ps. 16:5
i shall be for ever. . .Ps. 37:18
i shall be ours. . .Mark 12:7
gave him none *i*. . .Acts 7:5
i be of the law. . .Gal. 3:18
we have obtained an *i*. . .Eph. 1:11
glory of his *i*. . .Eph. 1:18
i in the kingdom. . .Eph. 5:5
partakers of the *i*. . .Col. 1:12
receive for an *i*. . .Heb. 11:8

482. Iniquity

i of the fathers. . .Exod. 20:5
without *i*, just and right. . .Deut. 32:4

O Lord, pardon mine *i*. . .Ps. 25:11
mine *i* have I not hid. . .Ps. 32:5
I was shapen in *i*. . .Ps. 51:5
If I regard *i*. . .Ps. 66:18
workers of *i* do flourish. . .Ps. 92:7
They also do no *i*. . .Ps. 119:3
He that soweth *i*. . .Prov. 22:8
her *i* is pardoned. . .Isa. 40:2
i of us all. . .Isa. 53:6
canst not look on *i*. . .Hab. 1:13
ye that work *i*. . .Matt. 7:23
mystery of *i*. . .2 Thess. 2:7
and hated *i*. . .Heb. 1:9

See *Sin.*

483. Innocent

i and righteous. . .Exod. 23:7
i blood be not shed. . .Deut. 19:10
slay an *i* person. . .Deut. 27:25
wilt not hold me *i*. . .Job 9:28
I shall be *i*. . .Ps. 19:13
rich shall not be *i*. . .Prov. 28:20
betrayed the *i* blood. . .Matt. 27:4
I am *i* of the blood. . .Matt. 27:24

484. Insects

it may become lice. . .Exod. 8:16
locust went up over. . .Exod. 10:14
beetle after his kind. . .Lev. 11:22
hornet before you. . .Josh. 24:12
dead dog, after a flea. . .1 Sam. 24:14
consume away like a moth. . .Ps. 39:11
increase unto the caterpiller. . .Ps. 78:46
Go to the ant. . .Prov. 6:6

ants are a people. . .Prov. 30:25
locust hath eaten. . .Joel 2:25
moth and rust doth. . .Matt. 6:19
strain at a gnat. . .Matt. 23:24
offer him a scorpion?. . .Luke 11:12
neither moth corrupteth. . .Luke 12:33
torment of a scorpion. . .Rev. 9:5

485. Instruction

seeing thou hatest *i*. . .Ps. 50:17
i of wisdom. . .Prov. 1:3
despise wisdom and *i*. . .Prov. 1:7
i of a father. . .Prov. 4:1
Take fast hold of *i*. . .Prov. 4:13
shall die without *i*. . .Prov. 5:23
Hear *i*, and be wise. . .Prov. 8:33
Give *i* to a wise man. . .Prov. 9:9
life that keepeth *i*. . .Prov. 10:17
Whoso loveth *i*. . .Prov. 12:1
He that refuseth *i*. . .Prov. 15:32
i of fools is folly. . .Prov. 16:22
i that causeth to err. . .Prov. 19:27
thine heart unto *i*. . .Prov. 23:12
i in righteousness. . .2 Tim. 3:16

486. Instruments of Musick

handle the harp and organ. . .Gen. 4:21
with tabret, and with harp?. . .Gen. 31:27
psaltery, and a tabret. . .1 Sam. 10:5
with joy, and with *i o m*. . .1 Sam. 18:6
fir wood, even on harps. . .2 Sam. 6:5
i o m, psalteries and harps. . .1 Chron. 15:16
cornet, and with trumpets. . .1 Chron. 15:28
musical instruments of God. . .1 Chron. 16:42
cymbals and *i o m*. . .2 Chron. 5:13
the singers with *i o m*. . .2 Chron. 23:13
could skill of *i o m*. . .2 Chron. 34:12
With trumpets and sound. . .Ps. 98:6
men, as musical instruments. . .Eccles. 2:8
cornet, flute, harp, sackbut. . .Dan. 3:7
neither were *i o m*. . .Dan. 6:18

See *Musick*.

487. Integrity

walked, in *i* of heart. . .1 Kings 9:4
still he holdeth fast his *i*. . .Job 2:3
still retain thine *i*?. . .Job 2:9
not remove mine *i*. . .Job 27:5
God may know mine *i*. . .Job 31:6
according to mine *i*. . .Ps. 7:8
i and uprightness. . .Ps. 25:21
walked in mine *i*. . .Ps. 26:1

upholdest me in mine *i*. . .Ps. 41:12

i of the upright. . .Prov. 11:3

walketh in his *i*. . .Prov. 19:1

walketh in his *i*. . .Prov. 20:7

488. Intercession/ Intercessions

my prayer returned. . .Ps. 35:13

i for the transgressors. . .Isa. 53:12

continually to prayer. . .Acts 6:4

prayer was made. . .Acts 12:5

maketh *i* for us. . .Rom. 8:26

i for the saints. . .Rom. 8:27

maketh *i* for us. . .Rom. 8:34

maketh *i* to God. . .Rom. 11:2

Praying always with all. . .Eph. 6:18

supplications, prayers, *i's*. . .1 Tim. 2:1

liveth to make *i*. . .Heb. 7:25

pray one for another. . .James 5:16

489. Israelites

all the *I* passed over. . .Josh. 3:17

I returned unto Ai. . .Josh. 8:24

I for an inheritance. . .Josh. 13:6

dwell among the *I*. . .Josh. 13:13

I went down. . .1 Sam. 13:20

I were gathered. . .1 Sam. 25:1

I pitched by a fountain. . .1 Sam. 29:1

I rose up. . .2 Kings 3:24

I, the priests, Levites. . .1 Chron. 9:2

Who are *I*. . .Rom. 9:4

Are they *I*?. . .2 Cor. 11:22

See *Hebrew/Hebrews*.

490. Jealous/Jealousy

God am a *j* God. . .Exod. 20:5

provoked him to *j'y*. . .Deut. 32:16

I will move them to *j'y*. . .Deut. 32:21

moved him to *j'y*. . .Ps. 78:58

j'y is the rage. . .Prov. 6:34

j'y is cruel. . .Song of Sol. 8:6

j for my holy name. . .Ezek. 39:25

j for his land. . .Joel 2:18

to provoke them to *j'y*. . .Rom. 11:11

provoke the Lord to *j'y*?. . .1 Cor. 10:22

with godly *j'y*. . .2 Cor. 11:2

491. Jesus Christ
As God

J C is the Son of God. . .Acts 8:37

one Lord *J C*. . .1 Cor. 8:6

J C is Lord. . .Phil. 2:11

J C the same. . .Heb.13:8

Belief in

in the name of *J C*. . .Acts 2:38

Believe on the Lord *J C*. . .Acts 16:31

by faith of *J C*. . .Rom. 3:22

Christian life and

through *J C* our Lord. . .Rom. 6:11
which is *J C*. . .1 Cor. 3:11
through our Lord *J C*. . .1 Cor. 15:57
to himself by *J C*. . .2 Cor. 5:18
the day of *J C*. . .Phil. 1:6
Spirit of *J C*. . .Phil. 1:19

Eternal life through

true God, and *J C*. . .John 17:3
eternal life through *J C*. . .Rom. 6:23

Grace of

truth came by *J C*. . .John 1:17
grace of our Lord *J C*. . .2 Cor. 8:9

Redemption of

J C, and him crucified. . .1 Cor. 2:2
cross of our Lord *J C*. . .Gal. 6:14
body of *J C*. . .Heb. 10:10
blood of *J C*. . .1 John 1:7
J C the righteous. . .1 John 2:1

See *Deity of Christ, Messiah.*

492. Jew/Jews

was a certain *J.*. . .Esther 2:5
Mordecai the *J.*. . .Esther 5:13
great among the *J's*. . .Esther 10:3
of a *J* his brother. . .Jer. 34:9
J, saying, We will go. . .Zech. 8:23
thou, being a *J.*. . .John 4:9
J to keep company. . .Acts 10:28
J named Aquila. . .Acts 18:2
J named Apollos. . .Acts 18:24
knew that he was a *J.*. . .Acts 19:34

J, born in Tarsus. . .Acts 22:3
to the *J* first. . .Rom. 1:16
he is not a *J.*. . .Rom. 2:28
then hath the *J?*. . .Rom. 3:1
neither *J* nor Greek. . .Gal. 3:28

See *Hebrew/Hebrews.*

493. Jewel/Jewels

j's of silver. . .Gen. 24:53
j's of gold. . .Exod. 3:22
j's of gold. . .Exod. 35:22
j's of gold, chains. . .Num. 31:50
j's of gold. . .1 Sam. 6:8
precious *j's*. . .2 Chron. 20:25
j of gold in a swine's. . .Prov. 11:22
herself with her *j's*. . .Isa. 61:10
j on thy forehead. . .Ezek. 16:12
make up my *j's*. . .Mal. 3:17

See *Jewelry.*

494. Jewelry

bracelets for her hands. . .Gen. 24:22
earring and bracelets. . .Gen. 24:30
signet, and thy bracelets. . .Gen. 38:18

ring from his hand. . .Gen. 41:42
Break off the golden earrings. . .Exod. 32:2
bracelets, and earrings. . .Exod. 35:22
gold, chains, and bracelets. . .Num. 31:50
earrings of his prey. . .Judg. 8:24
sealed with the king's ring. . .Esther 8:8
an earring of gold. . .Job 42:11
ornament of fine gold. . .Prov. 25:12
their tinkling ornaments. . .Isa. 3:18
earrings and her jewels. . .Hosea 2:13
ring on his hand. . .Luke 15:22
man with a gold ring. . .James 2:2

See *Jewel/Jewels.*

495. Jobs

In the biblical era, people worked at many different trades and jobs. Here is a sampling of some of their lifework.

Deborah Rebekah's nurse died. . .Gen. 35:8
against the chief of the bakers. . .Gen. 40:2
shepherds, for their trade hath. . .Gen. 46:32
do the office of a midwife. . .Exod. 1:16
embroiderer, in blue, and in purple. . .Exod. 35:35
the work of the apothecary. . .Exod. 37:29
confectionaries, and to be cooks. . .1 Sam. 8:13
carpenters, and masons: and they built. . .2 Sam. 5:11
watchman called unto the porter. . .2 Sam. 18:26
a wise man, and a scribe. . .1 Chron. 27:32

skilful to work in gold. . .2 Chron. 2:14
overseers to set the people. . .2 Chron. 2:18
plowman plow all day to sow?. . .Isa. 28:24
thy mariners, and thy pilots, thy calkers. . .Ezek. 27:27
all the pilots of the sea. . .Ezek. 27:29
silversmith, which made silver shrines. . .Acts 19:24
townclerk had appeased the people. . .Acts 19:35
potter power over the clay. . .Rom. 9:21

See *Employment, Labour, Work.*

496. Joking
See *Humor, Laugh/Laughter.*

497. Joy
j, of the Lᴏʀᴅ is your strength. . .Neh. 8:10
j, and honour. . .Esther 8:16
see his face with *j.* . .Job 33:26
shouted for *j*?. . .Job 38:7
ever shout for *j.* . .Ps. 5:11
fulness of *j.* . .Ps. 16:11
j cometh in the morning. . .Ps. 30:5
hear *j* and gladness. . .Ps. 51:8
j of thy salvation. . .Ps. 51:12
shall reap in *j.* . .Ps. 126:5
A man hath *j.* . .Prov. 15:23
good tidings of great *j.* . .Luke 2:10
leap for *j.* . .Luke 6:23
j shall be in heaven. . .Luke 15:7
your *j* might be full. . .John 15:11
we also *j* in God. . .Rom. 5:11
j, peace, longsuffering. . .Gal. 5:22
count it all *j.* . .James 1:2

See *Joyful.*

498. Joyful

be *j* in thee. . .Ps. 5:11
my soul shall be *j*. . .Ps. 35:9
j noise unto God. . .Ps. 66:1
j mother of children. . .Ps. 113:9
j in their King. . .Ps. 149:2
Let the saints be *j*. . .Ps. 149:5
my soul shall be *j*. . .Isa. 61:10
j in all our tribulation. . .2 Cor. 7:4

See *Joy.*

499. Jubile/Jubilee

God proclaimed every fiftieth year a jubile (or jubilee). In these celebration years, no crops were planted, giving the land a rest, and all property in Israel that had been sold was to be returned to the original owner. Slaves were freed in the year of jubilee.

be a *j* unto you. . .Lev. 25:10
j shall that fiftieth year be. . .Lev. 25:11
until the year of *j*. . .Lev. 25:28
not go out in the *j*. . .Lev. 25:30
unto the year of *j*. . .Lev. 25:40
j: and the price. . .Lev. 25:50
from the year of *j*. . .Lev. 27:17

j the field shall return. . .Lev. 27:24
j of the children of Israel. . .Num. 36:4

500. Judge/Judgest/Judgeth/Judging

j thy neighbour. . .Lev. 19:15
j not for man. . .2 Chron. 19:6
do ye *j* uprightly. . .Ps. 58:1
J not, that ye be. . .Matt. 7:1
j'ing the twelve tribes. . .Matt. 19:28
J not according to. . .John 7:24
j after the flesh. . .John 8:15
thou *j'st* another. . .Rom. 2:1
man, that *j'st* them. . .Rom. 2:3
not *j* him that eateth. . .Rom. 14:3
j thy brother?. . .Rom. 14:10
spiritual *j'th* all things. . .1 Cor. 2:15
j not mine own self. . .1 Cor. 4:3
we shall *j* angels?. . .1 Cor. 6:3
j between his brethren?. . .1 Cor. 6:5

501. Judge, God as/Judgeth

Shall not the *J*. . .Gen. 18:25
Lord shall *j*. . .Deut. 32:36

wilt thou not *j* them?. . .2 Chron. 20:12

The Lᴏʀᴅ shall *j*. . .Ps. 7:8

he shall *j* the world. . .Ps. 9:8

j the fatherless. . .Ps. 10:18

God is the *j*, . . .Ps. 75:7

j the people righteously. . .Ps. 96:10

j among the nations. . .Isa. 2:4

Lᴏʀᴅ is our *j*. . .Isa. 33:22

Father *j'th* no man. . .John 5:22

as I hear, I *j*. . .John 5:30

yet if I *j*. . .John 8:16

not to *j* the world. . .John 12:47

j the secrets of men. . .Rom. 2:16

See *Judgment, God's/Judgments.*

502. Judgment, Day of

Gomorrha in the *d o j*. . .Matt. 10:15

Sidon at the *d o j*. . .Matt. 11:22

account thereof in the *d o j*. . .Matt. 12:36

day of wrath and revelation. . .Rom. 2:5

unjust unto the *d o j*. . .2 Pet. 2:9

j and perdition. . .2 Pet. 3:7

boldness in the *d o j*. . .1 John 4:17

j of the great day. . .Jude 1:6

See *Judgment, God's/Judgments.*

503. Judgment, God's/Judgments

Ye shall do my *j's*. . .Lev. 18:4

the *j* is God's. . .Deut. 1:17

all his ways are *j*. . .Deut. 32:4

shall not stand in the *j*. . .Ps. 1:5

righteousness and *j*. . .Ps. 33:5

Justice and *j*. . .Ps. 89:14

every work into *j*. . .Eccles. 12:14

j; not in thine anger. . .Jer. 10:24

j run down as waters. . .Amos 5:24

in danger of the *j*. . .Matt. 5:22

j unto victory. . .Matt. 12:20

For *j* I am come. . .John 9:39

j of God. . .Rom. 1:32

j was by one to. . .Rom. 5:16

j seat of Christ. . .Rom. 14:10

after this the *j*. . .Heb. 9:27

See *Judge, God as/Judgeth; Judgment, Day of.*

504. Judgment, Human

do justice and *j*. . .Gen. 18:19

j of thy poor. . .Exod. 23:6

unrighteousness in *j*. . .Lev. 19:35

not pervert the *j*. . .Deut. 24:17

perverted *j*. . .1 Sam. 8:3

guide in *j*. . .Ps. 25:9

Teach me good *j*. . .Ps. 119:66

I have done *j*. . .Ps. 119:121

wisdom, justice, and *j*. . .Prov. 1:3
the righteous in *j*. . .Prov. 18:5
To do justice and *j*. . .Prov. 21:3
understand not *j*. . .Prov. 28:5
what *j* ye judge. . .Matt. 7:2
j, mercy, and faith. . .Matt. 23:23

505. Justice

in plenty of *j*. . .Job 37:23
do *j* to the afflicted. . .Ps. 82:3
J and judgment. . .Ps. 89:14
done judgment and *j*. . .Ps. 119:121
wisdom, *j*, and judgment. . .Prov. 1:3
princes decree *j*. . .Prov. 8:15
To do *j* and judgment. . .Prov. 21:3
None calleth for *j*. . .Isa. 59:4
execute judgment and *j*. . .Jer. 23:5

See *Fairness*.

506. Justify/ Justification/Justified/ Justifieth

I will not *j* the wicked. . .Exod. 23:7
thou shalt be *j'ied*. . .Matt. 12:37
to his house *j'ied*. . .Luke 18:14
j'ied from all things. . .Acts 13:39

the law shall be *j'ied*. . .Rom. 2:13
shall no flesh be *j'ied*. . .Rom. 3:20
j'ied freely by his grace. . .Rom. 3:24
j'ied by faith. . .Rom. 3:28
j the circumcision. . .Rom. 3:30
j'ieth the ungodly. . .Rom. 4:5
raised again for our *j'ication*. . .Rom. 4:25
j'ied by faith. . .Rom. 5:1
j'ication of life. . .Rom. 5:18
whom he *j'ied*. . .Rom. 8:30
not *j'ied* by the works. . .Gal. 2:16
no man is *j'ied*. . .Gal. 3:11
might be *j'ied* by faith. . .Gal. 3:24
j'ied by his grace. . .Titus 3:7
works a man is *j'ied*. . .James 2:24

507. Kidnapping

he that stealeth a man. . .Exod. 21:16
stealing any of his brethren. . .Deut. 24:7

508. Kill/Killed/ Killeth

Thou shalt not *k*. . .Exod. 20:13
he that *k'eth* any man. . .Lev. 24:17
he that *k'eth* a beast. . .Lev. 24:18
Whoso *k'eth* any person. . .Num. 35:30
k his neighbour unawares. . .Deut. 4:42
k'eth any person unawares. . .Josh. 20:3
The Lord *k'eth*. . .1 Sam. 2:6
A time to *k*. . .Eccles. 3:3
them which *k* the body. . .Matt. 10:28
they shall *k* him. . .Matt. 17:23
and shall *k* you. . .Matt. 24:9
go ye about to *k* me?. . .John 7:19
k'ed the Prince of life. . .Acts 3:15

day and night to *k* him. . .Acts 9:24
k'ed the just. . .James 5:6

See *Murder/Murders.*

509. Kind/Kindly/ Kindness

his merciful *k'ness* is great. . .Ps. 117:2
a man is his *k'ness*. . .Prov. 19:22
the law of *k'ness*. . .Prov. 31:26
of great *k'ness*. . .Joel 2:13
k unto the unthankful. . .Luke 6:35
Be *k'ly* affectioned. . .Rom. 12:10
suffereth long, and is *k*. . .1 Cor. 13:4
longsuffering, by *k'ness*. . .2 Cor. 6:6
grace in his *k'ness*. . .Eph. 2:7
k one to another. . .Eph. 4:32
k'ness, humbleness of mind. . .Col. 3:12
k'ness and love of God. . .Titus 3:4
to godliness brotherly *k'ness*. . .2 Pet. 1:7

510. King, Earthly

Melchizedek *k* of Salem. . .Gen. 14:18
Pharaoh *k* of Egypt. . .Gen. 41:46
no *k* in Israel. . .Judg. 17:6
Give us a *k*. . .1 Sam. 8:6

k whom ye have chosen. . .1 Sam. 12:13
hid from the *k*. . .1 Kings 10:3
k Solomon exceeded. . .1 Kings 10:23
k Ahasuerus sat on. . .Esther 1:2
giveth he to his *k*. . .Ps. 18:50
k trusteth in the LORD. . .Ps. 21:7
k shall rejoice in God. . .Ps. 63:11
wise *k* scattereth the wicked. . .Prov. 20:26
great *k*, the *k* of Assyria. . .Isa. 36:4
k of Assyria departed. . .Isa. 37:37
Nebuchadnezzar the *k*. . .Jer. 27:8

See *Government, Leader/Leaders, Ruler/Rulers.*

511. King, God as

your God was your *k*. . .1 Sam. 12:12
The LORD is *K*. . .Ps. 10:16
K of glory shall come in. . .Ps. 24:7
K over all the earth. . .Ps. 47:2
Holy One of Israel is our *k*. . .Ps. 89:18
great *K* above all gods. . .Ps. 95:3
the *K*, the LORD of hosts. . .Isa. 6:5
the LORD is our *k*. . .Isa. 33:22
an everlasting *k*. . .Jer. 10:10
righteous Branch, and a *K*. . .Jer. 23:5
behold, thy *K* cometh. . .John 12:15
K eternal, immortal. . .1 Tim. 1:17
K of *k*, and Lord of lords. . .1 Tim. 6:15

512. Kingdom of God

seek ye first the *k o G*. . .Matt. 6:33
enter into the *k o G*. . .Matt. 19:24
k o G is at hand. . .Mark 1:15
mystery of the *k o G*. . .Mark 4:11
enter into the *k o G*. . .Mark 9:47

of such is the *k o G*. . .Mark 10:14
enter into the *k o G*. . .Mark 10:25
yours is the *k o G*. . .Luke 6:20
preach the *k o G*. . .Luke 9:2
seek ye the *k o G*. . .Luke 12:31
cannot see the *k o G*. . .John 3:3
k o G is not in word. . .1 Cor. 4:20
shall not inherit the *k o G*?. . .1 Cor. 6:9
cannot inherit the *k o G*. . .1 Cor. 15:50

See *Kingdom of Heaven*.

---

513. Kingdom of Heaven

k o h is at hand. . .Matt. 3:2
theirs is the *k o h*. . .Matt. 5:3
theirs is the *k o h*. . .Matt. 5:10
enter into the *k o h*. . .Matt. 5:20
enter into the *k o h*. . .Matt. 7:21
mysteries of the *k o h*. . .Matt. 13:11
keys of the *k o h*. . .Matt. 16:19
greatest in the *k o h*?. . .Matt. 18:1
enter into the *k o h*. . .Matt. 18:3
of such is the *k o h*. . .Matt. 19:14
shut up the *k o h*. . .Matt. 23:13

See *Kingdom of God*.

---

514. Knowing God

know that my redeemer liveth. . .Job 19:25
they that know thy name. . .Ps. 9:10
know that I am God. . .Ps. 46:10
Know ye that the Lord. . .Ps. 100:3
delight to know my ways. . .Isa. 58:2
thou shalt know the Lord. . .Hosea 2:20
for all shall know me. . .Heb. 8:11
know that we know him. . .1 John 2:3
He that saith, I know him. . .1 John 2:4
know we that we are in him. . .1 John 2:5
dwelleth in him, and he in him. . .1 John 3:24

See *Conversion*, *New Life*, *Salvation*.

---

515. Knowledge

Lord is a God of *k*. . .1 Sam. 2:3
workers of iniquity no *k*?. . .Ps. 14:4
good judgment and *k*. . .Ps. 119:66
Such *k* is too wonderful. . .Ps. 139:6
is the beginning of *k*. . .Prov. 1:7
find the *k* of God. . .Prov. 2:5
k rather than choice gold. . .Prov. 8:10
k of the holy. . .Prov. 9:10
Wise men lay up *k*. . .Prov. 10:14
loveth instruction loveth *k*. . .Prov. 12:1
To give *k* of salvation. . .Luke 1:77
law is the *k* of sin. . .Rom. 3:20

to another the word of *k*. . .1 Cor. 12:8
whether there be *k*. . .1 Cor. 13:8
against the *k* of God. . .2 Cor. 10:5

See *Learn/Learned/Learning*.

516. Labour

Six days shalt thou *l*. . .Exod. 20:9
they *l* in vain. . .Ps. 127:1
l of the righteous. . .Prov. 10:16
he that gathereth by *l*. . .Prov. 13:11
In all *l* there is profit. . .Prov. 14:23
L not to be rich. . .Prov. 23:4
good reward for their *l*. . .Eccles. 4:9
good of all his *l*. . .Eccles. 5:18
l for that which satisfieth not?. . .Isa. 55:2
all ye that *l*. . .Matt. 11:28
L not for the meat. . .John 6:27
according to his own *l*. . .1 Cor. 3:8

See *Jobs*, *Work*.

517. Lack/Lacked

thou hast *l'ed* nothing. . .Deut. 2:7
young lions do *l*. . .Ps. 34:10
unto the poor shall not *l*. . .Prov. 28:27
any among them that *l'ed*. . .Acts 4:34
gathered little had no *l*. . .2 Cor. 8:15

See *Beggar/Begging*; *Poor, the*; *Poverty*.

518. Lamb of God

In the Old Testament era, a lamb was sacrificed during Passover and, later, as part of the regular temple sin offerings. This picture of Christ's sacrifice was fulfilled in the Crucifixion. The book of Revelation describes Jesus as the glorified Lamb.

every man a lamb. . .Exod. 12:3
offer a lamb for his offering. . .Lev. 3:7
as a lamb to the slaughter. . .Isa. 53:7
Behold the *L o G*. . .John 1:29
Behold the *L o G*!. . .John 1:36
a lamb without blemish. . .1 Pet. 1:19
Lamb as it had been slain. . .Rev. 5:6
fell down before the Lamb. . .Rev. 5:8
Worthy is the Lamb. . .Rev. 5:12
unto the Lamb for ever. . .Rev. 5:13
marriage supper of the Lamb. . .Rev. 19:9

519. Lame

was *l* of his feet. . .2 Sam. 4:4
l on his feet. . .2 Sam. 9:3
l man leap as an hart. . .Isa. 35:6
the *l* walk. . .Matt. 11:5
l, blind, dumb, maimed. . .Matt. 15:30
the *l* to walk. . .Matt. 15:31

blind and the *l*. . .Matt. 21:14
maimed, the *l*, the blind. . .Luke 14:13
a certain man *l*. . .Acts 3:2
l, were healed. . .Acts 8:7
l be turned out. . .Heb. 12:13

520. Lasciviousness

deceit, *l*, an evil eye. . .Mark 7:22
fornication and *l*. . .2 Cor. 12:21
fornication, uncleanness, *l*. . .Gal. 5:19
themselves over unto *l*. . .Eph. 4:19
walked in *l*, lusts. . .1 Pet. 4:3
grace of our God into *l*. . .Jude 1:4

See *Adultery*, *Debauchery*.

521. Last Day

again at the *l d*. . .John 6:39
raise him up at the *l d*. . .John 6:40
raise him up at the *l d*. . .John 6:44
raise him up at the *l d*. . .John 6:54
resurrection at the *l d*. . .John 11:24
judge him in the *l d*. . .John 12:48

See *Second Coming of Christ*.

522. Laugh/Laughter

God hath made me to *l*. . .Gen. 21:6
our mouth filled with *l'ter*. . .Ps. 126:2
Even in *l'ter* the heart. . .Prov. 14:13
a time to *l*. . .Eccles. 3:4
in the house of mirth. . .Eccles. 7:4
feast is made for *l'ter*. . .Eccles. 10:19
for ye shall *l*. . .Luke 6:21

you that *l* now!. . .Luke 6:25
l'ter be turned to mourning. . .James 4:9

See *Humor*.

523. Law

The Law consists of the commandments God gave Moses, which are contained in the first five books of the Bible.

the *l* which Moses. . .Deut. 4:44
this book of the *l*. . .Deut. 30:10
the *l* shall not depart. . .Josh. 1:8
copy of the *l* of Moses. . .Josh. 8:32
the *l* of the LORD. . .Ps. 1:2
the *l* of the LORD. . .Ps. 19:7
the *l* is light. . .Prov. 6:23
come to destroy the *l*. . .Matt. 5:17
the *l* and the prophets. . .Matt. 7:12
great commandment in the *l?*. . .Matt. 22:36
weightier matters of the *l*. . .Matt. 23:23
The *l* and the prophets. . .Luke 16:16

judged by the *l*. . .Rom. 2:12
the *l* worketh wrath. . .Rom. 4:15
strength of sin is the *l*. . .1 Cor. 15:56

See *Commandment/Commandments, Rules.*

524. Laws

my statutes, and my *l*. . .Gen. 26:5
ordinances and *l*. . .Exod. 18:20
right judgments, and true *l*. . .Neh. 9:13
statutes, and keep his *l*. . .Ps. 105:45
transgressed the *l*. . .Isa. 24:5
l into their hearts. . .Heb. 10:16

See *Commandment/Commandments,
Rules, Statutes.*

525. Lawsuits

counsel of the ungodly. . .Ps. 1:1
the LORD giveth wisdom. . .Prov. 2:6
Agree with thine adversary. . .Matt. 5:25
any man will sue thee. . .Matt. 5:40
brother shall trespass against thee. . .Matt. 18:15
judgeth all things. . .1 Cor. 2:15
go to law before the unjust. . .1 Cor. 6:1
saints shall judge the world?. . .1 Cor. 6:2
goeth to law with brother. . .1 Cor. 6:6
suffer yourselves to be defrauded?. . .1 Cor. 6:7
him that judgeth righteously. . .1 Pet. 2:23

See *Divorce/Divorced/Divorcement.*

526. Laziness

See *Slothful/Slothfulness.*

527. Leader/Leaders

and with every *l*. . .1 Chron. 13:1
l's of this people. . .Isa. 9:16
l and commander to the people. . .Isa. 55:4
blind *l's* of the blind. . .Matt. 15:14

See *Government; King, Earthly; Ruler/Rulers.*

528. Learn/ Learned/Learning

that ye may *l* them. . .Deut. 5:1
thou shalt not *l* to do. . .Deut. 18:9
l to fear the LORD. . .Deut. 31:13
l'ed thy righteous judgments. . .Ps. 119:7
I might *l* thy statutes. . .Ps. 119:71
l thy commandments. . .Ps. 119:73
will increase *l'ing*. . .Prov. 1:5
L to do well. . .Isa. 1:17
world will *l* righteousness. . .Isa. 26:9
murmured shall *l* doctrine. . .Isa. 29:24
ye have not so *l'ed* Christ. . .Eph. 4:20
which ye have both *l'ed*. . .Phil. 4:9
l'ed, in whatsoever state I am. . .Phil. 4:11
l first to shew piety. . .1 Tim. 5:4
l'ed and hast been assured. . .2 Tim. 3:14
l to maintain good works. . .Titus 3:14

See *Edify/Edification/Edifieth/Edifying*, *Education*, *Knowledge*, *Literacy*.

529. Leaven/Leavened

In the Bible, leaven is a picture of sin. During Passover, the Hebrews were to clean their homes of leaven.

put away *l*. . .Exod. 12:15
no *l* found. . .Exod. 12:19
before it was *l'ed*. . .Exod. 12:34
for it was not *l'ed*. . .Exod. 12:39
no *l'ed* bread be eaten. . .Exod. 13:3
kingdom of heaven is like unto *l*. . .Matt. 13:33
beware of the *l*. . .Matt. 16:6
Purge out therefore the old *l*. . .1 Cor. 5:7
with the *l* of malice. . .1 Cor. 5:8

530. Legalism

Legalism is faith gone wrong, because it puts more emphasis on following the letter of the law than on following the Spirit. Legalists bind themselves and others up in keeping track of their ability to do all the "right" things instead of having an obedient and loving spirit that follows the Lord. This rigid attitude that seeks to earn salvation is

not the faith Jesus demands of His followers, who should have warm hearts as well as obedient ones.

bind heavy burdens. . .Matt. 23:4
within full of dead men's bones. . .Matt. 23:27
Now to him that worketh. . .Rom. 4:4
unto another gospel. . .Gal. 1:6
now made perfect by the flesh?. . .Gal. 3:3
yoke of bondage. . .Gal. 5:1
the law is fulfilled in one word. . .Gal. 5:14
ye are not under the law. . .Gal. 5:18
an Hebrew of the Hebrews. . .Phil. 3:5
which is in the law, blameless. . .Phil. 3:6
are ye subject to ordinances. . .Col. 2:20
Touch not; taste not; handle not. . .Col. 2:21

See *Pharisee/Pharisee's/Pharisees*.

531. Lend/Lendeth

If thou *l* money. . .Exod. 22:25
nor *l* him thy victuals. . .Lev. 25:37
l him sufficient. . .Deut. 15:8
ever merciful, and *l'eth*. . .Ps. 37:26
sheweth favour, and *l'eth*. . .Ps. 112:5
l'eth unto the Lord. . .Prov. 19:17
l, hoping for nothing. . .Luke 6:35

See *Usury*.

532. Lies

not bear false witness. . .Exod. 20:16
false witness that speaketh *l*. . .Prov. 6:19
a false witness deceit. . .Prov. 12:17
will utter *l*. . .Prov. 14:5

speaketh / shall perish. . .Prov. 19:9

If a ruler hearken to /. . .Prov. 29:12

thefts, false witness. . .Matt. 15:19

Speaking / in hypocrisy. . .1 Tim. 4:2

533. Life, Breath of

the *b o l*. . .Gen. 2:7

wherein is the *b o l*. . .Gen. 6:17

wherein is the *b o l*. . .Gen. 7:15

nostrils was the *b o l*. . .Gen. 7:22

breath of the Almighty. . .Job 33:4

giveth to all life, and breath. . .Acts 17:25

534. Life, Brevity of

I should prolong my *l?*. . .Job 6:11

My days are swifter. . .Job 7:6

my / is wind. . .Job 7:7

teach us to number our days. . .Ps. 90:12

l? It is even a vapour. . .James 4:14

535. Life Eternal

righteous into / e. . .Matt. 25:46

gathereth fruit unto / e. . .John 4:36

keep it unto / e. . .John 12:25

And this is / e. . .John 17:3

See *Eternal Life; Everlasting Life/Life Everlasting; Immortal/Immortality; Reward, Eternal; Salvation.*

536. Lifestyle

Live joyfully with the wife. . .Eccles. 9:9

Take no thought for your life. . .Matt. 6:25

Labour not for the meat. . .John 6:27

The just shall live by faith. . .Rom. 1:17

mortify the deeds of the body. . .Rom. 8:13

live peaceably with all men. . .Rom. 12:18

not henceforth live unto themselves. . .2 Cor. 5:15

live in peace. . .2 Cor. 13:11

live by the faith. . .Gal. 2:20

be sober, putting on the breastplate. . .1 Thess. 5:8

we should live soberly. . .Titus 2:12

live unto righteousness. . .1 Pet. 2:24

live the rest of his time. . .1 Pet. 4:2

537. Light

Let there be /. . .Gen. 1:3

Wherefore is / given. . .Job 3:20

The Lord is my /. . .Ps. 27:1

/ in the darkness. . .Ps. 112:4

/ unto my path. . .Ps. 119:105

the law is /. . .Prov. 6:23

Gentiles shall come to thy /. . .Isa. 60:3

Ye are the / of the world. . .Matt. 5:14

The / of the body. . .Matt. 6:22

A / to lighten the Gentiles. . .Luke 2:32

life was the / of men. . .John 1:4

That was the true *L*. . .John 1:9

a / into the world. . .John 12:46
/ of the glorious gospel. . .2 Cor. 4:4
God is /. . .1 John 1:5

man of unclean /. . .Isa. 6:5
honoureth me with their /. . .Matt. 15:8

539. Listen

hearken unto me. . .Ps. 34:11
Come and hear, all ye. . .Ps. 66:16
if thou wilt hearken unto me. . .Ps. 81:8
had hearkened unto me. . .Ps. 81:13
Hear, O my son, and receive. . .Prov. 4:10
heareth his father's instruction. . .Prov. 13:1
Hear counsel, and receive. . .Prov. 19:20
they would not hear. . .Zech. 7:13
hear ye him. . .Matt. 17:5
if he will not hear thee. . .Matt. 18:16
My sheep hear my voice. . .John 10:27
be swift to hear. . .James 1:19
and not hearers only. . .James 1:22
knoweth God heareth us. . .1 John 4:6

See *Hear/Hearer/Heareth.*

538. Lips

gone out of thy /. . .Deut. 23:23
my / shall utter knowledge. . .Job 33:3
Let the lying /. . .Ps. 31:18
thy / from speaking guile. . .Ps. 34:13
my / shall praise thee. . .Ps. 63:3
gone out of my /. . .Ps. 89:34
keep the door of my /. . .Ps. 141:3
perverse / put far. . .Prov. 4:24
/ of a strange woman. . .Prov. 5:3
hideth hatred with lying /. . .Prov. 10:18
talk of the /. . .Prov. 14:23
A fool's / enter. . .Prov. 18:6
flattereth with his /. . .Prov. 20:19

540. Literacy

book of the covenant, and read. . .Exod. 24:7
thou shalt read this law. . .Deut. 31:11
read all the words. . .Josh. 8:34
read in their ears. . .2 Kings 23:2
read in the book. . .Neh. 8:8
I am not learned. . .Isa. 29:12
never read in the scriptures. . .Matt. 21:42
read that which was spoken. . .Matt. 22:31
read every sabbath day. . .Acts 13:27
epistle is read among you. . .Col. 4:16

See *Learn/Learned/Learning.*

541. Livestock

Having a large herd of livestock was a sign of wealth in the biblical era. God also used sheep as a picture of His people.

Abel was a keeper of sheep. . .Gen. 4:2
sheep, and oxen, and he asses. . .Gen. 12:16
took sheep, and oxen. . .Gen. 20:14
ewes, and twenty rams. . .Gen. 32:14
ox, or ass, or sheep. . .Exod. 22:4
calf and a lamb. . .Lev. 9:3
ass said unto Balaam. . .Num. 22:30
his ox, or his ass. . .Deut. 5:21
thy kine, and the flocks. . .Deut. 7:13
ox, the sheep, and the goat. . .Deut. 14:4
An horse is a vain thing. . .Ps. 33:17
sheep of thy pasture. . .Ps. 79:13
and a colt with her. . .Matt. 21:2
the sheep follow him. . .John 10:4
blood of bulls and of goats. . .Heb. 9:13

See *Mammals*.

542. Living Together

if a man entice a maid. . .Exod. 22:16
men of her city shall stone her. . .Deut. 22:21
lying with a woman married. . .Deut. 22:22
ravished with a strange woman. . .Prov. 5:20
keep thee from the evil woman. . .Prov. 6:24
Marriage is honourable. . .Heb. 13:4

See *Fornication/Fornications, Marriage/Marry/Marrying, Virgin/Virginity/Virgins*.

543. Loneliness

man should be alone. . .Gen. 2:18
I am desolate and afflicted. . .Ps. 25:16
trust in him shall be desolate. . .Ps. 34:22
the solitary in families. . .Ps. 68:6
as a sparrow alone. . .Ps. 102:7
my heart within me is desolate. . .Ps. 143:4
widow indeed, and desolate. . .1 Tim. 5:5
never leave thee, nor forsake
    thee. . .Heb. 13:5

544. Longeth/Longing

panteth my soul after thee. . .Ps. 42:1
my flesh *l* for thee. . .Ps. 63:1
My soul *l*, yea. . .Ps. 84:2
satisfieth the *l'ing* soul. . .Ps. 107:9
My soul breaketh for the *l'ing*. . .Ps. 119:20

545. Longsuffering

gracious, *l*, and abundant. . .Exod. 34:6

The LORD is *l*. . .Num. 14:18

forbearance and *l*. . .Rom. 2:4

endured with much *l*. . .Rom. 9:22

peace, *l*, gentleness. . .Gal. 5:22

l, forbearing one another. . .Eph. 4:2

patience and *l*. . .Col. 1:11

of mind, meekness, *l*. . .Col. 3:12

shew forth all *l*. . .1 Tim. 1:16

l, charity, patience. . .2 Tim. 3:10

l of God waited. . .1 Pet. 3:20

but is *l* to us-ward. . .2 Pet. 3:9

l of our Lord is salvation. . .2 Pet. 3:15

See *Forbearance/Forbearing, Patience/Patient/Patiently*.

546. Lord of Hosts

ark of the covenant of the *L o h*. . .1 Sam. 4:4

L o h was with him. . .1 Chron. 11:9

L o h, he is the King. . .Ps. 24:10

Sanctify the *L o h*. . .Isa. 8:13

L o h is his name. . .Isa. 47:4

Mighty God, the *L o h*. . .Jer. 32:18

Thus speaketh the *L o h*. . .Zech. 7:9

messenger of the *L o h*. . .Mal. 2:7

saith the *L o h*. . .Mal. 3:10

547. Lordship of Christ

why call ye me, Lord, Lord. . .Luke 6:46

he is Lord of all. . .Acts 10:36

the Lord shall be saved. . .Rom. 10:13

on the Lord Jesus Christ. . .Rom. 13:14

Jesus Christ is Lord. . .Phil. 2:11

he is Lord of lords. . .Rev. 17:14

548. Lord's Supper

Take, eat; this is my body. . .Matt. 26:26

Drink ye all of it. . .Matt. 26:27

which is shed for many. . .Matt. 26:28

not to eat the Lord's supper. . .1 Cor. 11:20

he was betrayed took bread. . .1 Cor. 11:23

Take, eat: this is my body. . .1 Cor. 11:24

this cup is the new testament. . .1 Cor. 11:25

See *Eucharist*.

549. Lose/Loss/Lost

salt have *l't* his savour. . .Matt. 5:13

findeth his life shall *l* it. . .Matt. 10:39

no wise *l* his reward. . .Matt. 10:42

save his life shall *l* it. . .Matt. 16:25

l his own soul?. . .Matt. 16:26

if he *l* one of them. . .Luke 15:4

if she *l* one piece. . .Luke 15:8

he shall suffer *l's*. . .1 Cor. 3:15

I count all things but *l's*. . .Phil. 3:8
we *l* not those things. . .2 John 1:8

550. Lost/Unsaved

save that which was *l*. . .Matt. 18:11
little ones should perish. . .Matt. 18:14
ye shall all likewise perish. . .Luke 13:3
go after that which is *l*. . .Luke 15:4
was *l*, and is found. . .Luke 15:24
in him should not perish. . .John 3:15
none of them is *l*. . .John 17:12
gavest me have I *l* none. . .John 18:9
hid to them that are *l*. . .2 Cor. 4:3
in them that perish. . .2 Thess. 2:10

See *Harvest, Unsaved.*

551. Lots, Cast

Lots were small objects used to determine God's will. Casting lots also determined some choices in the Bible, including the allotment of land inherited by each of Israel's tribes and the choice of Matthias to take the place of the apostle Judas.

c l upon the two goats. . .Lev. 16:8
land shall be divided by lot. . .Num. 26:55

divide the land by lot. . .Num. 33:54
c l for them in Shiloh. . .Josh. 18:10
C l between me. . .1 Sam. 14:42
they *c l*; and his lot. . .1 Chron. 26:14
people also *c l*. . .Neh. 11:1
c l upon my vesture. . .Ps. 22:18
The lot is cast into the lap. . .Prov. 16:33
lot causeth contentions. . .Prov. 18:18
Come, and let us *c l*. . .Jon. 1:7
parted his garments, *c l*. . .Matt. 27:35
they gave forth their lots. . .Acts 1:26

552. Love, Brotherly

be of one mind, live in peace. . .2 Cor. 13:11
being knit together in love. . .Col. 2:2
as touching *b l*. . .1 Thess. 4:9
Love the brotherhood. . .1 Pet. 2:17
dwelleth the love of God in him?. . .1 John 3:17
let us love one another. . .1 John 4:7
ought also to love one another. . .1 John 4:11
loveth God love his brother also. . .1 John 4:21
love the children of God. . .1 John 5:2

See *Emotions, Feelings.*

553. Love, God's

Lord loved Israel for ever. . .1 Kings 10:9
he will rest in his *l*. . .Zeph. 3:17

judgment and the *l* of God. . .Luke 11:42
For God so loved the world. . .John 3:16
Father himself loveth you. . .John 16:27
l of God is shed abroad. . .Rom. 5:5
God commendeth his *l*. . .Rom. 5:8
from the *l* of God. . .Rom. 8:39
and the *l* of God. . .2 Cor. 13:14
God, who loved me, and gave. . .Gal. 2:20
great *l* wherewith he loved us. . .Eph. 2:4
l of Christ, which passeth. . .Eph. 3:19
our Father, which hath loved us. . .2 Thess. 2:16
l the Father hath bestowed. . .1 John 3:1
for God is *l*. . .1 John 4:8
For this is the *l* of God. . .1 John 5:3

554. Loving God

love the Lᴏʀᴅ thy God. . .Deut. 6:5
mercy with them that love him. . .Deut. 7:9
and to love him. . .Deut. 10:12
love the Lᴏʀᴅ thy God. . .Deut. 11:1
love the Lᴏʀᴅ thy God. . .Deut. 30:20
love the Lord thy God. . .Matt. 22:37
ye would love me. . .John 8:42
to them that love God. . .Rom. 8:28
for them that love him. . .1 Cor. 2:9
But if any man love God. . .1 Cor. 8:3
to them that love him?. . .James 2:5

555. Lovingkindness

Shew thy marvellous *l*. . .Ps. 17:7
How excellent is thy *l*. . .Ps. 36:7
I have not concealed thy *l*. . .Ps. 40:10
his *l* in the day time. . .Ps. 42:8
according to thy *l*. . .Ps. 51:1
thy *l* is better than life. . .Ps. 63:3

thy *l* is good. . .Ps. 69:16
l will I not utterly take. . .Ps. 89:33
To shew forth thy *l*. . .Ps. 92:2
crowneth thee with *l*. . .Ps. 103:4
shall understand the *l*. . .Ps. 107:43
Quicken me after thy *l*. . .Ps. 119:88
Cause me to hear thy *l*. . .Ps. 143:8
exercise *l*, judgment. . .Jer. 9:24
l unto thousands. . .Jer. 32:18

556. Lust/Lusts

L not after her beauty. . .Prov. 6:25
looketh on a woman to *l*. . .Matt. 5:28
the *l*'s of their own hearts. . .Rom. 1:24
burned in their *l*. . .Rom. 1:27
obey it in the *l*'s thereof. . .Rom. 6:12
to fulfil the *l*'s thereof. . .Rom. 13:14
not fulfil the *l* of the flesh. . .Gal. 5:16
in the *l*'s of our flesh. . .Eph. 2:3
the *l* of concupiscence. . .1 Thess. 4:5
Flee also youthful *l*'s. . .2 Tim. 2:22
drawn away of his own *l*. . .James 1:14
abstain from fleshly *l*'s. . .1 Pet. 2:11
through the *l*'s of the flesh. . .2 Pet. 2:18
the *l* of the flesh. . .1 John 2:16

See Entice/Enticed/Enticeth.

557. Luxuries

fat, and their meat plenteous. . .Hab. 1:16
not arrayed like one of these. . .Matt. 6:29
gorgeously apparelled. . .Luke 7:25
purple and fine linen, and fared. . .Luke 16:19
lived in pleasure on the earth. . .James 5:5
lived deliciously. . .Rev. 18:7

558. Lying

I will be a *l* spirit. . .1 Kings 2:22
that regard *l* vanities. . .Ps. 31:6
l lips be put to silence. . .Ps. 31:18
and *l* rather than. . .Ps. 52:3
and for cursing and *l*. . .Ps. 59:12
from me the way of *l*. . .Ps. 119:29
A proud look, a *l* tongue. . .Prov. 6:17
hideth hatred with *l* lips. . .Prov. 10:18
l tongue is but. . .Prov. 12:19
L lips are abomination. . .Prov. 12:22
A righteous man hateth *l*. . .Prov. 13:5
treasures by a *l* tongue. . .Prov. 21:6
A *l* tongue hateth. . .Prov. 26:28
Wherefore putting away *l*. . .Eph. 4:25

559. Mad/Madness

Scripture gives us examples of real and feigned madness, but it was not uncommon
to accuse someone of madness, in the same way that we say, "Are you crazy?" when we doubt others' wisdom.

Lord shall smite thee with *m'ness*. . .Deut. 28:28
feigned himself *m* in their hands. . .1 Sam. 21:13
Have I need of *m* men. . .1 Sam. 21:15
wherefore came this *m* fellow. . .2 Kings 9:11
they were filled with *m'ness*. . .Luke 6:11
hath a devil, and is *m*. . .John 10:20
much learning doth make thee *m*. . .Acts 26:24
not *m*, most noble Festus. . .Acts 26:25
not say that ye are *m*?. . .1 Cor. 14:23

560. Magic/Magicians

called for all the *m'ians* of Egypt. . .Gen. 41:8
m'ians of Egypt did so. . .Exod. 7:22
the *m'ians* said unto Pharaoh. . .Exod. 8:19
the soothsayer, did the children. . .Josh. 13:22
ten times better than all the *m'ians*. . .Dan. 1:20
astrologers, the *m'ians*, the soothsayers. . .Dan. 2:27
made master of the *m'ians*. . .Dan. 5:11
shalt have no more soothsayers. . .Mic. 5:12
much gain by soothsaying. . .Acts 16:16

See *Astrologers; Occult, the; Sorcery/Sorcerer/ Sorcerers; Witch/Witchcraft/Witchcrafts.*

561. Majesty

the victory, and the *m*. . .1 Chron. 29:11
such royal *m*. . .1 Chron. 29:25
with God is terrible *m*. . .Job 37:22
the Lord is full of *m*. . .Ps. 29:4
he is clothed with *m*. . .Ps. 93:1
Honour and *m* are. . .Ps. 96:6

glorious *m* of his kingdom. . .Ps. 145:12

behold the *m* of the LORD. . .Isa. 26:10

excellent *m* was added. . .Dan. 4:36

hand of the *M* on high. . .Heb. 1:3

throne of the *M*. . .Heb. 8:1

eyewitnesses of his *m*. . .2 Pet. 1:16

m, dominion and power. . .Jude 1:25

because he was a thief. . .John 12:6

If he were not a *m*. . .John 18:30

desired a murderer. . .Acts 3:14

drunkard, or an extortioner. . .1 Cor. 5:11

Nor thieves, nor covetous. . .1 Cor. 6:10

suffer as a murderer. . .1 Pet. 4:15

hateth his brother is a murderer. . .1 John 3:15

562. Malefactor/ Malefactors

By definition, a malefactor can be an offender against the law (especially a felon) or simply one who does ill toward another person.

murderer shall surely be put. . .Num. 35:16

children of the murderers. . .2 Kings 14:6

Whoso is partner with a thief. . .Prov. 29:24

thieves break through and steal. . .Matt. 6:19

made it a den of thieves. . .Matt. 21:13

crucified him, and the *m's*. . .Luke 23:33

one of the *m's*. . .Luke 23:39

He was a murderer. . .John 8:44

563. Malice/ Malicious/ Maliciousness

The King James Version of the Bible sometimes uses the word "hatred" where a more modern translation uses "malice."

thrust him of hatred. . .Num. 35:20

but mischief is in their hearts. . .Ps. 28:3

Whose hatred is covered by deceit. . .Prov. 26:26

wickedness, covetousness, *m'iousness*. . .Rom. 1:29

leaven of *m* and wickedness. . .1 Cor. 5:8

in *m* be ye children. . .1 Cor. 14:20

away from you, with all *m*. . .Eph. 4:31

anger, wrath, *m*, blasphemy. . .Col. 3:8

living in *m* and envy. . .Titus 3:3

laying aside all *m*. . .1 Pet. 2:1

liberty for a cloke of *m'iousness*. . .1 Pet. 2:16

against us with *m'ious* words. . .3 John 1:10

See *Spite/Spitefully*.

564. Mammals

beast of the earth. . .Gen. 1:24

every beast of the field. . .Gen. 2:19

clean beast thou shalt take. . .Gen. 7:2

fallow deer, and the wild goat. . .Deut. 14:5

there came a lion. . .1 Sam. 17:34
my feet like hinds' feet. . .2 Sam. 22:34
and apes, and peacocks. . .1 Kings 10:22
lions roar after their prey. . .Ps. 104:21
regardeth the life of his beast. . .Prov. 12:10
taketh a dog by the ears. . .Prov. 26:17
Take us the foxes. . .Song of Sol. 2:15
living dog is better than. . .Eccles. 9:4
leopard shall lie down. . .Isa. 11:6
foxes have holes. . .Matt. 8:20
dogs eat of the crumbs. . .Matt. 15:27

See *Animals*, *Livestock*.

565. Man

m became a living soul. . .Gen. 2:7
shall a *m* leave his father. . .Gen. 2:24
Behold, the *m* is become. . .Gen. 3:22
God is not a man. . .Num. 23:19
what can *m* do unto me?. . .Ps. 118:6
Behold the *m*!. . .John 19:5
things of God knoweth no *m*. . .1 Cor. 2:11
since by *m* came death. . .1 Cor. 15:21
first *m* is of the earth. . .1 Cor. 15:47
our outward *m* perish. . .2 Cor. 4:16
found in fashion as a *m*. . .Phil. 2:8
the *m* Christ Jesus. . .1 Tim. 2:5
m of God may be perfect. . .2 Tim. 3:17
hidden *m* of the heart. . .1 Pet. 3:4

566. Man/Mankind

created *m* in his own image. . .Gen. 1:27
shall not always strive with *m*. . .Gen. 6:3
I will destroy *m*. . .Gen. 6:7
image of God made he *m*. . .Gen. 9:6
Thou shalt not lie with *m'kind*. . .Lev. 18:22
Yet *m* is born unto trouble. . .Job 5:7
breath of all *m'kind*. . .Job 12:10
What is *m*, that thou art mindful. . .Ps. 8:4
hath been tamed of *m'kind*. . .James 3:7

567. Manna

It is *m*: for they wist. . .Exod. 16:15
an omer full of *m*. . .Exod. 16:33
eat *m* forty years. . .Exod. 16:35
m, before our eyes. . .Num. 11:6
the *m* fell upon it. . .Num. 11:9
in the wilderness with *m*. . .Deut. 8:16
m ceased on the morrow. . .Josh. 5:12
withheldest not thy *m*. . .Neh. 9:20
rained down *m* upon them. . .Ps. 78:24
Our fathers did eat *m*. . .John 6:31
golden pot that had *m*. . .Heb. 9:4
eat of the hidden *m*. . .Rev. 2:17

568. Marriage/Marry/Marrying

m'ing strange wives?. . .Neh. 13:27
m'y her that is divorced. . .Matt. 5:32
and shall *m'y* another. . .Matt. 19:9
nor are given in *m*. . .Matt. 22:30
m in Cana of Galilee. . .John 2:1
better to *m'y* than to burn. . .1 Cor. 7:9
But and if thou *m'y*. . .1 Cor. 7:28
giveth her in *m*. . .1 Cor. 7:38

Forbidding to m'y. . .1 Tim. 4:3
they will m'y. . .1 Tim. 5:11
younger women m'y. . .1 Tim. 5:14
love their husbands. . .Titus 2:4
M is honourable in all. . .Heb. 13:4
m of the Lamb. . .Rev. 19:7

See *Betroth/Betrothed, Courtship, Dating, Husband/Husbands, Living Together, Unequally Yoked, Wife/Wives.*

569. Martyr/Martyrs

And they stoned Stephen. . .Acts 7:59
blood of thy m Stephen. . .Acts 22:20
Antipas was my faithful m. . .Rev. 2:13
m's of Jesus. . .Rev. 17:6

570. Master/Masters

Though Christians most often associate this word with Jesus, who was called Master by His disciples, it's also used in the Bible to describe one who ruled over a household, or a slave owner.

thigh of Abraham his m. . .Gen. 24:9
house of his m the Egyptian. . .Gen. 39:2

I love my m. . .Exod. 21:5
shalt not deliver unto his m. . .Deut. 23:15
your m, the Lord's anointed. . .1 Sam. 26:16
take away thy m. . .2 Kings 2:3
unto the hand of their m's. . .Ps. 123:2
not a servant unto his m. . .Prov. 30:10
No man can serve two m's. . .Matt. 6:24
M, I will follow thee. . .Matt. 8:19
Why eateth your M. . .Matt. 9:11
disciple is not above his m. . .Matt. 10:24
M, we would see a sign. . .Matt. 12:38
Good M, what good thing. . .Matt. 19:16
Neither be ye called m's. . .Matt. 23:10
Hail, m; and kissed him. . .Matt. 26:49
Art thou a m of Israel. . .John 3:10
them that are your m's. . .Eph. 6:5
M's, give unto your servants. . .Col. 4:1
be subject to your m's. . .1 Pet. 2:18

571. Materialism

doth persecute the poor. . .Ps. 10:2
Wherefore do ye spend money. . .Isa. 55:2
kept back part of the price. . .Acts 5:2
God may be purchased with money. . .Acts 8:20
love of money is the root. . .1 Tim. 6:10

See *Greed/Greedily/Greediness/Greedy, Usury.*

572. Meanness

mine enemy sharpeneth his eyes. . .Job 16:9
doth persecute the poor. . .Ps. 10:2
hate me with cruel hatred. . .Ps. 25:19
of the wicked are cruel. . .Prov. 12:10
trial of cruel mockings. . .Heb. 11:36

573. Measurements

in a cubit shalt thou. . .Gen. 6:16
mete it with an omer. . .Exod. 16:18
omer is the tenth part of. . .Exod. 16:36
two cubits and a half. . .Exod. 25:17
span shall be the length. . .Exod. 28:16
an hin of beaten oil. . .Exod. 29:40
three pound of gold. . .1 Kings 10:17
thickness of it was an handbreadth. . .2 Chron. 4:5
vineyard shall yield one bath. . .Isa. 5:10
just ephah, and a just bath. . .Ezek. 45:10
tenth part of an homer. . .Ezek. 45:11
ten baths are an homer. . .Ezek. 45:14
compel thee to go a mile. . .Matt. 5:41
add one cubit unto his stature?. . .Matt. 6:27
pound of ointment of spikenard. . .John 12:3

574. Meddle/ Meddled/Meddleth/ Meddling

before it be *m'd* with. . .Prov. 17:14
every fool will be *m'ing*. . .Prov. 20:3

m not with him. . .Prov. 20:19
m not with them. . .Prov. 24:21
m'th with strife. . .Prov. 26:17

575. Mediator, Christ as

m is not a *m* of one. . .Gal. 3:20
one God, and one *m*. . .1 Tim. 2:5
m of a better covenant. . .Heb. 8:6
m of the new testament. . .Heb. 9:15
Jesus the *m*. . .Heb. 12:24

576. Medicine/ Medicines

doeth good like a *m*. . .Prov. 17:22
neither mollified with ointment. . .Isa. 1:6
for a plaister upon the boil. . .Isa. 38:21
Is there no balm in Gilead. . .Jer. 8:22
thou hast no healing *m's*. . .Jer. 30:13
use many *m's*. . .Jer. 46:11
take balm for her pain. . .Jer. 51:8
leaf thereof for *m*. . .Ezek. 47:12
wine mingled with myrrh. . .Mark 15:23
pouring in oil and wine. . .Luke 10:34
wine for thy stomach's sake. . .1 Tim. 5:23

577. Meditate/ Meditation

thou shalt *m* therein. . .Josh. 1:8
doth he *m* day and night. . .Ps. 1:2
consider my *m'ion*. . .Ps. 5:1
m'ion of my heart. . .Ps. 19:14
m'ion of my heart. . .Ps. 49:3
m on thee. . .Ps. 63:6
m also of all thy work. . .Ps. 77:12
m'ion of him shall be sweet. . .Ps. 104:34
m in thy precepts. . .Ps. 119:15
m in thy statutes. . .Ps. 119:23
thy law! it is my *m'ion*. . .Ps. 119:97
testimonies are my *m'ion*. . .Ps. 119:99
might *m* in thy word. . .Ps. 119:148
I *m* on all thy works. . .Ps. 143:5
M upon these things. . .1 Tim. 4:15

578. Meek/Meekness

Moses was very *m*. . .Num. 12:3
m shall eat and be satisfied. . .Ps. 22:26
The *m* will he guide. . .Ps. 25:9
m shall inherit the earth. . .Ps. 37:11
Lord lifteth up the *m*. . .Ps. 147:6
beautify the *m* with salvation. . .Ps. 149:4
m also shall increase their joy. . .Isa. 29:19
good tidings unto the *m*. . .Isa. 61:1
Blessed are the *m*. . .Matt. 5:5
m and lowly in heart. . .Matt. 11:29
m, and sitting upon an ass. . .Matt. 21:5
m'ness and gentleness. . .2 Cor. 10:1
M'ness, temperance: against such. . .Gal. 5:23
spirit of *m'ness*. . .Gal. 6:1
love, patience, *m'ness*. . .1 Tim. 6:11
ornament of a *m* and quiet spirit. . .1 Pet. 3:4
with *m'ness* and fear. . .1 Pet. 3:15

579. Membership, Church

That ye love one another. . .John 15:12
every one members one of another. . .Rom. 12:5
there should be no schism in the body. . .1 Cor. 12:25
Bear ye one another's burdens. . .Gal. 6:2
forbearing one another in love. . .Eph. 4:2
we are members one of another. . .Eph. 4:25
be ye kind one to another. . .Eph. 4:32
Submitting yourselves one to another. . .Eph. 5:21
Forbearing one another. . .Col. 3:13
teaching and admonishing one another. . .Col. 3:16
in love one toward another. . .1 Thess. 3:12
edify one another. . .1 Thess. 5:11
But exhort one another daily. . .Heb. 3:13
provoke unto love. . .Heb. 10:24
Not forsaking the assembling. . .Heb. 10:25
Confess your faults one to another. . .James 5:16

580. Memorial

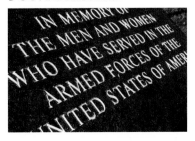

my *m* unto all generations. . .Exod. 3:15
shall be unto you for a *m*. . .Exod. 12:14
ephod for stones of *m*. . .Exod. 28:12
m before your God. . .Num. 10:10
these stones shall be for a *m*. . .Josh. 4:7
keep my name in remembrance. . .2 Sam. 18:18
nor the *m* of them perish. . .Esther 9:28
cut off the remembrance of them. . .Ps. 34:16

be in everlasting remembrance. . .Ps. 112:6

remembrance of thee. . .Isa. 26:8

told for a *m* of her. . .Matt. 26:13

in remembrance of his mercy. . .Luke 1:54

or a *m* before God. . .Acts 10:4

do in remembrance of me. . .1 Cor. 11:24

581. Mental Illness

See *Mad/Madness*.

582. Mercy/Mercies

I will shew *m* on whom. . .Exod. 33:19

for his *m'ies* are great. . .2 Sam. 24:14

make supplication to my judge. . .Job 9:15

heard my supplication. . .Ps. 6:9

thy tender *m'ies*. . .Ps. 40:11

Have *m* upon me, O God. . .Ps. 51:1

The poor useth intreaties. . .Prov. 18:23

forsaketh them shall have *m*. . .Prov. 28:13

I desired *m*, and not sacrifice. . .Hosea 6:6

delighteth in *m*. . .Mic. 7:18

they shall obtain *m*. . .Matt. 5:7

son of David, have *m* on us. . .Matt. 9:27

judgment, *m*, and faith. . .Matt. 23:23

his *m* is on them. . .Luke 1:50

m'ies of God, that ye present. . .Rom. 12:1

583. Message/ Messenger

put a word in Balaam's mouth. . .Num. 23:5

the Lᴏʀᴅ hath not spoken. . .Deut. 18:22

wicked *m'enger* falleth into mischief. . .Prov. 13:17

m by the hand of a fool. . .Prov. 26:6

m'enger of the covenant. . .Mal. 3:1

send my *m'enger* before thy face. . .Matt. 11:10

m'enger of Satan. . .2 Cor. 12:7

m which we have heard. . .1 John 1:5

m that ye heard from the beginning. . .1 John 3:11

584. Messiah

The Messiah, or "anointed one," was chosen by God to be the King and Redeemer of His people. The Messiah was foretold throughout the Old Testament in many prophecies. "Christ" is the Greek translation of this word.

in thy seed shall all the nations. . .Gen. 22:18

unto him shall the gathering. . .Gen. 49:10

I know that my redeemer liveth. . .Job 19:25

Thou art my Son. . .Ps. 2:7

from the power of the grave. . .Ps. 49:15

Thy seed will I establish for ever. . .Ps. 89:4

Blessed be he that cometh. . .Ps. 118:26

he shall judge among the nations. . .Isa. 2:4

a virgin shall conceive. . .Isa. 7:14

government shall be upon. . .Isa. 9:6

he bare the sin of many. . .Isa. 53:12

Gentiles shall come to thy light. . .Isa. 60:3

their affliction he was afflicted. . .Isa. 63:9

M the Prince. . .Dan. 9:25

shall *M* be cut off. . .Dan. 9:26

See *Jesus Christ*.

585. Metals

artificer in brass and iron. . .Gen. 4:22

gold, and silver, and brass. . .Exod. 25:3

Moses made a serpent of brass. . .Num. 21:9

the iron, the tin, and the lead. . .Num. 31:22

hills thou mayest dig brass. . .Deut. 8:9

brass and iron, are consecrated. . .Josh. 6:19

with silver, and with gold. . .Josh. 22:8

five thousand shekels of brass. . .1 Sam. 17:5

took exceeding much brass. . .2 Sam. 8:8

work all works in brass. . .1 Kings 7:14

hundred thousand talents of gold. . .1 Chron. 22:14

gold, and in silver, in brass. . .2 Chron. 2:14

an altar of brass. . .2 Chron. 4:1

iron, tin, and lead. . .Ezek. 27:12

head was of fine gold. . .Dan. 2:32

586. Might/Mighty

and thy *m'y* hand. . .Deut. 3:24

with all thy *m*. . .Deut. 6:5

m of mine hand. . .Deut. 8:17

his *m'y* power to be known. . .Ps. 106:8

do it with thy *m*. . .Eccles. 9:10

greatness of his *m*. . .Isa. 40:26

to them that have no *m*. . .Isa. 40:29

neither let the *m'y* man glory. . .Jer. 9:23

wisdom and *m* are his. . .Dan. 2:20

Not by *m*, nor by power. . .Zech. 4:6

m, and dominion. . .Eph. 1:21

in the power of his *m*. . .Eph. 6:10

Strengthened with all *m*. . .Col. 1:11

greater in power and *m*. . .2 Pet. 2:11

587. Mind

good or bad of mine own *m*. . .Num. 24:13

imaginations of the thoughts. . .1 Chron. 28:9

with a wicked *m*?. . .Prov. 21:27

A fool uttereth all his *m*. . .Prov. 29:11

whose *m* is stayed on thee. . .Isa. 26:3

and with all thy *m*. . .Matt. 22:37

neither be ye of doubtful *m*. . .Luke 12:29

with all readiness of *m*. . .Acts 17:11

over to a reprobate *m*. . .Rom. 1:28

against the law of my *m*. . .Rom. 7:23

carnal *m* is enmity. . .Rom. 8:7

by the renewing of your *m*. . .Rom. 12:2

Be of the same *m*. . .Rom. 12:16

one *m* and one mouth. . .Rom. 15:6

have the *m* of Christ. . .1 Cor. 2:16

588. Minister/ Ministry/Ministering

let him be your *m*. . .Matt. 20:26

take part of this *m'ry*. . .Acts 1:25

m'ry of the word. . .Acts 6:4

they had fulfilled their *m'ry*. . .Acts 12:25

joy, and the *m'ry*. . .Acts 20:24

m and a witness. . .Acts 26:16

let us wait on our *m'ing*. . .Rom. 12:7

he is the *m* of God. . .Rom. 13:4

m of the circumcision. . .Rom. 15:8

m of Jesus Christ. . .Rom. 15:16
m'ry of reconciliation. . .2 Cor. 5:18
for the work of the *m'ry*. . .Eph. 4:12
Take heed to the *m'ry*. . .Col. 4:17
full proof of thy *m'ry*. . .2 Tim. 4:5

589. Miracle/Miracles

Shew a *m* for you. . .Exod. 7:9
man which shall do a *m*. . .Mark 9:39
This beginning of *m's*. . .John 2:11
saw the *m's* which he did. . .John 2:23
no man can do these *m's*. . .John 3:2
second *m* that Jesus did. . .John 4:54
heard that he had done this *m*. . .John 12:18
had done so many *m's*. . .John 12:37
m's and wonders and signs. . .Acts 2:22
notable *m* hath been done. . .Acts 4:16
m of healing was shewed. . .Acts 4:22
did great wonders and *m's*. . .Acts 6:8
beholding the *m's* and signs. . .Acts 8:13
m's by the hands of Paul. . .Acts 19:11
with divers *m's*. . .Heb. 2:4

See *Signs*.

590. Miscarriage

hurt a woman with child. . .Exod. 21:22
if any mischief follow. . .Exod. 21:23

as an hidden untimely birth. . .Job 3:16
untimely birth of a woman. . .Ps. 58:8
fearfully and wonderfully made. . .Ps. 139:14
when I was made in secret. . .Ps. 139:15
untimely birth is better than he. . .Eccles. 6:3
Before I formed thee in the belly. . .Jer. 1:5

591. Mischief/Mischiefs

practised *m* against him. . .1 Sam. 23:9
this man seeketh *m*. . .1 Kings 20:7
away the *m* of Haman. . .Esther 8:3
They conceive *m*. . .Job 15:35
and hath conceived *m*. . .Ps. 7:14
His *m* shall return. . .Ps. 7:16
under his tongue is *m*. . .Ps. 10:7
m is in their hearts. . .Ps. 28:3
deviseth *m* upon his bed. . .Ps. 36:4
The tongue deviseth *m's*. . .Ps. 52:2
they have done *m*. . .Prov. 4:16
deviseth *m* continually. . .Prov. 6:14
swift in running to *m*. . .Prov. 6:18
he that seeketh *m*. . .Prov. 11:27
tongue falleth into *m*. . .Prov. 17:20

592. Misery

grieved for the *m* of Israel. . .Judg. 10:16
given to him that is in *m*. . .Job 3:20
thou shalt forget thy *m*. . .Job 11:16
cast down, O my soul?. . .Ps. 42:5
cast down, O my soul?. . .Ps. 42:11
remember his *m* no more. . .Prov. 31:7
mine affliction and my *m*. . .Lam. 3:19
Destruction and *m* are. . .Rom. 3:16

593. Mock/Mocked/ Mocker/Mockers/ Mocketh/Mocking/ Mockings

born unto Abraham, *m'ing*. . .Gen. 21:9

Elijah *m'ed* them. . .1 Kings 18:27

out of the city, and *m'ed* him. . .2 Kings 2:23

m'ed the messengers of God. . .2 Chron. 36:16

m'ed the Jews. . .Neh. 4:1

Fools make a *m* at sin. . .Prov. 14:9

Wine is a *m'er*. . .Prov. 20:1

m'eth at his father. . .Prov. 30:17

every one *m'eth* me. . .Jer. 20:7

him to the Gentiles to *m*. . .Matt. 20:19

m'ed him, saying, Hail, King. . .Matt. 27:29

some *m'ed*: and others said. . .Acts 17:32

God is not *m'ed*. . .Gal. 6:7

trial of cruel *m'ings*. . .Heb. 11:36

m'ers in the last time. . .Jude 1:18

594. Moderation

eat so much as is sufficient. . .Prov. 25:16

not good to eat much honey. . .Prov. 25:27

m be known unto all. . .Phil. 4:5

595. Modest/Modesty

she took a vail, and covered. . .Gen. 24:65

adorn themselves in *m* apparel. . .1 Tim. 2:9

To be discreet, chaste. . .Titus 2:5

your chaste conversation. . .1 Pet. 3:2

See *Chaste/Chastity*, *Virgin/Virginity/Virgins*.

596. Money

m as it is worth. . .Gen. 23:9

m failed in the land of Egypt. . .Gen. 47:15

If thou lend *m*. . .Exod. 22:25

m to repair the house. . .2 Chron. 24:5

not out his *m* to usury. . .Ps. 15:5

m is a defence. . .Eccles. 7:12

Wherefore do ye spend *m*. . .Isa. 55:2

cannot serve God and mammon. . .Matt. 6:24

Shew me the tribute *m*. . .Matt. 22:19

neither bread, neither *m*. . .Luke 9:3

the unrighteous mammon. . .Luke 16:11

brought the *m*. . .Acts 4:37

purchased with *m*. . .Acts 8:20

love of *m* is the root. . .1 Tim. 6:10

not for filthy lucre. . .1 Pet. 5:2

See *Currency*, *Financial Gain*, *Gambling*, *Wealth*.

597. Morning

m were the first day. . .Gen. 1:5
m ye shall be filled with bread. . .Exod. 16:12
m to thank and praise the Lord. . .1 Chron. 23:30
For the *m* is to them. . .Job 24:17
m stars sang together. . .Job 38:7
shalt thou hear in the *m*. . .Ps. 5:3
joy cometh in the *m*. . .Ps. 30:5
m, and at noon, will I pray. . .Ps. 55:17
In the *m* it flourisheth. . .Ps. 90:6
lovingkindness in the *m*. . .Ps. 92:2
that watch for the *m*. . .Ps. 130:6
take the wings of the *m*. . .Ps. 139:9
In the *m* sow thy seed. . .Eccles. 11:6
They are new every *m*. . .Lam. 3:23
bright and *m* star. . .Rev. 22:16

598. Mortal/Mortality

Shall *m* man be more. . .Job 4:17
reign in your *m* body. . .Rom. 6:12
quicken your *m* bodies. . .Rom. 8:11
m must put on immortality. . .1 Cor. 15:53
incorruption, and this *m*. . .1 Cor. 15:54
manifest in our *m* flesh. . .2 Cor. 4:11
m'ity might be swallowed. . .2 Cor. 5:4

See *Bury/Burial/Buried, Death.*

599. Mother/Mother's

leave his father and his *m*. . .Gen. 2:24
m of all living. . .Gen. 3:20
m of nations. . .Gen. 17:16
Honour thy father and thy *m*. . .Exod. 20:12
curseth his father, or his *m*. . .Exod. 21:17
fear every man his *m*. . .Lev. 19:3

out of my *m's* womb. . .Job 1:21
my God from my *m's* belly. . .Ps. 22:10
my *m* forsake me. . .Ps. 27:10
joyful *m* of children. . .Ps. 113:9
forsake not the law of thy *m*. . .Prov. 1:8
despise not thy *m*. . .Prov. 23:22
his *m* Mary was espoused. . .Matt. 1:18
loveth father or *m* more. . .Matt. 10:37
Behold my *m*. . .Matt. 12:49

See *Family, Parents.*

600. Mountain/ Mountains

and the *m's* were covered. . .Gen. 7:20
m's of Ararat. . .Gen. 8:4
m did burn with fire. . .Deut. 5:23
m Abarim, unto mount Nebo. . .Deut. 32:49
therefore give me this *m*. . .Josh. 14:12
overturneth the *m's*. . .Job 28:9

though the *m*'s shake. . .Ps. 46:3
Before the *m*'s were. . .Ps. 90:2
As the *m*'s are round. . .Ps. 125:2
get thee up into the high *m*. . .Isa. 40:9
How beautiful upon the *m*'s. . .Isa. 52:7
For the *m*'s shall depart. . .Isa. 54:10
For in mine holy *m*. . .Ezek. 20:40
exceeding high *m*. . .Matt. 4:8
to a great and high *m*. . .Rev. 21:10

m shall shew forth thy praise. . .Ps. 51:15
The words of his *m*. . .Ps. 55:21
m of the foolish. . .Prov. 10:14
The *m* of the just. . .Prov. 10:31
He that keepeth his *m*. . .Prov. 13:3
flattering *m* worketh ruin. . .Prov. 26:28
open my *m* in parables. . .Matt. 13:35
every *m* may be stopped. . .Rom. 3:19
Whose *m*'s must be stopped. . .Titus 1:11

601. Mourn/Mourning

grave unto my son *m'ing*. . .Gen. 37:35
made a *m'ing*. . .Gen. 50:10
m'ing unto all the people. . .2 Sam. 19:2
m'ing among the Jews. . .Esther 4:3
m'ing into dancing. . .Ps. 30:11
m'ing all the day long. . .Ps. 38:6
beareth rule, the people *m*. . .Prov. 29:2
a time to *m*. . .Eccles. 3:4
to comfort all that *m*. . .Isa. 61:2
weeping, and great *m'ing*. . .Matt. 2:18
Blessed are they that *m*. . .Matt. 5:4
tribes of the earth *m*. . .Matt. 24:30
ye shall *m* and weep. . .Luke 6:25
Be afflicted, and *m*. . .James 4:9

see *Grief/Griefs*.

602. Mouth/Mouths

Who hath made man's *m*?. . .Exod. 4:11
own *m* shall condemn me. . .Job 9:20
lay mine hand upon my *m*. . .Job 40:4
His *m* is full of cursing. . .Ps. 10:7
The *m* of the righteous. . .Ps. 37:30
m shall speak of wisdom. . .Ps. 49:3

603. Murder/Murders

doth he *m* the innocent. . .Ps. 10:8

m the fatherless. . .Ps. 94:6
m's, adulteries, fornications. . .Matt. 15:19
Thou shalt do no *m*. . .Matt. 19:18
m in the insurrection. . .Mark 15:7
full of envy, *m*, debate. . .Rom. 1:29
Envyings, *m*'s, drunkenness. . .Gal. 5:21
Neither repented they of their *m*'s. . .Rev. 9:21

See *Crime, Criminals, Kill/Killed/Killeth,
Murderer/Murderers*.

604. Murderer/ Murderers

m shall surely be put. . .Num. 35:16
m shall be put to death. . .Num. 35:30

children of the *m's*. . .2 Kings 14:6
The *m* rising with the light. . .Job 24:14
He was a *m*. . .John 8:44
desired a *m* to be granted. . .Acts 3:14
betrayers and *m's*. . .Acts 7:52
for *m's* of fathers. . .1 Tim. 1:9
suffer as a *m*. . .1 Pet. 4:15
hateth his brother is a *m*. . .1 John 3:15
the abominable, and *m's*. . .Rev. 21:8
m's, and idolaters. . .Rev. 22:15

See *Murder/Murders*.

---

605. Murmur/ Murmured/ Murmurers/ Murmuring/ Murmurings

m'ed against Moses and Aaron. . .Exod. 16:2
m'ings of the children. . .Exod. 16:12
which *m* against me?. . .Num. 14:27
made all the congregation to *m*. . .Num. 14:36
ye *m* against him?. . .Num. 16:11
take away their *m'ings*. . .Num. 17:10
m'ed against the princes. . .Josh. 9:18
m'ed in their tents. . .Ps. 106:25
m'ed shall learn doctrine. . .Isa. 29:24
they *m'ed* against her. . .Mark 14:5
m'ed against his disciples. . .Luke 5:30
Pharisees and scribes *m'ed*. . .Luke 15:2
m'ing of the Grecians. . .Acts 6:1
without *m'ings* and disputings. . .Phil. 2:14
These are *m'ers*, complainers. . .Jude 1:16

See *Complain/Complained/Complainers/Complaint,
Contention/Contentions/Contentious, Quarrel*.

606. Musick

I will sing unto the Lord. . .Exod. 15:1
noise of them that sing. . .Exod. 32:18
sing unto the Lord. . .Judg. 5:3
singing and dancing. . .1 Sam. 18:6
I will sing praises. . .2 Sam. 22:50
with singing, and with harps. . .1 Chron. 13:8
sing praise to the name. . .Ps. 7:17
Sing praises to the Lord. . .Ps. 9:11
daughters of *m*. . .Eccles. 12:4
young men from their *m*. . .Lam. 5:14
all kinds of *m*. . .Dan. 3:5
he heard *m* and dancing. . .Luke 15:25
sing unto thy name. . .Rom. 15:9
sing with the spirit. . .1 Cor. 14:15
singing and making melody. . .Eph. 5:19

See *Instruments of Musick*.

---

607. Mystery/ Mysteries

m of the kingdom of God. . .Mark 4:11
ignorant of this *m*. . .Rom. 11:25
revelation of the *m*. . .Rom. 16:25
wisdom of God in a *m*. . .1 Cor. 2:7
m'ies of God. . .1 Cor. 4:1

Behold, I shew you a *m*. . .1 Cor. 15:51
the *m* of his will. . .Eph. 1:9
in the *m* of Christ. . .Eph. 3:4
fellowship of the *m*. . .Eph. 3:9
This is a great *m*. . .Eph. 5:32
the *m* of the gospel. . .Eph. 6:19
m which hath been hid. . .Col. 1:26
this *m* among the Gentiles. . .Col. 1:27
acknowledgement of the *m* of God. . .Col. 2:2
to speak the *m* of Christ. . .Col. 4:3
m of iniquity doth already work. . .2 Thess. 2:7
Holding the *m* of the faith. . .1 Tim. 3:9
great is the *m* of godliness. . .1 Tim. 3:16
the *m* of God should be finished. . .Rev. 10:7

See *Secret/Secrets*.

608. Naked/ Nakedness

In scripture, nakedness not only describes a lack of physical clothing but also refers to our own spiritual inadequacy before God.

knew that they were *n*. . .Gen. 3:7
saw the *n'ness* of his. . .Gen. 9:22
to uncover their *n'ness*. . .Lev. 18:6
lay down *n* all that day. . .1 Sam. 19:24
N came I out of my mother's. . .Job 1:21
n and barefoot. . .Isa. 20:4
Thy *n'ness* shall be uncovered. . .Isa. 47:3
they have seen her *n'ness*. . .Lam. 1:8
thy *n'ness* discovered through. . .Ezek. 16:36
n'ness of thy whoredoms. . .Ezek. 23:29
mayest look on their *n'ness*!. . .Hab. 2:15
N, and ye clothed me. . .Matt. 25:36
or *n'ness*, or peril. . .Rom. 8:35

all things are *n*. . .Heb. 4:13
shame of thy *n'ness*. . .Rev. 3:18

609. Name

make thy *n* great. . .Gen. 12:2
A Good *n* is rather to be. . .Prov. 22:1
A good *n* is better than. . .Eccles. 7:1

610. Name of God

God's name reveals who He is to His people. Various names are used to describe God, each showing some part of His nature. The most often used in biblical times was His covenant name, Yahweh, or Jehovah, "the One who is always present." It is often translated as "LORD."

called upon the *n*. . .Gen. 12:8
dost ask after my *n*?. . .Gen. 32:29
this is my *n* for ever. . .Exod. 3:15
n o G Almighty. . .Exod. 6:3
my *n* may be declared. . .Exod. 9:16
n of the LORD thy God. . .Exod. 20:7
my *n* is in him. . .Exod. 23:21
whose *n* is Jealous. . .Exod. 34:14
in the *n* of the LORD. . .Deut. 18:22
call on the *n* of the LORD. . .1 Kings 18:24
holy and reverend is his *n*. . .Ps. 111:9

Hallowed be thy *n*. . .Matt. 6:9
n of the Father. . .Matt. 28:19
Father, glorify thy *n*. . .John 12:28
I have manifested thy *n*. . .John 17:6

none other *n* under heaven. . .Acts 4:12
call upon the *n*. . .Rom. 10:13
n which is above every *n*. . .Phil. 2:9
a more excellent *n*. . .Heb. 1:4
thou holdest fast my *n*. . .Rev. 2:13

See *"I Am" Statements of Jesus.*

611. Name of Jesus/ Name's

call his *n* JESUS. . .Matt. 1:21
shall call his *n* Emmanuel. . .Matt. 1:23
in his *n* shall the Gentiles trust. . .Matt. 12:21
in my *n*, receiveth me. . .Mark 9:37
for my *n*'s sake. . .Mark 13:13
that believe on his *n*. . .John 1:12
n of the only begotten. . .John 3:18
shall ask in my *n*. . .John 14:13
will send in my *n*. . .John 14:26
have life through his *n*. . .John 20:31

612. Nation/Nations

families, in their *n*'s. . .Gen. 10:5
make of thee a great *n*. . .Gen. 12:2
n's of the earth shall. . .Gen. 18:18
priests, and an holy *n*. . .Exod. 19:6
what one *n* in the earth. . .2 Sam. 7:23
Righteousness exalteth a *n*. . .Prov. 14:34
n shall not lift up sword. . .Isa. 2:4
n and kingdom that will. . .Isa. 60:12
n that was not called. . .Isa. 65:1
in the midst of the *n*'s. . .Ezek. 5:5
I will make them one *n*. . .Ezek. 37:22
wanderers among the *n*'s. . .Hosea 9:17
hated of all *n*'s. . .Matt. 24:9
teach all *n*'s. . .Matt. 28:19
whole *n* perish not. . .John 11:50
holy *n*, a peculiar people. . .1 Pet. 2:9

613. Nativity, the

Thy seed will I establish for ever. . .Ps. 89:4
Behold, a virgin shall conceive. . .Isa. 7:14
he that is born King of the Jews?. . .Matt. 2:2
young child with Mary his mother. . .Matt. 2:11
Hail, thou that art highly favoured. . .Luke 1:28
thou shalt conceive in thy womb. . .Luke 1:31
born of thee shall be called. . .Luke 1:35
she brought forth her firstborn son. . .Luke 2:7

unto you is born this day. . .Luke 2:11

this child is set for the fall. . .Luke 2:34

See *Virgin Birth.*

614. Natural Man

The old or natural man refers to a person who has not yet been redeemed by Christ. In our natural state, humans habitually sin. Only Christ brings us salvation.

our old man is crucified. . .Rom. 6:6

n m receiveth not. . .1 Cor. 2:14

old things are passed away. . .2 Cor. 5:17

by nature the children of wrath. . .Eph. 2:3

old man, which is corrupt. . .Eph. 4:22

old man with his deeds. . .Col. 3:9

615. Nazarite/ Nazarites

a vow of a *N.* . .Num. 6:2

this is the law of the *N.* . .Num. 6:13

N shall shave the head. . .Num. 6:18

upon the hands of the *N.* . .Num. 6:19

N may drink wine. . .Num. 6:20

This is the law of the *N.* . .Num. 6:21

child shall be a *N.* . .Judg. 13:5

N to God from the womb. . .Judg. 13:7

for I have been a *N.* . .Judg. 16:17

your young men for *N's.* . .Amos 2:11

gave the *N's* wine to drink. . .Amos 2:12

See *Vow/Vowed/Vowest/Vows.*

616. Nearness to God

Draw nigh unto my soul. . .Ps. 69:18

draw near to God. . .Ps. 73:28

people draw near me. . .Isa. 29:13

and come unto me. . .Isa. 55:3

we draw nigh unto God. . .Heb. 7:19

draw near with a true heart. . .Heb. 10:22

I will never leave thee. . .Heb. 13:5

Draw nigh to God. . .James 4:8

Come unto me, all ye that labour. . .Matt. 11:28

them not, to come unto me. . .Matt. 19:14

617. Necessities of Life

They shall be abundantly satisfied. . .Ps. 36:8

I not seen the righteous forsaken. . .Ps. 37:25

satisfy her poor with bread. . .Ps. 132:15

every man should eat and drink. . .Eccles. 3:13

Give us this day our daily bread. . .Matt. 6:11

what ye shall drink. . .Matt. 6:25

why take ye thought for raiment?. . .Matt. 6:28

Come unto me, all ye that labour. . .Matt. 11:28

man shall not live by bread alone. . .Luke 4:4

not one of them is forgotten. . .Luke 12:6

bread from heaven to eat. . .John 6:31

618. Neglect/ Neglected/Neglecting

forsake my statutes. . .2 Chron. 7:19
not forsake the house of our God. . .Neh. 10:39
house of God forsaken?. . .Neh. 13:11
forsaken the poor. . .Job 20:19
I will not forget thy word. . .Ps. 119:16
not mercy and truth forsake thee. . .Prov. 3:3
n to hear them. . .Matt. 18:17
not to leave the other undone. . .Matt. 23:23
n'ed in the daily ministration. . .Acts 6:1
n'ing of the body. . .Col. 2:23
N not the gift. . .1 Tim. 4:14
n so great salvation. . .Heb. 2:3

619. Neighbour/ Neighbour's

false witness against thy *n*. . .Exod. 20:16
not covet thy *n's* house. . .Exod. 20:17
thy *n's* raiment to pledge. . .Exod. 22:26
shalt not defraud thy *n*. . .Lev. 19:13

rebuke thy *n*. . .Lev. 19:17
love thy *n* as thyself. . .Lev. 19:18
not evil against thy *n*. . .Prov. 3:29
despiseth his *n* sinneth. . .Prov. 14:21
not a witness against thy *n*. . .Prov. 24:28
Withdraw thy foot from thy *n's*. . .Prov. 25:17
better is a *n* that is near. . .Prov. 27:10
n's service without wages. . .Jer. 22:13
who is my *n*?. . .Luke 10:29
Love worketh no ill to his *n*. . .Rom. 13:10
please his *n*. . .Rom. 15:2

620. New Life

Except a man be born again. . .John 3:3
born of water and of the Spirit. . .John 3:5
Ye must be born again. . .John 3:7
but have eternal life. . .John 3:15
walk in newness of life. . .Rom. 6:4
in Christ, he is a new creature. . .2 Cor. 5:17
but a new creature. . .Gal. 6:15
Being born again. . .1 Pet. 1:23

See *Born Again, Conversion, Knowing God, Regeneration, Salvation.*

621. Night

the darkness he called *N*. . .Gen. 1:5
divide the day from the *n*. . .Gen. 1:14
n shall not cease. . .Gen. 8:22
a *n* to be much observed. . .Exod. 12:42
giveth songs in the *n*. . .Job 35:10
n unto *n* sheweth knowledge. . .Ps. 19:2
even the *n* shall be light. . .Ps. 139:11
desired thee in the *n*. . .Isa. 26:9
came to Jesus by *n*. . .John 3:2

the *n* cometh. . .John 9:4
if a man walk in the *n*. . .John 11:10
cometh as a thief in the *n*. . .1 Thess. 5:2
we are not of the *n*. . .1 Thess. 5:5
prayers *n* and day. . .1 Tim. 5:5
there shall be no *n*. . .Rev. 21:25

622. Noise, Joyful

Make a *j n* unto God. . .Ps. 66:1
j n unto the God of Jacob. . .Ps. 81:1
j n to the rock. . .Ps. 95:1
make a *j n* unto him. . .Ps. 95:2
j n unto the Lord. . .Ps. 98:4
sound of cornet make a *j n*. . .Ps. 98:6
j n unto the Lord. . .Ps. 100:1

See *Sing/Singing, Worship/Worshipped.*

623. None Righteous

thoughts of his heart was only evil. . .Gen. 6:5
man's heart is evil from his youth. . .Gen. 8:21
I was shapen in iniquity. . .Ps. 51:5
The heart is deceitful. . .Jer. 17:9
There is *n r*. . .Rom. 3:10
For all have sinned. . .Rom. 3:23
for that all have sinned. . .Rom. 5:12
captivity to the law of sin. . .Rom. 7:23
carnal mind is enmity against God. . .Rom. 8:7

natural man receiveth not. . .1 Cor. 2:14
dead in trespasses and sins. . .Eph. 2:1
by nature the children of wrath. . .Eph. 2:3
alienated from the life of God. . .Eph. 4:18
If we say that we have no sin. . .1 John 1:8

624. Nourishment

and good for food. . .Gen. 2:9
thou mayest freely eat. . .Gen. 2:16
neither shall ye eat any flesh. . .Exod. 22:31
food out of the earth. . .Ps. 104:14
It is not good to eat much honey. . .Prov. 25:27
she bringeth her food from afar. . .Prov. 31:14
man shall not live by bread alone. . .Luke 4:4
neither to eat flesh. . .Rom. 14:21
having food and raiment. . .1 Tim. 6:8

See *Eat/Eateth/Eating, Food.*

625. Numbers

Various numbers have special meanings in the Bible, for example, seven, a number indicating perfection; twelve (and its multiples); and forty, which indicated a generation or completion.

seventh day God ended. . .Gen. 2:2
forty days and forty nights. . .Gen. 7:12
not destroy it for ten's sake. . .Gen. 18:32

Jacob served seven years. . .Gen. 29:20
seven well favoured kine. . .Gen. 41:2
seven other kine. . .Gen. 41:3
seventh year shall be a sabbath. . .Lev. 25:4
twelve chargers of silver. . .Num. 7:84
golden spoons were twelve. . .Num. 7:86
called unto him his twelve disciples. . .Matt. 10:1
Until seventy times seven. . .Matt. 18:22
seven golden candlesticks. . .Rev. 2:1
an hundred and forty and four thousand. . .Rev. 7:4
had twelve gates. . .Rev. 21:12
twelve manner of fruits. . .Rev. 22:2

626. Oath/Oaths

In biblical times an oath was a promise, often made in the name of the Lord. Keeping an oath made in His name was serious, since God would judge the outcome.

o which I sware. . .Gen. 26:3
Joseph took an *o*. . .Gen. 50:25
an *o* of the LORD. . .Exod. 22:11
this covenant and this *o*. . .Deut. 29:14
blameless of this thine *o*. . .Josh. 2:17
for the people feared the *o*. . .1 Sam. 14:26
LORD's *o* that was between. . .2 Sam. 21:7
That I may perform the *o*. . .Jer. 11:5
despised the *o*. . .Ezek. 16:59
love no false *o*. . .Zech. 8:17
perform unto the Lord thine *o's*. . .Matt. 5:33
promised with an *o* to give. . .Matt. 14:7
sworn with an *o* to him. . .Acts 2:30
neither by any other *o*. . .James 5:12

See *Swear/Swearers/Sweareth/Swearing, Vow/
Vowed/Vowest/Vows*.

627. Obedience

for *o* to the faith. . .Rom. 1:5
so by the *o* of one. . .Rom. 5:19
o unto righteousness?. . .Rom. 6:16
For your *o* is come abroad. . .Rom. 16:19
for the *o* of faith. . .Rom. 16:26
commanded to be under *o*. . .1 Cor. 14:34
the *o* of you all. . .2 Cor. 7:15
thought to the *o* of Christ. . .2 Cor. 10:5
when your *o* is fulfilled. . .2 Cor. 10:6
confidence in thy *o*. . .Philem. 1:21
yet learned he *o*. . .Heb. 5:8
unto *o* and sprinkling. . .1 Pet. 1:2

See *Discipline*.

628. Obesity

neither desire thou his dainty meats. . .Prov. 23:6
glutton shall come to poverty. . .Prov. 23:21
life is more than meat. . .Luke 12:23
sin therefore reign in your mortal body. . .Rom. 6:12
if ye live after the flesh. . .Rom. 8:13
body is the temple of the Holy Ghost. . .1 Cor. 6:19
glorify God in your body. . .1 Cor. 6:20
body, and bring it into subjection. . .1 Cor. 9:27

See *Glutton/Gluttonous*.

629. Obey/Obeyed

Abraham *o'ed* my voice. . .Gen. 26:5
if ye will *o* my voice. . .Exod. 19:5
if ye *o* the commandments. . .Deut. 11:27
thou mayest *o* his voice. . .Deut. 30:20
o'ed not the voice. . .Josh. 5:6
to *o* is better than sacrifice. . .1 Sam. 15:22
If they *o* and serve him. . .Job 36:11
despiseth to *o* his mother. . .Prov. 30:17
O my voice. . .Jer. 7:23
that it *o* not my voice. . .Jer. 18:10
shall serve and *o* him. . .Dan. 7:27
unclean spirits, and they do *o* him. . .Mark 1:27
given to them that *o* him. . .Acts 5:32
yield yourselves servants to *o*. . .Rom. 6:16
Children, *o* your parents. . .Eph. 6:1

630. Oblation/ Oblations

An oblation is a sacrificial offering that is not a blood offering.

o of a meat offering. . .Lev. 2:4
to offer their *o's*. . .Lev. 7:38
o for all his vows. . .Lev. 22:18
brought an *o*. . .Num. 31:50
Bring no more vain *o's*. . .Isa. 1:13
firstfruits of your *o's*. . .Ezek. 20:40

every sort of your *o's*. . .Ezek. 44:30
they should offer an *o*. . .Dan. 2:46
the *o* to cease. . .Dan. 9:27

See *Offering/Offerings, Sacrifice/Sacrifices.*

631. Obscenity

lewdness and folly in Israel. . .Judg. 20:6
filthiness of the people. . .Ezra 9:11
abominable and filthy is man. . .Job 15:16
all together become filthy. . .Ps. 14:3
altogether become filthy. . .Ps. 53:3
lewdness of thy whoredom. . .Jer. 13:27
ashamed of thy lewd way. . .Ezek. 16:27
another hath lewdly defiled. . .Ezek. 22:11
bear thou also thy lewdness. . .Ezek. 23:35
cause lewdness to cease. . .Ezek. 23:48
In thy filthiness is lewdness. . .Ezek. 24:13
filthiness of the flesh. . .2 Cor. 7:1
Neither filthiness, nor foolish. . .Eph. 5:4
abominations and filthiness. . .Rev. 17:4

See *Abomination.*

632. Occult, the

not suffer a witch to live. . .Exod. 22:18
neither shall ye use enchantment. . .Lev. 19:26
such as have familiar spirits. . .Lev. 20:6
or an enchanter, or a witch. . .Deut. 18:10
or a wizard, or a necromancer. . .Deut. 18:11
priests and the diviners. . .1 Sam. 6:2
familiar spirits, and the wizards. . .1 Sam. 28:3
hath a familiar spirit. . .1 Sam. 28:7
soothsayers like the Philistines. . .Isa. 2:6
your enchanters, nor to your sorcerers. . .Jer. 27:9

prophets and your diviners. . .Jer. 29:8
soothsayers, shew unto the king. . .Dan. 2:27
shalt have no more soothsayers. . .Mic. 5:12
bewitched them with sorceries. . .Acts 8:11
Idolatry, witchcraft, hatred. . .Gal. 5:20

See *Magic/Magicians, Sorcery/Sorcerer/Sorcerers, Witch/Witchcraft/Witchcrafts.*

more than all whole burnt *o's.* . .Mark 12:33
given himself for us an *o.* . .Eph. 5:2
Sacrifice and *o* thou wouldest not. . .Heb. 10:5
o he hath perfected. . .Heb. 10:14
no more *o* for sin. . .Heb. 10:18

See *Oblation/Oblations, Sacrifice/Sacrifices, Tithe/Tithes.*

633. Offence/Offences

yielding pacifieth great *o's.* . .Eccles. 10:4
for a rock of *o.* . .Isa. 8:14
thou art an *o.* . .Matt. 16:23
be that *o's* come. . .Matt. 18:7
conscience void to *o.* . .Acts 24:16
Who was delivered for our *o's.* . .Rom. 4:25
But not as the *o.* . .Rom. 5:15
by one man's *o* death. . .Rom. 5:17
the *o* might abound. . .Rom. 5:20
stumblingstone and rock of *o.* . .Rom. 9:33
man who eateth with *o.* . .Rom. 14:20
divisions and *o's* contrary. . .Rom. 16:17
Giving no *o.* . .2 Cor. 6:3
o of the cross. . .Gal. 5:11
without *o* till. . .Phil. 1:10

635. Oil

The Bible describes oil as one of the blessings God gave His obedient people. It was used in lamps, to provide light, and in cooking; oil was added to spices to create anointing oil and was used as a medication and in healing services. It was also a valuable trading commodity.

O for the light. . .Exod. 25:6
o of holy ointment. . .Exod. 30:25

634. Offering/Offerings

Abel and to his *o.* . .Gen. 4:4
for a burnt *o.* . .Gen. 22:2
lamb for a burnt *o.* . .Gen. 22:8
Sacrifice and *o* thou didst. . .Ps. 40:6
delightest not in burnt *o.* . .Ps. 51:16
freewill *o's* of my mouth. . .Ps. 119:108
o in righteousness. . .Mal. 3:3

flour unleavened, mingled with *o*. . .Lev. 2:5
thy wine, and thine *o*. . .Deut. 7:13
land of *o* olive, and honey. . .Deut. 8:8
Samuel took the horn of *o*. . .1 Sam. 16:13
twenty measures of pure *o*. . .1 Kings 5:11
the cruse of *o* fail. . .1 Kings 17:14
meat, and drink, and *o*. . .Ezra 3:7
anointest my head with *o*. . .Ps. 23:5
o to make his face to shine. . .Ps. 104:15
he that loveth wine and *o*. . .Prov. 21:17
o of joy for mourning. . .Isa. 61:3
wounds, pouring in *o* and wine. . .Luke 10:34
anointing him with *o*. . .James 5:14

---

636. Opportunity

*Scripture speaks of our opportunities to do
good or evil and encourages us to make the
most of our time and situation.*

sought *o* to betray him. . .Matt. 26:16
taking occasion. . .Rom. 7:8
we have therefore *o*. . .Gal. 6:10
Redeeming the time. . .Eph. 5:16
but ye lacked *o*. . .Phil. 4:10
redeeming the time. . .Col. 4:5
none occasion to the adversary. . .1 Tim. 5:14
o to have returned. . .Heb. 11:15

---

637. Oppose/ Opposed/Opposeth/ Oppositions

hate thee, which persecuted thee. . .Deut. 30:7
all them that persecute me. . .Ps. 7:1
persecutors and mine enemies. . .Ps. 119:157
persecuted for righteousness' sake. . .Matt. 5:10

use you, and persecute you. . .Matt. 5:44
persecute you in this city. . .Matt. 10:23
persecute them from city to city. . .Matt. 23:34
and persecute you. . .Luke 21:12
the Jews persecute Jesus. . .John 5:16
If they have persecuted me. . .John 15:20
persecution against the church. . .Acts 8:1
when they *o'd* themselves. . .Acts 18:6
Who *o'th* and exalteth himself. . .2 Thess. 2:4
o'itions of science falsely. . .1 Tim. 6:20
instructing those that *o* themselves. . .2 Tim. 2:25

See *Oppression/Oppressions, Persecute/Persecuted/
Persecutest, Persecution/Persecutions.*

---

638. Oppression/ Oppressions

I have also seen the *o*. . .Exod. 3:9
our labour, and our *o*. . .Deut. 26:7
openeth their ears in *o*. . .Job 36:15
For the *o* of the poor. . .Ps. 12:5
o of the enemy?. . .Ps. 42:9
Trust not in *o*. . .Ps. 62:10
brought low through *o*. . .Ps. 107:39
Deliver me from the *o*. . .Ps. 119:134
o maketh a wise man mad. . .Eccles. 7:7
despiseth the gain of *o's*. . .Isa. 33:15

thou shalt be far from *o*. . .Isa. 54:14

people's inheritance by *o*. . .Ezek. 46:18

See *Oppose/Opposed/Opposeth/Oppositions, Persecute/Persecuted/Persecutest, Persecution/ Persecutions.*

639. Ordain/Ordained

o a place for my people. . .1 Chron. 17:9

which thou hast *o'ed*. . .Ps. 8:3

o'ed them for judgment. . .Hab. 1:12

chosen you, and *o'ed* you. . .John 15:16

he which was *o'ed* of God. . .Acts 10:42

o'ed to eternal life. . .Acts 13:48

powers that be are *o'ed* of God. . .Rom. 13:1

hidden wisdom, which God *o'ed*. . .1 Cor. 2:7

Even so hath the Lord *o'ed*. . .1 Cor. 9:14

o'ed that we should walk. . .Eph. 2:10

o'ed to this condemnation. . .Jude 1:4

640. Orphans

or fatherless child. . .Exod. 22:22

the judgment of the fatherless. . .Deut. 10:18

nor of the fatherless. . .Deut. 24:17

for the fatherless. . .Deut. 24:19

fatherless, and the widow. . .Deut. 26:12

thou art the helper of the fatherless. . .Ps. 10:14

fatherless and the oppressed. . .Ps. 10:18

A father of the fatherless. . .Ps. 68:5

Defend the poor and fatherless. . .Ps. 82:3

We are *o* and fatherless. . .Lam. 5:3

widow, and the fatherless. . .Mal. 3:5

To visit the fatherless. . .James 1:27

641. Outcast/Outcasts

Cast out this bondwoman. . .Gen. 21:10

I will cast out the nations. . .Exod. 34:24

I cast out of my sight. . .1 Kings 9:7

cast out the priests. . .2 Chron. 13:9

together the *o's* of Israel. . .Ps. 147:2

assemble the *o's* of Israel. . .Isa. 11:12

hide the *o's*. . .Isa. 16:3

o's in the land of Egypt. . .Isa. 27:13

gathereth the *o's* of Israel. . .Isa. 56:8

because they called thee an *O*. . .Jer. 30:17

o's of Elam. . .Jer. 49:36

642. Outward Appearance

man looketh on the *o a*. . .1 Sam. 16:7

them which glory in appearance. . .2 Cor. 5:12

things after the *o a*?. . .2 Cor. 10:7

adorn themselves in modest apparel. . .1 Tim. 2:9

not be that outward adorning. . .1 Pet. 3:3

See *Appearance, Physical.*

643. Overcome/ Overcometh

I have *o* the world. . .John 16:33

o evil with good. . .Rom. 12:21
ye have *o* the wicked one. . .1 John 2:13
and have *o* them. . .1 John 4:4
whatsoever is born of God *o'th*. . .1 John 5:4
he that *o'th* the world. . .1 John 5:5
To him that *o'th*. . .Rev. 2:7
He that *o'th* shall not be hurt. . .Rev. 2:11
o'th will I give to eat. . .Rev. 2:17
o'th, and keepeth my works. . .Rev. 2:26
He that *o'th*, the same shall be. . .Rev. 3:5
Him that *o'th* will I make. . .Rev. 3:12
that *o'th* will I grant. . .Rev. 3:21
the Lamb shall *o* them. . .Rev. 17:14
He that *o'th* shall inherit. . .Rev. 21:7

See *Triumph/Triumphed/Triumphing*.

644. Overwhelm/ Overwhelmed
Yea, ye *o* the fatherless. . .Job 6:27
horror hath *o'ed* me. . .Ps. 55:5
when my heart is *o'ed*. . .Ps. 61:2
my spirit was *o'ed*. . .Ps. 77:3
the sea *o'ed* their enemies. . .Ps. 78:53
waters had *o'ed* us. . .Ps. 124:4
When my spirit was *o'ed*. . .Ps. 142:3
my spirit *o'ed* within me. . .Ps. 143:4

See *Struggles*.

645. Pacifism
Thou shalt not kill. . .Exod. 20:13
beat their swords into plowshares. . .Mic. 4:3
Blessed are the peacemakers. . .Matt. 5:9
That ye resist not evil. . .Matt. 5:39

shall perish with the sword. . .Matt. 26:52
My kingdom is not of this world. . .John 18:36
avenge not yourselves. . .Rom. 12:19
overcome evil with good. . .Rom. 12:21
none render evil for evil. . .1 Thess. 5:15
ye should follow his steps. . .1 Pet. 2:21
Not rendering evil for evil. . .1 Pet. 3:9

646. Pagan
"Pagan" is not a word used in the King James Version of the Bible, but there are many references to the heathen and Gentiles—people who worshipped idols instead of the one God.

in the sight of the heathen. . .Lev. 26:45
went after the heathen. . .2 Kings 17:15
put down the idolatrous priests. . .2 Kings 23:5
Declare his glory among the heathen. . .1 Chron. 16:24
Why do the heathen rage. . .Ps. 2:1
scattered us among the heathen. . .Ps. 44:11
heathen entered into her sanctuary. . .Lam. 1:10
vain repetitions, as the heathen do. . .Matt. 6:7
these things do the Gentiles seek. . .Matt. 6:32
heathen man and a publican. . .Matt. 18:17
named among the Gentiles. . .1 Cor. 5:1
Neither be ye idolaters. . .1 Cor. 10:7

things which the Gentiles sacrifice. . .1 Cor. 10:20
Ye know that ye were Gentiles. . .1 Cor. 12:2
honest among the Gentiles. . .1 Pet. 2:12
taking nothing of the Gentiles. . .3 John 1:7

See *Gentiles, Heathen.*

647. Pain/Pained

wicked man travaileth with *p*. . .Job 15:20
mine affliction and my *p*. . .Ps. 25:18
My heart is sore *p'ed* within me. . .Ps. 55:4
I found trouble and sorrow. . .Ps. 116:3
p'ed at my very heart. . .Jer. 4:19
p, as of a woman. . .Jer. 6:24

See *Sorrow/Sorrowed/Sorrows.*

648. Parables

mote that is in thy brother's eye. . .Matt. 7:3
wise man, which built his house. . .Matt. 7:24
unclean spirit is gone out of a man. . .Matt. 12:43
sower went forth to sow. . .Matt. 13:3
a grain of mustard seed. . .Matt. 13:31
one pearl of great price. . .Matt. 13:46
sheep, and one of them be gone astray. . .Matt. 18:12
labourers into his vineyard. . .Matt. 20:1
A certain man had two sons. . .Matt. 21:28
householder, which planted a vineyard. . .Matt. 21:33
king, which made a marriage for his son. . .Matt. 22:2
ten virgins, which took their lamps. . .Matt. 25:1
one he gave five talents. . .Matt. 25:15
creditor which had two debtors. . .Luke 7:41
I am the true vine. . .John 15:1

649. Paradoxes

Blessed are the poor in spirit. . .Matt. 5:3
Blessed are ye, when men shall revile. . .Matt. 5:11
He that findeth his life shall lose it. . .Matt. 10:39
So the last shall be first. . .Matt. 20:16
exalteth himself shall be abased. . .Luke 14:11
the good that I would I do not. . .Rom. 7:19
weep, as though they wept not. . .1 Cor. 7:30
as dying, and, behold, we live. . .2 Cor. 6:9
as poor, yet making many rich. . .2 Cor. 6:10
I am weak, then am I strong. . .2 Cor. 12:10
to live is Christ, and to die is gain. . .Phil. 1:21
the poor of this world rich. . .James 2:5

650. Parents

rise up against their *p*. . .Matt. 10:21
p brought in the child Jesus. . .Luke 2:27
no man that hath left house, or *p*. . .Luke 18:29
who did sin, this man, or his *p*. . .John 9:2
Therefore said his *p*. . .John 9:23
disobedient to *p*. . .Rom. 1:30
p for the children. . .2 Cor. 12:14

Children, obey your *p*. . .Eph. 6:1
obey your *p* in all things. . .Col. 3:20
to requite their *p*. . .1 Tim. 5:4
disobedient to *p*. . .2 Tim. 3:2

See *Family*, *Father/Fathers*, *Mother/Mother's*.

651. Partner/Partners

Whoso is *p* with a thief. . .Prov. 29:24
which were *p's* with Simon. . .Luke 5:10
not unequally yoked together. . .2 Cor. 6:14
my *p* and fellowhelper. . .2 Cor. 8:23
count me therefore a *p*. . .Philem. 1:17

See *Business*.

652. Passion of Christ

*"Passion" is used only once in scripture, by
Luke in Acts 1:3, to describe Jesus' suffering in
the last days of His earthly life. The events of
His passion were foretold in the Prophets.*

I am poured out like water. . .Ps. 22:14
He is despised and rejected of men. . .Isa. 53:3
he was wounded for our transgressions. . .Isa. 53:5
oppressed, and he was afflicted. . .Isa. 53:7

pleased the LORD to bruise him. . .Isa. 53:10
poured out his soul unto death. . .Isa. 53:12
whom they have pierced. . .Zech. 12:10
suffer many things of the elders. . .Matt. 16:21
to give his life a ransom for many. . .Matt. 20:28
that he must suffer many things. . .Mark 9:12
first must he suffer many things. . .Luke 17:25
shewed himself alive after his *p*. . .Acts 1:3
Christ must needs have suffered. . .Acts 17:3
That Christ should suffer. . .Acts 26:23
sin by the sacrifice of himself. . .Heb. 9:26

653. Passover

it is the LORD's *p*. . .Exod. 12:11
This is the ordinance of the *p*. . .Exod. 12:43
forbeareth to keep the *p*. . .Num. 9:13
Thou shalt therefore sacrifice the *p*. . .Deut. 16:2
Then they killed the *p*. . .2 Chron. 30:15
did they eat the *p* otherwise. . .2 Chron. 30:18

keep such a *p* as Josiah kept. . .2 Chron. 35:18
p, and the Son of man. . .Matt. 26:2
and they made ready the *p*. . .Matt. 26:19
at the feast of the *p*. . .Luke 2:41
I have desired to eat this *p*. . .Luke 22:15
that they might eat the *p*. . .John 18:28
release unto you one at the *p*. . .John 18:39
Christ our *p* is sacrificed. . .1 Cor. 5:7
Through faith he kept the *p*. . .Heb. 11:28

654. Pastor

See *Church Leaders.*

655. Path/Paths/ Path of Life

The *p's* of their way. . .Job 6:18

p's of all that forget God. . .Job 8:13

lookest narrowly unto all my *p's*. . .Job 13:27

shew me the *p o l*. . .Ps. 16:11

p's of righteousness. . .Ps. 23:3

lead me in a plain *p*. . .Ps. 27:11

a light unto my *p*. . .Ps. 119:105

Thou compassest my *p*. . .Ps. 139:3

thou knewest my *p*. . .Ps. 142:3

refrain thy foot from their *p*. . .Prov. 1:15

her *p's* unto the dead. . .Prov. 2:18

he shall direct thy *p's*. . .Prov. 3:6

the *p* of the just. . . Prov. 4:18

ponder the *p o l*. . .Prov. 5:6

weigh the *p* of the just. . .Isa. 26:7

destruction are in their *p's*. . .Isa. 59:7

ask for the old *p's*. . .Jer. 6:16

we will walk in his *p's*. . .Mic. 4:2

make straight *p's*. . .Heb. 12:13

656. Patience/ Patient/Patiently

the Lord, and wait *p'tly*. . .Ps. 37:7

p't in spirit is better. . .Eccles. 7:8

bring forth fruit with *p*. . .Luke 8:15

p possess ye your souls. . .Luke 21:19

tribulation worketh *p*. . .Rom. 5:3

we with *p* wait for it. . .Rom. 8:25

p and comfort of the scriptures. . .Rom. 15:4

God of *p* and consolation. . .Rom. 15:5

be *p't* toward all men. . .1 Thess. 5:14

p't waiting for Christ. . .2 Thess. 3:5

p't, not a brawler. . .1 Tim. 3:3

love, *p*, meekness. . .1 Tim. 6:11

p inherit the promises. . .Heb. 6:12

ye have need of *p*. . .Heb. 10:36

run with *p* the race. . .Heb. 12:1

let *p* have her perfect work. . .James 1:4

and to temperance *p*. . .2 Pet. 1:6

See *Delay/Delayed, Longsuffering, Perseverance, Wait/Waited/Waiteth/Waiting.*

657. Pay/Payeth

p for the loss of his time. . .Exod. 21:19

let him *p* double. . .Exod. 22:7

p double unto his neighbour. . .Exod. 22:9

p money according to the dowry. . .Exod. 22:17

shalt not slack to *p* it. . .Deut. 23:21

sell the oil, and *p*. . .2 Kings 4:7

Haman had promised to *p*. . .Esther 4:7

wicked borroweth, and *p'eth* not. . .Ps. 37:21

given will he *p* him again. . .Prov. 19:17

your master *p* tribute?. . .Matt. 17:24

as he had not to *p*. . .Matt. 18:25

till he should *p* all. . .Matt. 18:34

ye *p* tithe of mint. . .Matt. 23:23

p ye tribute also. . .Rom. 13:6

658. Peace

unto him my covenant of *p*. . .Num. 25:12
bless his people with *p*. . .Ps. 29:11
the end of that man is *p*. . .Ps. 37:37
speak *p* unto his people. . .Ps. 85:8
Pray for the *p* of Jerusalem. . .Ps. 122:6
keep him in perfect *p*. . . Isa. 26:3
thy *p* been as a river. . .Isa. 48:18
P, p; when there is no *p*. . .Jer. 6:14
feet into the way of *p*. . .Luke 1:79
p, good will toward men. . .Luke 2:14
come to give *p* on earth?. . .Luke 12:51
P I leave with you. . .John 14:27
ye might have *p*. . .John 16:33
we have *p* with God. . .Rom. 5:1
p of God, which passeth. . .Phil. 4:7
let the *p* of God rule. . .Col. 3:15

See *Harmony*, *Peacemakers*.

659. Peacemakers

work of righteousness shall be peace. . .Isa. 32:17
that publisheth peace!. . .Nah. 1:15
Blessed are the *p*. . .Matt. 5:9
have peace one with another. . .Mark 9:50
live peaceably with all men. . .Rom. 12:18
things which make for peace. . .Rom. 14:19
live in peace. . .2 Cor. 13:11
preparation of the gospel of peace. . .Eph. 6:15
be at peace among yourselves. . .1 Thess. 5:13
Follow peace with all men. . .Heb. 12:14
them that make peace. . .James 3:18
let him seek peace. . .1 Pet. 3:11

See *Peace*.

660. Peer Pressure

Scripture clearly advises Christians to choose their friends carefully and to live in a way that glorifies God, no matter what others think.

thy friend, which is as thine own soul. . .Deut. 13:6
Thou shalt not consent unto him. . .Deut. 13:8
Depart from evil, and do good. . .Ps. 34:14
companion of all them that fear thee. . .Ps. 119:63
Depart from me, ye evildoers. . .Ps. 119:115
keep thee from the evil woman. . .Prov. 6:24
a companion of fools. . .Prov. 13:20
A friend loveth at all times. . .Prov. 17:17
a companion of riotous men. . .Prov. 28:7
companion of a destroyer. . .Prov. 28:24
Whoso is partner with a thief. . .Prov. 29:24
please his neighbour. . .Rom. 15:2
please all men in all things. . .1 Cor. 10:33
do I seek to please men?. . .Gal. 1:10
not as pleasing men, but God. . .1 Thess. 2:4
ye ought to walk and to please God. . .1 Thess. 4:1

See *Pleasing God*.

661. People of God

chosen thee to be a peculiar people. . .Deut. 14:2
this day to be his peculiar people. . .Deut. 26:18

assembly of the *p o G*. . .Judg. 20:2

a people to himself. . .2 Sam. 7:23

a thing against the *p o G*?. . .2 Sam. 14:13

unto himself a peculiar people. . .Titus 2:14

a rest to the *p o G*. . .Heb. 4:9

suffer affliction with the *p o G*. . .Heb. 11:25

an holy nation, a peculiar people. . .1 Pet. 2:9

are now the *p o G*. . .1 Pet. 2:10

be revealed, the son of *p*. . .2 Thess. 2:3

drown men in destruction and *p*. . .1 Tim. 6:9

them who draw back unto *p*. . .Heb. 10:39

day of judgment and *p*. . .2 Pet. 3:7

and go into *p*. . .Rev. 17:8

and goeth into *p*. . .Rev. 17:11

See *Hell*.

662. Perceive

hath not given you an heart to *p*. . .Deut. 29:4

that ye may *p* and see. . .1 Sam. 12:17

but I cannot *p* him. . .Job 23:8

p the words of understanding. . .Prov. 1:2

I *p* that there is nothing better. . .Eccles. 3:22

see ye indeed, but *p* not. . .Isa. 6:9

ye shall see, and shall not *p*. . .Matt. 13:14

Do ye not *p*. . .Mark 7:18

I *p* that virtue is gone out. . .Luke 8:46

I *p* that thou art a prophet. . .John 4:19

I *p* that God is no respecter. . .Acts 10:34

p that in all things ye. . .Acts 17:22

Hereby *p* we the love of God. . .1 John 3:16

664. Perfect

In our own power, as Christians, we are certainly not perfect. Our perfection comes from God, who is perfect; only as His Spirit works in us are we perfected.

Noah was a just man and *p*. . .Gen. 6:9

before me, and be thou *p*. . .Gen. 17:1

shalt be *p* with the Lord. . .Deut. 18:13

his work is *p*. . .Deut. 32:4

As for God, his way is *p*. . .2 Sam. 22:31

he maketh my way *p*. . .2 Sam. 22:33

serve him with a *p* heart. . .1 Chron. 28:9

man was *p* and upright. . .Job 1:1

God will not cast away a *p* man. . .Job 8:20

he that is *p* in knowledge. . .Job 36:4

The law of the Lord is *p*. . .Ps. 19:7

Mark the *p* man. . .Ps. 37:37

Be ye therefore *p*. . .Matt. 5:48

If thou wilt be *p*. . .Matt. 19:21

they may be made *p* in one. . .John 17:23

acceptable, and *p*, will of God. . .Rom. 12:2

when that which is *p* is come. . .1 Cor. 13:10

made *p* in weakness. . .2 Cor. 12:9

now made *p* by the flesh?. . .Gal. 3:3

unto a *p* man. . .Eph. 4:13

p in Christ Jesus. . .Col. 1:28

663. Perdition

lost, but the son of *p*. . .John 17:12

to them an evident token of *p*. . .Phil. 1:28

p, thoroughly furnished. . .2 Tim. 3:17

good gift and every *p* gift. . .James 1:17

p love casteth out fear. . .1 John 4:18

See *Perfection*.

665. Perfection

the Almighty unto *p*?. . .Job 11:7

searcheth out all *p*. . .Job 28:3

Zion, the *p* of beauty. . .Ps. 50:2

I have seen an end of all *p*. . .Ps. 119:96

we wish, even your *p*. . .2 Cor. 13:9

let us go on unto *p*. . .Heb. 6:1

p were by the Levitical. . .Heb. 7:11

See *Perfect*.

666. Perish/ Perished/Perisheth

ye shall surely *p*. . .Deut. 8:19

So let all thine enemies *p*. . .Judg. 5:31

to cause to *p*, all Jews. . .Esther 3:13

if I *p*, I *p*. . .Esther 4:16

the ungodly shall *p*. . .Ps. 1:6

are far from thee shall *p*. . .Ps. 73:27

have *p'ed* in mine affliction. . .Ps. 119:92

wicked *p*, there is shouting. . .Prov. 11:10

is no vision, the people *p*. . .Prov. 29:18

strive with thee shall *p*. . .Isa. 41:11

The righteous *p'eth*. . .Isa. 57:1

one of thy members should *p*. . .Matt. 5:29

Lord, save us: we *p*. . .Matt. 8:25

shall *p* with the sword. . .Matt. 26:52

shall all likewise *p*. . .Luke 13:3

not an hair of your head *p*. . .Luke 21:18

not *p*, but have eternal life. . .John 3:15

not for the meat which *p'eth*. . . John 6:27

they shall never *p*. . .John 10:28

whole nation *p* not. . .John 11:50

though our outward man *p*. . .2 Cor. 4:16

not willing that any should *p*. . .2 Pet. 3:9

667. Persecute/ Persecuted/ Persecutest

hate thee, which *p'd* thee. . .Deut. 30:7

all them that *p* me. . .Ps. 7:1

wicked in his pride doth *p*. . .Ps. 10:2

Princes have *p'd* me. . .Ps. 119:161

p'd for righteousness' sake. . .Matt. 5:10

so *p'd* they the prophets. . .Matt. 5:12

use you, and *p* you. . .Matt. 5:44

p you in this city. . .Matt. 10:23

p them from city to city. . .Matt. 23:34

and *p* you. . .Luke 21:12

the Jews *p* Jesus. . .John 5:16

If they have *p'd* me. . .John 15:20

I am Jesus whom thou *p'st*. . .Acts 9:5

p'd the church of God. . .1 Cor. 15:9

P'd, but not forsaken. . .2 Cor. 4:9

born after the flesh *p'd* him. . .Gal. 4:29
and others were tortured. . .Heb. 11:35

See *Oppose/Opposed/Opposeth/Oppositions,
Oppression/Oppressions, Persecution/Persecutions.*

668. Persecution/ Persecutions

p ariseth for the word's sake. . .Mark 4:17
children, and lands, with *p's*. . .Mark 10:30
p against the church. . .Acts 8:1
scattered abroad upon the *p*. . .Acts 11:19
raised *p* against Paul. . .Acts 13:50
distress, or *p*, or famine. . .Rom. 8:35
in *p's*, in distresses. . .2 Cor. 12:10
p for the cross of Christ. . .Gal. 6:12
your *p's* and tribulations. . .2 Thess. 1:4
what *p's* I endured. . .2 Tim. 3:11
in Christ Jesus shall suffer *p*. . .2 Tim. 3:12

See *Oppose/Opposed/Opposeth/Oppositions,
Oppression/Oppressions, Persecute/Persecuted/
Persecutest.*

669. Perseverance

endureth all things. . .1 Cor. 13:7

with all *p* and supplication. . .Eph. 6:18
continue in them. . .1 Tim. 4:16
for he endured, as seeing. . .Heb. 11:27
let us run with patience. . .Heb. 12:1
trying of your faith worketh patience. . .James 1:3
Blessed is the man that endureth. . .James 1:12
we count them happy which endure. . .James 5:11
And hast borne, and hast patience. . .Rev. 2:3

See *Endure/Endured/Endureth/Enduring, Patience/
Patient/Patiently.*

670. Persuade/ Persuaded/ Persuadeth/ Persuasion

Hezekiah make you trust. . .2 Kings 18:30
With her much fair speech. . .Prov. 7:21
is a prince *p'd*. . .Prov. 25:15
makest this people to trust. . .Jer. 28:15
elders *p'd* the multitude. . .Matt. 27:20
And to him they agreed. . .Acts 5:40
Then they suborned men. . .Acts 6:11
she besought us. . .Acts 16:15
some of them believed . . .Acts 17:4
and *p'd* the Jews and Greeks. . .Acts 18:4
p'th men to worship. . .Acts 18:13
Being fully *p'd* that. . .Rom. 4:21
not with enticing words. . .1 Cor. 2:4
we *p* men. . .2 Cor. 5:11
This *p'sion* cometh not. . .Gal. 5:8

671. Perversion

*The word "perversion" does not appear in the
King James Bible. Where a modern translation*

would use that word, the King James Version uses "confusion" or explains the kind of perversion that occurred in biblical times.

lie down thereto: it is confusion. . .Lev. 18:23
they have wrought confusion. . .Lev. 20:12
recompence of their error. . .Rom. 1:27
them over to a reprobate mind. . .Rom. 1:28
except ye be reprobates?. . .2 Cor. 13:5
defile themselves with mankind. . .1 Tim. 1:10
reprobate concerning the faith. . .2 Tim. 3:8
unto every good work reprobate. . .Titus 1:16
going after strange flesh. . .Jude 1:7

the *P's* began to reason. . .Luke 5:21
he went into the *P's* house. . .Luke 7:36
spake unto the lawyers and *P's*. . .Luke 14:3
P's also, who were covetous. . .Luke 16:14
to pray; the one a *P*. . .Luke 18:10
P's, named Nicodemus. . .John 3:1
P's therefore said unto him. . .John 8:13
P's him that aforetime was blind. . .John 9:13
P's they did not confess him. . .John 12:42
P, named Gamaliel. . .Acts 5:34
P, the son of a *P*. . .Acts 23:6

See *Legalism*.

672. Pharisee/ Pharisee's/Pharisees

The Pharisees were the legalists of Israel. They sought to follow every letter of the Law, but missed the truth that Jesus was the Messiah. Instead, they became His major opposition. While they contended with Him, the Pharisees missed out on God's love and grace.

saw many of the *P's*. . .Matt. 3:7
of the scribes and *P's*. . .Matt. 5:20
when the *P's* saw it. . .Matt. 9:11
we and the *P's* fast. . .Matt. 9:14
when the *P's* saw it. . .Matt. 12:2
when the *P's* heard it. . .Matt. 12:24
the *P's* were offended. . .Matt. 15:12
beware of the leaven of the *P's*. . .Matt. 16:6
doctrine of the *P's*. . .Matt. 16:12
P's had heard. . .Matt. 22:34
woe unto you, scribes and *P's*. . .Matt. 23:13
Woe unto you, scribes and *P's*. . .Matt. 23:29
P's came together unto Pilate. . .Matt. 27:62

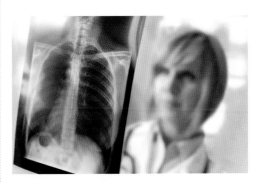

673. Physician/ Physicians

but to the *p's*. . .2 Chron. 16:12
ye are all *p's* of no value. . .Job 13:4
is there no *p* there?. . .Jer. 8:22
whole need not a p. . .Matt. 9:12
P, heal thyself. . .Luke 4:23
whole need not a *p*. . .Luke 5:31
spent all her living upon *p's*. . .Luke 8:43
Luke, the beloved *p*. . .Col. 4:14

See *Heal/Healing*.

674. Piety

in all godliness and honesty. . .1 Tim. 2:2
women professing godliness. . .1 Tim. 2:10
great is the mystery of godliness. . .1 Tim. 3:16
thyself rather unto godliness. . .1 Tim. 4:7
godliness is profitable. . .1 Tim. 4:8
shew *p* at home. . .1 Tim. 5:4
according to godliness. . .1 Tim. 6:3
supposing that gain is godliness. . .1 Tim. 6:5
godliness with contentment. . .1 Tim. 6:6
righteousness, godliness, faith. . .1 Tim. 6:11
Having a form of godliness. . .2 Tim. 3:5
truth which is after godliness. . .Titus 1:1
that pertain unto life and godliness. . .2 Pet. 1:3
and to patience godliness. . .2 Pet. 1:6
And to godliness brotherly kindness. . .2 Pet. 1:7
in all holy conversation and godliness. . .2 Pet. 3:11

675. Pity

have no *p* upon them. . .Deut. 7:16
Thine eye shall not *p* him. . .Deut. 19:13
And thine eye shall not *p*. . .Deut. 19:21
because he had no *p*. . .2 Sam. 12:6
To him that is afflicted *p*. . .Job 6:14
looked for some to take *p*. . .Ps. 69:20
hath *p* upon the poor. . .Prov. 19:17
for him that will *p* the poor. . .Prov. 28:8
in his *p* he redeemed them. . .Isa. 63:9
I will not *p*, nor spare. . .Jer. 13:14
For who shall have *p* upon thee. . .Jer. 15:5
neither have *p*, nor have mercy. . .Jer. 21:7
neither will I have any *p*. . .Ezek. 5:11
Thou hast had *p* on the gourd. . .Jon. 4:10
even as I had *p* on thee?. . .Matt. 18:33

See *Compassion/Compassions.*

676. Plant/Plants

the herb yielding seed. . .Gen. 1:11
every *p* of the field. . .Gen. 2:5
bush was not consumed. . .Exod. 3:2
leeks, and the onions. . .Num. 11:5
He causeth the grass to grow. . .Ps. 104:14
Thy *p*'s are an orchard. . .Song of Sol. 4:13
whether the vine flourished. . .Song of Sol. 6:11
A bruised reed shall he not break. . .Isa. 42:3
before him as a tender *p*. . .Isa. 53:2
as hemlock in the furrows. . .Hosea 10:4
God prepared a gourd. . .Jon. 4:6
sowed tares among the wheat. . .Matt. 13:25
grain of mustard seed. . .Matt. 13:31
p, which my heavenly Father. . .Matt. 15:13
mint and rue and all manner of herbs. . .Luke 11:42
If then God so clothe the grass. . .Luke 12:28

See *Crops, Food.*

677. Pleasing God

hast pleasure in uprightness. . .1 Chron. 29:17
This also shall please the LORD. . .Ps. 69:31
that do his pleasure. . .Ps. 103:21
pleasure in them that fear him. . .Ps. 147:11
a man's ways please the LORD. . .Prov. 16:7
in the flesh cannot please God. . .Rom. 8:8
how he may please the Lord. . .1 Cor. 7:32
worthy of the Lord unto all pleasing. . .Col. 1:10
well pleasing unto the Lord. . .Col. 3:20
not as pleasing men, but God. . .1 Thess. 2:4
they please not God. . .1 Thess. 2:15
ought to walk and to please God. . .1 Thess. 4:1
that he pleased God. . .Heb. 11:5
impossible to please him. . .Heb. 11:6
God is well pleased. . .Heb. 13:16

See *Peer Pressure.*

678. Pleasure/ Pleasures

at thy right hand there are *p's*. . .Ps. 16:11
the river of thy *p's*. . .Ps. 36:8
all them that have *p* therein. . .Ps. 111:2
He that loveth *p*. . .Prov. 21:17
thou that art given to *p's*. . .Isa. 47:8
from doing thy *p*. . .Isa. 58:13
and *p's* of this life. . .Luke 8:14
I take *p* in infirmities. . .2 Cor. 12:10
had *p* in unrighteousness. . .2 Thess. 2:12
she that liveth in *p*. . .1 Tim. 5:6
lovers of *p's*. . .2 Tim. 3:4
serving divers lusts and *p's*. . .Titus 3:3
Ye have lived in *p*. . .James 5:5
count it *p* to riot. . .2 Pet. 2:13

679. Plenty

p of corn and wine. . .Gen. 27:28
seven years of great *p*. . .Gen. 41:29
p shall be forgotten. . .Gen. 41:30
p shall not be known. . .Gen. 41:31
great *p* of almug trees. . .1 Kings 10:11
and have left *p*. . .2 Chron. 31:10
thou shalt have *p* of silver. . .Job 22:25
in *p* of justice. . .Job 37:23
thy barns be filled with *p*. . .Prov. 3:10
shall have *p* of bread. . .Prov. 28:19
And ye shall eat in *p*. . .Joel 2:26

680. Pollution
See *Ecology.*

681. Poor, the

any of my people that is *p*. . .Exod. 22:25
wrest the judgment of thy *p*. . .Exod. 23:6
p of thy people may eat. . .Exod. 23:11
p shall never cease. . .Deut. 15:11
The LORD maketh *p*. . .1 Sam. 2:7

the *p* hath hope. . .Job 5:16

He delivereth the *p*. . .Job 36:15

he that considereth the *p*. . .Ps. 41:1

the Lord heareth the *p*. . .Ps. 69:33

Defend the *p* and fatherless. . .Ps. 82:3

He becometh *p* that dealeth. . .Prov. 10:4

p, yet hath great riches. . .Prov. 13:7

He that oppresseth the *p*. . .Prov. 14:31

p that walketh in his integrity. . .Prov. 19:1

He that hath pity upon the *p*. . .Prov.19:17

plead the cause of the *p*. . .Prov. 31:9

stretcheth out her hand to the *p*. . .Prov. 31:20

a strength to the *p*. . .Isa. 25:4

p among men shall rejoice. . .Isa. 29:19

have the *p* always with you. . .Matt. 26:11

p of this world rich in faith. . .James 2:5

See *Beggar/Begging*, *Give/Given/Giveth*, *Haves and Have Nots*, *Lack/Lacked*, *Poverty*, *Welfare.*

682. Popularity

despise me shall be lightly
  esteemed. . .1 Sam. 2:30

poor man, and lightly esteemed?. . .1 Sam. 18:23

regardeth the rich. . .Job 34:19

he that shutteth his lips is esteemed. . .Prov. 17:28

we esteemed him not. . .Isa. 53:3

we did esteem him stricken. . .Isa. 53:4

esteemed as earthen pitchers. . .Lam. 4:2

let each esteem other better. . .Phil. 2:3

683. Pornography

rejoice with the wife of thy youth. . .Prov. 5:18

Lust not after her beauty. . .Prov. 6:25

looketh on a woman to lust. . .Matt. 5:28

lusts of their own hearts. . .Rom. 1:24

Let not sin therefore reign. . .Rom. 6:12

make not provision for the flesh. . .Rom. 13:14

not fulfil the lust of the flesh. . .Gal. 5:16

fulfilling the desires of the flesh. . .Eph. 2:3

Not in the lust of concupiscence. . .1 Thess. 4:5

abstain from fleshly lusts. . .1 Pet. 2:11

walked in lasciviousness, lusts. . .1 Pet. 4:3

lust of the eyes. . .1 John 2:16

684. Possession, Demon

possessed with devils. . .Matt. 4:24

were possessed with devils. . .Matt. 8:16

two possessed with devils. . .Matt. 8:28

dumb man possessed with a devil. . .Matt. 9:32

possessed with a devil, blind. . .Matt. 12:22

unclean spirit had torn him. . .Mark 1:26

which hath a dumb spirit. . .Mark 9:17

he was casting out a devil. . .Luke 11:14

many that were possessed. . .Acts 8:7

possessed with a spirit. . .Acts 16:16

because it was not possible. . .Acts 2:24

in the flesh cannot please God. . .Rom. 8:8

If it be possible. . .Rom. 12:18

he cannot deny himself. . .2 Tim. 2:13

God, that cannot lie. . .Titus 1:2

For it is not possible. . .Heb. 10:4

God cannot be tempted with evil. . .James 1:13

685. Possession/ Possessions/Possessing

for an everlasting *p*. . .Gen. 48:4

p's of flocks and herds. . .2 Chron. 32:29

for he had great *p's*. . .Matt. 19:22

things which he possesseth. . .Luke 12:15

sold their *p's*. . . Acts 2:45

which he possessed was his own. . .Acts 4:32

possessors of lands or houses. . .Acts 4:34

Sapphira his wife, sold a *p*. . .Acts 5:1

give it to him for a *p*. . .Acts 7:5

and yet *p'ing* all things. . .2 Cor. 6:10

redemption of the purchased *p*. . .Eph. 1:14

686. Possibilities/ Impossibilities

heavens cannot contain thee. . .1 Kings 8:27

I cannot attain unto it. . .Ps. 139:6

Many waters cannot quench love. . .Song of Sol. 8:7

a god that cannot save. . .Isa. 45:20

Ye cannot serve God and mammon. . .Matt. 6:24

Ask, and it shall be given you. . .Matt. 7:7

all things are possible. . .Matt. 19:26

if it were possible. . .Matt. 24:24

believe, all things are possible. . .Mark 9:23

things are possible unto thee. . .Mark 14:36

cannot be my disciple. . .Luke 14:27

cannot enter into the kingdom. . .John 3:5

687. Potter, God as/ Potter's/Potters'

pieces like a *p's* vessel. . .Ps. 2:9

esteemed as the *p's* clay. . .Isa. 29:16

breaking of the *ps'* vessel. . .Isa. 30:14

the clay, and thou our *p*. . .Isa. 64:8

cannot I do with you as this *p*?. . .Jer. 18:6

as one breaketh a *p's* vessel. . .Jer. 19:11

work of the hands of the *p!*. . .Lam. 4:2

p power over the clay. . .Rom. 9:21

as the vessels of a *p*. . .Rev. 2:27

688. Poverty

regard the prayer of the destitute. . .Ps. 102:17

So shall thy *p* come. . .Prov. 6:11

poor is their *p*. . .Prov. 10:15

but it tendeth to *p*. . .Prov. 11:24

P and shame shall be. . .Prov. 13:18

lest thou come to *p*. . .Prov. 20:13

glutton shall come to *p*. . .Prov. 23:21

shall have *p* enough. . .Prov. 28:19

p shall come upon him. . .Prov. 28:22

give me neither *p* nor riches. . .Prov. 30:8

and forget his *p*. . .Prov. 31:7

p abounded unto the riches. . .2 Cor. 8:2

through his *p* might be rich. . .2 Cor. 8:9

destitute of daily food. . .James 2:15

and *p*, (but thou art rich). . .Rev. 2:9

See *Beggar/Begging; Lack/Lacked; Poor, the.*

689. Power, God's

The Father's

shew in thee my *p*. . .Exod. 9:16

is become glorious in *p*. . .Exod. 15:6

giveth thee *p* to get wealth. . .Deut. 8:18

God is my strength and *p*. . .2 Sam. 22:33

p and a stretched out arm. . .2 Kings 17:36

p, and the glory. . .1 Chron. 29:11

there not *p* and might. . .2 Chron. 20:6

God hath *p* to help. . .2 Chron. 25:8

his *p* and his wrath. . .Ezra 8:22

redeemed by thy great *p*. . .Neh. 1:10

his *p* who can understand?. . .Job 26:14

God exalteth by his *p*. . .Job 36:22

he is excellent in *p*. . .Job 37:23

p belongeth unto God. . .Ps. 62:11

p shall thine enemies submit. . .Ps. 66:3

He ruleth by his *p* for ever. . .Ps. 66:7

p of thine anger?. . .Ps. 90:11

he is strong in *p*. . .Isa. 40:26

He giveth *p* to the faint. . .Isa. 40:29

made the earth by his *p*. . .Jer. 10:12

slow to anger, and great in *p*. . .Nah. 1:3

kingdom, and the *p*. . .Matt. 6:13

his eternal *p* and Godhead. . .Rom. 1:20

to make his *p* known. . .Rom. 9:22

there is no *p* but of God. . .Rom. 13:1

but in the *p* of God. . .1 Cor. 2:5

raise up us by his own *p*. . .1 Cor. 6:14

liveth by the *p* of God. . .2 Cor. 13:4

Christ's

Son of man hath *p*. . .Matt. 9:6

p and great glory. . .Matt. 24:30

All *p* is given unto me. . .Matt. 28:18

his word was with *p*. . .Luke 4:32

p he commandeth. . .Luke 4:36

p over all flesh. . .John 17:2

the Son of God with *p*. . .Rom. 1:4

not be afraid of the *p*?. . .Rom. 13:3

p to stablish you. . .Rom. 16:25

Christ the *p* of God. . .1 Cor. 1:24

p of our Lord Jesus Christ. . .1 Cor. 5:4

p of Christ may rest upon me. . .2 Cor. 12:9

p, and riches, and wisdom. . .Rev. 5:12

The Spirit's

in the *p* of the Spirit. . .Luke 4:14
p of the Holy Ghost. . .Rom. 15:13
p of the Spirit of God. . .Rom. 15:19

690. Power, Human

It is very clear in scripture that man's power always comes from God.

as a prince hast thou *p*. . .Gen. 32:28
ye shall have no *p* to stand. . .Lev. 26:37
My *p* and the might. . .Deut. 8:17
seeth that their *p* is gone. . .Deut. 32:36
a mighty man of *p*. . .1 Sam. 9:1
have *p* over them. . .Esther 9:1
all the acts of his *p*. . .Esther 10:2
are mighty in *p*?. . .Job 21:7
seen the wicked in great *p*. . .Ps. 37:35
p unto his people. . .Ps. 68:35
hath *p* over the spirit. . .Eccles. 8:8
it is in the *p* of their hand. . .Mic. 2:1
gave them *p* and authority. . .Luke 9:1
unto you *p* to tread. . .Luke 10:19
p to become the sons . . .John 1:12
I have *p* to crucify thee. . .John 19:10
ye shall receive *p*. . .Acts 1:8
full of faith and *p*. . .Acts 6:8
The wife hath not *p*. . .1 Cor. 7:4
p which the Lord hath given . . .2 Cor. 13:10

greatly to be *p'd*. . .1 Chron. 16:25
I will *p* the Lord. . .Ps. 7:17
sing *p's* unto thy name. . .Ps. 18:49
inhabitest the *p's* of Israel. . .Ps. 22:3
p the Lord that seek him. . .Ps. 22:26
p is comely for the upright. . .Ps. 33:1
p shall continually be. . .Ps. 34:1
make his *p* glorious. . .Ps. 66:2
heaven and earth *p* him. . .Ps. 69:34
p thy great and terrible name. . .Ps. 99:3
who can shew forth all his *p*?. . .Ps. 106:2
his *p* endureth for ever. . .Ps. 111:10
Lord's name is to be *p'd*. . .Ps. 113:3
The dead *p* not the Lord. . .Ps. 115:17
kings of the earth shall *p* thee. . .Ps. 138:4
p thee; for I am fearfully. . .Ps. 139:14
neither my *p* to graven images. . .Isa. 42:8
thou art my *p*. . .Jer. 17:14
more than the *p* of God. . .John 12:43
offer the sacrifice of *p*. . .Heb. 13:15

692. Pray/Prayed/Praying

I *p'ed* therefore unto the Lord. . .Deut. 9:26
in bitterness of soul, and *p'ed*. . .1 Sam. 1:10
ceasing to *p* for you. . .1 Sam. 12:23
p, and make supplication. . .1 Kings 8:33

691. Praise/Praises/Praised

fearful in *p's*. . .Exod. 15:11
He is thy *p*. . .Deut. 10:21
who is worthy to be *p'd*. . .2 Sam. 22:4

p'ing all this prayer. . .1 Kings 8:54
p unto thee in a time when thou. . .Ps. 32:6
will I *p*, and cry aloud. . .Ps. 55:17
P for the peace of Jerusalem. . .Ps. 122:6
p for them which despitefully. . .Matt. 5:44
p to thy Father. . .Matt. 6:6
manner therefore *p* ye. . .Matt. 6:9
to *p*, and not to faint. . .Luke 18:1
know not what we should *p*. . .Rom. 8:26
P without ceasing. . .1 Thess. 5:17
that men *p* every where. . .1 Tim. 2:8
afflicted? let him *p*. . .James 5:13
p one for another. . .James 5:16

693. Prayer/Prayers

hear thou in heaven their *p*. . .1 Kings 8:45
have heard thy *p*. . .1 Kings 9:3
I have heard thy *p*. . .2 Kings 20:5
I have heard thy *p*. . .2 Chron. 7:12
attent unto the *p*. . .2 Chron. 7:15
we made our *p*. . .Neh. 4:9
morning will I direct my *p*. . .Ps. 5:3
regard the *p* of the destitute. . .Ps. 102:17
p of the upright is his delight. . .Prov. 15:8
p of the righteous. . .Prov. 15:29
house of *p* for all people. . .Isa. 56:7
but by *p* and fasting. . .Matt. 17:21
ye shall ask in *p*. . .Matt. 21:22
continuing instant in *p*. . .Rom. 12:12
every thing by *p* and supplication. . .Phil. 4:6
supplications, *p's*, intercessions. . .1 Tim. 2:1
p of faith shall save the sick. . .James 5:15

See *Devotions*, *Word of God*.

694. Preach/Preached/Preaching

p good tidings unto the meek. . .Isa. 61:1
p'ing that I bid thee. . .Jon. 3:2
John the Baptist, *p'ing*. . .Matt. 3:1
p'ing the gospel of the kingdom. . .Matt. 4:23
p ye upon the housetops. . .Matt. 10:27
p'ed in all the world. . .Matt. 24:14
send them forth to *p*. . .Mark 3:14
p the gospel to the poor. . .Luke 4:18
teach and *p* Jesus Christ. . .Acts 5:42
the word of faith, which we *p*. . .Rom. 10:8
p'ing of the cross. . .1 Cor. 1:18
foolishness of *p'ing*. . .1 Cor. 1:21
But we *p* Christ crucified. . .1 Cor. 1:23
p'ing was not with enticing. . .1 Cor. 2:4
p the gospel, I may make. . .1 Cor. 9:18
then is our *p'ing* vain. . .1 Cor. 15:14
For we *p* not ourselves. . .2 Cor. 4:5
p any other gospel. . .Gal. 1:8
P the word. . .2 Tim. 4:2
p'ed unto the spirits in prison. . .1 Pet. 3:19

See *Witness/Witnessing*.

695. Predestinate/ Predestinated

p to be conformed. . .Rom. 8:29

p, them he also called. . .Rom. 8:30

Having *p'd* us unto. . .Eph. 1:5

p'd according to the purpose. . .Eph. 1:11

See *Election, Foreknowledge of God, Sovereignty of God.*

696. Premarital Sex

See *Adultery, Fornication/Fornications, Living Together, Marriage/Marry/Marrying.*

697. Presence of God

p o the Lord G. . .Gen. 3:8

My presence shall go. . .Exod. 33:14

at the presence of the Lord. . .1 Chron. 16:33

went forth from the presence of the Lord. . .Job 1:12

perish at the *p o G.* . .Ps. 68:2

at the presence of the Lord. . .Ps. 97:5

at the presence of the Lord. . .Ps. 114:7

from the presence of the Lord. . .Jon. 1:3

stand in the *p o G.* . .Luke 1:19

come from the presence of the Lord. . .Acts 3:19

from the presence of the Lord. . .2 Thess. 1:9

the *p o G* for us. . .Heb. 9:24

698. Prevail/Prevailed

his hand, that Israel *p'ed.* . .Exod. 17:11

house of Joseph *p'ed.* . .Judg. 1:35

p'ed against Chushan-rishathaim. . .Judg. 3:10

p'ed against Jabin the king. . .Judg. 4:24

Midian *p'ed* against Israel. . .Judg. 6:2

what means we may *p.* . .Judg. 16:5

by strength shall no man *p.* . .1 Sam. 2:9

David *p'ed* over the Philistine. . .1 Sam. 17:50

and also shalt still *p.* . .1 Sam. 26:25

children of Judah *p'ed.* . .2 Chron. 13:18

thou shalt not *p* against him. . .Esther 6:13

if one *p* against him. . .Eccles. 4:12

and they shall not *p.* . .Jer. 20:11

hell shall not *p* against it. . .Matt. 16:18

that he could *p* nothing. . .Matt. 27:24

the word of God and *p'ed.* . .Acts 19:20

Root of David, hath *p'ed.* . .Rev. 5:5

699. Pride

break the *p* of your power. . .Lev. 26:19

for the *p* of his heart. . .2 Chron. 32:26

wicked in his *p* doth persecute. . .Ps. 10:2

the *p* of his countenance. . .Ps. 10:4

p, and arrogancy, and the evil. . .Prov. 8:13

p cometh, then cometh shame. . .Prov. 11:2

by *p* cometh contention. . .Prov. 13:10

foolish is a rod of *p*. . .Prov. 14:3

P goeth before destruction. . .Prov. 16:18

A man's *p* shall bring. . .Prov. 29:23

those that walk in *p*. . .Dan. 4:37

blasphemy, *p*, foolishness. . .Mark 7:22

lest being lifted up with *p*. . .1 Tim. 3:6

and the *p* of life. . .1 John 2:16

700. Priesthood of Believers

The Old Testament line of the priesthood ended with Christ's sacrifice on the cross, as the temple veil tore from top to bottom. From that time, each believer had direct access to God through Jesus Christ and took up the position of the priesthood described in Exodus 19:6. In 1 Corinthians 12:7–11 and Ephesians 4:11–16, scripture describes the ministries of this priesthood of believers.

kingdom of priests, and an holy nation. . .Exod. 19:6

veil of the temple was rent. . .Matt. 27:51

the Spirit is given to every man. . .1 Cor. 12:7

And he gave some, apostles. . .Eph. 4:11

one mediator between God and men. . .1 Tim. 2:5

we have a great high priest. . .Heb. 4:14

holy priesthood, to offer up. . .1 Pet. 2:5

royal priesthood, an holy nation. . .1 Pet. 2:9

unto our God kings and priests. . .Rev. 5:10

they shall be priests of God. . .Rev. 20:6

701. Prince/Princes

He poureth contempt upon *p's*. . .Job 12:21

put confidence in *p's*. . .Ps. 118:9

P's have persecuted me. . .Ps. 119:161

By me *p's* rule. . .Prov. 8:16

destruction of the *p*. . .Prov. 14:28

much less do lying lips a *p*. . .Prov. 17:7

forbearing is a *p* persuaded. . .Prov. 25:15

p that wanteth understanding. . .Prov. 28:16

The *P* of Peace. . .Isa. 9:6

p's also shall worship. . .Isa. 49:7

unto the Messiah the *P*. . .Dan. 9:25

p of this world be cast out. . .John 12:31

killed the *P* of life . . .Acts 3:15

P and a Saviour. . .Acts 5:31

p of the kings of the earth. . .Rev. 1:5

See *Government, Ruler/Rulers.*

702. Prisoner/ Prisoners

where the king's *p's* were bound. . .Gen. 39:20

despiseth not his *p's*. . .Ps. 69:33

sighing of the *p* come. . .Ps. 79:11

groaning of the *p*. . .Ps. 102:20

The LORD looseth the *p's*. . .Ps. 146:7

to bring out the *p's*. . .Isa. 42:7

all the *p's* of the earth. . .Lam. 3:34

release unto the people a *p*. . .Matt. 27:15

notable *p*, called Barabbas. . .Matt. 27:16

the *p's* heard them. . .Acts 16:25

p's had been fled. . .Acts 16:27

Paul the *p* called me. . .Acts 23:18

counsel was to kill the *p's*. . .Acts 27:42

p of Jesus Christ. . .Eph. 3:1

See *Captive/Captives, Captive/Captivity, Imprisonment.*

703. Procrastination

See *Idle/Idleness, Slothful/Slothfulness.*

704. Profane/Profanity

p the name of thy God. . .Lev. 19:12

His mouth is full of cursing. . .Ps. 10:7

the sin of their mouth. . .Ps. 59:12

every idle word that. . .Matt. 12:36

cometh out of the mouth, this defileth. . .Matt. 15:11

mouth come forth from the heart. . .Matt. 15:18

mouth is full of cursing. . .Rom. 3:14

no corrupt communication proceed. . .Eph. 4:29

blasphemy, filthy communication. . .Col. 3:8

shun *p* and vain babblings. . .2 Tim. 2:16

See *Curse/Cursed/Cursing.*

705. Profit/Profitable/ Profited/Profiteth

which cannot *p* nor deliver. . .1 Sam. 12:21

thy righteousness may *p*. . .Job 35:8

wickedness *p* nothing. . .Prov. 10:2

Riches *p* not in the day. . .Prov. 11:4

In all labour there is *p*. . .Prov. 14:23

What *p* hath a man. . .Eccles. 1:3

by it there is *p*. . .Eccles. 7:11

which teacheth thee to *p*. . .Isa. 48:17

after things that do not *p*. . .Jer. 2:8

lying words, that cannot *p*. . .Jer. 7:8

p'able for thee that one. . .Matt. 5:29

For what is a man *p'ed*. . .Matt. 16:26

the flesh *p'eth* nothing. . .John 6:63

to every man to *p* withal. . .1 Cor. 12:7

charity, it *p'eth* me nothing. . .1 Cor. 13:3

bodily exercise *p'eth* little. . .1 Tim. 4:8

p'able for doctrine. . .2 Tim. 3:16

What doth it *p*, my brethren. . .James 2:14

706. Promise/ Promised/Promises
God's

God of thy fathers hath *p'd*. . .Deut. 6:3

LORD thy God *p'd* him. . .Deut. 10:9

blesseth thee, as he *p'd* thee. . .Deut. 15:6

as he hath *p'd* thee. . .Deut. 26:18
as he hath *p'd* you. . .Josh. 23:10
your God *p'd* you. . .Josh. 23:15
Solomon wisdom, as he *p'd*. . .1 Kings 5:12
p'd to David thy father. . .1 Kings 9:5
doth his *p* fail for evermore?. . . Ps. 77:8
good that I have *p'd* them. . .Jer. 32:42
mercy *p'd* to our fathers. . .Luke 1:72
p of my Father. . .Luke 24:49
p of the Holy Ghost. . .Acts 2:33
For the *p* is unto you. . .Acts 2:39
p raised unto Israel. . .Acts 13:23
he had *p'd*, he was able. . .Rom. 4:21
children of the *p*. . .Rom. 9:8
p's of God in him. . .2 Cor. 1:20
Having therefore these *p's*. . .2 Cor. 7:1
p of the Spirit. . .Gal. 3:14
when God made *p*. . .Heb. 6:13
not slack concerning his *p*. . .2 Pet. 3:9
p'd us, even eternal life. . .1 John 2:25

Humans'
which thou hast *p'd*. . .Deut. 23:23
he *p'd* with an oath. . .Matt. 14:7
he *p'd*, and sought. . .Luke 22:6

See *Promised Land*.

I will make of thee a great nation. . .Gen. 12:2
seed will I give this land. . .Gen. 12:7
all the land which thou seest. . .Gen. 13:15
walk through the land. . .Gen. 13:17
I will give unto thee. . .Gen. 17:8
Unto thy seed will I give this land. . .Gen. 24:7
I will give all these countries. . .Gen. 26:3
to thee will I give it. . .Gen. 28:13
bring thee again into this land. . .Gen. 28:15
the land which I gave Abraham. . .Gen. 35:12
give this land to thy seed. . .Gen. 48:4
land which he sware to Abraham. . .Gen. 50:24
land which the LORD will give you. . .Exod. 12:25
sojourned in the land of promise. . .Heb. 11:9

See *Promise/Promised/Promises*.

707. Promised Land
Though the words "Promised Land" do not appear in the King James Bible, the promise runs throughout the book of Genesis, and the writer of Hebrews reminds readers of this "land of promise."

unto a land that I will shew thee. . .Gen. 12:1

708. Proof/Proofs
by many infallible *p's*. . .Acts 1:3
might know the *p* of you. . .2 Cor. 2:9
the *p* of your love. . .2 Cor. 8:24
Since ye seek a *p* of Christ. . .2 Cor. 13:3
ye know the *p* of him. . .Phil. 2:22
make full *p* of thy ministry. . .2 Tim. 4:5

709. Prophecy/ Prophecies

seal up the vision and *p*. . .Dan. 9:24
fulfilled the *p* of Esaias. . .Matt. 13:14
whether *p*, let us prophesy. . .Rom. 12:6
to another *p*. . .1 Cor. 12:10
though I have the gift of *p*. . .1 Cor. 13:2
p'ies, they shall fail. . .1 Cor. 13:8
given thee by *p*. . .1 Tim. 4:14
a more sure word of *p*. . .2 Pet. 1:19
no *p* of the scripture. . .2 Pet. 1:20
p came not in old time. . .2 Pet. 1:21
hear the words of this *p*. . .Rev. 1:3
is the spirit of *p*. . .Rev. 19:10
keepeth the sayings of the *p*. . .Rev. 22:7
words of the book of this *p*. . .Rev. 22:19

710. Prophet/ Prophetess/Prophets

for he is a *p*. . .Gen. 20:7
Miriam the *p'ess*. . .Exod. 15:20
Lᴏʀᴅ's people were *p's*. . .Num. 11:29

a *p* among you. . .Num. 12:6
unto thee a P. . .Deut. 18:15
p, which shall presume. . .Deut. 18:20
many *p's* and righteous men. . .Matt. 13:17
A *p* is not without honour. . .Matt. 13:57
false *p's* shall rise. . .Matt. 24:11
false *p's*, and shall shew. . .Matt. 24:24
p of the Highest. . .Luke 1:76
of Galilee ariseth no *p*. . .John 7:52
are all *p's*?. . .1 Cor. 12:29
apostles; and some, *p's*. . .Eph. 4:11
But there were false *p's*. . .2 Pet. 2:1

711. Propitiation

God hath set forth to be a *p*. . .Rom. 3:25
he is the *p* for our sins. . .1 John 2:2
his Son to be the *p*. . .1 John 4:10

See *Finished Work of Christ*.

712. Prosperity

thy wisdom and *p*. . .1 Kings 10:7
in *p* the destroyer shall. . .Job 15:21
spend their days in *p*. . .Job 36:11
in my *p* I said. . .Ps. 30:6
in the *p* of his servant. . .Ps. 35:27
saw the *p* of the wicked. . .Ps. 73:3
send now *p*. . .Ps. 118:25
p within thy palaces. . .Ps. 122:7
p of fools shall destroy them. . .Prov. 1:32
In the day of *p* be joyful. . .Eccles. 7:14
I spake unto thee in thy *p*. . .Jer. 22:21
all the *p* that I procure. . .Jer. 33:9
I forgat *p*. . .Lam. 3:17
My cities through *p* shall yet. . .Zech. 1:17

713. Prostitution

See *Harlot/Harlot's/Harlots, Whore/Whoredom/Whoremonger/Whoremongers.*

714. Protection

and be your *p.* . .Deut. 32:38
my rock, and my fortress. . .2 Sam. 22:2
made an hedge about him. . .Job 1:10
broken down all his hedges. . .Ps. 89:40
my refuge and my fortress. . .Ps. 91:2
my fortress; my high tower. . .Ps. 144:2
The Lord is good, a strong hold. . .Nah. 1:7

715. Provision, God's

God will provide himself. . .Gen. 22:8
I have provided me a king. . .1 Sam. 16:1
not seen the righteous forsaken. . .Ps. 37:25
when thou hast so provided. . .Ps. 65:9
can he provide flesh for his people?. . .Ps. 78:20
abundantly bless her *p.* . .Ps. 132:15
Father knoweth that ye have need. . .Matt. 6:32
always having all sufficiency. . .2 Cor. 9:8
supply of the Spirit of Jesus. . .Phil. 1:19
God shall supply all your need. . .Phil. 4:19
provided some better thing. . .Heb. 11:40

716. Provocation/ Provocations

p wherewith he provoked. . .1 Kings 15:30
p wherewith thou hast provoked. . .1 Kings 21:22
all the *p's* that Manasseh. . .2 Kings 23:26
had wrought great *p's*. . .Neh. 9:18
they wrought great *p's*. . .Neh. 9:26
continue in their *p*?. . .Job 17:2

your heart, as in the *p.* . .Ps. 95:8
vexed his holy Spirit. . .Isa. 63:10
a *p* of mine anger. . .Jer. 32:31
p of their offering. . .Ezek. 20:28
hearts, as in the *p.* . .Heb. 3:15

717. Prudence/ Prudent/Prudently

and *p't* in matters. . .1 Sam. 16:18
I wisdom dwell with *p.* . .Prov. 8:12
p't man covereth shame. . .Prov. 12:16
p't man concealeth knowledge. . .Prov. 12:23
p't man dealeth with knowledge. . .Prov. 13:16
The wisdom of the *p't* . . .Prov. 14:8
the *p't* man looketh well. . .Prov. 14:15
p't are crowned with knowledge. . .Prov. 14:18
he that regardeth reproof is *p't* . . .Prov. 15:5
wise in heart shall be called *p't* . . .Prov. 16:21
heart of the *p't* getteth knowledge. . .Prov. 18:15
a *p't* wife is from the Lord. . .Prov. 19:14
A *p't* man foreseeth the evil. . .Prov. 22:3
and *p't* in their own sight!. . .Isa. 5:21
Behold, my servant shall deal *p'ly*. . .Isa. 52:13
Therefore the *p't* shall keep silence. . .Amos 5:13
things from the wise and *p't*. . .Matt. 11:25
the understanding of the *p't*. . .1 Cor. 1:19
in all wisdom and *p.* . .Eph. 1:8

718. Punish/ Punished/Punishment

p'ment is greater. . .Gen. 4:13

p you seven times more. . .Lev. 26:18

accept of the *p'ment*. . .Lev. 26:41

God hast *p'ed* us less. . .Ezra 9:13

p the just is not good. . .Prov. 17:26

wrath shall suffer *p'ment*. . .Prov. 19:19

When the scorner is *p'ed*. . .Prov. 21:11

simple pass on, and are *p'ed*. . .Prov. 22:3

p you according to the fruit. . .Jer. 21:14

man for the *p'ment* of his sins?. . .Lam. 3:39

will not turn away the *p'ment*. . .Amos 2:6

go away into everlasting *p'ment*. . .Matt. 25:46

p'ed with everlasting destruction. . .2 Thess. 1:9

Of how much sorer *p'ment*. . .Heb. 10:29

for the *p'ment* of evildoers. . .1 Pet. 2:14

719. Purpose/ Purposed/Purposes/ Purposeth

I am *p'd* that my mouth. . .Ps. 17:3

p'd to overthrow my goings. . .Ps. 140:4

Without counsel *p's* are disappointed. . .Prov. 15:22

Every *p* is established by counsel. . .Prov. 20:18

time to every *p* under the heaven. . .Eccles. 3:1

for every *p* and for every work. . .Eccles. 3:17

to every *p* there is time. . .Eccles. 8:6

the *p* that is *p'd* upon the. . .Isa. 14:26

Lord of hosts hath *p'd*. . .Isa. 14:27

with *p* of heart they. . .Acts 11:23

appeared unto thee for this *p*. . .Acts 26:16

I *p'd* to come unto you. . .Rom. 1:13

called according to his *p*. . .Rom. 8:28

p of God according to election. . .Rom. 9:11

for this same *p* have I raised thee up. . .Rom. 9:17

Every man according as he *p'th*. . .2 Cor. 9:7

which he hath *p'd* in himself. . .Eph. 1:9

predestinated according to the *p*. . .Eph. 1:11

p which he *p'd* in Christ. . .Eph. 3:11

according to his own *p* and grace. . .2 Tim. 1:9

For this *p* the Son of God. . .1 John 3:8

720. Quarrel

avenge the *q* of my covenant. . .Lev. 26:25

he seeketh a *q* against me. . .2 Kings 5:7

Herodias had a *q* against him. . .Mark 6:19

man have a *q* against any. . .Col. 3:13

See *Contention/Contentions/Contentious, Murmur/ Murmured/Murmurers/Murmuring/Murmurings*.

721. Queen

when the *q* of Sheba heard. . .1 Kings 10:1

Solomon gave unto the *q*. . .1 Kings 10:13

removed from being *q*. . .1 Kings 15:13

Vashti the *q* made a feast. . .Esther 1:9

heard of the deed of the *q*. . .Esther 1:18

q instead of Vashti. . .Esther 2:4

head, and made her *q*. . .Esther 2:17

who told it unto Esther the *q*. . .Esther 2:22

the king saw Esther the *q*. . .Esther 5:2

Esther the *q* answered. . .Esther 7:3

request for his life to Esther the *q*. . .Esther 7:7

enemy unto Esther the *q*. . .Esther 8:1

Ahasuerus said unto Esther the *q*. . .Esther 8:7

and Esther the *q*. . .Esther 9:31
Candace *q* of the Ethiopians. . .Acts 8:27
her heart, I sit a *q*. . .Rev. 18:7

722. Quench

that thou *q* not the light of Israel. . .2 Sam. 21:17
Many waters cannot *q* love. . .Song of Sol. 8:7
smoking flax shall he not *q*. . .Isa. 42:3
burn that none can *q* it. . .Jer. 4:4
there be none to *q* it. . .Amos 5:6
q all the fiery darts. . .Eph. 6:16
Q not the Spirit. . .1 Thess. 5:19

723. Ransom

give every man a *r* for his soul. . .Exod. 30:12
I have found a *r*. . .Job 33:24
then a great *r* cannot deliver thee. . .Job 36:18
nor give to God a *r* for him. . .Ps. 49:7
He will not regard any *r*. . .Prov. 6:35
r for the righteous. . .Prov. 21:18
I gave Egypt for thy *r*. . .Isa. 43:3
I will *r* them from the power of the
    grave. . .Hosea 13:14
to give his life a *r* for many. . .Matt. 20:28
to give his life a *r* for many. . .Mark 10:45
Who gave himself a *r* for all. . .1 Tim. 2:6

724. Rape

lay with her, and defiled her. . .Gen. 34:2
and lie with her. . .Exod. 22:16
force her, and lie with her. . .Deut. 22:25
lay hold on her, and lie. . .Deut. 22:28
knew her, and abused her. . .Judg. 19:25
forced her, and lay with her. . .2 Sam. 13:14

their wives ravished. . .Isa. 13:16
They ravished the women. . .Lam. 5:11
and the women ravished. . .Zech. 14:2

See *Abuse/Abusers/Abused, Adultery*.

725. Reaping/Sowing

Not only does scripture describe an agricultural reaping and sowing; it also tells people that they sow and reap a spiritual reward.

reap the harvest of your land. . .Lev. 19:9
not sow, neither reap. . .Lev. 25:11
wickedness, reap the same. . .Job 4:8
sow in tears shall reap in joy. . .Ps. 126:5
soweth iniquity shall reap vanity. . .Prov. 22:8
sown wheat, but shall reap thorns. . .Jer. 12:13
shall reap the whirlwind. . .Hosea 8:7
reap in mercy. . .Hosea 10:12
ye have reaped iniquity. . .Hosea 10:13
sow not, neither do they reap. . .Matt. 6:26

One soweth, and another reapeth. . .John 4:37

soweth sparingly shall reap. . .2 Cor. 9:6

soweth, that shall he also reap. . .Gal. 6:7

in due season we shall reap. . .Gal. 6:9

726. Rebel/Rebelled/ Rebellion/Rebellious

Only r not ye against. . .Num. 14:9

ye r'led against my word. . .Num. 20:24

then ye r'led against the commandment. . .Deut. 9:23

Ye have been r'lious. . .Deut. 9:24

a stubborn and r'lious son. . .Deut. 21:18

thy r'lion, and thy stiff neck. . .Deut. 31:27

Whosoever he be that doth r. . .Josh. 1:18

r'lion is as the sin. . .1 Sam. 15:23

disobedient, and r'led against thee. . .Neh. 9:26

those that r against the light. . .Job 24:13

he addeth r'lion unto his sin. . .Job 34:37

but the r'lious dwell in a dry land. . .Ps. 68:6

An evil man seeketh only r'lion. . .Prov. 17:11

Woe to the r'lious children. . .Isa. 30:1

we have r'led against him. . .Dan. 9:9

727. Rebuke/ Rebuked/Rebuketh

thou shalt in any wise r. . .Lev. 19:17

cursing, vexation, and r. . .Deut. 28:20

O Lord, r me not in thine anger. . .Ps. 6:1

Thou hast r'd the heathen. . .Ps. 9:5

Thou hast r'd the proud. . .Ps. 119:21

he that r'th a wicked man. . .Prov. 9:7

r a wise man. . .Prov. 9:8

a scorner heareth not r. . .Prov. 13:1

the poor heareth not r. . .Prov. 13:8

But to them that r him. . .Prov. 24:25

Open r is better. . .Prov. 27:5

He that r'th a man. . .Prov. 28:23

hear the r of the wise. . .Eccles. 7:5

the r of his people. . .Isa. 25:8

the sons of God, without r. . .Phil. 2:15

R not an elder. . .1 Tim. 5:1

Them that sin r before all. . .1 Tim. 5:20

reprove, r, exhort. . .2 Tim. 4:2

Wherefore r them sharply. . .Titus 1:13

speak, and exhort, and r. . .Titus 2:15

nor faint when thou art r'd. . .Heb. 12:5

As many as I love, I r. . .Rev. 3:19

728. Recompense/ Recompensed/ Recompensest

thou shalt not slack to pay it. . .Deut. 23:21

The Lord r thy work. . .Ruth 2:12

hath he r'd me. . .2 Sam. 22:21

the righteous shall be r'd. . .Prov. 11:31

I will r evil. . .Prov. 20:22

shouldest vow and not pay. . .Eccles. 5:5

r'st the iniquity of the fathers. . .Jer. 32:18

upon thee all thine abominations. . .Ezek. 7:3

shall r your lewdness. . .Ezek. 23:49

the labourer is worthy of his hire. . .Luke 10:7

for they cannot r thee. . .Luke 14:14

R to no man evil for evil. . .Rom. 12:17

r tribulation to them that trouble. . .2 Thess. 1:6

I will *r*, saith the Lord. . .Heb. 10:30

729. Reconcile/ Reconciled/ Reconciliation/ Reconciling

tabernacle of the congregation to *r*. . .Lev. 6:30

to make *r'iation* upon it. . .Lev. 8:15

end of *r'ing* the holy place. . .Lev. 16:20

r himself unto his master?. . .1 Sam. 29:4

they made *r'iation* with their blood. . .2 Chron. 29:24

to make *r'iation* for them. . .Ezek. 45:15

r'iation for the house of Israel. . .Ezek. 45:17

so shall ye *r* the house. . .Ezek. 45:20

to make *r'iation* for iniquity. . .Dan. 9:24

be *r'd* to thy brother. . .Matt. 5:24

we were *r'd* to God. . .Rom. 5:10

be the *r'ing* of the world. . .Rom. 11:15

be *r'd* to her husband. . .1 Cor. 7:11

hath *r'd* us to himself by Jesus Christ. . .2 Cor. 5:18

r'ing the world unto himself. . .2 Cor. 5:19

be ye *r'd* to God. . .2 Cor. 5:20

that he might *r* both unto God. . .Eph. 2:16

r all things unto himself. . .Col. 1:20

yet now hath he *r'd*. . .Col. 1:21

to make *r'iation* for the sins. . .Heb. 2:17

See *Finished Work of Christ*.

730. Recover/ Recovered/Recovering

he would *r* him of his leprosy. . .2 Kings 5:3

Shall I *r* of this disease?. . .2 Kings 8:8

that I may *r* strength. . .Ps. 39:13

was *r'ed* of his sickness. . .Isa. 38:9

so wilt thou *r* me. . .Isa. 38:16

and he shall *r*. . .Isa. 38:21

daughter of my people *r'ed*?. . .Jer. 8:22

the sick, and they shall *r*. . .Mark 16:18

r'ing of sight to the blind. . .Luke 4:18

See *Heal/Healing*.

731. Redeem/ Redeemed/Redeemeth

I will *r* you with a. . .Exod. 6:6

people which thou hast *r'ed*. . .Exod. 15:13

the Lord thy God *r'ed* thee. . .Deut. 15:15

r'ed my soul out of all adversity. . .2 Sam. 4:9

whom God went to *r*. . .2 Sam. 7:23

R Israel, O God. . .Ps. 25:22

r me, and be merciful. . .Ps. 26:11

thou hast *r'ed* me. . .Ps. 31:5

r'eth the soul of his servants. . .Ps. 34:22

r us for thy mercies' sake. . .Ps. 44:26

r my soul from the power. . .Ps. 49:15

unto my soul, and *r* it. . .Ps. 69:18

He shall *r* their soul. . .Ps. 72:14

r'eth thy life from destruction. . .Ps. 103:4

r'ed them from the hand. . .Ps. 106:10

Let the *r'ed* of the Lord. . .Ps. 107:2

hath *r'ed* us from our enemies. . .Ps. 136:24

I have *r'ed* thee . . .Isa. 43:1

for I have *r'ed* thee. . .Isa. 44:22

that it cannot *r*?. . .Isa. 50:2

ye shall be *r'ed* without money. . .Isa. 52:3

The holy people, The *r'ed*. . .Isa. 62:12

in his pity he *r'ed*. . .Isa. 63:9

he hath visited and *r'ed*. . .Luke 1:68

r'ed us from the curse. . .Gal. 3:13

r us from all iniquity. . .Titus 2:14

not *r'ed* with corruptible things. . .1 Pet. 1:18

r'ed us to God by thy blood. . .Rev. 5:9

r'ed from among men. . .Rev. 14:4

732. Redeemer

I know that my *r* liveth. . .Job 19:25

Lord, my strength, and my *r*. . .Ps. 19:14

the high God their *r*. . .Ps. 78:35

For their *r* is mighty. . .Prov. 23:11

thy *r*, the Holy One. . .Isa. 41:14

his *r* the Lord of hosts. . .Isa. 44:6

thy *r*, and he that formed. . .Isa. 44:24

R, the Holy One of Israel. . .Isa. 48:17

thy *R* the Holy One. . .Isa. 54:5

saith the Lord thy *R*. . .Isa. 54:8

the *R* shall come to Zion. . .Isa. 59:20

art our father, our *r*. . .Isa. 63:16

Their *R* is strong. . .Jer. 50:34

733. Redemption

r of their soul is precious. . .Ps. 49:8

He sent *r* unto his people. . .Ps. 111:9

with him is plenteous *r*. . .Ps. 130:7

looked for *r* in Jerusalem. . .Luke 2:38

for your *r* draweth nigh. . .Luke 21:28

r that is in Christ Jesus. . .Rom. 3:24

the *r* of our body. . .Rom. 8:23

righteousness, and sanctification,
    and *r*. . .1 Cor. 1:30

have *r* through his blood. . .Eph. 1:7

until the *r* of the purchased. . .Eph. 1:14

sealed unto the day of *r*. . .Eph. 4:30

we have *r* through his blood. . .Col. 1:14

having obtained eternal *r* for us. . .Heb. 9:12

the *r* of the transgressions. . .Heb. 9:15

See *Finished Work of Christ*.

734. Refreshed/ Refresheth/Refreshing, Spiritual

and the stranger, may be *r'ed*. . .Exod. 23:12

he rested, and was *r*. . .Exod. 31:17

Saul was *r*, and was well. . .1 Sam. 16:23

he *r'eth* the soul. . .Prov. 25:13

and this is the *r'ing*. . .Isa. 28:12

times of *r'ing* shall come. . .Acts 3:19

may with you be *r*. . .Rom. 15:32

they have *r* my spirit and yours. . .1 Cor. 16:18

his spirit was *r* by you all. . .2 Cor. 7:13

bowels of the saints are *r* by thee. . .Philem. 1:7

735. Refuge, Spiritual

The eternal God is thy r. . .Deut. 33:27
my r, my saviour. . .2 Sam. 22:3
a r for the oppressed. . .Ps. 9:9
because the LORD is his r. . .Ps. 14:6
God is our r and strength. . .Ps. 46:1
the God of Jacob is our r. . .Ps. 46:11
thy wings will I make my r. . .Ps. 57:1
r in the day. . .Ps. 59:16
my strength, and my r. . .Ps. 62:7
God is a r for us. . .Ps. 62:8
thou art my strong r . . .Ps. 71:7
He is my r and my fortress. . .Ps. 91:2
the LORD, which is my r. . .Ps. 91:9
the rock of my r. . .Ps. 94:22
my r and my portion. . .Ps. 142:5
shall have a place of r. . .Prov. 14:26
a r from the storm. . .Isa. 25:4
r in the day of affliction. . .Jer. 16:19
who have fled for r. . .Heb. 6:18

736. Regeneration

have followed me, in the r. . .Matt. 19:28
Except a man be born again. . .John 3:3
that which is born of the Spirit. . .John 3:6
alive unto God through Jesus. . .Rom. 6:11
cleanse it with the washing. . .Eph. 5:26
by the washing of r. . .Titus 3:5
Son cleanseth us from all sin. . .1 John 1:7

See *Born Again*, *New Life*, *Salvation*.

737. Reincarnation

Religions that believe in reincarnation teach
that after death, a person is reborn in another
body, not necessarily a human one. Various
Eastern religions have interpreted this belief
differently. In Hinduism, the soul that does
good in one life can improve its position in
the next one, while the soul that does wrong
will move into a lower life-form. The concepts
of a sinless Redeemer, the Resurrection, and
a heaven-or-hell judgment that follows one
life are foreign ideas to faiths that believe in

reincarnation.

our righteousnesses are as filthy rags. . .Isa. 64:6
righteous into life eternal. . .Matt. 25:46
thou be with me in paradise. . .Luke 23:43
before the judgment seat of Christ. . .Rom. 14:10
but ye are sanctified. . .1 Cor. 6:11
no resurrection of the dead?. . .1 Cor. 15:12
to be present with the Lord. . .2 Cor. 5:8
deliver us from this present evil world. . .Gal. 1:4
like as we are, yet without sin. . .Heb. 4:15
appointed unto men once to die. . .Heb. 9:27
faith and hope might be in God. . .1 Pet. 1:21

738. Reject/ Rejected/Rejecteth

they have r'ed me. . .1 Sam. 8:7

this day r'ed your God. . .1 Sam. 10:19

thou hast r'ed the. . .1 Sam. 15:23

I have r'ed him from reigning. . .1 Sam. 16:1

And they r'ed his statutes. . .2 Kings 17:15

despised and r'ed of men. . .Isa. 53:3

my law, but r'ed it. . .Jer. 6:19

LORD hath r'ed and forsaken. . .Jer. 7:29

they have r'ed the word. . .Jer. 8:9

I will also r thee. . .Hosea 4:6

ye r the commandment of God. . .Mark 7:9

suffer many things, and be r'ed. . .Luke 9:22

be r'ed of this generation. . .Luke 17:25

The stone which the builders r'ed. . .Luke 20:17

He that r'eth me. . .John 12:48

the first and second admonition r. . .Titus 3:10

he was r'ed. . .Heb. 12:17

739. Rejoice/Rejoiced/ Rejoiceth/Rejoicing

let the heart of them r. . .1 Chron. 16:10

and r with trembling. . .Ps. 2:11

glad and r in thee. . .Ps. 9:2

are right, r'ing the heart. . .Ps. 19:8

therefore my heart greatly r'th. . .Ps. 28:7

glad and r in thy mercy. . .Ps. 31:7

thou hast broken may r. . .Ps. 51:8

thy wings will I r. . .Ps. 63:7

Let the heavens r. . .Ps. 96:11

r and be glad in it. . .Ps. 118:24

I r at thy word. . .Ps. 119:162

r with the wife. . .Prov. 5:18

saw the star, they r'd. . .Matt. 2:10

R, and be exceeding glad. . .Matt. 5:12

many shall r at his birth. . .Luke 1:14

r in hope of the glory. . .Rom. 5:2

R'ing in hope. . .Rom. 12:12

R with them that do rejoice. . .Rom. 12:15

R in the Lord always. . .Phil. 4:4

R evermore. . .1 Thess. 5:16

r with joy unspeakable. . .1 Pet. 1:8

740. Relatives

See *Brother/Brother's/Brotherly/Brotherhood, Father/Fathers, Mother/Mother's.*

741. Religion

straitest sect of our r. . .Acts 26:5

in time past in the Jews' r. . .Gal. 1:13

profited in the Jews' r. . .Gal. 1:14

this man's r is vain. . .James 1:26

Pure r and undefiled before God. . .James 1:27

See *Faith.*

742. Remember/ Remembered/ Remembereth

I may *r* the everlasting covenant. . .Gen. 9:16

R the sabbath day. . .Exod. 20:8

r'ed before the LORD your God. . .Num. 10:9

r, and do all my commandments. . .Num. 15:40

r the LORD thy God. . .Deut. 8:18

the LORD *r'ed* her. . .1 Sam. 1:19

R his marvellous works. . .1 Chron. 16:12

r the name of the LORD. . .Ps. 20:7

R, O LORD, thy tender mercies. . .Ps. 25:6

I *r* thee upon my bed. . .Ps. 63:6

r'ed that God was their rock. . .Ps. 78:35

r not against us former iniquities. . .Ps. 79:8

he *r'eth* that we are dust. . .Ps. 103:14

wonderful works to be *r'ed*. . . Ps. 111:4

R now thy Creator. . .Eccles. 12:1

I will *r* their sin no more. . .Jer. 31:34

righteousnesses shall not be *r'ed*. . .Ezek. 33:13

r me when thou comest. . .Luke 23:42

iniquities will I *r* no more. . .Heb. 10:17

743. Remission

To remit is to release from guilt or penalty. The word also carries the idea of making payment for a demand.

for the *r* of sins. . .Matt. 26:28

repentance for the *r* of sins. . .Mark 1:4

by the *r* of their sins. . .Luke 1:77

repentance for the *r* of sins. . .Luke 3:3

r of sins should be preached. . .Luke 24:47

Jesus Christ for the *r* of sins. . .Acts 2:38

in him shall receive *r* of sins. . .Acts 10:43

r of sins that are past. . .Rom. 3:25

shedding of blood is no *r*. . .Heb. 9:22

Now where *r* of these is. . .Heb. 10:18

744. Remnant

The concept of a remnant of people who escape destruction by God's providence is not an uncommon theme in scripture. When sin destroys His people, God lifts up a few with whom to start again. When Babylon and Assyria attacked and carried off the Jews, a remnant returned to Israel. But those who disobeyed God and fled into Egypt were destroyed.

all the *r* of Israel. . .2 Chron. 34:9

r of their brethren the priests. . .Ezra 3:8

that the *r* of Israel. . .Isa. 10:20

The *r* shall return. . .Isa. 10:21

second time to recover the *r*. . .Isa. 11:11

the *r* that is escaped. . .Isa. 37:31

gather the *r* of my flock. . .Jer. 23:3

captive into Babylon the *r*. . .Jer. 39:9

ye *r* of Judah. . .Jer. 42:15

take the *r* of Judah. . .Jer. 44:12

Yet will I leave a *r*. . .Ezek. 6:8

r of Israel shall not. . .Zeph. 3:13

r of this people to possess. . .Zech. 8:12

a *r* shall be saved. . .Rom. 9:27

r according to the election. . .Rom. 11:5

745. Renew/ Renewed/Renewing

r a right spirit within me. . .Ps. 51:10

shall *r* their strength. . .Isa. 40:31

r our days as of old. . .Lam. 5:21

transformed by the *r'ing*. . .Rom. 12:2

inward man is *r'ed*. . .2 Cor. 4:16

be *r'ed* in the spirit. . .Eph. 4:23

is *r'ed* in knowledge. . .Col. 3:10

r'ing of the Holy Ghost. . .Titus 3:5

to *r* them again unto repentance. . .Heb. 6:6

See *Revive*, *Self-Help*.

746. Repentance

fruits meet for *r*. . .Matt. 3:8

baptize you with water unto *r*. . .Matt. 3:11

but sinners to *r*. . .Matt. 9:13

just persons, which need no *r*. . .Luke 15:7

r and remission of sins. . .Luke 24:47

to give *r* to Israel. . .Acts 5:31

to the Gentiles granted *r*. . .Acts 11:18

r toward God, and faith. . .Acts 20:21

do works meet for *r*. . .Acts 26:20

God leadeth thee to *r*?. . .Rom. 2:4

godly sorrow worketh *r*. . .2 Cor. 7:10

will give them *r*. . .2 Tim. 2:25

not laying again the foundation of *r*. . .Heb. 6:1

to renew them again unto *r*. . .Heb. 6:6

he found no place of *r*. . .Heb. 12:17

but that all should come to *r*. . .2 Pet. 3:9

See *Believe/Believed/Believeth/Believest*, *Coming to Christ*, *Conversion*, *Salvation*.

747. Reproach/ Reproached/ Reproaches/ Reproacheth

the *r* of Egypt from off you. . .Josh. 5:9

taketh away the *r* from Israel?. . .1 Sam. 17:26

to *r* the living God. . .2 Kings 19:4

Whom hast thou *r'ed*. . .2 Kings 19:22

r of the heathen our enemies?. . .Neh. 5:9

ten times have ye *r'ed* me. . .Job 19:3

my heart shall not *r* me. . .Job 27:6

the *r* of the foolish. . .Ps. 39:8

R hath broken my heart. . .Ps. 69:20

Remove from me *r* and contempt. . .Ps. 119:22

r'eth his Maker. . .Prov. 14:31

a *r* to any people. . .Prov. 14:34

take away my *r* among men. . .Luke 1:25

and shall *r* you. . .Luke 6:22

that *r'ed* thee fell on me. . .Rom. 15:3

in infirmities, in *r'es*. . .2 Cor. 12:10

lest he fall into *r*. . .1 Tim. 3:7

both labour and suffer *r*. . .1 Tim. 4:10

Esteeming the *r* of Christ. . .Heb. 11:26

bearing his *r*. . .Heb. 13:13

r'ed for the name of Christ. . .1 Pet. 4:14

See *Humiliation*.

748. Reproof/Reproofs

in whose mouth are no *r's*. . .Ps. 38:14

Turn you at my *r*. . .Prov. 1:23

would none of my *r*. . .Prov. 1:25

they despised all my *r*. . .Prov. 1:30

my heart despised *r*. . .Prov. 5:12

r's of instruction are the way. . .Prov. 6:23

he that refuseth *r* erreth. . .Prov. 10:17

he that hateth *r* is brutish. . .Prov. 12:1

he that regardeth *r* shall be
  honoured. . .Prov. 13:18

749. Reptiles

Lᴏʀᴅ God said unto the serpent. . .Gen. 3:14

became a serpent; and Moses fled. . .Exod. 4:3

and the tortoise after his kind. . .Lev. 11:29

the chameleon, and the lizard. . .Lev. 11:30

And the Lᴏʀᴅ sent fiery serpents. . .Num. 21:6

the cruel venom of asps. . .Deut. 32:33

on the hole of the asp. . .Isa. 11:8

shall come forth a cockatrice. . .Isa. 14:29

the viper and fiery flying serpent. . .Isa. 30:6

They hatch cockatrice' eggs. . .Isa. 59:5

I will send serpents, cockatrices. . .Jer. 8:17

fish, will he give him a serpent?. . .Matt. 7:10

therefore wise as serpents. . .Matt. 10:16

came a viper out of the heat. . .Acts 28:3

poison of asps is under . . .Rom. 3:13

that old serpent, which is the Devil. . .Rev. 20:2

See *Animals, Sea Creatures*.

750. Reputation

poor that walketh in his integrity. . .Prov. 19:1

good name is rather. . .Prov. 22:1

good name is better than precious. . .Eccles. 7:1

in *r* for wisdom and honour. . .Eccles. 10:1

in *r* among all the people. . .Acts 5:34

them which were of *r*. . .Gal. 2:2

But made himself of no *r*. . .Phil. 2:7

hold such in *r*. . .Phil. 2:29

751. Respect

When the Bible prohibits respect for a person, it is not telling us to treat others badly, but rather not to give someone who has a high position or stature or plenty of money more respect than a poor but honest believer—or to treat the poor well while belittling the person in a high position. Every person is to be treated as one who is important to God and is to be dealt with honestly.

shalt not *r* the person of the poor. . .Lev. 19:15

For I will have *r* unto you. . .Lev. 26:9

not *r* persons in judgment. . .Deut. 1:17

thou shalt not *r* persons. . .Deut. 16:19

had *r* unto them. . .2 Kings 13:23

Have *r* therefore to the prayer. . .2 Chron. 6:19

Have *r* unto the covenant. . .Ps. 74:20

r unto all thy commandments. . .Ps. 119:6

have *r* unto thy statutes. . .Ps. 119:117

r unto the lowly. . .Ps. 138:6

To have *r* of persons. . .Prov. 28:21

have *r* to the Holy One. . .Isa. 17:7

in *r* of an holyday. . .Col. 2:16

r unto the recompence. . .Heb. 11:26

And ye have *r* to him. . .James 2:3

See *Honour/Honoureth*.

752. Rest

the *r* of the holy sabbath. . .Exod. 16:23

seventh day thou shalt *r*. . .Exod. 23:12

I will give thee *r*. . .Exod. 33:14

seventh year shall be a sabbath of *r*. . .Lev. 25:4

not as yet come to the *r*. . .Deut. 12:9

given thee *r* from all thine enemies. . .Deut. 25:19

Lord gave them *r* round about. . .Josh. 21:44

my flesh also shall *r* in hope. . .Ps. 16:9

R in the Lord. . .Ps. 37:7

his *r* shall be glorious. . .Isa. 11:10

find *r* for your souls. . .Jer. 6:16

I will give you *r*. . .Matt. 11:28

shall not enter into my *r*. . .Heb. 3:11

a *r* to the people of God. . .Heb. 4:9

enter into that *r*. . .Heb. 4:11

753. Restitution

he should make full *r*. . .Exod. 22:3

shall he make *r*. . .Exod. 22:5

shall surely make *r*. . .Exod. 22:6

r unto the owner thereof. . .Exod. 22:12

according to his substance shall the *r*. . .Job 20:18

times of *r* of all things. . .Acts 3:21

754. Restore/ Restored/Restorer/ Restoreth

son he had *r'd* to life. . .2 Kings 8:5

He *r'th* my soul. . .Ps. 23:3

R unto me the joy. . .Ps. 51:12

r the preserved of Israel. . .Isa. 49:6

r comforts unto him. . .Isa. 57:18

r'r of paths to dwell in. . .Isa. 58:12

bring them up, and *r* them. . .Jer. 27:22

For I will *r* health unto thee. . .Jer. 30:17

I will *r* to you the years. . .Joel 2:25

r'd whole, like as the other. . .Matt. 12:13

first come, and *r* all things. . .Matt. 17:11

was *r'd*, and saw every man. . .Mark 8:25

I *r* him fourfold. . .Luke 19:8

r again the kingdom to Israel?. . .Acts 1:6

spiritual, *r* such an one. . .Gal. 6:1

755. Restrictions

thou shalt not eat of it. . .Gen. 2:17

shalt not make unto thee. . .Exod. 20:4

Thou shalt not bow down thyself. . .Exod. 20:5

not take the name of the Lord. . .Exod. 20:7

thou shalt not do any work. . .Exod. 20:10

Thou shalt not kill. . .Exod. 20:13

Thou shalt not commit adultery. . .Exod. 20:14

Thou shalt not steal. . .Exod. 20:15

Thou shalt not bear false witness. . .Exod. 20:16

Thou shalt not covet. . .Exod. 20:17

Thou shalt not follow a multitude. . .Exod. 23:2

shalt thou not uncover. . .Lev. 18:7

Thou shalt not lie with mankind. . .Lev. 18:22

Thou shalt not lend. . .Deut. 23:19

Thou shalt not tempt the Lord. . .Matt. 4:7

shalt not be as the hypocrites. . .Matt. 6:5

See *Forbidden Fruit*.

756. Resurrection

that there is no *r*. . .Matt. 22:23

in the *r* they neither marry. . .Matt. 22:30

touching the *r* of the dead. . .Matt. 22:31

the *r* of the just. . .Luke 14:14

unto the *r* of damnation. . .John 5:29

r at the last day. . .John 11:24

the *r* of the dead. . .Acts 17:32

hope and *r* of the dead. . .Acts 23:6

say that there is no *r*. . .Acts 23:8

r of the dead, both of. . .Acts 24:15

r of the dead. . .Acts 24:21

is the *r* of the dead. . .1 Cor. 15:42

unto the *r* of the dead. . .Phil. 3:11

saying that the *r* is past. . .2 Tim. 2:18

of *r* of the dead. . .Heb. 6:2

they might obtain a better *r*. . .Heb. 11:35

This is the first *r*. . .Rev. 20:5

hath part in the first *r*. . .Rev. 20:6

See *Resurrection, Christ's*.

757. Resurrection, Christ's

graves after his *r*. . .Matt. 27:53

I am the *r*, and the life. . .John 11:25

witness with us of his *r*. . .Acts 1:22

spake of the *r* of Christ. . .Acts 2:31

through Jesus the *r* from the dead. . .Acts 4:2

witness of the *r* of the Lord Jesus. . .Acts 4:33

Jesus, and the *r*. . .Acts 17:18

by the *r* from the dead. . .Rom. 1:4

in the likeness of his *r*. . .Rom. 6:5

is no *r* of the dead?. . .1 Cor. 15:12

be no *r* of the dead. . .1 Cor. 15:13

by man came also the *r*. . .1 Cor. 15:21

the power of his *r*. . .Phil. 3:10

r of Jesus Christ from the dead. . .1 Pet. 1:3

by the *r* of Jesus Christ. . .1 Pet. 3:21

See *Resurrection*.

758. Retirement

Today's retirement is not a biblical idea. Older people, in the Bible, have active lifestyles that include work and ministry, even when they are elderly. But scripture also makes it clear that families are to help their senior family members and that God will never desert them.

Sarah, that is ninety years old, bear?. . .Gen. 17:17

strong this day as I was. . .Josh. 14:11

not seen the righteous forsaken. . .Ps. 37:25

trust in the mercy of God. . .Ps. 52:8

in the time of old age. . .Ps. 71:9

when I am old and grayheaded. . .Ps. 71:18

bring forth fruit in old age. . .Ps. 92:14

the crown of old men. . .Prov. 17:6

thy mother when she is old. . .Prov. 23:22

to hoar hairs will I carry you. . .Isa. 46:4

conceived a son in her old age. . .Luke 1:36

she was of a great age. . .Luke 2:36

Mnason of Cyprus, an old disciple. . .Acts 21:16

to requite their parents. . .1 Tim. 5:4

widow be taken into the number. . .1 Tim. 5:9

never leave thee, nor forsake thee. . .Heb. 13:5

759. Revelation/ Revelations

the day of wrath and *r*. . .Rom. 2:5

r of the mystery. . .Rom. 16:25

speak to you either by *r*. . .1 Cor. 14:6

hath a *r*, hath an interpretation. . .1 Cor. 14:26

visions and *r's* of the Lord. . .2 Cor. 12:1

the abundance of the *r's*. . .2 Cor. 12:7

the *r* of Jesus Christ. . .Gal. 1:12

And I went up by *r*. . .Gal. 2:2

spirit of wisdom and *r*. . .Eph. 1:17

by *r* he made known. . .Eph. 3:3

at the *r* of Jesus Christ. . .1 Pet. 1:13

The *R* of Jesus Christ. . .Rev. 1:1

760. Revelry

drunkenness, revellings, and such like. . .Gal. 5:21

excess of wine, revellings, banquetings. . .1 Pet. 4:3

See *Alcohol, Banquet/Banqueting/Banquetings, Drink/Drinking, Drunkenness*.

761. Revenge/ Revenged/ Revenger/Revenges/ Revengeth

r'r of blood himself shall slay. . .Num. 35:19

beginning of *r's* upon the enemy. . .Deut. 32:42

r me of my persecutors. . .Jer. 15:15

we shall take our *r* on him. . .Jer. 20:10

r'd himself upon them. . .Ezek. 25:12

Philistines have dealt by *r*. . .Ezek. 25:15
the LORD *r'th*. . .Nah. 1:2
a *r'r* to execute wrath. . .Rom. 13:4
what zeal, yea, what *r!*. . .2 Cor. 7:11
readiness to *r* all disobedience. . .2 Cor. 10:6

See *Vengeance*.

762. Revile/Reviled/Revilers/Revilest/Revilings

Thou shalt not *r* the gods. . .Exod. 22:28
afraid of their *r'ings*. . .Isa. 51:7
when men shall *r* you. . .Matt. 5:11
they that passed by *r'd* him. . .Matt. 27:39
crucified with him *r'd* him. . .Mark 15:32
Then they *r'd* him. . .John 9:28
R'est thou God's high priest?. . .Acts 23:4
being *r'd*, we bless. . .1 Cor. 4:12
nor drunkards, nor *r'rs*. . .1 Cor. 6:10
when he was *r'd*, *r'd* not. . .1 Pet. 2:23

763. Revive

Wilt thou not *r* us again. . .Ps. 85:6
thou wilt *r* me. . .Ps. 138:7
to *r* the heart of the contrite ones. . .Isa. 57:15
After two days will he *r* us. . .Hosea 6:2
they shall *r* as the corn. . .Hosea 14:7
O LORD, *r* thy work. . .Hab. 3:2

See *Renew/Renewed/Renewing*.

764. Reward, Eternal

your *r* in heaven. . .Matt. 5:12
he shall *r* every man. . .Matt. 16:27
away into everlasting punishment. . .Matt. 25:46
danger of eternal damnation. . .Mark 3:29
the *r* of the inheritance. . .Col. 3:24
in Christ Jesus with eternal glory. . .2 Tim. 2:10
the author of eternal salvation. . .Heb. 5:9
vengeance of eternal fire. . .Jude 1:7

See *Eternity, Eternal Life, Heaven/Heavenly/Heavens, Life Eternal*.

765. Rich/Riches

LORD maketh poor, and maketh *r*. . .1 Sam. 2:7
neither hast asked *r'es*. . .1 Kings 3:11
both *r'es*, and honour. . .1 Kings 3:13
r'es of many wicked. . .Ps. 37:16
afraid when one is made *r*. . .Ps. 49:16
if *r'es* increase, set not. . .Ps. 62:10
earth is full of thy *r'es*. . .Ps. 104:24
hand of the diligent maketh *r*. . .Prov. 10:4
R'es profit not. . .Prov. 11:4
trusteth in his *r'es* shall fall. . .Prov. 11:28
Labour not to be *r*. . .Prov. 23:4

r'es certainly make themselves wings. . .Prov. 23:5

maketh haste to be r. . .Prov. 28:20

neither poverty nor r'es. . .Prov. 30:8

eye satisfied with r'es. . .Eccles. 4:8

given r'es and wealth. . .Eccles. 5:19

r man glory in his r'es. . .Jer. 9:23

r man shall hardly enter. . .Matt. 19:23

deceitfulness of r'es. . .Mark 4:19

woe unto you that are r!. . .Luke 6:24

is not r toward God. . .Luke 12:21

though he was r. . .2 Cor. 8:9

r'es of his grace. . .Eph. 1:7

according to his r'es in glory. . .Phil. 4:19

them that are r. . .1 Tim. 6:17

See *Financial Gain, Wealth.*

---

766. Right

that which is r in his sight. . .Exod. 15:26

r in his own eyes. . .Deut. 12:8

just and r is he. . .Deut. 32:4

gavest them r judgments. . .Neh. 9:13

statutes of the LORD are r. . .Ps. 19:8

seemeth r unto a man. . .Prov. 14:12

do that which is lawful and r. . .Ezek. 18:21

ways of the LORD are r. . .Hosea 14:9

for this is r. . .Eph. 6:1

---

767. Righteousness

counted it to him for r. . .Gen. 15:6

in r shalt thou judge. . .Lev. 19:15

I put on r. . .Job 29:14

LORD loveth r. . .Ps. 11:7

according to my r. . .Ps. 18:20

in the paths of r. . .Ps. 23:3

speak of thy r. . .Ps. 35:28

r hath he openly shewed. . .Ps. 98:2

The LORD executeth r. . .Ps. 103:6

doeth r at all times. . .Ps. 106:3

r delivereth from death. . .Prov. 10:2

R exalteth a nation. . .Prov. 14:34

Better is a little with r. . .Prov. 16:8

turneth away from his r. . .Ezek. 18:26

hunger and thirst after r. . .Matt. 5:6

persecuted for r' sake. . .Matt. 5:10

his r; and all these things. . .Matt. 6:33

faith is counted for r. . .Rom. 4:5

members as instruments of r. . .Rom. 6:13

believeth unto r. . .Rom. 10:10

hath r with unrighteousness?. . .2 Cor. 6:14

follow after r. . .1 Tim. 6:11

for instruction in r. . .2 Tim. 3:16

worketh not the r of God. . .James 1:20

doeth r is righteous. . .1 John 3:7

---

768. Riot/Rioting/Riotous

among r'ous eaters of flesh. . .Prov. 23:20

companion of r'ous men. . .Prov. 28:7

not in r'ing and drunkenness. . .Rom. 13:13

not accused of r or unruly. . .Titus 1:6

to the same excess of r. . .1 Pet. 4:4

pleasure to r in the day time. . .2 Pet. 2:13

769. River

Some of these rivers, like the Chebar and Ulai, may actually have been canals. The Hiddekel was another name for the Tigris River.

r went out of Eden. . .Gen. 2:10

The name of the first is Pison. . .Gen. 2:11

the second *r* is Gihon. . .Gen. 2:13

the fourth *r* is Euphrates. . .Gen. 2:14

the great *r*, the *r* Euphrates. . .Gen. 15:18

even unto the *r* Arnon. . .Deut. 3:16

the great *r*, the *r* Euphrates. . .Josh. 1:4

r Arnon unto mount Hermon. . .Josh. 12:1

descended unto the *r* Kanah. . .Josh. 17:9

unto thee to the *r* Kishon Sisera. . .Judg. 4:7

by the *r* of Gozan. . .2 Kings 17:6

captives by the *r* of Chebar. . .Ezek. 1:1

I was by the *r* of Ulai. . .Dan. 8:2

great *r*, which is Hiddekel. . .Dan. 10:4

in the *r* of Jordan. . .Mark 1:5

770. Rob/Robbed/Robber/Robbery/Robbeth

neither *r* him. . .Lev. 19:13

r'bed all that came along. . .Judg. 9:25

they *r* the threshingfloors. . .1 Sam. 23:1

become not vain in *r'bery*. . .Ps. 62:10

The *r'bery* of the wicked. . .Prov. 21:7

R not the poor. . .Prov. 22:22

Whoso *r'beth* his father. . .Prov. 28:24

Will a man *r* God?. . .Mal. 3:8

Now Barabbas was a *r'ber*. . .John 18:40

thought it not *r'bery*. . .Phil. 2:6

771. Rock, God as

He is the *R*. . .Deut. 32:4

the *R* of his salvation. . .Deut. 32:15

Of the *R* that begat thee. . .Deut. 32:18

rock is not as our *R*. . .Deut. 32:31

there any *r* like our God. . .1 Sam. 2:2

The Lord is my *r*. . .2 Sam. 22:2

my *r*; in him will I . . .2 Sam. 22:3

who is a *r*, save our God?. . .2 Sam. 22:32

blessed be my *r*. . .2 Sam. 22:47

my *r*, and my fortress. . .Ps. 18:2

my *r*; be not silent. . .Ps. 28:1

remembered that God was their *r*. . .Ps. 78:35

God is the *r* of my refuge. . .Ps. 94:22

stumblingstone and *r* of offence. . .Rom. 9:33

and that *R* was Christ. . .1 Cor. 10:4

772. Ruin

they were the *r* of him. . .2 Chron. 28:23
brought his strong holds to *r*. . .Ps. 89:40
knoweth the *r* of them both?. . .Prov. 24:22
flattering mouth worketh *r*. . .Prov. 26:28
and he brought it to *r*. . .Isa. 23:13
of a defenced city a *r*. . .Isa. 25:2
so iniquity shall not be your *r*. . .Ezek. 18:30
the *r* of that house was great. . .Luke 6:49

773. Ruler/Rulers

r over all the land. . .Gen. 41:43
to be *r's* of thousands. . .Exod. 18:21
nor curse the *r*. . .Exod. 22:28
man to be *r* in Israel. . .2 Chron. 7:18
r's take counsel together. . .Ps. 2:2
so is a wicked *r*. . .Prov. 28:15
If a *r* hearken to lies. . .Prov. 29:12
third *r* in the kingdom. . .Dan. 5:29
r's of the synagogue, Jairus. . .Mark 5:22
brought before *r's* and kings. . .Mark 13:9
our *r's* delivered him. . .Luke 24:20
Nicodemus, a *r* of the Jews. . .John 3:1
chief *r's* also many believed. . .John 12:42
r's are not a terror. . .Rom. 13:3
against the *r's* of the darkness. . .Eph. 6:12

See *King, Earthly; Prince/Princes.*

774. Rules

commandments, my statutes, and
  my laws. . .Gen. 26:5
keep my statutes, and my judgments. . .Lev. 18:5
good statutes and commandments. . .Neh. 9:13
The statutes of the Lord are right. . .Ps. 19:8

delight myself in thy statutes. . .Ps. 119:16
Let my heart be sound in thy statutes. . .Ps. 119:80
and keep all my statutes. . .Ezek. 18:21
the decrees for to keep. . .Acts 16:4
many as walk according to this rule. . .Gal. 16:6
let us walk by the same rule. . .Phil. 3:16

See *Law, Laws; Statutes.*

775. Rumour/ Rumours

he shall hear a *r*. . .2 Kings 19:7
heard a *r* from the Lord. . .Jer. 49:14
the *r* that shall be heard. . .Jer. 51:46
r shall be upon *r*. . .Ezek. 7:26
hear of wars and *r's* of wars. . .Matt. 24:6
r of him went forth. . .Luke 7:17

776. Sabbath, the/ Sabbaths

During the Exodus, God established a holy rest day called the sabbath.

rest of the holy s. . .Exod. 16:23
Remember the s day. . .Exod. 20:8
the seventh day is the s. . .Exod. 20:10
blessed the s day . . .Exod. 20:11
the seventh is the s of rest. . .Exod. 31:15
Ye shall keep my s's. . .Lev. 19:30
upon Israel by profaning the s. . .Neh. 13:18
gave them my s's. . .Ezek. 20:12
on the s day through the corn. . .Matt. 12:1
Lord even of the s day. . .Matt. 12:8
to heal on the s days?. . .Matt. 12:10
do well on the s days. . .Matt. 12:12
In the end of the s. . .Matt. 28:1
from this bond on the s. . .Luke 13:16
three s days reasoned with them. . .Acts 17:2
or of the s days. . .Col. 2:16

no more s for sins. . .Heb. 10:26
more excellent s than Cain. . .Heb. 11:4
offer the s of praise. . .Heb. 13:15
offer up spiritual s's. . .1 Pet. 2:5

See *Oblation/Oblations, Offering/Offerings.*

778. Sadness

See *Sorrow/Sorrowed/Sorrows.*

779. Safe/Safely/ Safety

dwell in the land in s'ty. . .Lev. 25:18
only makest me dwell in s'ty. . .Ps. 4:8
I will set him in s'ty. . .Ps. 12:5
horse is a vain thing for s'ty. . .Ps. 33:17
And he led them on s'ly . . .Ps. 78:53
and I shall be s. . .Ps. 119:117
hearkeneth unto me shall dwell s'ly. . .Prov. 1:33
thou walk in thy way s'ly . . .Prov. 3:23
multitude of counsellors there is s'ty . . .Prov. 11:14
runneth into it, and is s. . .Prov. 18:10
but s'ty is of the LORD. . .Prov. 21:31
LORD shall be s. . .Prov. 29:25
Peace and s'ty. . .1 Thess. 5:3

777. Sacrifice/ Sacrifices

to obey is better than s. . .1 Sam. 15:22
s's of joy; I will sing. . .Ps. 27:6
S and offering thou didst not. . .Ps. 40:6
s's of God are a broken. . .Ps. 51:17
acceptable to the LORD than s. . .Prov. 21:3
will have mercy, and not s. . .Matt. 9:13
present your bodies a living s. . .Rom. 12:1
offering and a s to God. . .Eph. 5:2
high priests, to offer up s. . .Heb. 7:27
put away sin by the s. . .Heb. 9:26
S and offering thou wouldest not. . .Heb. 10:5
one s for sins. . .Heb. 10:12

780. Saints

In the Bible, saints are not some super-holy brand of believer; instead this word describes the everyday faithful believers who make up the church. Everyone who has accepted Jesus as Savior is a saint.

He will keep the feet of his s. . .1 Sam. 2:9
fear the LORD, ye his s. . .Ps. 34:9
in the assembly of the s. . .Ps. 89:7
preserveth the souls of his s. . .Ps. 97:10
is the death of his s. . . Ps. 116:15
Let the s be joyful. . .Ps. 149:5
s which slept arose. . .Matt. 27:52
maketh intercession for the s. . .Rom. 8:27
called to be s. . .1 Cor. 1:2
s shall judge the world?. . .1 Cor. 6:2
his inheritance in the s. . .Eph. 1:18
For the perfecting of the s. . .Eph. 4:12
as becometh s. . .Eph. 5:3
supplication for all s. . .Eph. 6:18

781. Salt

The salt sea is another name for the Dead Sea. Sowing land with salt was a method conquerors used to ruin the land for agriculture for a long time to come.

she became a pillar of s. . .Gen. 19:26
shalt thou season with s. . .Lev. 2:13
outmost coast of the s sea. . .Num. 34:3
and sowed it with s. . .Judg. 9:45
Syrians in the valley of s. . .2 Sam. 8:13
and cast the s in there. . .2 Kings 2:21
by a covenant of s?. . .2 Chron. 13:5
wheat, s, wine, and oil. . .Ezra 6:9
unsavoury be eaten without s?. . .Job 6:6
the s of the earth. . .Matt. 5:13
s have lost his saltness. . .Mark 9:50
with grace, seasoned with s. . .Col. 4:6
both yield s water and fresh. . .James 3:12

782. Salvation

see the s of the LORD. . .Exod. 14:13
he is become my s. . .Exod. 15:2
Rock of his s. . .Deut. 32:15
S belongeth unto the LORD. . .Ps. 3:8
shall rejoice in thy s. . .Ps. 13:5
my s, and my high tower. . .Ps. 18:2
the God of his s. . .Ps. 24:5
my light and my s. . .Ps. 27:1
s of the righteous. . .Ps. 37:39
from him cometh my s. . .Ps. 62:1
King of old, working s. . .Ps. 74:12
shew forth his s. . .Ps. 96:2
my s shall be for ever. . .Isa. 51:6
quietly wait for the s. . .Lam. 3:26
s unto his people. . .Luke 1:77
shall see the s of God. . .Luke 3:6
power of God unto s. . .Rom. 1:16
confession is made unto s. . .Rom. 10:10
sorrow worketh repentance to s. . .2 Cor. 7:10
take the helmet of s. . .Eph. 6:17
work out your own s. . .Phil. 2:12
to wrath, but to obtain s. . .1 Thess. 5:9

chosen you to s. . .2 Thess. 2:13

if we neglect so great s. . .Heb. 2:3

even the s of your souls. . .1 Pet. 1:9

See *Born Again, Coming to Christ, Conversion, Eternal Life, Everlasting Life/Life Everlasting, Immortal/Immortality, Knowing God, Life Eternal, New Life, Regeneration, Repentance.*

783. Sanctify/ Sanctification/ Sanctified/Sanctifieth

S yourselves therefore. . .Lev. 20:7

sabbath day to s it. . .Deut. 5:12

temple that s*'ieth* the gold?. . .Matt. 23:17

whom the Father hath s*'ied*. . .John 10:36

S them through thy truth. . .John 17:17

being s*'ied* by the Holy Ghost. . .Rom. 15:16

to them that are s*'ied*. . .1 Cor. 1:2

righteousness, and s*'ication*, and
   redemption. . .1 Cor. 1:30

ye are s*'ied*. . .1 Cor. 6:11

husband is s*'ied* by the wife. . .1 Cor. 7:14

he might s and cleanse it. . .Eph. 5:26

will of God, even your s*'ication*. . .1 Thess. 4:3

possess his vessel in s*'ication*. . .1 Thess. 4:4

God of peace s you wholly. . .1 Thess. 5:23

through s*'ication* of the Spirit. . .2 Thess. 2:13

s*'ied* by the word of God. . .1 Tim. 4:5

s*'ied*, and meet for the master's. . .2 Tim. 2:21

s*'ieth* and they who are s*'ied*. . .Heb. 2:11

s*'ieth* to the purifying. . .Heb. 9:13

are s*'ied* through the offering. . .Heb. 10:10

for ever them that are s*'ied*. . .Heb. 10:14

covenant, wherewith he was s*'ied*. . .Heb. 10:29

s the people with his own blood. . .Heb. 13:12

through s*'ication* of the Spirit. . .1 Pet. 1:2

s the Lord God in your hearts. . .1 Pet. 3:15

784. Satan

And S stood up against Israel. . .1 Chron. 21:1

S came also among them. . .Job 1:6

S, Hast thou considered my servant Job. . .Job 2:3

went S forth from the presence. . .Job 2:7

S standing at his right hand. . .Zech. 3:1

The Lord rebuke thee, O S. . .Zech. 3:2

Get thee hence, S. . .Matt. 4:10

if S cast out S. . .Matt. 12:26

Get thee behind me, S. . .Matt. 16:23

forty days, tempted of S. . .Mark 1:13

I beheld S as lightning. . .Luke 10:18

whom S hath bound. . .Luke 13:16

Then entered S into Judas. . .Luke 22:3

S hath desired to have you. . .Luke 22:31

why hath S filled thine heart. . .Acts 5:3

shall bruise S under your feet. . .Rom. 16:20

deliver such an one unto S. . .1 Cor. 5:5

that S tempt you not. . .1 Cor. 7:5

S himself is transformed. . .2 Cor. 11:14

working of S with all power. . .2 Thess. 2:9

turned aside after S. . .1 Tim. 5:15

called the Devil, and S. . .Rev. 12:9

S shall be loosed. . .Rev. 20:7

See *Tempter*.

Who hath *s'd* us, and called. . .2 Tim. 1:9

according to his mercy he *s'd* us. . .Titus 3:5

able also to *s* them. . .Heb. 7:25

can faith *s* him?. . .James 2:14

prayer of faith shall *s* the sick. . .James 5:15

785. Satisfy/Satisfying

O *s* us early. . .Ps. 90:14

With long life will I *s*. . .Ps. 91:16

I will *s* her poor with bread. . .Ps. 132:15

let her breasts *s* thee. . .Prov. 5:19

if he steal to *s* his soul. . .Prov. 6:30

eateth to the *s'ing* of his soul. . .Prov. 13:25

and *s* the afflicted soul. . .Isa. 58:10

s thy soul in drought. . .Isa. 58:11

they shall not *s* their souls. . .Ezek. 7:19

s these men with bread. . .Mark 8:4

to the *s'ing* of the flesh. . .Col. 2:23

786. Save/Saved

he shall *s* his people. . .Matt. 1:21

to the end shall be *s'd*. . .Matt. 10:22

whosoever will *s* his life. . .Matt. 16:25

s that which was lost. . .Matt. 18:11

is baptized shall be *s'd*. . .Mark 16:16

world through him might be *s'd*. . .John 3:17

name of the Lord shall be *s'd*. . .Acts 2:21

such as should be *s'd*. . .Acts 2:47

whereby we must be *s'd*. . .Acts 4:12

we shall be *s'd* from wrath. . .Rom. 5:9

Lord shall be *s'd*. . .Rom. 10:13

whether thou shalt *s* thy husband?. . .1 Cor. 7:16

For by grace are ye *s'd*. . .Eph. 2:8

the world to *s* sinners. . .1 Tim. 1:15

will have all men to be *s'd*. . .1 Tim. 2:4

787. Saviour/Saviours

and my refuge, my *s*. . .2 Sam. 22:3

s's, who saved them out of. . .Neh. 9:27

They forgat God their *s*. . .Ps. 106:21

he shall send them a *s*. . .Isa. 19:20

beside me there is no *s*. . .Isa. 43:11

a just God and a *S*. . .Isa. 45:21

thy *S* and thy Redeemer. . .Isa. 49:26

rejoiced in God my *S*. . .Luke 1:47

S, which is Christ the Lord. . .Luke 2:11

Christ, the *S* of the world. . .John 4:42

to be a Prince and a *S*. . .Acts 5:31

raised unto Israel a *S*, Jesus. . .Acts 13:23

he is the *s* of the body. . .Eph. 5:23

sight of God our *S*. . .1 Tim. 2:3

who is the *S* of all men. . .1 Tim. 4:10

S Jesus Christ, who hath abolished. . .2 Tim. 1:10

788. Scolding

See *Reproach/Reproached/Reproaches/ Reproacheth, Revile/Reviled/Revilers/ Revilest/Revilings.*

789. Scorn/Scorner/ Scorners/Scornest/ Scorneth/Scornful/ Scorning

laughed us to *s*, and despised. . .Neh. 2:19
in the seat of the *s'ful*. . .Ps. 1:1
laugh me to *s*. . .Ps. 22:7
s'ers delight in their *s'ing*. . .Prov. 1:22
Surely he *s'eth* the *s'ers*. . .Prov. 3:34
He that reproveth a *s'er*. . .Prov. 9:7
if thou *s'est*. . .Prov. 9:12
a *s'er* heareth not rebuke. . .Prov. 13:1
A *s'er* seeketh wisdom. . .Prov. 14:6
s'er loveth not one that reproveth. . .Prov. 15:12
Judgments are prepared for *s'ers*. . .Prov. 19:29
When the *s'er* is punished. . .Prov. 21:11
Cast out the *s'er*. . .Prov. 22:10
s'er is an abomination to men. . .Prov. 24:9
S'ful men bring a city. . .Prov. 29:8
And they laughed him to *s*. . .Mark 5:40

790. Scripture/ Scriptures

not knowing the *s's*. . .Matt. 22:29
s's of the prophets. . .Matt. 26:56
s was fulfilled, which saith. . .Mark 15:28
s's the things concerning himself. . .Luke 24:27
that they might understand the *s's*. . .Luke 24:45
they believed the *s*. . .John 2:22
Search the *s's*. . .John 5:39

s cannot be broken. . .John 10:35
searched the *s's* daily. . .Acts 17:11
s's that Jesus was Christ. . .Acts 18:28
s's might have hope. . .Rom. 15:4
by the *s's* of the prophets. . .Rom. 16:26
our sins according to the *s's*. . .1 Cor. 15:3
known the holy *s's*. . .2 Tim. 3:15
All *s* is given by inspiration. . .2 Tim. 3:16
royal law according to the *s*. . .James 2:8
s is of any private interpretation. . .2 Pet. 1:20

See *Searching the Scriptures, Word of God.*

791. Sea Creatures

And God created great whales. . .Gen. 1:21
over the fish of the sea. . .Gen. 1:26
upon all the fishes of the sea. . .Gen. 9:2
Am I a sea, or a whale. . .Job 7:12
Canst thou draw out leviathan. . .Job 41:1
there is that leviathan. . .Ps. 104:26
fishes that are taken. . .Eccles. 9:12
nights in the whale's belly. . .Matt. 12:40

See *Animals, Reptiles.*

792. Searching for God

See *Seeking God*.

793. Searching the Scriptures

Search the scriptures. . .John 5:39
searched the scriptures daily. . .Acts 17:11

See *Scripture/Scriptures, Seeking God, Word of God*.

794. Seasons of Life

wilderness a long season. . .Josh. 24:7
for a long season Israel hath. . .2 Chron. 15:3
his fruit in his season. . .Ps. 1:3
every thing there is a season. . .Eccles. 3:1
speak a word in season. . .Isa. 50:4
season; there shall be showers of
    blessing. . .Ezek. 34:26

in due season we shall reap. . .Gal. 6:9
in season, out of season. . .2 Tim. 4:2
rejoice, though now for a season. . .1 Pet. 1:6

See *Age; Elderly, the; Youth*.

795. Second Coming of Christ

cometh in the name of the Lord. . .Matt. 23:39
hour your Lord doth come. . .Matt. 24:42
hour wherein the Son of man cometh. . .Matt. 25:13
When the Son of man shall come. . .Matt. 25:31
shall so come in like manner. . .Acts 1:11
the Lord's death till he come. . .1 Cor. 11:26
that are Christ's at his coming. . .1 Cor. 15:23
Lord Jesus Christ at his coming?. . .1 Thess. 2:19
coming of our Lord Jesus Christ. . .1 Thess. 3:13
Jesus shall be revealed from heaven. . .2 Thess. 1:7
the brightness of his coming. . .2 Thess. 2:8
glorious appearing of the great God. . .Titus 2:13
power and coming of our Lord. . .2 Pet. 1:16
day of the Lord will come as a thief. . .2 Pet. 3:10
coming of the day of God. . .2 Pet. 3:12
when he shall appear. . .1 John 3:2

See *Last Day*.

796. Secret/Secrets

s things belong unto the Lord. . .Deut. 29:29
my name, seeing it is s?. . .Judg. 13:18
He made darkness his s place. . .Ps. 18:11
The s of the Lord. . .Ps. 25:14
s place of the most High. . .Ps. 91:1
his s is with the righteous. . .Prov. 3:32
revealeth the deep and s things. . .Dan. 2:22

God in heaven that revealeth s's. . .Dan. 2:28
revealeth his s unto his servants. . .Amos 3:7
thy Father which is in s. . .Matt. 6:6
things which have been kept s. . .Matt. 13:35
neither was any thing kept s. . .Mark 4:22

See *Mystery/Mysteries.*

797. Security

he will not forsake thee. . .Deut. 4:31
he it is that doth go with thee. . .Deut. 31:6
none of them that trust in him. . .Ps. 34:22
God is a refuge for us. . .Ps. 62:8
Even there shall thy hand lead me. . .Ps. 139:10
runneth into it, and is safe. . .Prov. 18:10
in the Lord shall be safe. . .Prov. 29:25
I will not turn away. . .Jer. 32:40
I will in no wise cast out. . .John 6:37
pluck them out of my hand. . .John 10:28
able to pluck them out. . .John 10:29
now no condemnation to them. . .Rom. 8:1
save them to the uttermost. . .Heb. 7:25
never leave thee, nor forsake thee. . .Heb. 13:5

798. Seduction

if a man entice a maid. . .Exod. 22:16
Entice thy husband. . .Judg. 14:15
if sinners entice thee. . .Prov. 1:10

ravished with a strange woman. . .Prov. 5:20

See *Harlot/Harlot's/Harlots.*

799. Seeking God

if thou seek him with all thy heart. . .Deut. 4:29
and pray, and seek my face. . .2 Chron. 7:14
all them for good that seek him. . .Ezra 8:22
hast not forsaken them that seek thee. . .Ps. 9:10
did understand, and seek God. . .Ps. 14:2
praise the Lord that seek him. . .Ps. 22:26
early will I seek thee. . .Ps. 63:1
your heart shall live that seek God. . .Ps. 69:32
that they may seek thy name. . .Ps. 83:16
seek me early shall find me. . .Prov. 8:17
they that seek the Lord understand. . .Prov. 28:5
Seek ye the Lord while he may. . .Isa. 55:6
ye shall seek me, and find me. . .Jer. 29:13
to the soul that seeketh him. . .Lam. 3:25
seek ye first the kingdom. . .Matt. 6:33
That they should seek the Lord. . .Acts 17:27
none that seeketh after God. . .Rom. 3:11
them that diligently seek him. . .Heb. 11:6

See *Searching the Scriptures.*

800. Self-Control

I have refrained my feet. . .Ps. 119:101
refrain thy foot from their path. . .Prov. 1:15
he that refraineth his lips. . .Prov. 10:19

He that hath no rule over. . .Prov. 25:28

righteousness, temperance, and

    judgment. . .Acts 24:25

you not for your incontinency. . .1 Cor. 7:5

and to temperance patience. . .2 Pet. 1:6

See *Self-Denial.*

801. Self-Denial

let him deny himself, and take. . .Matt. 16:24

not to please ourselves. . .Rom. 15:1

esteem other better than themselves. . .Phil. 2:3

denying ungodliness and worldly lusts. . .Titus 2:12

See *Self-Control.*

802. Self-Esteem

Every Christian's self-esteem must be centered in the value God gives each person. He created us in His image, and Christ died for us; each of us has a high value. But believers must also live humbly, putting others before themselves, as Christ gave Himself for them.

God created man in his own image. . .Gen. 1:27

he that hath made us. . .Ps. 100:3

Christ died for us. . .Rom. 5:8

not to think of himself more highly. . .Rom. 12:3

For ye are bought with a price. . .1 Cor. 6:20

Ye are bought with a price. . .1 Cor. 7:23

image and glory of God. . .1 Cor. 11:7

loved me, and gave himself for me. . .Gal. 2:20

church, and gave himself for it. . .Eph. 5:25

esteem other better than themselves. . .Phil. 2:3

Who gave himself for us. . .Titus 2:14

803. Self-Help

The Bible doesn't really speak of self-help. Instead, it reminds us that God is our help in every trouble and that we should help and serve one another. As we live for God, our lives are renewed.

God hath power to help. . .2 Chron. 25:8

he is our help and our shield. . .Ps. 33:20

very present help in trouble. . .Ps. 46:1

vain is the help of man. . .Ps. 60:11

help is in the name of the Lord. . .Ps. 124:8

shall be added unto you. . .Matt. 6:33

helpeth our infirmities. . .Rom. 8:26

gifts of healings, helps. . .1 Cor. 12:28

we should not trust in ourselves. . .2 Cor. 1:9

are sufficient of ourselves. . .2 Cor. 3:5

let us cleanse ourselves. . .2 Cor. 7:1

by love serve one another. . .Gal. 5:13

find grace to help. . .Heb. 4:16

See *Renew/Renewed/Renewing.*

804. Sell/Seller/ Selleth

S me this day thy birthright. . .Gen. 25:31

s ought unto thy neighbour. . .Lev. 25:14

or *s'eth* him. . .Deut. 24:7
Go, *s* the oil. . .2 Kings 4:7
on the sabbath day to *s*. . .Neh. 10:31
Buy the truth, and *s*. . .Prov. 23:23
s that thou hast. . .Matt. 19:21
S that ye have, and give. . .Luke 12:33
Lydia, a *s'er* of purple. . .Acts 16:14
buy and *s*, and get gain. . .James 4:13
no man might buy or *s*. . . Rev. 13:17

805. Separate/ Separated

s'd you from other people. . .Lev. 20:24
s themselves unto the LORD. . .Num. 6:2
s yourselves from the people. . .Ezra 10:11
s them one from another. . .Matt. 25:32
s you from their company. . .Luke 6:22
S me Barnabas and Saul. . .Acts 13:2
s'd unto the gospel of God. . .Rom. 1:1
s us from the love of Christ?. . .Rom. 8:35
shall be able to *s* us. . .Rom. 8:39
be ye *s*, saith the Lord. . .2 Cor. 6:17
undefiled, *s* from sinners. . .Heb. 7:26

806. Seriousness

let us watch and be sober. . .1 Thess. 5:6
sober, putting on the breastplate. . .1 Thess. 5:8
vigilant, sober, of good behaviour. . .1 Tim. 3:2
in subjection with all gravity. . .1 Tim. 3:4
must the deacons be grave. . .1 Tim. 3:8
their wives be grave. . .1 Tim. 3:11
sober, just, holy, temperate. . .Titus 1:8
sober, grave, temperate. . .Titus 2:2
young women to be sober. . .Titus 2:4
exhort to be sober minded. . .Titus 2:6

uncorruptness, gravity. . .Titus 2:7
sober, and hope to the end. . .1 Pet. 1:13
be ye therefore sober. . .1 Pet. 4:7
Be sober, be vigilant. . .1 Pet. 5:8

807. Servant/Servants

In the biblical era, servants were slaves.

I am thy *s*. . .Ps. 119:125
therefore thy *s* loveth it. . .Ps. 119:140
nor the *s* above his lord. . .Matt. 10:24
the *s* as his lord. . .Matt. 10:25
Behold my *s*. . .Matt. 12:18
let him be your *s*. . .Matt. 20:27
you shall be your *s*. . .Matt. 23:11
is a faithful and wise *s*. . .Matt. 24:45
Blessed is that *s*. . .Matt. 24:46
last of all, and *s* of all. . .Mark 9:35
No *s* can serve two masters. . .Luke 16:13
committeth sin is the *s*. . .John 8:34
s abideth not in the house. . .John 8:35
I call you not *s's*. . .John 15:15
I made myself *s* unto all. . .1 Cor. 9:19
be the *s* of Christ. . .Gal. 1:10
no more a *s*, but a son. . .Gal. 4:7
the form of a *s*. . .Phil. 2:7

See *Bondage, Serve.*

808. Serve

LORD thy God, and s him. . .Deut. 6:13
s the LORD thy God. . .Deut. 10:12
him shalt thou s. . .Deut. 10:20
whom ye will s. . .Josh. 24:15
S the LORD with fear. . .Ps. 2:11
all nations shall s him. . .Ps. 72:11
s the LORD with gladness. . .Ps. 100:2
No man can s two masters. . .Matt. 6:24
If any man s me. . .John 12:26
whom I s with my spirit. . .Rom. 1:9
we should not s sin. . .Rom. 6:6
s in newness of spirit. . .Rom. 7:6
by love s one another. . .Gal. 5:13
for ye s the Lord Christ. . .Col. 3:24
s God acceptably with reverence. . .Heb. 12:28
his servants shall s him. . .Rev. 22:3

See *Servant/Servants*.

809. Shame

will ye turn my glory into s?. . .Ps. 4:2
put them to s that hated us. . .Ps. 44:7
s of my face hath covered. . .Ps. 44:15
will I clothe with s. . .Ps. 132:18
s shall be the promotion. . .Prov. 3:35
a son that causeth s. . .Prov. 10:5
pride cometh, then cometh s. . .Prov. 11:2
a prudent man covereth s. . .Prov. 12:16
loathsome, and cometh to s. . .Prov. 13:5
Poverty and s shall be. . .Prov. 13:18
suffer s for his name. . .Acts 5:41
s them that have not?. . .1 Cor. 11:22
s even to speak. . .Eph. 5:12
glory is in their s. . .Phil. 3:19
cross, despising the s. . .Heb. 12:2

810. Shining/ Glory of God

The bright physical sign of His presence, God's Shekinah glory was shown in the pillar of cloud by day and the pillar of fire by night that protected His people as they left Egypt, and in various other manifestations. It was a sign of His glory.

pillar of the cloud went. . .Exod. 14:19
it gave light by night. . .Exod. 14:20
through the pillar of fire. . .Exod. 14:24
the glory of the LORD abode. . .Exod. 24:16
sight of the glory of the LORD. . .Exod. 24:17
glory of the LORD filled. . .Exod. 40:34
the glory of the LORD. . .Num. 14:21
glory of the LORD appeared. . .Num. 20:6
glory of the LORD had filled. . .1 Kings 8:11
fire came down from heaven. . .2 Chron. 7:1
glory of the LORD had filled. . .2 Chron. 7:2

s of a flaming fire. . .Isa. 4:5

likeness as the appearance of fire. . .Ezek. 8:2

his raiment became s. . .Mark 9:3

glory of the Lord shone round. . .Luke 2:9

See *Glory*.

811. Sick/Sickly/ Sickness/Sicknesses

his *s'ness* was so sore. . .1 Kings 17:17

was s: and he sent. . .2 Kings 1:2

Hezekiah s unto death. . .2 Kings 20:1

healing all manner of *s'ness*. . .Matt. 4:23

s of the palsy. . .Matt. 8:6

s of a fever. . .Matt. 8:14

and bare our *s'nesses*. . .Matt. 8:17

s of the palsy. . .Matt. 9:2

Heal the s, cleanse the lepers. . .Matt. 10:8

I was s, and ye visited. . .Matt. 25:36

many are weak and *s'ly*. . .1 Cor. 11:30

Is any s among you?. . .James 5:14

save the s, and the Lord. . .James 5:15

See *Ailments, Disabilitites, Diseases, Heal/Healing*.

812. Sight/Sights

pleasant to the s. . .Gen. 2:9

see this great s. . .Exod. 3:3

s of the glory of the LORD. . .Exod. 24:17

in the s of their fathers. . .Ps. 78:12

in the s of the heathen. . .Ps. 98:2

Better is the s of the eyes. . .Eccles. 6:9

in the s of thine eyes. . .Eccles. 11:9

The blind receive their s. . .Matt. 11:5

that I might receive my s. . .Mark 10:51

recovering of s to the blind. . .Luke 4:18

fearful *s's* and great signs. . .Luke 21:11

and I received s. . .John 9:11

received him out of their s. . .Acts 1:9

mightest receive thy s. . .Acts 9:17

walk by faith, not by s. . .2 Cor. 5:7

so terrible was the s. . .Heb. 12:21

813. Signs

wherewith thou shalt do s. . .Exod. 4:17

multiply my s and my wonders. . .Exod. 7:3

my s which I have done. . .Exod. 10:2

by s, and by wonders. . .Deut. 4:34

How great are his *s!*. . .Dan. 4:3

shew great s and wonders. . .Matt. 24:24

shall shew s and wonders. . .Mark 13:22

s shall follow them. . .Mark 16:17

s shall there be from heaven. . .Luke 21:11

Except ye see s and wonders. . .John 4:48

many other s truly did Jesus. . .John 20:30

many wonders and s. . .Acts 2:43

s and lying wonders. . .2 Thess. 2:9

s and wonders, and with divers. . .Heb. 2:4

See *Miracle/Miracles, Wonders*.

814. Silence

Let the lying lips be put to s. . .Ps. 31:18

I kept s, my bones waxed old. . .Ps. 32:3

I was dumb with s. . .Ps. 39:2
and shall not keep s. . .Ps. 50:3
soul had almost dwelt in s. . .Ps. 94:17
any that go down into s. . .Ps. 115:17
a time to keep s. . .Eccles. 3:7
let all the earth keep s. . .Hab. 2:20
put the Sadducees to s. . .Matt. 22:34
let him keep s. . .1 Cor. 14:28
put to s the ignorance. . .1 Pet. 2:15

815. Simple/Simplicity

*Though scripture sometimes uses the word
"simple" to describe an uneducated or foolish
person, it is also used to describe a sincere one.*

making wise the s. . .Ps. 19:7
The LORD preserveth the s. . .Ps. 116:6
giveth understanding unto the s. . .Ps. 119:130
To give subtilty to the s. . .Prov. 1:4
will ye love s'icity?. . .Prov. 1:22
turning away of the s. . .Prov. 1:32
O ye s, understand wisdom. . .Prov. 8:5
she is s, and knoweth nothing. . .Prov. 9:13
Whoso is s. . .Prov. 9:16
The s believeth every word. . .Prov. 14:15
The s inherit folly. . .Prov. 14:18
the s will beware. . .Prov. 19:25
the s pass on. . .Prov. 22:3

let him do it with s'icity. . .Rom. 12:8
deceive the hearts of the s. . .Rom. 16:18
good, and s concerning evil. . .Rom. 16:19
in s'icity and godly sincerity. . .2 Cor. 1:12
from the s'icity that is in Christ. . .2 Cor. 11:3

816. Sin

Dangers of

s lieth at the door. . .Gen. 4:7
my bones because of my s. . .Ps. 38:3
wages of s is death. . .Rom. 6:23
law of s and death. . .Rom. 8:2
sting of death is s. . .1 Cor. 15:56

Humanity and

in s did my mother conceive. . .Ps. 51:5
my brother s against me. . .Matt. 18:21
is without s among you. . .John 8:7
committeth s is the servant. . .John 8:34
by one man s entered. . .Rom. 5:12
captivity to the law of s. . .Rom. 7:23
not of faith is s. . .Rom. 14:23
For if we s wilfully. . .Heb. 10:26
every weight, and the s. . .Heb. 12:1
it bringeth forth s. . .James 1:15
say that we have no s. . .1 John 1:8
doth not commit s. . .1 John 3:9

Redemption and

If I s, then thou markest me. . .Job 10:14
whose s is covered. . .Ps. 32:1
cleanse me from my s. . .Ps. 51:2
he bare the s of many. . .Isa. 53:12
remember their s no more. . .Jer. 31:34
taketh away the s. . .John 1:29
Lord will not impute s. . .Rom. 4:8

where *s* abounded, grace. . .Rom. 5:20
made him to be *s* for us. . .2 Cor. 5:21
as we are, yet without *s*. . .Heb. 4:15
sacrifices for *s*. . .Heb. 10:6

Wickedness and

transgression and my *s*. . .Job 13:23
fruit of the wicked to *s*. . .Prov. 10:16
s is a reproach. . .Prov. 14:34
manner of *s* and blasphemy. . .Matt. 12:31

See various kinds of sin, such as *Adultery*; *Sin of Anger/Anger*; also *Iniquity*; *Sinner/Sinners*; *Transgression/Transgressions*; *Trespass/Trespassed/ Trespasses*; *Wrongdoing*.

817. Sing/Singing

I will *s* unto the Lᴏʀᴅ. . .Exod. 15:1
s'ing and dancing. . .1 Sam. 18:6
S unto him, *s* psalms. . .1 Chron. 16:9
S unto the Lᴏʀᴅ. . .1 Chron. 16:23
trees of the wood *s* out. . .1 Chron. 16:33
began to *s* and to praise. . .2 Chron. 20:22
s unto the Lᴏʀᴅ, because he. . .Ps. 13:6
S unto the Lᴏʀᴅ, O ye. . .Ps. 30:4

S forth the honour of his name. . .Ps. 66:2
s unto the Lᴏʀᴅ: let us. . .Ps. 95:1
S unto the Lᴏʀᴅ, bless. . .Ps. 96:2
s the Lᴏʀᴅ's song. . .Ps. 137:4
S unto the Lᴏʀᴅ a new. . .Isa. 42:10
Gentiles, and *s* unto thy name. . .Rom. 15:9
church will I *s* praise. . .Heb. 2:12

See *Noise, Joyful*.

818. Sinner/Sinners

standeth in the way of *s's*. . .Ps. 1:1
he teach *s's* in the way. . .Ps. 25:8
wickedness overthroweth the *s*. . .Prov. 13:6
wealth of the *s* is laid. . .Prov. 13:22
to the *s* he giveth travail. . .Eccles. 2:26
one *s* destroyeth much good. . .Eccles. 9:18
but *s's* to repentance. . .Matt. 9:13
over one *s* that repenteth. . .Luke 15:7
be merciful to me a *s*. . .Luke 18:13
we were yet *s's*, Christ died. . .Rom. 5:8
Cleanse your hands, ye *s's*. . .James 4:8
he which converteth the *s*. . .James 5:20

See *Sin*.

819. Sincere/Sincerely/ Sincerity

in *s'ity* and in truth. . .Josh. 24:14
whose spirit there is no guile. . .Ps. 32:2
in whom is no guile!. . .John 1:47
bread of *s'ity* and truth. . .1 Cor. 5:8
in simplicity and godly *s'ity*. . .2 Cor. 1:12
s'ity, but as of God. . .2 Cor. 2:17
to prove the *s'ity* of your love. . .2 Cor. 8:8

that ye may be *s*. . .Phil. 1:10

preach Christ of contention, not *s'ly*. . .Phil. 1:16

shewing uncorruptness, gravity, *s'ity*. . .Titus 2:7

desire the *s* milk of the word. . .1 Pet. 2:2

they speak no guile. . .1 Pet. 3:10

their mouth was found no guile. . .Rev. 14:5

820. Singleness

eunuchs, which have made
    themselves. . .Matt. 19:12

neither marry, nor are given. . .Luke 20:35

to the unmarried and widows. . .1 Cor. 7:8

let her remain unmarried. . .1 Cor. 7:11

He that is unmarried careth. . .1 Cor. 7:32

The unmarried woman careth. . .1 Cor. 7:34

Forbidding to marry. . .1 Tim. 4:3

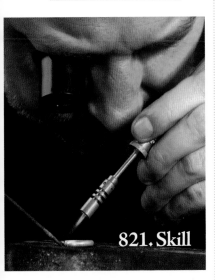

821. Skill

s to hew timber. . .1 Kings 5:6

s to grave with the cunning men. . .2 Chron. 2:7

s of instruments of musick. . .2 Chron. 34:12

nor yet favour to men of *s*. . .Eccles. 9:11

God gave them knowledge and *s*. . .Dan. 1:17

come forth to give thee *s*. . .Dan. 9:22

See *Ability*.

822. Slander/Slandered/Slanderers/Slanderest/Slandereth/Slanderously/Slanders

a *s* upon the land. . .Num. 14:36

he hath *s'ed* thy servant. . .2 Sam. 19:27

I have heard the *s* of many. . .Ps. 31:13

thou *s'est* thine own mother's son. . .Ps. 50:20

Whoso privily *s'eth* his neighbour. . .Ps. 101:5

he that uttereth a *s*. . .Prov. 10:18

walking with *s's*. . .Jer. 6:28

every neighbour will walk with *s's*. . .Jer. 9:4

as we be *s'ously* reported. . .Rom. 3:8

grave, not *s'ers*, sober. . .1 Tim. 3:11

823. Slavery

See *Bondage, Servant/Servants*.

824. Sleep/Sleepest/Sleepeth

deep *s* to fall upon Adam. . .Gen. 2:21

he may *s* in his own raiment. . .Deut. 24:13

deep *s* from the LORD. . .1 Sam. 26:12

could not the king *s*. . .Esther 6:1

me down in peace, and *s*. . .Ps. 4:8

shall neither slumber nor *s*. . .Ps. 121:4

so he giveth his beloved *s*. . .Ps. 127:2

wilt thou *s*, O sluggard?. . .Prov. 6:9

when thou *s'est*, it shall keep thee. . .Prov. 6:22

he that *s'eth* in harvest. . .Prov. 10:5

Slothfulness casteth into a deep *s*. . .Prov. 19:15

Love not *s*. . .Prov. 20:13

The *s* of a labouring man. . .Eccles. 5:12

Joseph being raised from *s*. . .Matt. 1:24

being fallen into a deep *s*. . .Acts 20:9

825. Slothful/ Slothfulness

s shall be under tribute. . .Prov. 12:24

s man roasteth not. . .Prov. 12:27

way of the *s* man. . .Prov. 15:19

s in his work. . .Prov. 18:9

S'ness casteth into. . .Prov. 19:15

desire of the *s* killeth. . .Prov. 21:25

The *s* man saith. . .Prov. 22:13

field of the *s*. . .Prov. 24:30

doth the *s* upon his bed. . .Prov. 26:14

By much *s'ness*. . .Eccles. 10:18

Not *s* in business. . .Rom. 12:11

That ye be not *s*. . .Heb. 6:12

See *Idle/ Idleness*.

826. Smoking

Though scripture does not specifically mention drugs, it condemns the kind of lifestyle that goes with illegal drug use and encourages believers to care for their bodies.

the servant of sin. . .John 8:34

temple of the Holy Ghost. . .1 Cor. 6:19

827. Snakes

See *Reptiles*.

828. Snare/ Snared/Snares

be a *s* unto thee. . .Exod. 23:33

wicked is *s'd* in the work. . .Ps. 9:16

wicked have laid a *s*. . .Ps. 119:110

as a bird out of the *s*. . .Ps. 124:7

s'd with the words. . .Prov. 6:2

depart from the *s's* of death. . .Prov. 14:27

the *s* of his soul. . .Prov. 18:7

s's are in the way of the froward. . .Prov. 22:5

evil man there is a *s*. . .Prov. 29:6

fear of man bringeth a *s*. . .Prov. 29:25

woman, whose heart is *s's*. . .Eccles. 7:26

as he that setteth *s's*. . .Jer. 5:26

the *s* of the devil. . .1 Tim. 3:7

fall into temptation and a *s*. . .1 Tim. 6:9

the *s* of the devil. . .2 Tim. 2:26

829. Sneakiness

hath deceived his neighbour. . .Lev. 6:2
disappointeth the devices of the crafty. . .Job 5:12
the tongue of the crafty. . .Job 15:5
They have taken crafty counsel. . .Ps. 83:3
and shall deceive many. . .Matt. 24:5
shall deceive the very elect. . .Matt. 24:24
they lie in wait to deceive. . .Eph. 4:14
Let no man deceive you. . .2 Thess. 2:3
but the woman being deceived. . .1 Tim. 2:14
deceiving, and being deceived. . .2 Tim. 3:13

830. Snobbery

respect of persons is not good. . .Prov. 28:21
Mind not high things. . .Rom. 12:16
no one of you be puffed up. . .1 Cor. 4:6
think himself to be something. . .Gal. 6:3
Sit thou here in a good place. . .James 2:3
love thy neighbour as thyself. . .James 2:8
if ye have respect to persons. . .James 2:9

831. Soft Answer

A s a turneth away wrath. . .Prov. 15:1
slow to anger appeaseth strife. . .Prov. 15:18
Charity suffereth long. . .1 Cor. 13:4

832. Son/Sons

For I was my father's s. . .Prov. 4:3
a foolish s is the heaviness. . .Prov. 10:1
A foolish s is a grief. . .Prov. 17:25
s's of the living God. . .Hosea 1:10
man spareth his own s. . .Mal. 3:17
Is not this the carpenter's s?. . .Matt. 13:55
The s's of thunder. . .Mark 3:17

the only s of his mother. . .Luke 7:12
become the s's of God. . .John 1:12
Woman, behold thy s!. . .John 19:26
receive the adoption of s's. . .Gal. 4:5
if a s, then an heir. . .Gal. 4:7
as a s with the father. . .Phil. 2:22
bringing many s's unto glory. . .Heb. 2:10
refused to be called the s. . .Heb. 11:24

See *Boys*, *Child/Children*, *Youth*.

833. Son of God

Thou art my S; this day have. . .Ps. 2:7
This is my beloved S. . .Matt. 3:17
no man knoweth the S. . .Matt. 11:27
thou art the S of God. . .Matt. 14:33
S of the living God. . .Matt. 16:16
I am the S of God. . .Matt. 27:43
the S of the Blessed?. . .Mark 14:61
the only begotten S. . .John 1:18
this is the S of God. . .John 1:34
S quickeneth whom he will. . .John 5:21
declared to be the S of God. . .Rom. 1:4
God sending his own S. . .Rom. 8:3
spared not his own S. . .Rom. 8:32
hath not the S of God. . .1 John 5:12
Jesus Christ, the S. . .2 John 1:3

godly *s* worketh repentance. . .2 Cor. 7:10

should have *s* upon *s*. . .Phil. 2:27

through with many *s's*. . .1 Tim. 6:10

neither *s*, nor crying. . .Rev. 21:4

See *Depression, Pain/Pained.*

834. Sorcery/ Sorcerer/Sorcerers

wise men and the *s'ers*. . .Exod. 7:11

nor to your *s'ers*. . .Jer. 27:9

astrologers, and the *s'ers*. . .Dan. 2:2

swift witness against the *s'ers*. . .Mal. 3:5

in the same city used *s*. . .Acts 8:9

s'er, a false prophet, a Jew. . .Acts 13:6

But Elymas the *s'er*. . .Acts 13:8

and *s'ers*, and idolaters. . .Rev. 21:8

For without are dogs, and *s'ers*. . .Rev. 22:15

See *Magic/Magicians; Occult, the;
Witch/Witchcraft/Witchcrafts.*

835. Sorrow/ Sorrowed/Sorrows

s is turned into joy. . .Job 41:22

s's shall be to the wicked. . .Ps. 32:10

my *s* is continually before me. . .Ps. 38:17

S is better than laughter. . .Eccles. 7:3

remove *s* from thy heart. . .Eccles. 11:10

s and sighing shall flee. . .Isa. 35:10

a man of *s's*. . .Isa. 53:3

and carried our *s's*. . .Isa. 53:4

any *s* like unto my *s*. . .Lam. 1:12

s hath filled your heart. . .John 16:6

s shall be turned into joy. . .John 16:20

s'ed to repentance. . .2 Cor. 7:9

836. Soul/Souls

man became a living *s*. . .Gen. 2:7

heart and with all your *s*. . .Deut. 11:13

My *s* shall make her boast. . .Ps. 34:2

my *s* shall be joyful. . .Ps. 35:9

cast down, O my *s*?. . .Ps. 42:5

my *s* waiteth upon God. . .Ps. 62:1

destroyeth his own *s*. . .Prov. 6:32

wrongeth his own *s*. . .Prov. 8:36

make his *s* an offering. . .Isa. 53:10

Behold, all *s's* are mine. . .Ezek. 18:4

not able to kill the *s*. . .Matt. 10:28

lose his own *s*?. . .Matt. 16:26

heart, and with all thy *s*. . .Matt. 22:37

his *s* was not left in hell. . .Acts 2:31

to the saving of the *s*. . .Heb. 10:39

even as thy *s* prospereth. . .3 John 1:2

837. Sound Mind/ Thinking

fool uttereth all his mind. . .Prov. 29:11

whose mind is stayed on thee. . .Isa. 26:3

and with all thy mind. . .Luke 10:27

neither be ye of doubtful mind. . .Luke 12:29

be spiritually minded is life. . .Rom. 8:6

renewing of your mind. . .Rom. 12:2

not to think of himself. . .Rom. 12:3

same mind one toward another. . .Rom. 12:16

with one mind and one mouth. . .Rom. 15:6

him that thinketh he standeth. . .1 Cor. 10:12

renewed in the spirit of your mind. . .Eph. 4:23

in lowliness of mind. . .Phil. 2:3

Let this mind be in you. . .Phil. 2:5

and of a *s m*. . .2 Tim. 1:7

838. Sovereignty of God

God created all things and is completely in control of them. He guides His people's paths and retains power even over those who do not know Him. Nothing is beyond His sovereign power.

the kingdom is the LORD's. . .Ps. 22:28

done whatsoever he hath pleased. . .Ps. 115:3

Whatsoever the LORD pleased. . .Ps. 135:6

the LORD directeth his steps. . .Prov. 16:9

disposing thereof is of the LORD. . .Prov. 16:33

I have made the earth. . .Isa. 45:12

I will direct all his ways. . .Isa. 45:13

an everlasting dominion. . .Dan. 4:34

doeth according to his will. . .Dan. 4:35

power over all flesh. . .John 17:2

determinate counsel and foreknowledge. . .Acts 2:23

determined the times before appointed. . .Acts 17:26

who hath resisted his will?. . .Rom. 9:19

hath chosen us in him. . .Eph. 1:4

by him were all things created. . .Col. 1:16

by him all things consist. . .Col. 1:17

by the word of his power. . .Heb. 1:3

See *Foreknowledge of God, Predestinate/ Predestinated.*

839. Spanking

Of course the Bible does not use this word, but it does provide direction on disciplining a child. Scripture also presents a rather tender picture of father-child relationships that is based on both kindness and discipline. A child is to listen to and obey parents. A father is to tenderly but firmly care for his children.

hear the instruction of thy father. . .Prov. 1:8

even as a father the son. . .Prov. 3:12

spareth his rod hateth his son. . .Prov. 13:24

Train up a child in the way. . .Prov. 22:6

Withhold not correction. . .Prov. 23:13

father, will he give him a stone?. . .Luke 11:11

Fathers, provoke not your children. . .Col. 3:21

as a father doth his children. . .1 Thess. 2:11

whom the father chasteneth not?. . .Heb. 12:7

See *Corporal Punishment.*

continued his *s* until midnight. . .Acts 20:7

not with excellency of *s*. . .1 Cor. 2:1

my *s* and my preaching. . .1 Cor. 2:4

we use great plainness of *s*. . .2 Cor. 3:12

Great is my boldness of *s*. . .2 Cor. 7:4

s be always with grace. . .Col. 4:6

Sound *s*, that cannot be. . .Titus 2:8

See *Tongue*.

842. Spending Money

foolish man spendeth it up. . .Prov. 21:20

with harlots spendeth his substance. . .Prov. 29:3

Wherefore do ye spend money. . .Isa. 55:2

counteth the cost, whether he have. . .Luke 14:28

love of money is the root. . .1 Tim. 6:10

843. Spice/Spiced/ Spices

honey, *s's*, and myrrh. . .Gen. 43:11

s's for anointing oil. . .Exod. 25:6

principal *s's*, of pure myrrh. . .Exod. 30:23

sweet *s's* with pure frankincense. . .Exod. 30:34

s's for anointing oil. . .Exod. 35:8

pure incense of sweet *s's*. . .Exod. 37:29

with camels that bare *s's*. . .1 Kings 10:2

traffick of the *s* merchants. . .1 Kings 10:15

the gold, and the *s's*. . .2 Kings 20:13

with all the chief *s's*. . .Song of Sol. 4:14

s'd wine of the juice. . .Song of Sol. 8:2

upon the mountains of *s's*. . .Song of Sol. 8:14

bought sweet *s's*. . .Mark 16:1

in linen clothes with the *s's*. . .John 19:40

840. Special to God

Thou knowest my downsitting. . .Ps. 139:2

laid thine hand upon me. . .Ps. 139:5

Thine eyes did see my substance. . .Ps. 139:16

loved thee with an everlasting love. . .Jer. 31:3

hairs of your head are all numbered. . .Luke 12:7

he hath chosen us in him. . .Eph. 1:4

unto the adoption of children. . .Eph. 1:5

I will never leave thee. . .Heb. 13:5

See *Beloved*.

841. Speech

one language, and of one *s*. . .Gen. 11:1

not understand one another's *s*. . .Gen. 11:7

I am slow of *s*. . .Exod. 4:10

hear my *s*. . .Ps. 17:6

There is no *s* nor language. . .Ps. 19:3

With her much fair *s*. . .Prov. 7:21

Excellent *s* becometh not. . .Prov. 17:7

thy *s* is comely. . .Song of Sol. 4:3

thy *s* bewrayeth thee. . .Matt. 26:73

an impediment in his *s*. . .Mark 7:32

844. Spirit, Holy

take not thy holy *s* from me. . .Ps. 51:11
vexed his holy S. . .Isa. 63:10
put his holy S within him?. . .Isa. 63:11
Holy S to them that ask him?. . .Luke 11:13
sealed with that holy S. . .Eph. 1:13
grieve not the holy S. . .Eph. 4:30
given unto us his holy S. . .1 Thess. 4:8

See *Holy Ghost*.

845. Spirit, Human

thine hand I commit my *s*. . .Ps. 31:5
be of a contrite *s*. . .Ps. 34:18
a right *s* within me. . .Ps. 51:10
are a broken *s*. . .Ps. 51:17
my *s* was overwhelmed. . .Ps. 77:3
my *s* made diligent search. . .Ps. 77:6
whose *s* was not stedfast. . .Ps. 78:8
Therefore is my *s*. . .Ps. 143:4
I will pour out my *s*. . .Prov. 1:23
no rule over his own *s*. . .Prov. 25:28
s shall return unto God. . .Eccles. 12:7
unto the Lord is one *s*. . .1 Cor. 6:17
s, which are God's. . .1 Cor. 6:20
my *s* prayeth. . .1 Cor. 14:14
was made a quickening *s*. . .1 Cor. 15:45

846. Spiritual

unto you some *s* gift. . .Rom. 1:11
the law is *s*. . .Rom. 7:14
partakers of their *s* things. . .Rom. 15:27
comparing *s* things with *s*. . .1 Cor. 2:13
that is *s* judgeth all things. . .1 Cor. 2:15
concerning *s* gifts, brethren. . .1 Cor. 12:1
desire *s* gifts. . .1 Cor. 14:1
zealous of *s* gifts. . .1 Cor. 14:12
it is raised a *s* body. . .1 Cor. 15:44
ye which are *s*, restore. . .Gal. 6:1
us with all *s* blessings. . .Eph. 1:3
against *s* wickedness in high places. . .Eph. 6:12
all wisdom and *s* understanding. . .Col. 1:9
psalms and hymns and *s* songs. . .Col. 3:16
are built up a *s* house. . .1 Pet. 2:5

847. Spite/Spitefully

thou beholdest mischief and *s*. . .Ps. 10:14
entreated them *s'fully*. . .Matt. 22:6
mocked, and *s'fully* entreated. . .Luke 18:32

See *Malice/Malicious/Maliciousness*.

848. Sports

See *Athletics*.

849. Spot/Spots

their *s* is not the *s*. . .Deut. 32:5
lift up thy face without *s*. . .Job 11:15
there is no *s* in thee. . .Song of Sol. 4:7
or the leopard his *s's*?. . .Jer. 13:23
not having *s*, or wrinkle. . .Eph. 5:27
keep this commandment without *s*. . .1 Tim. 6:14
offered himself without *s* to God. . .Heb. 9:14
without blemish and without *s*. . .1 Pet. 1:19
S's they are and blemishes. . .2 Pet. 2:13
without *s*, and blameless. . .2 Pet. 3:14
s's in your feasts of charity. . .Jude 1:12

850. Spouse/Spouses

me from Lebanon, my *s*. . .Song of Sol. 4:8
my *s*; thou hast ravished my heart. . .Song of Sol. 4:9
thy love, my sister, my *s*!. . .Song of Sol. 4:10
Thy lips, O my *s*. . .Song of Sol. 4:11
inclosed is my sister, my *s*. . .Song of Sol. 4:12
my sister, my *s*. . .Song of Sol. 5:1

your *s's* shall commit adultery. . .Hosea 4:13
your *s's* when they commit adultery. . .Hosea 4:14

See *Husband/Husbands*, *Wife/Wives*.

851. Star/Stars

he made the *s's* also. . .Gen. 1:16
multiply your seed as the *s's*. . .Exod. 32:13
s's are not pure. . .Job 25:5
When the morning *s's* sang together. . .Job 38:7
Pleiades, or loose the bands of Orion?. . .Job 38:31
the moon and the *s's*. . .Ps. 8:3
telleth the number of the *s's*. . .Ps. 147:4
we have seen his *s*. . .Matt. 2:2
the *s*, which they saw. . .Matt. 2:9
s's shall fall from heaven. . .Matt. 24:29
day *s* arise in your hearts. . .2 Pet. 1:19
in his right hand seven *s's*. . .Rev. 1:16
The mystery of the seven *s's*. . .Rev. 1:20
s's of heaven fell unto the earth. . .Rev. 6:13
the bright and morning *s*. . .Rev. 22:16

852. Stargazers

See *Astrologers*.

853. Stand Fast

my covenant shall s f. . .Ps. 89:28
They s f for ever. . .Ps. 111:8
Watch ye, s f in the faith. . .1 Cor. 16:13
S f therefore in the liberty. . .Gal. 5:1
ye s f in one spirit. . .Phil. 1:27
s f in the Lord. . .Phil. 4:1
if ye s f in the Lord. . .1 Thess. 3:8
s f, and hold the traditions. . .2 Thess. 2:15

854. Stature

are men of a great s. . .Num. 13:32
the height of his s. . .1 Sam. 16:7
man of great s. . .2 Sam. 21:20
Egyptian, a man of great s. . .1 Chron. 11:23
s is like to a palm. . .Song of Sol. 7:7
s shall be hewn. . .Isa. 10:33
Sabeans, men of s. . .Isa. 45:14
and of an high s. . .Ezek. 31:3
add one cubit unto his s?. . .Matt. 6:27
Jesus increased in wisdom and s. . .Luke 2:52
he was little of s. . .Luke 19:3
s of the fulness of Christ. . .Eph. 4:13

855. Statutes

A statute is a law or decree created by either God or a ruler. The Old Testament commands believers to follow God's statutes.

my s, and my laws. . .Gen. 26:5
and keep all his s. . .Exod. 15:26
Ye shall therefore keep my s. . .Lev. 18:5
to do all these s. . .Deut. 6:24
keep his charge, and his s. . .Deut. 11:1
do these s and judgments. . .Deut. 26:16

s which are written. . .Deut. 30:10
walking in the s of David. . .1 Kings 3:3
to keep my s. . .1 Kings 3:14
teach in Israel s and judgments. . .Ezra 7:10
nor the s, nor the judgments. . .Neh. 1:7
not put away his s. . .Ps. 18:22
s of the Lord are right. . .Ps. 19:8
to declare my s. . .Ps. 50:16
teach me thy s. . .Ps. 119:12
them that err from thy s. . .Ps. 119:118

See *Laws, Rules.*

856. Steadfastness

renew a right spirit within me. . .Ps. 51:10
My heart is fixed, O God. . .Ps. 57:7
O God, my heart is fixed. . .Ps. 108:1
They stand fast for ever. . .Ps. 111:8
his heart is fixed, trusting. . .Ps. 112:7
directed to keep thy statutes!. . .Ps. 119:5
whose mind is stayed on thee. . .Isa. 26:3
stablish, strengthen, settle you. . .1 Pet. 5:10

857. Steal/Stealeth

Thou shalt not s. . .Exod. 20:15
he that s'eth a man. . .Exod. 21:16

man shall s an ox. . .Exod. 22:1

Ye shall not s. . .Lev. 19:11

if he s to satisfy his soul. . .Prov. 6:30

for every one that s'eth. . .Zech. 5:3

thieves break through and s. . .Matt. 6:19

not break through nor s. . .Matt. 6:20

Thou shalt not s. . .Matt. 19:18

and s him away. . .Matt. 27:64

but for to s. . .John 10:10

not s, dost thou s?. . .Rom. 2:21

Thou shalt not s. . .Rom. 13:9

him that stole s no more. . .Eph. 4:28

858. Steward/ Stewards

s's of the mysteries of God. . .1 Cor. 4:1

it is required in s's. . .1 Cor. 4:2

blameless, as the s of God. . .Titus 1:7

as good s's of the manifold grace. . .1 Pet. 4:10

859. Strange Woman

A "strange woman" was an immoral woman, possibly an adulteress.

art the son of a s w. . .Judg. 11:2

deliver thee from the s w. . .Prov. 2:16

lips of a s w drop. . .Prov. 5:3

ravished with a s w. . .Prov. 5:20

tongue of a s w. . .Prov. 6:24

keep thee from the s w. . .Prov. 7:5

pledge of him for a s w. . .Prov. 20:16

s w is a narrow pit. . .Prov. 23:27

pledge of him for a s w. . .Prov. 27:13

860. Stranger/ Strangers

In many verses that describe God's care for strangers, scripture makes it clear that strangers, or aliens, are to be treated fairly by believers. Israel was never to forget that its people had been strangers in Egypt for four hundred years.

thy seed shall be a s. . .Gen. 15:13

land wherein thou art a s. . .Gen. 17:8

s shall sojourn with thee. . .Exod. 12:48

unto the s that sojourneth. . .Exod. 12:49

Thou shalt neither vex a s. . .Exod. 22:21

for the poor and s. . .Lev. 19:10

And if a s sojourn. . .Lev. 19:33

But the s that dwelleth. . .Lev. 19:34

and loveth the s. . .Deut. 10:18

perverteth the judgment of the s. . .Deut. 27:19

seeing I am a s?. . .Ruth 2:10

S's shall submit themselves. . .2 Sam. 22:45

The s did not lodge. . .Job 31:32

I am a *s* in the earth. . .Ps. 119:19

Lᴏʀᴅ preserveth the *s's*. . .Ps. 146:9

s, and ye took me in. . .Matt. 25:35

no more *s's* and foreigners. . .Eph. 2:19

Be not forgetful to entertain *s's*. . .Heb. 13:2

to the *s's* scattered. . .1 Pet. 1:1

beseech you as *s's*. . .1 Pet. 2:11

doest to the brethren, and to *s's*. . .3 John 1:5

See *Alien*.

861. Strength of God

The Lᴏʀᴅ is my *s* and song. . .Exod. 15:2

God is my *s* and power. . .2 Sam. 22:33

Seek the Lᴏʀᴅ and his *s*. . .1 Chron. 16:11

s and gladness are. . .1 Chron. 16:27

to give *s* unto all. . .1 Chron. 29:12

heart, and mighty in *s*. . .Job 9:4

With him is wisdom and *s*. . .Job 12:13

God is our refuge and *s*. . .Ps. 46:1

declared thy *s* among the people. . .Ps. 77:14

been a *s* to the poor. . .Isa. 25:4

Jᴇʜᴏᴠᴀʜ is everlasting *s*. . .Isa. 26:4

my *s* is made perfect. . .2 Cor. 12:9

862. Strength, Physical/Strengthen/ Strengthened

even so is my *s* now. . .Josh. 14:11

wherein thy great *s* lieth. . .Judg. 16:6

by *s* shall no man prevail. . .1 Sam. 2:9

s'ened their hands with vessels. . .Ezra 1:6

s'en their hands in the work. . .Ezra 6:22

For thou hast girded me with *s*. . .Ps. 18:39

My *s* is dried up like. . .Ps. 22:15

with sighing: my *s* faileth. . .Ps. 31:10

not delivered by much *s*. . .Ps. 33:16

deliver any by his great *s*. . .Ps. 33:17

not when my *s* faileth. . .Ps. 71:9

by reason of *s* they be. . .Ps. 90:10

in the *s* of the horse. . .Ps. 147:10

young men is their *s*. . .Prov. 20:29

girdeth her loins with *s*. . .Prov. 31:17

Wisdom is better than *s*. . .Eccles. 9:16

s of Pharaoh be your shame. . .Isa. 30:3

no might he increaseth *s*. . .Isa. 40:29

shall renew their *s*. . .Isa. 40:31

863. Strength, Spiritual/ Strengthen/ Strengthened/ Strengtheneth

joy of the Lᴏʀᴅ is your *s*. . .Neh. 8:10

hast *s'ened* the weak hands. . .Job 4:3

What is my *s*. . .Job 6:11

I will love thee, O Lᴏʀᴅ, my *s*. . .Ps. 18:1

my *s*, and my redeemer. . .Ps. 19:14

s in the time of trouble. . .Ps. 37:39

made not God his *s*. . .Ps. 52:7

the rock of my *s*. . .Ps. 62:7

the *s* of my heart. . .Ps. 73:26

whose *s* is in thee. . .Ps. 84:5

s'en thou me according unto. . .Ps. 119:28

LORD is *s* to the upright. . .Prov. 10:29

confidence shall be your *s*. . .Isa. 30:15

and with all thy *s*. . .Mark 12:30

s'en thy brethren. . .Luke 22:32

Christ which *s'eneth* me. . .Phil. 4:13

S'ened with all might. . .Col. 1:11

864. Stress

See *Overwhelm/Overwhelmed, Strife/Strifes, Struggles, Trouble.*

865. Strife/Strifes

Hatred stirreth up *s's*. . .Prov. 10:12

A wrathful man stirreth up *s*. . .Prov. 15:18

full of sacrifices with *s*. . .Prov. 17:1

man to cease from *s*. . .Prov. 20:3

s and reproach shall cease. . .Prov. 22:10

meddleth with *s* belonging not. . .Prov. 26:17

no talebearer, the *s* ceaseth. . .Prov. 26:20

contentious man to kindle *s*. . .Prov. 26:21

proud heart stirreth up *s*. . .Prov. 28:25

also a *s* among them. . Luke 22:24

not in *s* and envying. . .Rom. 13:13

envying, and *s*, and divisions. . .1 Cor. 3:3

nothing be done through *s*. . .Phil. 2:3

knowing that they do gender *s's*. . .2 Tim. 2:23

bitter envying and *s* in your hearts. . .James 3:14

For where envying and *s* is. . .James 3:16

866. Strive/Striveth/Striving/Strivings

shall not always *s* with man. . .Gen. 6:3

from the *s'ings* of the people. . .Ps. 18:43

them that *s* with me. . .Ps. 35:1

S not with a man. . .Prov. 3:30

Go not forth hastily to *s*. . .Prov. 25:8

him that *s'th* with his Maker!. . .Isa. 45:9

He shall not *s*, nor cry. . .Matt. 12:19

S to enter in. . .Luke 13:24

And every man that *s'th*. . .1 Cor. 9:25

s'ing together for the faith. . .Phil. 1:27

s'ing according to his working. . .Col. 1:29

they *s* not about words. . .2 Tim. 2:14

must not *s*; but be gentle. . .2 Tim. 2:24

and *s'ings* about the law. . .Titus 3:9

s'ing against sin. . .Heb. 12:4

See *Struggles.*

867. Struggles

to frustrate their purpose. . .Ezra 4:5

we wrestle not against flesh. . .Eph. 6:12

Having the same conflict. . .Phil. 1:30

striving according to his working. . .Col. 1:29

great conflict I have for you. . .Col. 2:1

Ye have not yet resisted. . .Heb. 12:4

See *Overwhelm/Overwhelmed, Strive/Striveth/Striving/Strivings, Trouble.*

868. Stubborn/ Stubbornness

it is a stiffnecked people. . .Exod. 32:9

be no more stiffnecked. . .Deut. 10:16

have a *s* and rebellious son. . .Deut. 21:18

nor from their *s* way. . .Judg. 2:19

s'ness is as iniquity and idolatry. . .1 Sam. 15:23

Now be ye not stiffnecked. . .2 Chron. 30:8

a *s* and rebellious generation. . .Ps. 78:8

She is loud and *s*. . .Prov. 7:11

I knew that thou art obstinate. . .Isa. 48:4

Ye stiffnecked and uncircumcised in heart. . .
    Acts 7:51

869. Study

much *s* is a weariness. . .Eccles. 12:12

that ye *s* to be quiet. . .1 Thess. 4:11

S to shew thyself approved. . .2 Tim. 2:15

870. Stumblingblock/ Stumblingblocks

s before the blind. . .Lev. 19:14

s out of the way. . .Isa. 57:14

lay *s's* before this people. . .Jer. 6:21

the *s* of their iniquity. . .Ezek. 7:19

the *s* of their iniquity. . .Ezek. 14:3

the *s* of his iniquity. . .Ezek. 14:4

the *s* of his iniquity. . .Ezek. 14:7

and a trap, and a *s*. . .Rom. 11:9

no man put a *s*. . .Rom. 14:13

unto the Jews a *s*. . .1 Cor. 1:23

s to them that are weak. . .1 Cor. 8:9

Balac to cast a *s*. . .Rev. 2:14

871. Subjection

s under their hand. . .Ps. 106:42

s for servants and for handmaids. . .Jer. 34:11

brought them into *s*. . .Jer. 34:16

and bring it into *s*. . .1 Cor. 9:27

s unto the gospel of Christ. . .2 Cor. 9:13

gave place by *s*. . .Gal. 2:5

in silence with all *s*. . .1 Tim. 2:11

children in *s* with all gravity. . .1 Tim. 3:4

in *s* the world to come. . .Heb. 2:5

all things in *s* under his feet. . .Heb. 2:8

in *s* unto the Father of spirits. . .Heb. 12:9

in *s* to your own husbands. . .1 Pet. 3:1

in *s* unto their own husbands. . .1 Pet. 3:5

872. Submit/ Submitted/Submitting

s thyself under her hands. . .Gen. 16:9

Strangers shall *s* themselves. . .2 Sam. 22:45

s'ted themselves unto Solomon. . .1 Chron. 29:24

strangers shall *s* themselves unto me. . .Ps. 18:44

enemies *s* themselves unto thee. . .Ps. 66:3

every one *s* himself. . .Ps. 68:30

s'ted themselves unto him. . .Ps. 81:15

have not *s'ted* themselves. . .Rom. 10:3

That ye *s* yourselves. . .1 Cor. 16:16

S'ting yourselves one to another. . .Eph. 5:21

Wives, *s* yourselves. . .Eph. 5:22

Wives, *s* yourselves. . .Col. 3:18

rule over you, and *s* yourselves. . .Heb. 13:17

S yourselves therefore to God. . .James 4:7

S yourselves to every ordinance. . .1 Pet. 2:13

younger, *s* yourselves unto the elder. . .1 Pet. 5:5

---

873. Substance Abuse

See *Addiction, Alcohol, Drink/Drinking*.

874. Success

giveth thee power to get wealth. . .Deut. 8:18

that ye may prosper in all. . .Deut. 29:9

then thou shalt have good *s*. . .Josh. 1:8

Then shalt thou prosper. . .1 Chron. 22:13

with all his heart, and prospered. . .2 Chron. 31:21

whatsoever he doeth shall prosper. . .Ps. 1:3

give thee the desires. . .Ps. 37:4

they shall prosper that love thee. . .Ps. 122:6

he that watereth shall be watered. . .Prov. 11:25

thy thoughts shall be established. . .Prov. 16:3

his enemies to be at peace. . .Prov. 16:7

riches, and honour, and life. . .Prov. 22:4

diligent in his business?. . .Prov. 22:29

humble himself shall be exalted. . .Matt. 23:12

Give, and it shall be given. . .Luke 6:38

least is faithful also in much. . .Luke 16:10

---

875. Suffering

See *Hurt/Hurtful, Pain/Pained*.

---

876. Suicide

Though the Bible does not condone suicide, it describes it and one act of what might be called euthanasia. God calls all His people to choose life and faithfully stand firm during troubles.

therefore choose life. . .Deut. 30:19

Draw thy sword, and slay me. . .Judg. 9:54

Let me die with the Philistines. . .Judg. 16:30

Saul took a sword, and fell upon it. . .1 Sam. 31:4

fell likewise upon his sword. . .1 Sam. 31:5

hanged himself, and died. . .2 Sam. 17:23

burnt the king's house over him. . .1 Kings 16:18

went and hanged himself. . .Matt. 27:5

would have killed himself. . .Acts 16:27

trying of your faith. . .James 1:3

those days shall men seek death. . .Rev. 9:6

877. Superstition/ Superstitious

Idolatry and superstition went hand in hand wherever pagan gods were worshipped. God consistently told His people not to become involved in such practices, but both Israel and Judah disobeyed Him.

Turn ye not unto idols. . .Lev. 19:4
Their idols are silver and gold. . .Ps. 115:4
For the idols have spoken vanity. . .Zech. 10:2
idol, and rejoiced in the works. . .Acts 7:41
against him of their own *s*. . .Acts 25:19
all things ye are too *s'us*. . .Acts 17:22
idols of gold, and silver. . .Rev. 9:20

See *Idol/Idolater/Idolaters/Idols, Idolatry.*

878. Supplication/ Supplications

s unto thee in this house. . .1 Kings 8:33
What prayer and *s* soever. . .1 Kings 8:38
their prayer and their *s*. . .1 Kings 8:45
make *s* to my judge. . .Job 9:15
hath heard my *s*. . .Ps. 6:9
heard my voice and my *s's*. . .Ps. 116:1
Let my *s* come. . .Ps. 119:170
Daniel praying and making *s*. . .Dan. 6:11
spirit of grace and of *s's*. . .Zech. 12:10
one accord in prayer and *s*. . .Acts 1:14
with all prayer and *s*. . .Eph. 6:18
s with thanksgiving. . .Phil. 4:6
s's, prayers, intercessions. . .1 Tim. 2:1

continueth in *s's* and prayers. . .1 Tim. 5:5
s's with strong crying. . .Heb. 5:7

879. Surety

One who is liable for another's debts or actions provides surety for the other.

Know of a *s* that thy seed. . .Gen. 15:13
Shall I of a *s* bear a child. . .Gen. 18:13
of a *s* she is thy wife. . .Gen. 26:9
I will be *s* for him. . .Gen. 43:9
become *s* for the lad. . .Gen. 44:32
put me in a *s* with thee. . .Job 17:3
Be *s* for thy servant. . .Ps. 119:122
if thou be *s* for thy friend. . .Prov. 6:1
He that is *s* for a stranger. . .Prov. 11:15
and becometh *s* in the presence. . .Prov. 17:18
that is *s* for a stranger. . .Prov. 20:16
I know of a *s*. . .Acts 12:11
Jesus made a *s*. . .Heb. 7:22

880. Sustain/ Sustained

and wine have I *s'd* him. . .Gen. 27:37
woman there to *s* thee. . .1 Kings 17:9
s them in the wilderness. . .Neh. 9:21

for the LORD *s'd* me. . .Ps. 3:5
he shall *s* thee. . .Ps. 55:22
will *s* his infirmity. . .Prov. 18:14
his righteousness, it *s'd* him. . .Isa. 59:16

shall *s* by the temple. . .Matt. 23:16
s not, neither by heaven. . .James 5:12

See *Oath/Oaths.*

881. Swear/Swearers/ Sweareth/Swearing

The Old Testament commanded God's people to swear by His name, which meant a believer was to be held accountable to God for keeping that vow. Failure to keep such a promise reflected badly on the Lord and opened the false swearer to His judgment. Oaths were sometimes made before an altar. Jesus told His disciples not to swear at all, but simply to tell the truth.

not *s* by my name falsely. . .Lev. 19:12
s an oath to bind his soul. . .Num. 30:2
shalt *s* by his name. . .Deut. 6:13
nor cause to *s* by them. . .Josh. 23:7
S now therefore unto me. . .1 Sam. 24:21
to cause him to *s*. . .1 Kings 8:31
s'eth to his own hurt. . .Ps. 15:4
that *s'eth* by him shall glory. . .Ps. 63:11
every tongue shall *s*. . .Isa. 45:23
I *s* by myself. . .Jer. 22:5
s'ing falsely in making a covenant. . .Hosea 10:4
and against false *s'ers*. . .Mal. 3:5
S not at all. . .Matt. 5:34

882. Synagogue/ Synagogues

During the biblical era, synagogues were places where Jewish believers gathered locally for prayer and study. No sacrifices took place in synagogues, since the temple was devoted to such worship. Jesus preached in the synagogues, and Paul visited a synagogue in each city first, until he was no longer welcomed by the Jews.

burned up all the *s's*. . .Ps. 74:8
teaching in their *s's*. . .Matt. 4:23
hypocrites do in the *s's*. . .Matt. 6:2
pray standing in the *s's*. . .Matt. 6:5
teaching in their *s's*. . .Matt. 9:35
scourge you in their *s's*. . .Matt. 10:17
put you out of the *s's*. . .John 16:2
preached Christ in the *s's*. . .Acts 9:20
gone out of the *s*. . .Acts 13:42
into the *s* of the Jews. . .Acts 14:1
entered into the *s*. . .Acts 18:19
And he went into the *s*. . .Acts 19:8
punished them oft in every *s*. . .Acts 26:11
but are the *s* of Satan. . .Rev. 2:9
them of the *s* of Satan. . .Rev. 3:9

883. Tabernacle/ Tabernacles

Following the Exodus, God commanded Moses to build the tabernacle, a tent that was a portable place of worship for the Israelites. The word is also used to describe the homes of the righteous, and the apostles use it to describe the human body.

after the pattern of the *t*. . .Exod. 25:9
thou shalt make the *t*. . .Exod. 26:1
In the *t* of the congregation. . .Exod. 27:21
anointed the *t*. . .Lev. 8:10
who shall abide in thy *t*?. . .Ps. 15:1
the holy place of the *t's*. . .Ps. 46:4
t of the upright shall flourish. . .Prov. 14:11
t that shall not be taken down. . .Isa. 33:20
make here three *t's*. . .Matt. 17:4
t of witness in the wilderness. . .Acts 7:44
build again the *t* of David. . .Acts 15:16
earthly house of this *t*. . .2 Cor. 5:1
true *t*, which the Lord pitched. . .Heb. 8:2
greater and more perfect *t*. . .Heb. 9:11
I am in this *t*. . .2 Pet. 1:13

884. Talebearer

as a *t* among thy people. . .Lev. 19:16
A *t* revealeth secrets. . .Prov. 11:13
The words of a *t*. . .Prov. 18:8
as a *t* revealeth secrets. . .Prov. 20:19
no *t*, the strife ceaseth. . .Prov. 26:20
t are as wounds. . .Prov. 26:22

See *Gossip*.

885. Tattoos

nor print any marks upon you. . .Lev. 19:28

886. Taxed/Taxes/Taxing

he *t* the land. . .2 Kings 23:35
raiser of *t'es* in the glory. . .Dan. 11:20
all the world should be *t*. . .Luke 2:1
this *t'ing* was first made. . .Luke 2:2
And all went to be *t*. . .Luke 2:3
To be *t* with Mary. . .Luke 2:5
in the days of the *t'ing*. . .Acts 5:37

887. Teach/Teaching

thou shalt *t* them ordinances. . .Exod. 18:20
t them diligently unto thy children. . .Deut. 6:7
t me thy paths. . .Ps. 25:4
he *t* sinners in the way. . .Ps. 25:8
Train up a child. . .Prov. 22:6
shall *t* no more every man. . .Jer. 31:34
t'ing in their synagogues. . .Matt. 4:23
but whosoever shall do and *t* them. . .Matt. 5:19
t'ing for doctrines the commandments. . .Matt. 15:9
Go ye therefore, and *t* all. . .Matt. 28:19
T'ing them to observe all things. . .Matt. 28:20

Holy Ghost shall *t* you. . .Luke 12:12
they ceased not to *t*. . .Acts 5:42
t'ing and admonishing one another. . .Col. 3:16
apt to *t*. . .1 Tim. 3:2
t the young women. . .Titus 2:4

See *Great Commission.*

888. Tears

prayer, I have seen thy *t*. . .2 Kings 20:5
eye poureth out *t* unto God. . .Job 16:20
water my couch with my *t*. . .Ps. 6:6
not thy peace at my *t*. . .Ps. 39:12
My *t* have been my meat. . .Ps. 42:3
my *t* into thy bottle. . .Ps. 56:8
mine eyes from *t*. . .Ps. 116:8
sow in *t* shall reap in joy. . .Ps. 126:5
said with *t*, Lord, I believe. . .Mark 9:24
wash his feet with *t*. . .Luke 7:38
with many *t*, and temptations. . .Acts 20:19
every one night and day with *t*. . .Acts 20:31
he sought it carefully with *t*. . .Heb. 12:17

God shall wipe away all *t*. . .Rev. 7:17
And God shall wipe away all *t*. . .Rev. 21:4

889. Temper
See *Sin of Anger/Anger.*

890. Temperance/ Temperate

righteousness, *t*, and judgment. . .Acts 24:25
mastery is *t'te* in all things. . .1 Cor. 9:25
Meekness, *t*: against such. . .Gal. 5:23
sober, just, holy, *t'te*. . .Titus 1:8
grave, *t'te*, sound in faith. . .Titus 2:2
t; and to *t* patience. . .2 Pet. 1:6

891. Temple
Before Solomon built the temple in Jerusalem, there was a temple to the Lord in Shiloh. Solomon's temple was destroyed when the Babylonians overran the city. After the Jews

returned to Jerusalem, the temple was rebuilt on a less grand scale. Herod the Great made the temple part of his extensive rebuilding program. This is the place Jesus and His disciples visited.

the *t* of the Lord. . .1 Sam. 1:9
laid the foundation of the *t*. . .Ezra 3:10
The Lord is in his holy *t*. . .Ps. 11:4
to enquire in his *t*. . .Ps. 27:4
his train filled the *t*. . .Isa. 6:1
taken out of the *t*. . .Dan. 5:2
But the Lord is in his holy *t*. . .Hab. 2:20
on a pinnacle of the *t*. . .Matt. 4:5
one greater than the *t*. . .Matt. 12:6
sold and bought in the *t*. . .Matt. 21:12
Whosoever shall swear by the *t*. . .Matt. 23:16
the buildings of the *t*. . .Matt. 24:1
veil of the *t* was rent. . .Matt. 27:51
And he taught daily in the *t*. . .Luke 19:47
ye are the *t* of God. . .1 Cor. 3:16

892. Temptation/Temptations

t in the wilderness. . .Ps. 95:8
lead us not into *t*. . .Matt. 6:13
that ye enter not into *t*. . .Matt. 26:41
devil had ended all the *t*. . .Luke 4:13
in time of *t* fall away. . .Luke 8:13
continued with me in my *t's*. . .Luke 22:28
with many tears, and *t's*. . .Acts 20:19
There hath no *t* taken you. . .1 Cor. 10:13
rich fall into *t*. . .1 Tim. 6:9
ye fall into divers *t's*. . .James 1:2
man that endureth *t*. . .James 1:12
in heaviness through manifold *t's*. . .1 Pet. 1:6
deliver the godly out of *t's*. . .2 Pet. 2:9

893. Tempter

when the *t* came to him. . .Matt. 4:3
the *t* have tempted you. . .1 Thess. 3:5

See *Satan*.

894. Tender/Tenderhearted

Because thine heart was *t*. . .2 Kings 22:19
thy *t* mercies and thy lovingkindnesses. . .Ps. 25:6
Withhold not thou thy *t* mercies. . .Ps. 40:11
t mercies blot out my transgressions. . .Ps. 51:1
shut up his *t* mercies?. . .Ps. 77:9
t mercies speedily prevent us. . .Ps. 79:8
t mercies are over all his works. . .Ps. 145:9
before him as a *t* plant. . .Isa. 53:2
t love with the prince. . .Dan. 1:9
the *t* mercy of our God. . .Luke 1:78
t'hearted, forgiving one another. . .Eph. 4:32
very pitiful, and of *t* mercy. . .James 5:11

895. Terrible

t thing that I will do. . .Exod. 34:10
a mighty God and *t*. . .Deut. 7:21
these great and *t* things. . .Deut. 10:21

with God is *t* majesty. . .Job 37:22
the glory of his nostrils is *t*. . .Job 39:20
shall teach thee *t* things. . .Ps. 45:4
LORD most high is *t*. . .Ps. 47:2
By *t* things in righteousness. . .Ps. 65:5
How *t* art thou. . .Ps. 66:3
he is *t* in his doing. . .Ps. 66:5
he is *t* to the kings. . .Ps. 76:12
thy great and *t* name. . .Ps. 99:3
the hand of the *t*. . .Jer. 15:21
t day of the LORD. . .Joel 2:31
And so *t* was the sight. . .Heb. 12:21

896. Terror/Terrors

t of God was. . .Gen. 35:5
even appoint over you *t*. . .Lev. 26:16
arm, and by great *t's*. . .Deut. 4:34
great *t* which Moses shewed. . .Deut. 34:12
your *t* is fallen upon us. . .Josh. 2:9
t's of God do set themselves. . .Job 6:4
T's shall make him afraid. . .Job 18:11
T's are turned upon me. . .Job 30:15
from God was a *t* to me. . .Job 31:23
t's of death are fallen. . .Ps. 55:4
afraid for the *t* by night. . .Ps. 91:5
Be not a *t* unto me. . .Jer. 17:17
rulers are not a *t*. . .Rom. 13:3
the *t* of the Lord. . .2 Cor. 5:11
be not afraid of their *t*. . .1 Pet. 3:14

897. Terrorism

See *Kidnapping, Murder/Murders, Murderer/ Murderers, Violence.*

898. Testify/Testifying

I *t* among you this day. . .Deut. 32:46
I will *t* against thee. . .Ps. 50:7
I will *t* unto thee. . .Ps. 81:8
our sins *t* against us. . .Isa. 59:12
though our iniquities *t* against us. . .Jer. 14:7
that any should *t* of man. . .John 2:25
t that we have seen. . .John 3:11
they are they which *t* of me. . .John 5:39
because I *t* of it. . .John 7:7
he shall *t* of me. . .John 15:26
did he *t* and exhort. . .Acts 2:40
to *t* that it is he. . .Acts 10:42
T'ing both to the Jews. . .Acts 20:21
do *t* that the Father. . .1 John 4:14
mine angel to *t* unto you. . .Rev. 22:16

899. Testimony, Believer's

for a *t* against them. . .Matt. 10:18
for a *t* unto them. . .Luke 5:14
no man receiveth his *t*. . .John 3:32
He that hath received his *t*. . .John 3:33
know that his *t* is true. . .John 21:24
t unto the word. . .Acts 14:3
not receive thy *t* concerning me. . .Acts 22:18
t of Christ was confirmed. . .1 Cor. 1:6
unto you the *t* of God. . .1 Cor. 2:1
the *t* of our conscience. . .2 Cor. 1:12
our *t* among you. . .2 Thess. 1:10
the *t* of our Lord. . .2 Tim. 1:8

for a *t* of those things. . .Heb. 3:5
for the *t* of Jesus Christ. . .Rev. 1:9
t which they held. . .Rev. 6:9

900. Thankful/ Thanksgiving/ Thanksgivings

both with *t'sgivings*. . .Neh. 12:27
with the voice of *t'sgiving*. . .Ps. 26:7
Offer unto God *t'sgiving*. . .Ps. 50:14
magnify him with *t'sgiving*. . .Ps. 69:30
before his presence with *t'sgiving*. . .Ps. 95:2
be *t* unto him, and bless. . .Ps. 100:4
neither were *t*; but became vain. . .Rom. 1:21
supplication with *t'sgiving*. . .Phil. 4:6
one body; and be ye *t*. . .Col. 3:15
if it be received with *t'sgiving*. . .1 Tim. 4:4

See *Thanks*.

901. Thanks

I will give *t* unto thee. . .2 Sam. 22:50
Give *t* unto the Lord. . .1 Chron. 16:8
O give *t* unto the Lord. . .1 Chron. 16:34
give *t* to thy holy name. . .1 Chron. 16:35
t at the remembrance. . .Ps. 30:4

give *t* unto thee for ever. . .Ps. 30:12
t in the great congregation. . .Ps. 35:18
t: for that thy name. . .Ps. 75:1
give thee *t* for ever. . .Ps. 79:13
O give *t* unto the Lord. . .Ps. 105:1
t unto the Lord. . .Ps. 106:1
I will rise to give *t*. . .Ps. 119:62
the righteous shall give *t*. . .Ps. 140:13
But *t* be to God. . .1 Cor. 15:57
Now *t* be unto God. . .2 Cor. 2:14
T be unto God. . .2 Cor. 9:15
but rather giving of *t*. . .Eph. 5:4
Giving *t* always for all things. . .Eph. 5:20
Giving *t* unto the Father. . .Col. 1:12
Lord Jesus, giving *t* to God. . .Col. 3:17
In every thing give *t*. . .1 Thess. 5:18
giving of *t*, be made. . .1 Tim. 2:1
fruit of our lips giving *t*. . .Heb. 13:15

See *Thankful/Thanksgiving/Thanksgivings*.

902. Theism/ Agnosticism

Theists believe that God is disconnected from the world He created or that He is all love and does not judge humankind. Agnostics believe they cannot know if there is a God.

I am the Lord thy God. . .Exod. 20:2
Lord hath wrought this?. . .Job 12:9
will not seek after God. . .Ps. 10:4
There is no God. . .Ps. 14:1
there is none that doeth good. . .Ps. 53:1
thou knowest it altogether. . .Ps. 139:4
all my members were written. . .Ps. 139:16
evil things come from within. . .Mark 7:23

his eternal power and Godhead. . .Rom. 1:20

any man have not the Spirit of Christ. . .Rom. 8:9

he did foreknow, he also did predestinate. . .Rom. 8:29

natural man receiveth not. . .1 Cor. 2:14

who were dead in trespasses. . .Eph. 2:1

worlds were framed by the word of God. . .Heb. 11:3

without faith it is impossible. . .Heb. 11:6

if he *t*, give him drink. . .Rom. 12:20

hunger, and *t*, and are naked. . .1 Cor. 4:11

neither *t* any more. . .Rev. 7:16

903. Thirst/Thirsteth/Thirsty

Thirst is often a biblical picture of a person's desire for God.

My soul *t'eth* for God. . .Ps. 42:2

Hungry and *t'y*, their soul fainted. . .Ps. 107:5

he be *t'y*, give him water. . .Prov. 25:21

their tongue faileth for *t*. . .Isa. 41:17

every one that *t'eth*. . .Isa. 55:1

hunger and *t* after righteousness. . .Matt. 5:6

t'y, and ye gave me drink. . .Matt. 25:35

give him shall never *t*. . .John 4:14

believeth on me shall never *t*. . .John 6:35

If any man *t*. . .John 7:37

saith, I *t*. . .John 19:28

904. Thought/Thoughts

every imagination of the *t's*. . .Gen. 6:5

God is not in all his *t's*. . .Ps. 10:4

t's within me thy comforts. . .Ps. 94:19

I hate vain *t's*. . .Ps. 119:113

understandest my *t* afar off. . .Ps. 139:2

try me, and know my *t's*. . .Ps. 139:23

t's of the righteous. . .Prov. 12:5

t's of the wicked. . .Prov. 15:26

thy *t's* shall be established. . .Prov. 16:3

t's of the diligent. . .Prov. 21:5

The *t* of foolishness is sin. . .Prov. 24:9

my *t's* are not your *t's*. . .Isa. 55:8

t's that I think toward you. . .Jer. 29:11

Take no *t* for your life. . .Matt. 6:25

Take therefore no *t*. . .Matt. 6:34

take no *t* how or what. . .Matt. 10:19

out of the heart proceed evil *t's*. . .Matt. 15:19

bringing into captivity every *t*. . .2 Cor. 10:5

t's and intents of the heart. . .Heb. 4:12

905. Threaten/Threatened/Threatening/Threatenings

against this place to destroy it?. . .2 Kings 18:25

let us straitly *t* them. . .Acts 4:17

they had further *t'ed* them. . .Acts 4:21

behold their *t'ings*: and grant. . .Acts 4:29

breathing out *t'ings* and slaughter. . .Acts 9:1

forbearing *t'ing*: knowing that. . .Eph. 6:9

he suffered, he *t'ed* not. . .1 Pet. 2:23

906. Time/Times

against the *t* of trouble. . .Job 38:23

My *t's* are in thy hand. . .Ps. 31:15

t when thou mayest be found. . .Ps. 32:6

deliver him in *t* of trouble. . .Ps. 41:1

What *t* I am afraid. . .Ps. 56:3

Lord, in an acceptable *t*. . .Ps. 69:13

Remember how short my *t* is. . .Ps. 89:47

a *t* to every purpose. . .Eccles. 3:1

t to seek the Lord. . .Hosea 10:12

My *t* is not yet come. . .John 7:6

the *t* is short. . .1 Cor. 7:29

Redeeming the *t*. . .Eph. 5:16

perilous *t's* shall come. . .2 Tim. 3:1

help in *t* of need. . .Heb. 4:16

the *t* of your sojourning. . .1 Pet. 1:17

907. Tiredness

when thou wast faint and weary. . .Deut. 25:18

there the weary be at rest. . .Job 3:17

My soul is weary of my life. . .Job 10:1

he hath made me weary. . .Job 16:7

I am weary with my groaning. . .Ps. 6:6

I am weary of my crying. . .Ps. 69:3

neither be weary of his correction. . .Prov. 3:11

lest he be weary of thee. . .Prov. 25:17

much study is a weariness. . .Eccles. 12:12

a great rock in a weary land. . .Isa. 32:2

fainteth not, neither is weary?. . .Isa. 40:28

run, and not be weary. . .Isa. 40:31

what a weariness is it!. . .Mal. 1:13

In weariness and painfulness. . .2 Cor. 11:27

not be weary in well doing. . .Gal. 6:9

908. Tithe/Tithes

And he gave him *t's* of all. . .Gen. 14:20

all the *t* of the land. . .Lev. 27:30

concerning the *t* of the herd. . .Lev. 27:32

robbed thee? In *t's* and offerings. . .Mal. 3:8

all the *t's* into the storehouse. . .Mal. 3:10

pay *t* of mint and anise. . .Matt. 23:23

I give *t's* of all. . .Luke 18:12

men that die receive *t's*. . .Heb. 7:8

payed *t's* in Abraham. . .Heb. 7:9

See *Offering/Offerings*.

909. To Day/ The Present

T d if ye will hear his voice. . .Ps. 95:7

t d is, and to morrow. . .Matt. 6:30

T d if ye will hear his voice. . .Heb. 3:7

daily, while it is called *T d*. . .Heb. 3:13

no chastening for *t p* seemeth. . .Heb. 12:11

same yesterday, and *t d*. . .Heb. 13:8

910. Tolerance

Scripture calls believers to more than "live and let live" tolerance for one another. God repeatedly calls Christians to love others, including their enemies.

Love your enemies, bless them. . .Matt. 5:44
That ye love one another. . .John 13:34
in honour preferring one another. . .Rom. 12:10
not therefore judge one another. . .Rom. 14:13
by love serve one another. . .Gal. 5:13
forbearing one another in love. . .Eph. 4:2
tenderhearted, forgiving one another. . .Eph. 4:32
Submitting yourselves one to another. . .Eph. 5:21
Husbands, love your wives. . .Eph. 5:25
same love, being of one accord. . .Phil. 2:2
Forbearing one another. . .Col. 3:13
And let us consider one another. . .Heb. 10:24
Let brotherly love continue. . .Heb. 13:1
be subject one to another. . .1 Pet. 5:5
ought also to love one another. . .1 John 4:11
I love God, and hateth his brother. . .1 John 4:20

See *Unity*.

flattery of the *t*. . .Prov. 6:24
The *t* of the just. . .Prov. 10:20
t of the wise is health. . .Prov. 12:18
lying *t* is but for a moment. . .Prov. 12:19
The *t* of the wise. . .Prov. 15:2
A wholesome *t* is a tree. . .Prov. 15:4
perverse *t* falleth into mischief. . .Prov. 17:20
keepeth his mouth and his *t*. . .Prov. 21:23
soft *t* breaketh the bone. . .Prov. 25:15
every *t* should confess. . .Phil. 2:11
bridleth not his *t*. . .James 1:26
the *t* is a little member. . .James 3:5
t can no man tame. . .James 3:8
neither in *t*. . .1 John 3:18

See *Speech*.

911. Tongue

nor my *t* utter deceit. . .Job 27:4
under his *t* is mischief. . .Ps. 10:7
t that speaketh proud things. . .Ps. 12:3
backbiteth not with his *t*. . .Ps. 15:3
Keep thy *t* from evil. . .Ps. 34:13
t shall speak of thy righteousness. . .Ps. 35:28
his *t* talketh of judgment. . .Ps. 37:30
I sin not with my *t*. . .Ps. 39:1
whet their *t* like a sword. . .Ps. 64:3
not a word in my *t*. . .Ps. 139:4

912. Tongues, Speaking in

they shall speak with new *t*. . .Mark 16:17
speak with other *t*. . .Acts 2:4
every man in our own tongue. . .Acts 2:8
speak with *t*, and magnify God. . .Acts 10:46
spake with *t*, and prophesied. . .Acts 19:6
another divers kinds of *t*. . .1 Cor. 12:10
diversities of *t*. . .1 Cor. 12:28

do all speak with *t*?...1 Cor. 12:30

t of men and of angels...1 Cor. 13:1

there be *t*, they shall cease...1 Cor. 13:8

speaketh in an unknown tongue...1 Cor. 14:2

unknown tongue edifieth himself...1 Cor. 14:4

ye all spake with *t*...1 Cor. 14:5

speaketh in an unknown tongue...1 Cor. 14:13

pray in an unknown tongue...1 Cor. 14:14

t are for a sign...1 Cor. 14:22

speak in an unknown tongue...1 Cor. 14:27

forbid not to speak with *t*...1 Cor. 14:39

913. Tool/Tools

lift up thy *t* upon it...Exod. 20:25

fashioned it with a graving *t*...Exod. 32:4

nether or the upper millstone...Deut. 24:6

not lift up any iron *t*...Deut. 27:5

his axe, and his mattock...1 Sam. 13:20

hammer nor axe nor any *t*...1 Kings 6:7

And the pots, and the shovels...1 Kings 7:45

spears into pruninghooks...Isa. 2:4

shall the saw magnify itself...Isa. 10:15

shovel and with the fan...Isa. 30:24

with nails and with hammers...Jer. 10:4

a wall made by a plumbline...Amos 7:7

axe is laid unto the root...Matt. 3:10

914. Torment/ Tormented/ Tormentors/Torments

divers diseases and *t's*...Matt. 4:24

t us before the time?...Matt. 8:29

delivered him to the *t'ors*...Matt. 18:34

that thou *t* me not...Mark 5:7

being in *t's*, and seeth...Luke 16:23

I am *t'ed* in this flame...Luke 16:24

and thou art *t'ed*...Luke 16:25

this place of *t*...Luke 16:28

being destitute, afflicted, *t'ed*...Heb. 11:37

because fear hath *t*...1 John 4:18

t of a scorpion...Rev. 9:5

two prophets *t'ed* them...Rev. 11:10

t'ed with fire and brimstone...Rev. 14:10

smoke of their *t* ascendeth...Rev. 14:11

for the fear of her *t*...Rev. 18:10

t'ed day and night for ever...Rev. 20:10

915. Tradition/ Traditions

Many first-century Jews were caught up in traditions that were not strictly biblical. The apostles encouraged Christians to follow God's Word instead of man-made traditions.

the *t* of the elders?...Matt. 15:2

commandment of God by your *t*?...Matt. 15:3

none effect by your *t*...Matt. 15:6

holding the *t* of the elders...Mark 7:3

ye hold the *t* of men...Mark 7:8

ye may keep your own *t*...Mark 7:9

t's of my fathers...Gal. 1:14

after the *t* of men...Col. 2:8

t's which ye have been taught...2 Thess. 2:15

not after the *t* which he. . .2 Thess. 3:6
received by *t* from your fathers. . .1 Pet. 1:18

916. Traitor/Traitors

Judas Iscariot, which also was the *t*. . .Luke 6:16
T's, heady, highminded. . .2 Tim. 3:4

917. Transformed/ Transforming

be ye *t* by the renewing. . .Rom. 12:2
deceitful workers, *t'ing* themselves. . .2 Cor. 11:13
Satan himself is *t*. . .2 Cor. 11:14
t as the ministers of righteousness. . .2 Cor. 11:15

918. Transgression/ Transgressions

he will not pardon your *t's*. . .Exod. 23:21
forgiving iniquity and *t*. . .Num. 14:18

innocent from the great *t*. . .Ps. 19:13
my youth, nor my *t's*. . .Ps. 25:7
he whose *t* is forgiven. . .Ps. 32:1
blot out my *t's*. . .Ps. 51:1
acknowledge my *t's*. . .Ps. 51:3
the *t* of his lips. . .Prov. 12:13
He that covereth a *t*. . .Prov. 17:9
He loveth *t* that loveth strife. . .Prov. 17:19
wicked are multiplied, *t* increaseth. . .Prov. 29:16
he was wounded for our *t's*. . .Isa. 53:5
turneth away from all his *t's*. . .Ezek. 18:28
t's and our sins be upon us. . .Ezek. 33:10
no law is, there is no *t*. . .Rom. 4:15
t and disobedience received. . .Heb. 2:2
sin is the *t*. . .1 John 3:4

See *Sin*, *Trespass/Trespassed/Trespasses*.

919. Treachery/ Treacherous/ Treacherously

Shechem dealt *t'ously* with Abimelech. . .Judg. 9:23
There is *t*, O Ahaziah. . .2 Kings 9:23
not spoiled; and dealest *t'ously*. . .Isa. 33:1
thou wouldest deal very *t'ously*. . .Isa. 48:8
her *t'ous* sister Judah. . .Jer. 3:10

wife *t'ously* departeth. . .Jer. 3:20

dealt very *t'ously* against me. . .Jer. 5:11

an assembly of *t'ous* men. . .Jer. 9:2

happy that deal very *t'ously*?. . .Jer. 12:1

have dealt *t'ously* with thee. . .Jer. 12:6

dealt *t'ously* against the LORD. . .Hosea 5:7

Her prophets are light and *t'ous*. . .Zeph. 3:4

why do we deal *t'ously*. . .Mal. 2:10

none deal *t'ously* against the wife. . .Mal. 2:15

920. Treason

Zimri, and his *t*. . .1 Kings 16:20

and cried, *T, T*. . .2 Kings 11:14

and said, *T, T*. . .2 Chron. 23:13

921. Treasure, Spiritual/Treasures

the righteous is much *t*. . .Prov. 15:6

t's upon earth, where moth. . .Matt. 6:19

t's in heaven, where. . .Matt. 6:20

For where your *t* is. . .Matt. 6:21

the good *t* of the heart. . .Matt. 12:35

heaven is like unto *t*. . .Matt. 13:44

shalt have *t* in heaven. . .Matt. 19:21

not rich toward God. . .Luke 12:21

this *t* in earthen vessels. . .2 Cor. 4:7

922. Tree/Trees

fruit *t* yielding fruit. . .Gen. 1:11

God to grow every *t*. . .Gen. 2:9

every *t* of the garden. . .Gen. 2:16

t of the knowledge of good. . .Gen. 2:17

threescore and ten palm *t's*. . .Exod. 15:27

thick *t's*, and willows. . .Lev. 23:40

vineyards and olive *t's*. . .Deut. 6:11

fig *t's*, and pomegranates. . .Deut. 8:8

beatest thine olive *t*. . .Deut. 24:20

palm *t* of Deborah. . .Judg. 4:5

tops of the mulberry *t's*. . .2 Sam. 5:24

slept under a juniper *t*. . .1 Kings 19:5

cedar *t's*, fir *t's*, and algum *t's*. . .2 Chron. 2:8

t planted by the rivers. . .Ps. 1:3

a green bay *t*. . .Ps. 37:35

As the apple *t*. . .Song of Sol. 2:3

And when he saw a fig *t*. . .Matt. 21:19

up into a sycomore *t*. . .Luke 19:4

being a wild olive *t*. . .Rom. 11:17

923. Trespass/ Trespassed/Trespasses

t'ed against the LORD God. . .2 Chron. 30:7

our *t* is grown up. . .Ezra 9:6

t that he hath *t'ed*. . .Ezek. 18:24

if ye forgive men their *t'es*. . .Matt. 6:14

forgive not men their *t'es*. . .Matt. 6:15

brother shall *t* against thee. . .Matt. 18:15

every one his brother their *t'es*. . .Matt. 18:35

may forgive you your *t'es*. . .Mark 11:25

If thy brother *t* against thee. . .Luke 17:3

t against thee seven times. . .Luke 17:4

not imputing their *t'es* unto them. . .2 Cor. 5:19

who were dead in *t'es*. . .Eph. 2:1

having forgiven you all *t'es*. . .Col. 2:13

See *Sin, Transgression/Transgressions*.

924. Trial

a great *t* of affliction. . .2 Cor. 8:2

t of cruel mockings. . .Heb. 11:36

That the *t* of your faith. . .1 Pet. 1:7

concerning the fiery *t*. . .1 Pet. 4:12

925. Tribulation/Tribulations

When thou art in *t*. . .Deut. 4:30

your adversities and your *t's*. . .1 Sam. 10:19

deliver me out of all *t*. . .1 Sam. 26:24

t or persecution ariseth. . .Matt. 13:21

then shall be great *t*. . .Matt. 24:21

Immediately after the *t*. . .Matt. 24:29

ye shall have *t*. . .John 16:33

through much *t* enter. . .Acts 14:22

T and anguish, upon. . .Rom. 2:9

glory in *t's* also. . .Rom. 5:3

shall *t*, or distress. . .Rom. 8:35

patient in *t*. . .Rom. 12:12

comforteth us in all our *t*. . .2 Cor. 1:4

God to recompense *t*. . .2 Thess. 1:6

thy works, and *t*. . .Rev. 2:9

came out of great *t*. . .Rev. 7:14

926. Triumph/Triumphed/Triumphing

he hath *t'ed* gloriously. . .Exod. 15:1

he hath *t'ed* gloriously. . .Exod. 15:21

daughters of the uncircumcised *t*. . .2 Sam. 1:20

t'ing of the wicked is short. . .Job 20:5

let not mine enemies *t*. . .Ps. 25:2

mine enemy doth not *t*. . .Ps. 41:11

with the voice of *t*. . .Ps. 47:1

Philistia, *t* thou because. . .Ps. 60:8

I will *t* in the works. . .Ps. 92:4

how long shall the wicked *t*?. . .Ps. 94:3
to *t* in thy praise. . .Ps. 106:47
over Philistia will I *t*. . .Ps. 108:9
causeth us to *t* in Christ. . .2 Cor. 2:14
t'ing over them in it. . .Col. 2:15

See *Overcome/Overcometh, Victory*.

927. Trouble

yet *t* came. . .Job 3:26
man is born unto *t*. . .Job 5:7
few days and full of *t*. . .Job 14:1
a refuge in times of *t*. . .Ps. 9:9
in times of *t*?. . .Ps. 10:1
time of *t* he shall hide. . .Ps. 27:5
preserve me from *t*. . .Ps. 32:7
strength in the time of *t*. . .Ps. 37:39
deliver him in time of *t*. . .Ps. 41:1
present help in *t*. . .Ps. 46:1
me in the day of *t*. . .Ps. 50:15
have *t* in the flesh. . .1 Cor. 7:28
which are in any *t*. . .2 Cor. 1:4
them that *t* you. . .2 Thess. 1:6
Wherein I suffer *t*. . .2 Tim. 2:9

See *Affliction/Afflictions, Struggles*.

928. Trust

in him will I *t*. . .2 Sam. 22:3
buckler to all them that *t*. . .2 Sam. 22:31
put their *t* in him. . .Ps. 2:12
put your *t* in the LORD. . .Ps. 4:5
t in thee rejoice. . .Ps. 5:11
in thee do I put my *t*. . .Ps. 7:1
name will put their *t*. . .Ps. 9:10

I will *t*; my buckler. . .Ps. 18:2
Some *t* in chariots. . .Ps. 20:7
T in the LORD. . .Ps. 37:3
afraid, I will *t* in thee. . .Ps. 56:3
Put not your *t* in princes. . .Ps. 146:3
T in the LORD. . .Prov. 3:5
husband doth safely *t* in her. . .Prov. 31:11
T ye in the LORD. . .Isa. 26:4
name shall the Gentiles *t*. . .Matt. 12:21
we should not *t* in ourselves. . .2 Cor. 1:9
t that he will yet deliver. . .2 Cor. 1:10
we *t* in the living God. . .1 Tim. 4:10

929. Truth

abundant in goodness and *t*. . .Exod. 34:6
God of *t* and without iniquity. . .Deut. 32:4
in sincerity and in *t*. . .Josh. 24:14
thou desirest *t*. . .Ps. 51:6
his *t* endureth to all generations. . .Ps. 100:5
speaketh *t* sheweth forth
    righteousness. . .Prov. 12:17
full of grace and *t*. . .John 1:14
grace and *t* came by Jesus. . .John 1:17
in spirit and in *t*. . .John 4:24
And ye shall know the *t*. . .John 8:32
the Spirit of *t*. . .John 16:13

Sanctify them through thy *t*. . .John 17:17

but rejoiceth in the *t*. . .1 Cor. 13:6

speaking the *t* in love. . .Eph. 4:15

speak every man *t*. . .Eph. 4:25

the knowledge of the *t*. . .1 Tim. 2:4

rightly dividing the word of *t*. . .2 Tim. 2:15

the *t* is not in him. . .1 John 2:4

930. Types

A type is an Old Testament person or thing that foreshadows someone or something in the New Testament. What we call types, scripture sometimes speaks of as "shadows" of what would come. For example, figures such as the angel of the Lord and the captain of the Lord's hosts are types of Christ when they are worshipped, when they act as God would, or when God is described as acting in that passage.

name of the Lord that spake. . .Gen. 16:13

I am the God of thy father. . .Exod. 3:6

send an Angel before thee. . .Exod. 23:20

he will not pardon your transgressions. . .Exod. 23:21

set it upon a pole. . .Num. 21:8

captain of the host. . .Josh. 5:14

And the angel of the Lord appeared. . .Judg. 6:12

And the Lord looked upon him. . .Judg. 6:14

Son of man be lifted up. . .John 3:14

figure of him that was to come. . .Rom. 5:14

after the similitude of Melchisedec. . .Heb. 7:15

shadow of heavenly things. . .Heb. 8:5

shadow of good things to come. . .Heb. 10:1

eight souls were saved by water. . .1 Pet. 3:20

even baptism doth also now save us. . .1 Pet. 3:21

931. Unbelief

ye did not believe the Lord. . .Deut. 1:32

because of their *u*. . .Matt. 13:58

Because of your *u*. . .Matt. 17:20

ye not then believe him?. . .Matt. 21:25

ye will not believe. . .Luke 22:67

him ye believe not. . .John 5:38

seen me, and believe not. . .John 6:36

some of you that believe not. . .John 6:64

if ye believe not. . .John 8:24

But ye believe not. . .John 10:26

I will not believe. . .John 20:25

u make the faith. . .Rom. 3:3

u they were broken off. . .Rom. 11:20

not still in *u*. . .Rom. 11:23

to them that believe not. . .1 Cor. 14:22

ignorantly in *u*. . .1 Tim. 1:13

we believe not. . .2 Tim. 2:13

evil heart of *u*. . .Heb. 3:12

See *Believe/Believed/Believeth/Believest.*

932. Uncertainty

See *Doubt/Doubted/Doubteth/Doubtful/Doubting/Doubts.*

933. Uncleanness

Scripture describes humanity's inability to live up to God's perfectly pure holiness by calling people's sinful acts and attitudes unclean.

Israel from their *u*. . .Lev. 15:31
According to their *u*. . .Ezek. 39:24
for sin and for *u*. . .Zech. 13:1
and of all *u*. . .Matt. 23:27
gave them up to *u*. . .Rom. 1:24
your members servants to *u*. . .Rom. 6:19
not repented of the *u*. . .2 Cor. 12:21
fornication, *u*, lasciviousness. . .Gal. 5:19
work all *u* with greediness. . .Eph. 4:19
fornication, and all *u*. . .Eph. 5:3
fornication, *u*, inordinate affection. . .Col. 3:5
nor of *u*, nor in guile. . .1 Thess. 2:3
not called us unto *u*. . .1 Thess. 4:7
in the lust of *u*. . .2 Pet. 2:10

934. Understanding

in *u*, and in knowledge. . .Exod. 31:3
give thee wisdom and *u*. . .1 Chron. 22:12
hid their heart from *u*. . .Job 17:4
to depart from evil is *u*. . .Job 28:28

give me *u*. . .Ps. 119:73
Through thy precepts I get *u*. . .Ps. 119:104
giveth *u* unto the simple. . .Ps. 119:130
his *u* is infinite. . .Ps. 147:5
not unto thine own *u*. . .Prov. 3:5
hath *u* wisdom is found. . .Prov. 10:13
is of great *u*. . .Prov. 14:29
with all the *u*. . .Mark 12:33
your *u* being enlightened. . .Eph. 1:18
which passeth all *u*. . .Phil. 4:7
hath given us an *u*. . .1 John 5:20

See *Comprehend/Comprehended.*

935. Unequally Yoked

Before they entered the Promised Land, God warned His people not to intermarry with the pagan peoples who inhabited the land. Ezra and Nehemiah had to deal with the people's disobedience in this matter when they returned to Jerusalem following the Babylonian exile. The New Testament prohibits Christians from marrying those who do not believe but does not command new believers to separate from their unbelieving spouses.

make no covenant with them. . .Exod. 23:32
their daughters unto thy sons. . .Exod. 34:16
Neither shalt thou make marriages. . .Deut. 7:3
give not your daughters. . .Ezra 9:12
have taken strange wives. . .Ezra 10:2
marrying strange wives?. . .Neh. 13:27
unbelieving husband is sanctified. . .1 Cor. 7:14
u y together with unbelievers. . .2 Cor. 6:14

See *Marriage/Marry/Marrying.*

936. Unity

dwell together in *u*!. . .Ps. 133:1
keep the *u* of the Spirit. . .Eph. 4:3
in the *u* of the faith. . .Eph. 4:13
body fitly joined together. . .Eph. 4:16
are one bread, and one body. . .1 Cor. 10:17

See *Tolerance.*

937. Unjust/Unjustly

deceitful and *u* man. . .Ps. 43:1
hope of *u* men perisheth. . .Prov. 11:7
by usury and *u* gain. . .Prov. 28:8
u man is an abomination. . .Prov. 29:27
uprightness will he deal *u'ly*. . .Isa. 26:10
u knoweth no shame. . .Zeph. 3:5
rain on the just and on the *u*. . .Matt. 5:45
u in the least is *u*. . .Luke 16:10
extortioners, *u*, adulterers. . .Luke 18:11
both of the just and *u*. . .Acts 24:15
go to law before the *u*. . .1 Cor. 6:1
the just for the *u*. . .1 Pet. 3:18
reserve the *u* unto the day. . .2 Pet. 2:9
u, let him be *u*. . .Rev. 22:11

938. Unleavened Bread
The feast of the unleavened bread was Passover, during which no yeast was allowed in the house and God's people ate only bread made without leavening.

did bake *u b*. . .Gen. 19:3
u b; and with bitter herbs. . .Exod. 12:8
shall ye eat *u b*. . .Exod. 12:15
observe the feast of *u b*. . .Exod. 12:17
shall ye eat *u b*. . .Exod. 12:20
eat *u b* seven days. . .Exod. 23:15
u b shall it be eaten. . .Lev. 6:16
And a basket of *u b*. . .Num. 6:15
kept the feast of *u b*. . .2 Chron. 30:21
u b shall be eaten. . .Ezek. 45:21
u b of sincerity and truth. . .1 Cor. 5:8

939. Unmerciful
nor shew mercy unto them. . .Deut. 7:2
remembered not to shew mercy. . .Ps. 109:16
neither shall have mercy. . .Isa. 9:17
not have mercy on them. . .Isa. 27:11
shew them no mercy. . .Isa. 47:6
cruel, and have no mercy. . .Jer. 6:23

will not shew mercy. . .Jer. 50:42

no more have mercy. . .Hosea 1:6

without natural affection, implacable, *u*. . .Rom. 1:31

died without mercy. . .Heb. 10:28

have judgment without mercy. . .James 2:13

940. Unrighteous/ Unrighteousness

to be an *u* witness. . .Exod. 23:1

no *u'ness* in judgment. . .Lev. 19:15

no *u'ness* in him. . .Ps. 92:15

decree *u* decrees. . .Isa. 10:1

u man his thoughts. . .Isa. 55:7

buildeth his house by *u'ness*. . .Jer. 22:13

faithful in the *u* mammon. . .Luke 16:11

all ungodliness and *u'ness*. . .Rom. 1:18

members as instruments of *u'ness*. . .Rom. 6:13

Is there *u'ness* with God?. . .Rom. 9:14

u shall not inherit the kingdom. . .1 Cor. 6:9

hath righteousness with *u'ness*?. . .2 Cor. 6:14

merciful to their *u'ness*. . .Heb. 8:12

cleanse us from all *u'ness*. . .1 John 1:9

All *u'ness* is sin. . .1 John 5:17

941. Unsaved

believeth not shall be damned. . .Mark 16:16

be damned who believed not. . .2 Thess. 2:12

See Damnation, Harvest, Hell, Lost/Unsaved.

942. Upright, Morally/ Uprightly/Uprightness

u'ness of thine heart. . .Deut. 9:5

u man thou wilt shew thyself. . .2 Sam. 22:26

hast pleasure in *u'ness*. . .1 Chron. 29:17

a perfect and an *u* man. . .Job 1:8

saveth the *u* in heart. . .Ps. 7:10

judgment to the people in *u'ness*. . .Ps. 9:8

knoweth the days of the *u*. . .Ps. 37:18

perfect man, and behold the *u*. . .Ps. 37:37

from them that walk *u'ly*. . .Ps. 84:11

gladness for the *u* in heart. . .Ps. 97:11

tabernacle of the *u* shall flourish. . .Prov. 14:11

The highway of the *u*. . .Prov. 16:17

poor that walketh in his *u'ness*. . .Prov. 28:6

u shall have good things. . .Prov. 28:10

Whoso walketh *u'ly* shall be saved. . .Prov. 28:18

943. Usury

In ancient times, usury could simply refer to the interest charged on borrowed money, or—as is common today—to excessive interest on a loan.

thou lay upon him *u*. . .Exod. 22:25

Take thou no *u* of him. . .Lev. 25:36

him thy money upon *u*. . .Lev. 25:37

not lend upon *u*. . .Deut. 23:19

thou mayest lend upon *u*. . .Deut. 23:20

Ye exact *u*, every one. . .Neh. 5:7

let us leave off this *u*. . .Neh. 5:10

not out his money to *u*. . .Ps. 15:5

u and unjust gain increaseth. . .Prov. 28:8
as with the taker of *u*. . .Isa. 24:2
hath not given forth upon *u*. . .Ezek. 18:8
Hath given forth upon *u*. . .Ezek. 18:13
hath not received *u* nor increase. . .Ezek. 18:17
thou hast taken *u* and increase. . .Ezek. 22:12

See *Lend/Lendeth, Materialism*.

944. Vanity

The Bible uses the word "vanity" to describe anything that is useless, empty, or futile. In comparison to God, everything humans do, or are, is vain.

they followed *v*, and became vain. . .2 Kings 17:15
Surely God will not hear *v*. . .Job 35:13
They speak *v* every one. . .Ps. 12:2
his soul unto *v*. . .Ps. 24:4
his best state is altogether *v*. . .Ps. 39:5
surely every man is *v*. . .Ps. 39:11
man, that they are *v*. . .Ps. 94:11
Man is like to. . .Ps. 144:4
Wealth gotten by *v*. . .Prov. 13:11

soweth iniquity shall reap *v*. . .Prov. 22:8
all is *v* and vexation of spirit. . .Eccles. 1:14
are all of them *v*. . .Isa. 44:9

fathers have inherited lies, *v*. . .Jer. 16:19
made subject to *v*. . .Rom. 8:20
great swelling words of *v*. . .2 Pet. 2:18

945. Vengeance

v shall be taken on him. . .Gen. 4:15
To me belongeth *v*. . .Deut. 32:35
render *v* to mine enemies. . .Deut. 32:41
render *v* to his adversaries. . .Deut. 32:43
when he seeth the *v*. . .Ps. 58:10
to whom *v* belongeth. . .Ps. 94:1
tookest *v* of their inventions. . .Ps. 99:8
spare in the day of *v*. . .Prov. 6:34
garments of *v* for clothing. . .Isa. 59:17
day of *v* of our God. . .Isa. 61:2
day of *v* is in mine heart. . .Isa. 63:4
these be the days of *v*. . .Luke 21:22
V is mine; I will repay. . .Rom. 12:19
taking *v* on them. . .2 Thess. 1:8
suffering the *v* of eternal fire. . .Jude 1:7

See *Revenge/Revenged/Revenger/Revenges/ Revengeth*.

946. Vexation/ Vexations

cursing, *v*, and rebuke. . .Deut. 28:20
great *v*'s were upon all. . .2 Chron. 15:5
vanity and *v* of spirit. . .Eccles. 1:14
this also is *v* of spirit. . .Eccles. 1:17
was vanity and *v* of spirit. . .Eccles. 2:11
vanity and *v* of spirit. . .Eccles. 2:17
the *v* of his heart. . .Eccles. 2:22
vanity and *v* of spirit. . .Eccles. 2:26
vanity and *v* of spirit. . .Eccles. 4:4

travail and *v* of spirit. . .Eccles. 4:6

vanity and *v* of spirit. . .Eccles. 4:16

also vanity and *v* of spirit. . .Eccles. 6:9

such as was in her *v*. . .Isa. 9:1

v only to understand the report. . .Isa. 28:19

shall howl for *v* of spirit. . .Isa. 65:14

See *Affliction/Afflictions, Frustration.*

947. Victory

v that day was turned. . .2 Sam. 19:2

LORD wrought a great *v*. . .2 Sam. 23:10

LORD wrought a great *v*. . .2 Sam. 23:12

the glory, and the *v*. . .1 Chron. 29:11

hath gotten him the *v*. . .Ps. 98:1

swallow up death in *v*. . .Isa. 25:8

send forth judgment unto *v*. . .Matt. 12:20

Death is swallowed up in *v*. . .1 Cor. 15:54

O grave, where is thy *v*?. . .1 Cor. 15:55

which giveth us the *v*. . .1 Cor. 15:57

v that overcometh the world. . .1 John 5:4

gotten the *v* over the beast. . .Rev. 15:2

See *Triumph/Triumphed/Triumphing.*

948. Vile/Viler/ Vilest

sons made themselves *v*. . .1 Sam. 3:13

they were *v'r* than the earth. . .Job 30:8

Behold, I am *v*. . .Job 40:4

when the *v'st* men are exalted. . .Ps. 12:8

a *v* person is contemned. . .Ps. 15:4

v person shall be no more. . .Isa. 32:5

v person will speak villany. . .Isa. 32:6

forth the precious from the *v*. . .Jer. 15:19

for I am become *v*. . .Lam. 1:11

stand up a *v* person. . .Dan. 11:21

thy grave; for thou art *v*. . .Nah. 1:14

and make thee *v*. . .Nah. 3:6

gave them up unto *v* affections. . .Rom. 1:26

Who shall change our *v* body. . .Phil. 3:21

949. Violence

earth was filled with *v*. . .Gen. 6:11

savest me from *v*. . .2 Sam. 22:3

that loveth *v* his soul hateth. . .Ps. 11:5

soul from deceit and *v*. . .Ps. 72:14

v covereth them as a garment. . .Ps. 73:6

v covereth the mouth. . .Prov. 10:6

transgressors shall eat *v*. . .Prov. 13:2

v to the blood. . .Prov. 28:17

he had done no *v*. . .Isa. 53:9

do no *v* to the stranger. . .Jer. 22:3

who store up *v* and robbery. . .Amos 3:10

Do *v* to no man. . .Luke 3:14

with *v* shall that great city. . .Rev. 18:21

950. Virgin Birth

Behold, a virgin shall conceive. . .Isa. 7:14

before they came together. . .Matt. 1:18

that which is conceived in her. . .Matt. 1:20
a virgin shall be with child. . .Matt. 1:23
a virgin espoused to a man. . .Luke 1:27
shalt conceive in thy womb. . .Luke 1:31
seeing I know not a man?. . .Luke 1:34

See *Nativity, the.*

951. Virgin/Virginity/Virgins

In Old Testament law, a woman who was not a virgin at marriage could be put aside by her husband. As persecution afflicted the first-century church, Paul advised believers not to marry unnecessarily.

I found her not a maid. . .Deut. 22:14
tokens of my daughter's *v'ity*. . .Deut. 22:17
concerning *v's* I have no commandment. . .1 Cor. 7:25
if a *v* marry, she hath not sinned. . .1 Cor. 7:28
between a wife and a *v*. . .1 Cor. 7:34
uncomely toward his *v*. . .1 Cor. 7:36
he will keep his *v*. . .1 Cor. 7:37
for they are *v's*. . .Rev. 14:4

See *Chaste/Chastity, Living Together, Modest/Modesty, Virgin Birth.*

952. Virtue/Virtuous

thou art a *v'ous* woman. . .Ruth 3:11
A *v'ous* woman is a crown. . .Prov. 12:4
Who can find a *v'ous* woman?. . .Prov. 31:10
if there be any *v*. . .Phil. 4:8
called us to glory and *v*. . .2 Pet. 1:3
add to your faith *v*. . .2 Pet. 1:5

953. Vision/Visions

came unto Abram in a *v*. . .Gen. 15:1
known unto him in a *v*. . .Num. 12:6
according to all this *v*. . .2 Sam. 7:17
no *v*, the people perish. . .Prov. 29:18
The *v* of Isaiah the son. . .Isa. 1:1

a false *v* and divination. . .Jer. 14:14
a *v* of their own heart. . .Jer. 23:16
Daniel had understanding in all *v's*. . .Dan. 1:17
your young men shall see *v's*. . .Joel 2:28
Tell the *v* to no man. . .Matt. 17:9
seen a *v* in the temple. . .Luke 1:22
seen a *v* of angels. . .Luke 24:23
Lord in a *v*, Ananias. . .Acts 9:10
He saw in a *v*. . .Acts 10:3
this *v* which he had seen. . .Acts 10:17
in a trance I saw a *v*. . .Acts 11:5
a *v* appeared to Paul. . .Acts 16:9
the night by a *v*. . .Acts 18:9

954. Vow/Vowed/Vowest/Vows

v a *v* of a Nazarite. . .Num. 6:2
Nazarite who hath *v'ed*. . .Num. 6:21
v a *v* unto the Lord. . .Num. 30:2

establisheth all her *v's*. . .Num. 30:14

When thou shalt *v* a *v*. . .Deut. 23:21

shalt forbear to *v*. . .Deut. 23:22

Jephthah *v'ed* a *v*. . .Judg. 11:30

And she *v'ed* a *v*. . .1 Sam. 1:11

pay thy *v's*. . .Ps. 50:14

God, hast heard my *v's*. . .Ps. 61:5

v'est a *v* unto God. . .Eccles. 5:4

for he had a *v*. . .Acts 18:18

See *Nazarite/Nazarites, Oath/Oaths.*

955. Wait/Waited/ Waiteth/Waiting

none that *w* on thee. . .Ps. 25:3

do I *w* all the day. . .Ps. 25:5

for I *w* on thee. . .Ps. 25:21

W on the Lord. . .Ps. 27:14

Our soul *w'eth* for the Lord. . .Ps. 33:20

w patiently for him. . .Ps. 37:7

those that *w* upon the Lord. . .Ps. 37:9

W on the Lord, and keep. . .Ps. 37:34

what *w* I for?. . .Ps. 39:7

I *w'ed* patiently for the Lord. . .Ps. 40:1

my soul doth *w*. . .Ps. 130:5

them that *w* for him. . .Lam. 3:25

quietly *w* for the salvation. . .Lam. 3:26

w'ing for the adoption. . .Rom. 8:23

with patience *w* for it. . .Rom. 8:25

through the Spirit *w*. . .Gal. 5:5

patient *w'ing* for Christ. . .2 Thess. 3:5

See *Delay/Delayed, Patience/Patient/Patiently.*

956. Wages

the *w* of him that is hired. . .Lev. 19:13

thou shalt give him his hire. . .Deut. 24:15

soweth righteousness shall be a
  sure reward. . . Prov. 11:18

his neighbour's service without *w*. . .Jer. 22:13

earneth *w* to put it. . .Hag. 1:6

oppress the hireling in his *w*. . .Mal. 3:5

be content with your *w*. . .Luke 3:14

labourer is worthy of his hire. . .Luke 10:7

he that reapeth receiveth *w*. . .John 4:36

957. Wages of Sin

the *w* of sin is death. . .Rom. 6:23

loved the *w* of unrighteousness. . .2 Pet. 2:15

See *Sin.*

958. Walk, Christian/ Walked/Walkest/ Walking

w in the steps of that faith. . .Rom. 4:12

w in newness of life. . .Rom. 6:4

w not after the flesh. . .Rom. 8:1

Let us *w* honestly. . .Rom. 13:13

w'est thou not charitably. . .Rom. 14:15

so let him *w*. . .1 Cor. 7:17

not *w'ing* in craftiness. . .2 Cor. 4:2

w by faith. . .2 Cor. 5:7

they *w'ed* not uprightly. . .Gal. 2:14

W in the Spirit. . .Gal. 5:16

also *w* in the Spirit. . .Gal. 5:25

we should *w* in them. . .Eph. 2:10

w worthy of the vocation. . .Eph. 4:1

And *w* in love. . .Eph. 5:2

w as children of light. . .Eph. 5:8

w worthy of the Lord. . .Col. 1:10

so *w* ye in him. . .Col. 2:6

if we *w* in the light. . .1 John 1:7

w after his commandments. . .2 John 1:6

959. Wander/ Wandered/ Wandereth/Wanderers/ Wandering/Wanderings

w'ed in the wilderness of Beersheba. . .Gen. 21:14

w in the wilderness forty years. . .Num. 14:33

w in the wilderness. . .Num. 32:13

Thou tellest my *w'ings*. . .Ps. 56:8

causeth them to *w*. . .Ps. 107:40

let me not *w*. . .Ps. 119:10

w'eth out of the way. . .Prov. 21:16

w'ing of the desire. . .Eccles. 6:9

My sheep *w'ed*. . .Ezek. 34:6

w'ers among the nations. . .Hosea 9:17

w'ing about from house. . .1 Tim. 5:13

w'ed about in sheepskins. . .Heb. 11:37

they *w'ed* in deserts. . .Heb. 11:38

960. Wants/Desires

thy *w* lie upon me. . .Judg. 19:20

the desires of thine heart. . .Ps. 37:4

the desires of the wicked. . .Ps. 140:8

desires of the flesh. . .Eph. 2:3

ministered to my *w*. . .Phil. 2:25

961. War/Battles

go to *w* in your land. . .Num. 10:9

making *w* against it. . .Deut. 20:19

shall not go out to *w*. . .Deut. 24:5

He teacheth my hands to *w*. . .2 Sam. 22:35

girded me with strength to battle. . .2 Sam. 22:40

people go out to battle. . .1 Kings 8:44

the *w* was of God. . .1 Chron. 5:22

in *w* from the power. . .Job 5:20

the LORD mighty in battle. . .Ps. 24:8

though *w* should rise against me. . .Ps. 27:3

but *w* was in his heart. . .Ps. 55:21

they are for *w*. . .Ps. 120:7

gathered together for *w*. . .Ps. 140:2

head in the day of battle. . .Ps. 140:7

time of *w*, and a time. . .Eccles. 3:8

nor the battle to the strong. . .Eccles. 9:11

better than weapons of *w*. . .Eccles. 9:18

shall they learn *w* any more. . .Isa. 2:4

make *w* with the Lamb. . .Rev. 17:14

962. Warfare, Spiritual

we do not war after the flesh. . .2 Cor. 10:3

mightest war a good *w*. . .1 Tim. 1:18

lusts that war in your members?. . .James 4:1

ye fight and war, yet ye. . .James 4:2

which war against the soul. . .1 Pet. 2:11

963. Wastefulness

him that is a great waster. . .Prov. 18:9

wasted his substance with riotous
     living. . .Luke 15:13

he had wasted his goods. . .Luke 16:1

964. Water, Living/Waters

the fountain of *l w's*. . .Jer. 2:13

fountain of *l w's*. . .Jer. 17:13

that *l w's* shall go out. . .Zech. 14:8

would have given thee *l w*. . .John 4:10

then hast thou that *l w*?. . .John 4:11

shall flow rivers of *l w*. . .John 7:38

unto *l* fountains of *w's*. . .Rev. 7:17

965. Way, the

The *w* of holiness. . .Isa. 35:8

the *w* of God in truth. . .Mark 12:14

into the *w* of peace. . .Luke 1:79

the *w* of the Lord. . .Luke 3:4

found any of this *w*. . .Acts 9:2

I am the *w*. . .John 14:6

the *w* of salvation. . .Acts 16:17

w of God more perfectly. . .Acts 18:26

no small stir about that *w*. . .Acts 19:23

I persecuted this *w*. . .Acts 22:4

more perfect knowledge of that *w*. . .Acts 24:22

And the *w* of peace. . .Rom. 3:17

the *w* of truth shall. . .2 Pet. 2:2

the *w* of righteousness. . .2 Pet. 2:21

966. Weak/Weaker/Weakness/Weakeneth

hast strengthened the *w* hands. . .Job 4:3

w'eneth the strength of the mighty. . .Job 12:21

O LORD; for I am *w*. . .Ps. 6:2

knees are *w* through fasting. . .Ps. 109:24

let the *w* say, I am strong. . .Joel 3:10

W and riches shall be. . .Ps. 112:3
w is his strong city. . .Prov. 10:15
W gotten by vanity. . .Prov. 13:11
w of the sinner. . .Prov. 13:22
w is his strong city. . .Prov. 18:11
W maketh many friends. . .Prov. 19:4
God hath given riches and w. . .Eccles. 5:19
given riches, w, and honour. . .Eccles. 6:2
love of money is the root. . .1 Tim. 6:10

See *Financial Gain, Money, Rich/Riches.*

968. Weapon/Weapons

w's, thy quiver and thy bow. . .Gen. 27:3
fall before you by the sword. . .Lev. 26:7
took a javelin in his hand. . .Num. 25:7
his sword drawn in his hand. . .Josh. 5:13
thy sword, nor with thy bow. . .Josh. 24:12
The sword of the Lord. . .Judg. 7:18
spear was like a weaver's beam. . .1 Sam. 17:7
And Saul cast the javelin. . .1 Sam. 18:11
sword of Goliath the Philistine. . .1 Sam. 21:9
shooting arrows out of a bow. . .1 Chron. 12:2
spears, and bucklers, and shields. . .2 Chron. 23:9
he the arrows of the bow. . .Ps. 76:3
better than w's of war. . .Eccles. 9:18
No w that is formed. . .Isa. 54:17
send peace, but a sword. . .Matt. 10:34
must be killed with the sword. . .Rev. 13:10

but the flesh is w. . .Matt. 26:41
ye ought to support the w. . .Acts 20:35
it was w through the flesh. . .Rom. 8:3
Him that is w. . .Rom. 14:1
offended, or is made w. . .Rom. 14:21
bear the infirmities of the w. . .Rom. 15:1
w'ness of God is stronger. . .1 Cor. 1:25
w things of the world. . .1 Cor. 1:27
to them that are w. . .1 Cor. 8:9
many are w and sickly. . .1 Cor. 11:30
when I am w. . .2 Cor. 12:10
crucified through w'ness. . .2 Cor. 13:4
support the w. . .1 Thess. 5:14
as unto the w'er vessel. . .1 Pet. 3:7

967. Wealth

hath gotten me this w. . .Deut. 8:17
giveth thee power to get w. . .Deut. 8:18
hast not asked riches, w. . .2 Chron. 1:11
spend their days in w. . .Job 21:13
They that trust in their w. . .Ps. 49:6
leave their w to others. . .Ps. 49:10

969. Weep/Weepest/ Weeping/Wept

and w before me. . .2 Chron. 34:27
noise of the w'ing of the people. . .Ezra 3:13
confessed, w'ing and casting himself. . .Ezra 10:1

For all the people w'pt. . .Neh. 8:9

fasting, and w'ing, and wailing. . .Esther 4:3

w'ing may endure for a night. . .Ps. 30:5

A time to w. . .Eccles. 3:4

For these things I w. . .Lam. 1:16

with fasting, and with w'ing. . .Joel 2:12

lamentation, and w'ing, and great
    mourning. . .Matt. 2:18

w'ing and gnashing of teeth. . .Matt. 8:12

Blessed are ye that w now. . .Luke 6:21

w'ing, and began to wash his feet. . .Luke 7:38

w not for me, but w. . .Luke 23:28

Woman, why w'est thou?. . .John 20:13

w with them that w. . .Rom. 12:15

Be afflicted, and mourn, and w. . .James 4:9

970. Welfare

*In Bible times, there was no public welfare
system as there is today, but believers were
encouraged by scripture to be generous to the
less fortunate, including widows, the fatherless, and strangers. Not only were they to give
to the poor; God's people were also to leave
some crops in the field for them.*

leave them unto the poor. . .Lev. 23:22

shall eat and be satisfied. . .Deut. 14:29

not go again to fetch it. . .Deut. 24:19

not go over the boughs again. . .Deut. 24:20

thou shalt not glean it afterward. . .Deut. 24:21

widows, let them relieve them. . .1 Tim. 5:16

See *Alms; Give/Given/Giveth; Poor, the.*

971. Whore/ Whoredom/ Whoremonger/ Whoremongers

*God calls His people to sexual and spiritual
purity. When believers are unfaithful to Him,
He calls that whoredom, too.*

cause her to be a w. . .Lev. 19:29

commit w'dom with Molech. . .Lev. 20:5

wife that is a w. . .Lev. 21:7

herself by playing the w. . .Lev. 21:9

There shall be no w. . .Deut. 23:17

For a w is a deep ditch. . .Prov. 23:27

W'dom and wine and new wine. . .Hosea 4:11

daughters shall commit w'dom. . .Hosea 4:13

no w'monger, nor unclean person. . . Eph. 5:5

w'mongers and adulterers. . .Heb. 13:4

See *Bastard, Harlot/Harlot's/Harlots, Prostitution.*

972. Whosoever Will

w w not hearken. . .Deut. 18:19

w w not do the law. . .Ezra 7:26

w w save his life. . .Matt. 16:25

w w be great among you. . .Matt. 20:26

And w w be chief. . .Matt. 20:27

W w come after me. . .Mark 8:34

w w save his life. . .Mark 8:35

w w be great among you. . .Mark 10:43
w w not receive you. . .Luke 9:5
w w save his life. . .Luke 9:24
w w, let him take. . .Rev. 22:17

973. Wickedness

w of man was great. . .Gen. 6:5
it is *w.* . .Lev. 18:17
land become full of *w.* . .Lev. 19:29
wife and her mother, it is *w.* . .Lev. 20:14
hath wrought *w.* . .Deut. 17:2
w of thy doings. . .Deut. 28:20
hath pleasure in *w.* . .Ps. 5:4
lovest righteousness, and hatest *w.* . .Ps. 45:7
Treasures of *w* profit nothing. . .Prov. 10:2
not be established by *w.* . .Prov. 12:3
turn not from his *w.* . .Ezek. 3:19
wicked turn from his *w.* . .Ezek. 33:19
Ye have plowed *w.* . .Hosea 10:13
unrighteousness, fornication, *w.* . .Rom. 1:29
spiritual *w* in high places. . .Eph. 6:12
whole world lieth in *w.* . .1 John 5:9

See *Evil.*

974. Widow/Widow's/Widows

Ye shall not afflict any *w.* . .Exod. 22:22
But every vow of a *w.* . .Num. 30:9
judgment of the fatherless and *w.* . .Deut. 10:18
w, which are within thy gates. . .Deut. 14:29
take a *w's* raiment to pledge. . .Deut. 24:17
fatherless, and for the *w.* . .Deut. 24:19
fatherless, and for the *w.* . .Deut. 24:21
the stranger, fatherless, and *w.* . .Deut. 27:19

a judge of the *w's.* . .Ps. 68:5
relieveth the fatherless and *w.* . .Ps. 146:9
establish the border of the *w.* . .Prov. 15:25
plead for the *w.* . .Isa. 1:17
let thy *w's* trust in me. . .Jer. 49:11
And oppress not the *w.* . .Zech. 7:10
came a certain poor *w.* . .Mark 12:42
to the unmarried and *w's.* . .1 Cor. 7:8
Honour *w's* that are *w's.* . .1 Tim. 5:3
that believeth have *w's.* . .1 Tim. 5:16

975. Wife/Wives

shall put away his *w.* . .Matt. 5:32
shall cleave to his *w.* . .Matt. 19:5
every man have his own *w.* . .1 Cor. 7:2
husband render unto the *w.* . .1 Cor. 7:3
w hath not power. . .1 Cor. 7:4
Let not the *w* depart. . .1 Cor. 7:10
husband put away his *w.* . .1 Cor. 7:11
w that believeth not. . .1 Cor. 7:12
husband is sanctified by the *w.* . .1 Cor. 7:14
how he may please his *w.* . .1 Cor. 7:33
the head of the *w.* . .Eph. 5:23
love their *w'ves.* . .Eph. 5:28
be joined unto his *w.* . .Eph. 5:31

love his *w* even as himself. . .Eph. 5:33
giving honour unto the *w*. . .1 Pet. 3:7

See *Family, Marriage/Marry/Marrying, Spouse/Spouses, Woman.*

976. Will of God
See *God's Will.*

977. Wine
Wine was used as a temple offering and medication. There are many warnings concerning its use in scripture.

w, and was drunken. . .Gen. 9:21
make our father drink *w*. . .Gen. 19:32
w for a drink offering. . .Exod. 29:40
not drink *w* nor strong drink. . .Lev. 10:9
separate himself from *w*. . .Num. 6:3
and thy *w*, and thine oil. . .Deut. 11:14
w that maketh glad the heart. . .Ps. 104:15
W is a mocker. . .Prov. 20:1
he that loveth *w* and oil. . .Prov. 21:17
Look not thou upon the *w*. . .Prov. 23:31
buy *w* and milk without money. . .Isa. 55:1
We will drink no *w*. . .Jer. 35:6
new *w* into old bottles. . .Matt. 9:17
w mingled with myrrh. . .Mark 15:23
wounds, pouring in oil and *w*. . .Luke 10:34
water that was made *w*. . .John 2:9
be not drunk with *w*. . .Eph. 5:18
Not given to *w*. . .1 Tim. 3:3
w for thy stomach's sake. . .1 Tim. 5:23

See *Alcohol, Drink/Drinking.*

978. Wisdom
your *w* and your understanding. . .Deut. 4:6
price of *w* is above rubies. . .Job 28:18
righteous speaketh *w*. . .Ps. 37:30
is the beginning of *w*. . .Ps. 111:10
by *w* made the heavens. . .Ps. 136:5
For the Lord giveth *w*. . .Prov. 2:6
sound *w* for the righteous. . .Prov. 2:7
man that findeth *w*. . .Prov. 3:13
Get *w*, get understanding. . .Prov. 4:5
For *w* is better than rubies. . .Prov. 8:11
cease from thine own *w*. . .Prov. 23:4

W strengtheneth the wise. . .Eccles. 7:19
W is better than weapons of war. . .Eccles. 9:18
wise man glory in his *w*. . .Jer. 9:23
increased in *w* and stature. . .Luke 2:52
w and knowledge of God!. . .Rom. 11:33
foolish the *w* of this world?. . .1 Cor. 1:20
not stand in the *w* of men. . .1 Cor. 2:5
w of this world is foolishness. . .1 Cor. 3:19
the word of *w*. . .1 Cor. 12:8
If any of you lack *w*. . .James 1:5
w that is from above. . .James 3:17

979. Wise/Wiser
w in their own craftiness. . .Job 5:13
making *w* the simple. . .Ps. 19:7

A *w* man will hear. . .Prov. 1:5

Be not *w* in thine own eyes. . .Prov. 3:7

Hear instruction, and be *w*. . .Prov. 8:33

Give instruction to a *w* man. . .Prov. 9:9

refraineth his lips is *w*. . .Prov. 10:19

with *w* men shall be *w*. . .Prov. 13:20

Every *w* woman buildeth her house. . .Prov. 14:1

A *w* man feareth. . .Prov. 14:16

w in their own eyes. . .Isa. 5:21

w as serpents. . .Matt. 10:16

Professing themselves to be *w*. . .Rom. 1:22

not *w* in your own conceits. . .Rom. 12:16

w unto that which is good. . .Rom. 16:19

foolishness of God is *w'r*. . .1 Cor. 1:25

to confound the *w*. . .1 Cor. 1:27

980. Witch/ Witchcraft/Witchcrafts

Thou shalt not suffer a *w* to live. . .Exod. 22:18

that hath a familiar spirit. . .Lev. 20:27

or an enchanter, or a *w*. . .Deut. 18:10

is as the sin of *w'craft*. . .1 Sam. 15:23

enchantments, and used *w'craft*. . .2 Chron. 33:6

I will cut off *w'crafts*. . .Mic. 5:12

the mistress of *w'crafts*. . .Nah. 3:4

Idolatry, *w'craft*, hatred. . .Gal. 5:20

See *Magic/Magicians; Occult, the; Sorcery/ Sorcerer/Sorcerers.*

981. Witness/ Witnessing

for a *w* unto all nations. . .Matt. 24:14

Go ye therefore, and teach. . .Matt. 28:19

every where preaching the word. . .Acts 8:4

testified to the Jews. . .Acts 18:5

his *w* unto all men. . .Acts 22:15

w'ing both to small and great. . .Acts 26:22

hear without a preacher?. . .Rom. 10:14

See *Harvest, Preach/Preached/Preaching.*

982. Woes of Jesus

Woe unto thee, Chorazin!. . .Matt. 11:21

Woe unto the world. . .Matt. 18:7

woe unto you, scribes and Pharisees. . .Matt. 23:13

Woe unto you, scribes and Pharisees. . .Matt. 23:14

Woe unto you, scribes and Pharisees. . .Matt. 23:15

Woe unto you, ye blind guides. . .Matt. 23:16

Woe unto you, scribes and Pharisees. . .Matt. 23:23

Woe unto you, scribes and Pharisees. . .Matt. 23:25

Woe unto you, scribes and Pharisees. . .Matt. 23:29

woe unto them that are with child. . .Matt. 24:19

woe unto that man by whom. . .Matt. 26:24

But woe unto you that are rich!. . .Luke 6:24

Woe unto you, when all men. . .Luke 6:26

Woe unto you also, ye lawyers!. . .Luke 11:46

983. Woman

made he a *w*. . .Gen. 2:22

she shall be called *W*. . .Gen. 2:23

enmity between thee and the *w*. . .Gen. 3:15

barren *w* to keep house. . .Ps. 113:9

foolish *w* is clamorous. . .Prov. 9:13

gracious *w* retaineth honour. . .Prov. 11:16

fair *w* which is without discretion. . .Prov. 11:22

virtuous *w* is a crown. . .Prov. 12:4

wise *w* buildeth her house. . .Prov. 14:1

contentious and an angry *w*. . .Prov. 21:19

contentious *w* are alike. . .Prov. 27:15

way of an adulterous *w*. . .Prov. 30:20

find a virtuous *w*?. . .Prov. 31:10

w that feareth the Lord. . .Prov. 31:30

looketh on a *w* to lust. . .Matt. 5:28

w shall put away her husband. . .Mark 10:12

head of the *w*. . .1 Cor. 11:3

man created for the *w*. . .1 Cor. 11:9

See *Daughter/Daughters, Wife/Wives.*

984. Wonders

smite Egypt with all my *w*. . .Exod. 3:20

my *w* may be multiplied. . .Exod. 11:9

fearful in praises, doing *w*?. . .Exod. 15:11

temptations, by signs, and by *w*. . .Deut. 4:34

Lord will do *w* among you. . .Josh 3:5

his *w*, and the judgments. . .1 Chron. 16:12

God that doest *w*. . .Ps. 77:14

his *w* among all people. . .Ps. 96:3

his *w* in the deep. . .Ps. 107:24

shew great signs and *w*. . .Matt. 24:24

miracles and *w* and signs. . .Acts 2:22

w and signs were done. . .Acts 2:43

great *w* and miracles. . .Acts 6:8

signs, and *w*, and mighty deeds. . .2 Cor. 12:12

signs and *w*, and with divers. . .Heb. 2:4

See *Signs.*

985. Word of God

word of the Lord is tried. . .Ps. 18:30

Every *w o G* is pure. . .Prov. 30:5

by every *w o G*. . .Luke 4:4

hear the *w o G*. . .Luke 11:28

In the beginning was the Word. . .John 1:1

spake the *w o G*. . .Acts 4:31

the *w o G* increased. . .Acts 6:7

hearing by the *w o G*. . .Rom. 10:17

which is the *w o G*. . .Eph. 6:17

w o G be not blasphemed. . .Titus 2:5

w o G is quick. . .Heb. 4:12

framed by the *w o G*. . .Heb. 11:3

w o G, which liveth. . .1 Pet. 1:23

w o G abideth in you. . .1 John 2:14

called The *W o G*. . .Rev. 19:13

See *Devotions, Prayer/Prayers, Scripture/Scriptures, Searching the Scriptures.*

986. Work

do all thy w. . .Exod. 20:9
shalt not do any w. . .Exod. 20:10
all the w of thine hand. . .Deut. 14:29
bless all the w of thine. . .Deut. 28:12
employed in that w. . .1 Chron. 9:33
people had a mind to w. . .Neh. 4:6
establish thou the w. . .Ps. 90:17
Barnabas and Saul for the w. . .Acts 13:2
the w of the ministry. . .Eph. 4:12
w with your own hands. . .1 Thess. 4:11
any would not w. . .2 Thess. 3:10
quietness they w, and eat. . .2 Thess. 3:12
do the w of an evangelist. . .2 Tim. 4:5

See *Employment, Hiring, Jobs, Labour.*

987. Work, of God/ Works

God ended his w. . .Gen. 2:2
And Israel saw that great w. . .Exod. 14:31
his w is perfect. . .Deut. 32:4
the Lord will w for us. . .1 Sam. 14:6
all his wondrous w's. . .1 Chron. 16:9
Remember his marvellous w's. . .1 Chron. 16:12

his marvellous w's among all
    nations. . .1 Chron. 16:24
w was wrought of our God. . .Neh. 6:16
the w of thy fingers. . .Ps. 8:3
are thy wonderful w's. . .Ps. 40:5
w's of his hands are verity. . .Ps. 111:7
w that God maketh. . .Eccles. 3:11
thy w, He hath no hands?. . .Isa. 45:9
such mighty w's are wrought. . .Mark 6:2
and to finish his w. . .John 4:34
I must w the w's. . .John 9:4
I have finished the w. . .John 17:4
which hath begun a good w. . .Phil. 1:6
are the w's of thine hands. . .Heb. 1:10

988. Workmanship, God's

are the work of his hands. . .Job 34:19
For we are his w. . .Eph. 2:10
God which worketh in you. . .Phil. 2:13

according to the working whereby. . .Phil. 3:21

989. Works, Good/ Work

they may see your *g w's*. . .Matt. 5:16

every man that worketh good. . .Rom. 2:10

not a terror to *g w's*. . .Rom. 13:3

abound to every *g w*. . .2 Cor. 9:8

fruitful in every *g w*. . .Col. 1:10

your work of faith. . .1 Thess. 1:3

every *g* word and *w*. . .2 Thess. 2:17

he desireth a *g w*. . .1 Tim. 3:1

g w's of some are manifest. . .1 Tim. 5:25

be rich in *g w's*. . .1 Tim. 6:18

prepared unto every *g w*. . .2 Tim. 2:21

furnished unto all *g w's*. . .2 Tim. 3:17

pattern of *g w's*. . .Titus 2:7

zealous of *g w's*. . .Titus 2:14

careful to maintain *g w's*. . .Titus 3:8

unto love and to *g w's*. . .Heb. 10:24

perfect in every *g w*. . .Heb. 13:21

faith without works. . .James 2:26

by your *g w's*. . .1 Pet. 2:12

990. Works of the Flesh

works thereof are evil. . .John 7:7

they that are in the flesh. . .Rom. 8:8

ye live after the flesh. . .Rom. 8:13

do not war after the flesh. . .2 Cor. 10:3

fulfil the lust of the flesh. . .Gal. 5:16

flesh lusteth against the Spirit. . .Gal. 5:17

w o t f are manifest. . .Gal. 5:19

crucified the flesh. . .Gal. 5:24

fulfilling the desires of the flesh. . .Eph. 2:3

991. World, the

Scripture uses "world" to describe both the physical earth and the spiritual realm that denies God and fails to follow Him. The New Testament warns Christians to avoid the attitudes and actions of this world, which denies its Lord.

shall judge the *w* in righteousness. . .Ps. 9:8

the *w*, and they that dwell. . .Ps. 24:1

he shall judge the *w*. . .Ps. 96:13

the light of the *w*. . .Matt. 5:14

he shall gain the whole *w*. . .Matt. 16:26

preached in all the *w*. . .Matt. 24:14

from the foundation of the *w*. . .Matt. 25:34

unto the end of the *w*. . .Matt. 28:20

in the *w* to come life. . .Luke 18:30

He was in the *w*. . .John 1:10

taketh away the sin of the *w*. . .John 1:29

God so loved the *w*. . .John 3:16

w to condemn the *w*. . .John 3:17

not as the *w* giveth. . .John 14:27

prince of this *w* cometh. . .John 14:30

If ye were of the *w*. . .John 15:19

I have overcome the *w*. . .John 16:33

sin entered into the *w*. . .Rom. 5:12

be not conformed to this *w*. . .Rom. 12:2

foolish things of the *w*. . .1 Cor. 1:27

not the spirit of the *w*. . .1 Cor. 2:12

wisdom of this *w* is foolishness. . .1 Cor. 3:19
saints shall judge the *w*?. . .1 Cor. 6:2
reconciling the *w* unto himself. . .2 Cor. 5:19
this present evil *w*. . .Gal. 1:4
sins of the whole *w*. . .1 John 2:2
Love not the *w*. . .1 John 2:15
all that is in the *w*. . .1 John 2:16
overcometh the *w*. . .1 John 5:4

---

992. Worry

Take no thought for your life. . .Matt. 6:25
taking thought can add one cubit. . .Matt. 6:27
take ye thought for raiment?. . .Matt. 6:28
Therefore take no thought. . .Matt. 6:31
no thought for the morrow. . .Matt. 6:34
deliver you up, take no thought. . .Matt. 10:19
Let not your heart be troubled. . .John 14:27
neither be troubled. . .1 Pet. 3:14

See *Anxiety*.

---

993. Worship/ Worshipped

thou shalt *w* no other god. . .Exod. 34:14
w the Lord in the beauty. . .1 Chron. 16:29
God of my salvation be exalted. . .Ps. 18:46
Be thou exalted, Lord. . .Ps. 21:13

nations shall *w* before thee. . .Ps. 22:27
let us exalt his name together. . .Ps. 34:3
All the earth shall *w* thee. . .Ps. 66:4
let us *w* and bow down. . .Ps. 95:6
men shall *w* him. . .Zeph. 2:11
are come to *w* him. . .Matt. 2:2
w the Lord thy God. . .Matt. 4:10
w the Father in spirit and in truth. . .John 4:23
Neither is *w'ped* with men's hands. . .Acts 17:25
w God in the spirit. . .Phil. 3:3
angels of God *w* him. . .Heb. 1:6
w him that liveth for ever. . .Rev. 4:10

See *Noise, Joyful*.

---

994. Worthy

who is *w* to be praised. . .2 Sam. 22:4
I am not *w* that thou. . .Matt. 8:8
workman is *w* of his meat. . .Matt. 10:10
enquire who in it is *w*. . .Matt. 10:11
is not *w* of me. . .Matt. 10:37
is not *w* of me. . .Matt. 10:38
fruits *w* of repentance. . .Luke 3:8
are *w* of death. . .Rom. 1:32
not *w* to be compared. . .Rom. 8:18
walk *w* of the vocation. . .Eph. 4:1
walk *w* of the Lord. . .Col. 1:10
ye would walk *w* of God. . .1 Thess. 2:12
w of the kingdom of God. . .2 Thess. 1:5
count you *w* of this calling. . .2 Thess. 1:11
w of all acceptation. . .1 Tim. 1:15

---

995. Wrath of God

no wrath any more upon. . .Num. 18:5
God of heaven unto wrath. . .Ezra 5:12

was published unto all people. . .Esther 3:14

w'ing for a commandment. . .Esther 8:13

the pen of a ready *w'r*. . .Ps. 45:1

the *w'ing* of the house of Israel. . .Ezek. 13:9

Whosoever shall read this *w'ing*. . .Dan. 5:7

w'ing was Jesus of Nazareth. . .John 19:19

forth to the day of wrath. . .Job 21:30

when his wrath is kindled. . .Ps. 2:12

taken away all thy wrath. . .Ps. 85:3

sware in my wrath. . .Ps. 95:11

wrath of the Lord kindled. . .Ps. 106:40

reserveth wrath for his enemies. . .Nah. 1:2

w o G abideth on him. . .John 3:36

w o G is revealed. . .Rom. 1:18

treasurest up unto thyself wrath. . .Rom. 2:5

the law worketh wrath. . .Rom. 4:15

willing to shew his wrath. . .Rom. 9:22

w o G upon the children. . .Eph. 5:6

from the wrath to come. . .1 Thess. 1:10

not appointed us to wrath. . .1 Thess. 5:9

day of his wrath is come. . .Rev. 6:17

See *Anger of the Lord.*

996. Write/Writer/Writing

W this for a memorial. . .Exod. 17:14

w'ing was the *w'ing* of God. . .Exod. 32:16

W thou these words. . .Exod. 34:27

w them upon the posts. . .Deut. 6:9

w him a copy of this law. . .Deut. 17:18

w her a bill of divorcement. . .Deut. 24:1

w ye this song for you. . .Deut. 31:19

handle the pen of the *w'r*. . .Judg. 5:14

sent letters into all the king's. . .Esther 1:22

997. Wrongdoing

have I done no wrong. . .Acts 25:10

Why do ye not rather take wrong?. . .1 Cor. 6:7

Nay, ye do wrong. . .1 Cor. 6:8

he that doeth wrong shall receive. . .Col. 3:25

See *Sin.*

998. Yielding to God

obey the voice of the Lord. . .Deut. 27:10

thou mayest obey his voice. . .Deut. 30:20

thine enemies submit themselves

unto thee. . .Ps. 66:3

but yield yourselves unto God. . .Rom. 6:13

whom ye yield yourselves servants. . .Rom. 6:16

present your bodies a living sacrifice. . .Rom. 12:1

be not conformed to this world. . .Rom. 12:2

Submit yourselves therefore to God. . .James 4:7

999. Youth

evil from his *y*. . .Gen. 8:21

fear the Lord from my *y*. . .1 Kings 18:12

the sins of my *y*. . .Ps. 25:7

my trust from my *y*. . .Ps. 71:5

taught me from my *y*. . .Ps. 71:17

y is renewed like the eagle's. . .Ps. 103:5

young man cleanse his way?. . .Ps. 119:9

The glory of young men. . .Prov. 20:29

young man, in thy *y*. . .Eccles. 11:9

childhood and *y* are vanity. . .Eccles. 11:10

in the days of thy *y*. . .Eccles. 12:1

young men shall see visions. . .Joel 2:28

Let no man despise thy *y*. . .1 Tim. 4:12

younger men as brethren. . .1 Tim. 5:1

younger as sisters. . .1 Tim. 5:2

Flee also youthful lusts. . .2 Tim. 2:22

See *Adolescence, Boys, Child/Children, Daughter/ Daughters, Girls, Seasons of Life, Son/Sons.*

1000. Zeal/Zealous/ Zealously

he was *z'ous* for my sake. . .Num. 25:11

he was *z'ous* for his God. . .Num. 25:13

z of the Lord of hosts. . .2 Kings 19:31

My *z* hath consumed me. . .Ps. 119:139

Lord have spoken it in my *z*. . .Ezek. 5:13

all *z'ous* of the law. . .Acts 21:20

was *z'ous* toward God. . .Acts 22:3

they have a *z* of God. . .Rom. 10:2

ye are *z'ous* of spiritual gifts. . .1 Cor. 14:12

what vehement desire, yea, what *z*. . .2 Cor. 7:11

your *z* hath provoked very many. . .2 Cor. 9:2

z'ous of the traditions. . .Gal. 1:14

z'ously affected always in a good thing. . .Gal. 4:18

Concerning *z*, persecuting the church. . .Phil. 3:6

peculiar people, *z'ous* of good works. . .Titus 2:14

be *z'ous* therefore, and repent. . .Rev. 3:19

1001. Zodiac

See *Astrologers, Star/Stars.*

Through-the-Bible-in-a-Year Reading Plan

If you'd like to put the 1,001 topics of The Bible Search Engine *into a "big picture" context, you might try reading through the Bible in a year. The following plan breaks scripture into 365 relatively equal readings, featuring a selection from the Old Testament, the New Testament, and the "wisdom books" of Psalms and Proverbs for every day. This plan will take the average reader about 20 minutes per day.*

Day 1	Gen. 1–2 • Matt. 1 • Ps. 1	**Day 29**	Exod. 7:25–9:35 • Matt. 17:1–9 • Ps. 24
Day 2	Gen. 3–4 • Matt. 2 • Ps. 2	**Day 30**	Exod. 10–11 • Matt. 17:10–27 • Ps. 25
Day 3	Gen. 5–7 • Matt. 3 • Ps. 3	**Day 31**	Exod. 12 • Matt. 18:1–20 • Ps. 26
Day 4	Gen. 8–10 • Matt. 4 • Ps. 4	**Day 32**	Exod. 13–14 • Matt. 18:21–35 • Ps. 27
Day 5	Gen. 11–13 • Matt. 5:1–20 • Ps. 5	**Day 33**	Exod. 15–16 • Matt. 19:1–15 • Ps. 28
Day 6	Gen. 14–16 • Matt. 5:21–48 • Ps. 6	**Day 34**	Exod. 17–19 • Matt. 19:16–30 • Ps. 29
Day 7	Gen. 17–18 • Matt. 6:1–18 • Ps. 7	**Day 35**	Exod. 20–21 • Matt. 20:1–19 • Ps. 30
Day 8	Gen. 19–20 • Matt. 6:19–34 • Ps. 8	**Day 36**	Exod. 22–23 • Matt. 20:20–34 • Ps. 31:1–8
Day 9	Gen. 21–23 • Matt. 7:1–11 • Ps. 9:1–8	**Day 37**	Exod. 24–25 • Matt. 21:1–27 • Ps. 31:9–18
Day 10	Gen. 24 • Matt. 7:12–29 • Ps. 9:9–20	**Day 38**	Exod. 26–27 • Matt. 21:28–46 • Ps. 31:19–24
Day 11	Gen. 25–26 • Matt. 8:1–17 • Ps. 10:1–11	**Day 39**	Exod. 28 • Matt. 22 • Ps. 32
Day 12	Gen. 27:1–28:9 • Matt. 8:18–34 • Ps. 10:12–18	**Day 40**	Exod. 29 • Matt. 23:1–36 • Ps. 33:1–12
Day 13	Gen. 28:10–29:35 • Matt. 9 • Ps. 11	**Day 41**	Exod. 30–31 • Matt. 23:37–24:28 • Ps. 33:13–22
Day 14	Gen. 30:1–31:21 • Matt. 10:1–15 • Ps. 12	**Day 42**	Exod. 32–33 • Matt. 24:29–51 • Ps. 34:1–7
Day 15	Gen. 31:22–32:21 • Matt. 10:16–36 • Ps. 13	**Day 43**	Exod. 34:1–35:29 • Matt. 25:1–13 • Ps. 34:8–22
Day 16	Gen. 32:22–34:31 • Matt. 10:37–11:6 • Ps. 14	**Day 44**	Exod. 35:30–37:29 • Matt. 25:14–30 • Ps. 35:1–8
Day 17	Gen. 35–36 • Matt. 11:7–24 • Ps. 15	**Day 45**	Exod. 38–39 • Matt. 25:31–46 • Ps. 35:9–17
Day 18	Gen. 37–38 • Matt. 11:25–30 • Ps. 16	**Day 46**	Exod. 40 • Matt. 26:1–35 • Ps. 35:18–28
Day 19	Gen. 39–40 • Matt. 12:1–29 • Ps. 17	**Day 47**	Lev. 1–3 • Matt. 26:36–68 • Ps. 36:1–6
Day 20	Gen. 41 • Matt. 12:30–50 • Ps. 18:1–15	**Day 48**	Lev. 4:1–5:13 • Matt. 26:69–27:26 • Ps. 36:7–12
Day 21	Gen. 42–43 • Matt. 13:1–9 • Ps. 18:16–29	**Day 49**	Lev. 5:14 -7:21 • Matt. 27:27–50 • Ps. 37:1–6
Day 22	Gen. 44–45 • Matt. 13:10–23 • Ps. 18:30–50	**Day 50**	Lev. 7:22–8:36 • Matt. 27:51–66 • Ps. 37:7–26
Day 23	Gen. 46:1–47:26 • Matt. 13:24–43 • Ps. 19	**Day 51**	Lev. 9–10 • Matt. 28 • Ps. 37:27–40
Day 24	Gen. 47:27–49:28 • Matt. 13:44–58 • Ps. 20	**Day 52**	Lev. 11–12 • Mark 1:1–28 • Ps. 38
Day 25	Gen. 49:29–Exod. 1:22 • Matt. 14 • Ps. 21	**Day 53**	Lev. 13 • Mark 1:29–39 • Ps. 39
Day 26	Exod. 2–3 • Matt. 15:1–28 • Ps. 22:1–21	**Day 54**	Lev. 14 • Mark 1:40–2:12 • Ps. 40:1–8
Day 27	Exod. 4:1–5:21 • Matt. 15:29–16:12 • Ps. 22:22–31	**Day 55**	Lev. 15 • Mark 2:13–3:35 • Ps. 40:9–17
Day 28	Exod. 5:22–7:24 • Matt. 16:13–28 • Ps. 23	**Day 56**	Lev. 16–17 • Mark 4:1–20 • Ps. 41:1–4

About the Author

Pamela L. McQuade is a freelance writer and editor with dozens of projects to her credit. She began her Barbour writing career with coauthor and good friend Toni Sortor, then moved on to write solo. She has also coauthored *The Top 100 Men of the Bible* with her husband, Drew, under the name Drew Josephs. Over the years, four basset hounds and three cats have made the McQuade turf their home. Pam and Drew volunteer with a local basset rescue and live within sight of Manhattan's Empire State Building.

Photo Credits

All images used in *The Bible Search Engine* are licensed from iStockphoto.com.